TRANSNATIONAL ENVIRONMENTAL REGULATION AND GOVERNANCE

A large and growing proportion of contemporary environmental regulation is transnational, which means that it is impossible to understand environmental governance without a firm grasp of the nature of transnational environmental regulation (TER). In this illuminating work, Veerle Heyvaert offers readers a comprehensive discussion of TER, including international environmental agreements, regional and EU regulation, private environmental regulation and governance networks. She argues that TER is highly diverse but sufficiently cohesive to allow the identification of shared characteristics that establish TER as a model of regulation. The book uncovers the key features of TER and analyses the various intentions of TER regulators, TER's governance principles and compliance strategies, using a newly developed activity-based methodology for regulatory analysis. This book should be read by anyone seeking to understand the strengths and weaknesses of transnational environmental governance and its contribution to sustainability.

VEERLE HEYVAERT is Associate Professor of Law at the London School of Economics and Political Science and co-founding Editor-in-Chief of the journal *Transnational Environmental Law*. She teaches and publishes extensively on transnational regulation, environmental law, and European Union law. She has an LL.M. from Harvard Law School and a PhD from the European University Institute (Florence, Italy). She has been in legal practice at Akin, Gump (Brussels) and has held various academic fellowships at the United Nations, Oxford University, and Colombo (Sri Lanka).

Transnational Environmental Regulation and Governance

PURPOSE, STRATEGIES AND PRINCIPLES

VEERLE HEYVAERT
London School of Economics and Political Science

CAMBRIDGE
UNIVERSITY PRESS

CAMBRIDGE
UNIVERSITY PRESS

Shaftesbury Road, Cambridge CB2 8EA, United Kingdom

One Liberty Plaza, 20th Floor, New York, NY 10006, USA

477 Williamstown Road, Port Melbourne, VIC 3207, Australia

314–321, 3rd Floor, Plot 3, Splendor Forum, Jasola District Centre, New Delhi – 110025, India

103 Penang Road, #05–06/07, Visioncrest Commercial, Singapore 238467

Cambridge University Press is part of Cambridge University Press & Assessment, a department of the University of Cambridge.

We share the University's mission to contribute to society through the pursuit of education, learning and research at the highest international levels of excellence.

www.cambridge.org
Information on this title: www.cambridge.org/9781108415743

DOI: 10.1017/9781108235099

First published 2019

A catalogue record for this publication is available from the British Library

Library of Congress Cataloging-in-Publication data
NAMES: Heyvaert, Veerle, author.
TITLE: Transnational environmental regulation and governance : purpose, strategies and principles / Veerle Heyvaert.
DESCRIPTION: Cambridge, United Kingdom ; New York, NY : Cambridge University Press, 2018. | Includes bibliographical references and index.
IDENTIFIERS: LCCN 2018022104 | ISBN 9781108415743 (hardback)
SUBJECTS: LCSH: Environmental law, International. | Environmental policy–International cooperation. | International and municipal law–European Union countries.
CLASSIFICATION: LCC K3585 .H497 2018 | DDC 344.04/6–dc23
LC record available at https://lccn.loc.gov/2018022104

ISBN 978-1-108-41574-3 Hardback

To Ghislaine, Fons & Carla

Contents

Preface

The study of environmental law and regulation is a rewarding but emotionally draining enterprise. The more we learn about the range, scale and intensity of environmental threats facing the planet, about the vulnerability of political processes to pressure from special interest groups eyeing short-term profits for an already grotesquely moneyed elite, about the difficulty and slowness of regulatory reform, and about the countless obstructions standing in the way of effective implementation and enforcement, the more environmental law and regulation resemble a battle-worn, exhausted David, facing an ever-regenerating Goliath with only a frayed catapult and no promise of divine intervention. Recent developments, including the election of a US President who is overtly hostile to environmental regulation and, in the European sphere, the potentially disruptive impact of Brexit on both UK and European Union environmental law and policy, do little to alleviate concerns that the coming years will be at least as challenging as the past.

It goes without saying that the environmental problems of the third millennium massively outstrip any individual's – or any institution's – capacity for problem solving. However, this does not relieve us from the responsibility of trying to make a small contribution, however incomplete and imperfect. This book is my attempt. It seeks to contribute to the prospect of better environmental governance by strengthening our understanding of transnational environmental regulation, which occupies an increasingly large space in the regulatory landscape. Better informed insights into why transnational environmental regulation happens, how it works, and how it is disciplined, support critical thinking and may ultimately help us formulate responses to transnational environmental regulation that harness its potential for good and mitigate its vulnerabilities.

This book has benefited from the support of many colleagues and peers, who have been generous with their feedback on draft chapters, presentations, and scores of half-formed ideas. To avoid inadvertent omissions, I am taking the easy way out with a blanket statement: I am deeply grateful to you all. I do want to single out a few people who have been especially important to me in writing this manuscript: Jonathan Golub, for supporting this work and supporting me, always and unconditionally; Thijs Etty, for shouldering the lion's share of *Transnational Environmental Law* editorial work during the last crucial months of readying the book for submission; Robert Baldwin, for giving stacks of constructive feedback and safeguarding me from 'dead words'; Joana Setzer, for her dedicated guardianship of my 'Law and the Environment' course which freed up invaluable writing time; Jacob and Lia Rose Golub, for putting up with (and only occasionally taking advantage of) epic levels of distraction and Sroyon Mukherjee, for swift and effective research assistance. Last but not least, I owe a special debt of gratitude to my wonderful students, past and present, at the London School of Economics and Political Science. Their intellectual curiosity, enthusiasm and desire to contribute to a better world are a powerful source of inspiration and hope.

Abbreviations

ACCCRN	Asian Cities Climate Change Resilience Network
APEC	Asia-Pacific Economic Cooperation
ASEAN	Association of Southeast Asian Nations
CAC	Codex Alimentarius Commission
CBD	Convention on Biological Diversity
CCR	Cost Containment Reserve
CCRF	Code of Conduct for Responsible Fisheries
CDM	Clean Development Mechanism
CDM EB	CDM Executive Board
CDP	Carbon Disclosure Project
CEN	European Committee for Standardization
CENELEC	European Committee for Electrotechnical Standardization
CITES	Convention on International Trade in Endangered Species of Wild Fauna and Flora
CJEU	Courts of Justice of the European Union
CLRTAP	Convention on Long-Range Transboundary Air Pollution
CNP	Carbon Neutral Protocol
COATS	CO_2 Allowance Tracking System
COMO	Covenant of Mayors Office
COP	Conference of the Parties
CSR	Corporate Social Responsibility
CSSD	Centre for Sustainable Shale Development
DECC	UK Department of Energy and Climate Change
DNA	Designated National Authority
DOE	Designated Operational Entity
DVGW	Deutsche Vereinigung des Gas- und Wasserfaches eV
EC	European Community
ECHA	European Chemicals Agency

ECHR	European Convention on Human Rights
ECtHR	European Court of Human Rights
EEC	European Economic Community
EMA	European Medicines Agency
EMAS	Eco-management and Audit Scheme
EP	Equator Principles
EPA	Environmental Protection Agency
EPFI	Equator Principles Financial Institutions
ERA	early reduction allowance
ESM	environmentally sound management
EU	European Union
EU ETD	EU Emissions Trading Directive
EU ETS	EU Emissions Trading System
EWG	Environmental Working Group
FAO	Food and Agriculture Organisation
FLEGT	Forest Law Enforcement, Governance and Trade Facility
FQD	Fuel Quality Directive
FSA	Fish Stocks Agreement
FSC	Forest Stewardship Council
GAL	global administrative law
GHG	greenhouse gas
GHS	Globally Harmonised System of Classification and Labelling of Chemicals
GSTC	Global Sustainable Tourism Council
IAHTS	International Agreement on Humane Trapping Standards
ICANN	Internet Corporation for Assigned Names and Numbers
ICCA	International Council of Chemicals Associations
ICGN	International Corporate Governance Network
ICLEI	Local Governments for Sustainability
IFOAM	International Federation of Organic Agricultural Movements
IGO	intergovernmental organisation
ILO	International Labour Organisation
IMO	International Maritime Organisation
IMPEL	EU Network for the Implementation and Enforcement of Environmental Law
IOC	Inter-American Convention for the Protection and Conservation of Sea Turtles
IOMC	Inter-Organisational Programme for the Sound Management of Chemicals
IOTC	Indian Ocean Tuna Committee
IPCC	Intergovernmental Panel on Climate Change
IRMA	Initiative for Responsible Mining Assurance

ISEAL	International Social and Environmental Accreditation and Labelling
ISO	International Organisation for Standardisation
LDC	least developed country
MARPOL	International Convention for the Prevention of Pollution from Ships
MEA	multilateral environmental agreement
MNE	multinational enterprise
MSC	Marine Stewardship Council
MSPEA	Maldives Seafood Processors and Exporters Association
NDC	Nationally Determined Contribution
NGO	non-governmental organisation
NSMD	non-state market-driven
OECD	Organisation of Economic Cooperation and Development
PA	Paris Agreement
PEFC	Programme for the Endorsement of Forest Certification
POP	persistent organic pollutant
PPMs	process and production methods
REDD	Reductions in Environmental Deforestation and Forest Degradation
RFMO	regional fisheries management organisation
RGGI	Regional Greenhouse Gas Initiative
RSPO	Roundtable on Sustainable Palm Oil
SADC	Southern African Development Community
SBT Convention	Southern Bluefin Tuna Convention
SEAP	Sustainable Energy Action Plan
SFI	Sustainable Forestry Initiative
SIDS	small island developing states
SIEF	Substance Information Exchange Forum
SRI	Socially Responsible Investment
TAC	total allowable catch
TED	turtle exclusion device
TER	transnational environmental regulation
TEU	Treaty of the European Union
TFEU	Treaty on the Functioning of the European Union
UK	United Kingdom
UN	United Nations
UNCED	United Nations Conference on Environment and Development
UNCLOS	United Nations Convention on the Law of the Sea
UNEP	United Nations Environment
UNFCCC	United Nations Framework Convention on Climate Change
UNGA	United Nations General Assembly
UNICEF	United Nations Children's Fund

UNITAR	United Nations Training and Research Program
US	United States
VPA	Voluntary Partnership Agreement
WCI	Western Climate Initiative
WHO	World Health Organisation
WTO	World Trade Organization

1

The Transformation of Environmental Regulation

1.1 THE QUEST FOR THE IDENTITY OF TRANSNATIONAL ENVIRONMENTAL REGULATION

Environmental regulation has undergone fundamental changes in the past forty years. A key factor in its transformation is the rapid expansion of environmental regulation 'beyond the state'. This is regulation that is not under the sole authorship and control of national public authorities which have received a mandate and competences to that effect in national law. This type of regulation is instead characterised by a pronounced and substantive involvement of non-state actors.[1]

The past decades have also taught us that what lies beyond the state is not a neat, discrete package of transnational regulatory regimes. Instead, we encounter a sprawling body of initiatives supported by public bodies, private commercial associations, public bodies operating in a private capacity, private bodies acting under a public mandate, independent agencies, offices attached to international, regional or national organisations, quasi legislative bodies, civil society organisations, networks of public and private actors, and any permutation imaginable. The initiatives, in turn, target a varied range of environmental protection goals, and are driven by a plethora of different motivations. Regulatory goals are pursued in a wealth of different instruments and addressed to an audience as diverse as their authorship.

The aim of this book is to develop a deep and systematic understanding of transnational environmental regulation (TER) as a model of regulation. It examines the intentions of transnational environmental regulators, the strategies through which they pursue their regulatory goals, the legal status of transnational environmental

[1] See Robert W. Hahn & Kenneth R. Richards, 'The Internationalisation of Environmental Regulation' (1989) 30(2) *Harvard International Law Journal*, pp. 421–446; Frank Biermann & Philipp Pattberg, *Global Environmental Governance Reconsidered* (2012, MIT Press); Neil Gunningham & Cameron Holley 'Next-generation Environment Regulation: Law, Regulation and Governance' (2016) 12 *Annual Review of Law and Social Science*, pp. 273–293.

regimes and the norms they generate, in order to build up a detailed picture of the distinctive character of environmental regulatory activity beyond the state. This picture will help to answer the vital question whether transnationality affects the functioning and impacts of environmental regulation in a knowable, predictable way. In response, the book confirms that, unsurprisingly, the quest for the identity of transnational environmental regulation does not yield simple or straightforward answers. TER initiatives are undertaken in pursuit of a various objectives; TER regimes deploy a range of regulatory strategies. The impacts of TER on law vary depending on the type of transnationality at issue, and TER embraces and proclaims a diversity of regulatory principles. Nevertheless, it is possible to discern a number of overlapping and recurrent characteristics which are sufficiently pronounced to justify and, indeed, demand the recognition of TER as a distinctive model of regulation. The motivations of TER regulators differ, but their desire to achieve regulatory authority outside the remit of the state will almost invariably result in coalition building and compromises that are likely to affect the speed and stringency of regulatory standard setting. Notwithstanding the variety in TER strategies, a number of distinctive regulatory techniques – such as frequent reliance on standardisation by reference, compliance building through reporting, and a heavy emphasis on facilitation – stand out. Some TER regimes frustrate conventional understandings of law more than others, but they are all 'irritants' to a degree. Principles for TER differ, but we see a clear trend towards both the proceduralisation and the managerialisation of regulatory principles across the board. In sum, notwithstanding its variety and complexity, TER constitutes a distinctive model of regulation.

Theorising TER makes an important contribution to both the practice and scholarship of law and regulation. Transnational terminology has deeply embedded itself in legal and regulatory parlance in the past fifteen years. A recent investigation by Gregory Shaffer indicates that, within the legal field alone, there are now fifty-four journals with the term 'transnational law/transnational legal' in the title. Journal articles with 'transnational' in the title have increased from sixty one in 1990 to over 1,500 in 2015.[2] Studies in environmental law and regulation are very well represented within this group. During the initial stages of this 'scholarly transnationalisation', it arguably would have been intellectually stifling to draw fixed definitional boundaries hemming in an emergent discipline that is still on a journey of self-discovery. Over time, however, the risk increases that the term 'transnational regulation' will become too ubiquitous and porous to retain any possible distinctive meaning. The development of an articulated understanding of what we mean when we say 'transnational environmental regulation' averts this risk and helps the scholarly community to recognise and explain the characteristic dynamics and functions of

[2] Gregory Shaffer, 'Theorizing Transnational Legal Ordering' (2016) 12 *Annual Review of Law and Social Science*, pp. 231–253.

transnational regimes. It thereby harnesses our ability to identify and predict strengths and weaknesses of different regulatory arrangements, to compare and critique regulatory strategies, and to formulate effective reform proposals.

Harnessing analytical strength is all the more important because, up to now, critiques of environmental regulation have been developed overwhelmingly with reference to state-based regulation. Our understanding of what amounts to 'good' regulation has been forged in a predominantly national context.[3] To gauge whether regulation is effective, we traditionally use indicators that were crafted to measure the performance of state regulation. The point here is not to disclaim the huge contribution that the state as regulator makes to the development of regulation theory. Neither is it to dismiss the usefulness of state-based environmental regulation as a comparator against which to eke out a first, rudimentary image of its transnational counterpart. However, state-based environmental regulation no longer offers the full picture, and this leaves us vulnerable to analytical blind spots. For example, if the reasons why transnational actors engage in regulation differ from those that traditionally motivate domestic regulators, then this will affect the choices made in regulatory design and implementation. If regulatory strategy is determined by different opportunities and constraints at the transnational level than at the national level, then those instruments that thrive in TER are not necessarily the most effective ones for national regulators to deploy, and vice versa. In both cases, a lack of awareness of the distinctiveness of TER cripples analytical capacity, which creates risks of misdiagnosis of regulatory challenges and raises the potential for regulatory failure. The lens of TER unlocks great potential for law and policymakers alike to think creatively and productively about optimal approaches towards effective environmental regulation in today's complex and fragmented regulatory landscape.

Theorising TER has potentially far-reaching benefits for lawmakers, policymakers and courts because it facilitates their understanding of the new circumstances in which they operate. It helps authorities to engage more effectively with new modes of environmental governance, but it is also vital in helping them manage environmental regulatory change at the national level. This book establishes TER as a model of governance that is distinctive from national environmental regulation. However, the rise of transnational regulatory activity inevitably reverberates domestically and thereby also changes the landscape of traditional, state-based environmental regulation. This is most obviously so where TER displaces national responses and thus redefines the state's regulatory mandate. For example,

[3] Cf. Anand Menon & Stephen Weatherill, 'Transnational Legitimacy in a Globalising World: How the European Union Rescues Its States' (2008) 31(3) *West European Politics*, pp. 397–416. Menon and Weatherill observe and challenge the prevailing attitude of measuring the EU's legitimacy against the yardstick of idealised notions of national democratic legitimacy. They offer the opposing view that the non-majoritarian features of EU decision making do not threaten but are instead constitutive of the EU's legitimacy, and that supranationalism boosts the legitimacy of its Member States.

commentators have explained the relative scarcity of national forest regulation measures in countries such as Guatemala and Bolivia as a consequence of the success of the Forest Stewardship Council (FSC) as an alternative regulatory force in these countries.[4] Secondly, transnational regulators' experimentation with new regulatory strategies that are different from those typically pursued at the national level does not only expand the regulatory toolbox in general terms, but it may also inspire state regulators towards a change of regulatory strategy.[5] Furthermore, evolving understandings of the meaning of environmental principles are likely to infiltrate discussions at the national level. This is evidently the case for contemporary scholarly inquiries; it is a rare work of environmental scholarship that does not at the very least show an awareness of the multiplicity of locations and scales at which environmental principles and decision-making standards are developed and applied. Beyond academic walls, in national policy-making documents, administrative decisions and court proceedings, too, authorities refer to and draw inspiration from transnational sources of legal interpretation.

The following sections offer a general discussion of the drivers behind the rapid growth of TER in recent times, followed by a sectoral introduction to the field. The latter consists of a sketch of the transnational dimensions of chemicals regulation. Later chapters will cover a much wider range of topics, running the gamut from climate change to sustainable banking, but the goal of the upcoming paragraphs on transnational chemicals regulation is to convey a first impression of the breadth and variety of transnational environmental regulatory activity. The introductory example is followed by an explanation of the methodological and normative choices embedded in this project. The final segment fleshes out the content of the different chapters of the book in greater detail.

1.2 DRIVERS OF TRANSNATIONAL ENVIRONMENTAL REGULATION

A wealth of different factors have been identified as contributing to the fast-growing field of TER, and views on the relevance and weight of different potential triggers diverge widely. Moreover, the relationship between TER and the social, economic, and political environment in which it unfolds is anything but linear. Hence, what is cause to some is effect to others. The brief overview that follows does not aim to deliver a definitive account of the transnationalisation debate, but it does identify and explain the most frequently cited drivers behind the proliferation of regulation beyond the state.

[4] Errol Meidinger, 'Beyond Westphalia: Competitive Legalization in Emerging Transnational Regulatory Systems', in Christian Brütsch & Dirk Lehmkuhl (eds.), *Law and Legalization in Transnational Regulation* (2007, Routledge), p. 131.

[5] Cf. Stuart Bell, Donald McGillivray & Ole W. Pedersen, *Environmental Law*, 8th edn. (2013, Oxford University Press), p. 288.

Before reviewing the key 'real-life' events that are commonly associated with the rise of TER, we should reflect on the important role of perception in the maturation of 'new' realities. After all, the state has never been the sole purveyor of environmental regulatory content.[6] Private governance and transnational initiatives have long played a part in steering our behaviour vis-à-vis the world around us, including the natural world.[7] Conversely, it would be myopic to dismiss the continuing importance of the state in environmental regulation today. The national is still prominent, but, in the past decades, our intellectual curiosity and attention has increasingly been diverted towards those modes of regulation that do not fit the classical mould. Stronger awareness of alternatives to state regulation sharpens our alertness to their existence and reduces the likelihood that non-state regulatory structures, formerly more easily dismissed as atypical disturbances in the regulatory landscape, will escape attention. The stronger our awareness of transnational regulation, the more frequently we will spot its manifestations, which lends further credence to our initial impression that there is more of it about. This process of mutual corroboration, moreover, does not only help to consolidate the phenomenon of transnational regulation itself, but equally characterises a number of its chief causes. The more we are aware of globalisation, the more readily we see its imprint in the conduct of daily life; the more we reflect on the emergence of new environmental risks with global reach, the more we realise that old risks, too, can reverberate across the planet. Understanding social transformations as a tight entanglement of shifts in reality and perception is important because it reminds us that, as the spotlight moves on, structures that are now in the penumbra do not cease to exist and continue to merit scholarly attention. Yet for the purpose of understanding regulatory transformations, it is equally important to appreciate that a change in perception can be as impactful as a shift in real-life events. If lawmakers, regulators, judges, private actors and commentators are sensibilised and react to the rise of transnational regulation – in their planning, decision making, and discussions – then its impact is very real, regardless of whether the initial realisation was predominantly a product of real or of perceived change. To study and contribute to our knowledge about these very real impacts lies at the heart of this book's mission.

Moving from the perceived to the tangible, a significant factor contributing to the rise of TER is the ongoing legalisation of world politics. The past fifty years have witnessed an explosion in reliance on law and regulation as instruments to manage cooperation between states. In *Law and Legalization in Transnational Regulation*, editors Christian Brütsch and Dirk Lehmkuhl report that, since 1946, the number of

[6] See, e.g., on the subnational roots of environmental regulation in France, Pierre Claude Reynard, 'Public Order and Privilege: Eighteenth-Century French Roots of Environmental Regulation' (2002) 43(1) *Technology and Culture*, pp. 1–28, at 6–10.

[7] See, e.g., Jonathan Lurie, *The Chicago Board of Trade 1895–1905: The Dynamics of Self-Regulation* (1979, University of Illinois Press); Daniel Bodanksy, *The Art and Craft of International Environmental Law* (2010, Harvard University Press), pp. 18–30.

bi- and multilateral treaties has risen from around 2,000 to over 55,000.[8] This data may seem to be a resounding confirmation of ever-expanding state power, which would disprove frivolous claims about rapidly expanding transnationalisation and the demise of the state as regulator. Counterintuitively, however, the data also lends itself to an alternative interpretation. The dramatic increase in laws and rules may be an indicator not so much of the growing prowess of the state, but of the growing popularity of the instruments themselves. In fact, growing reliance on law and regulation could be the signature of a weakening state, which governs through commanding and steering rather than through ownership and occupation.[9] In line with this reasoning, the turn to lighter-touch, facilitating regulatory instruments over more direct, intrusive forms of regulation in the past decades becomes a further manifestation of the gradual alienation of the state from its regulated subjects; it represents the next degree of separation in state governance as the state resorts to ever more indirect mechanisms through which to exercise its control. Moreover, the now favoured mechanisms depend less on the unique attributes of the state to function, namely the power to coerce and the monopoly of violence. This shift towards less coercive, more flexible modes of control fosters opportunities for non-state actors to get in on the game and to assume regulatory functions alongside or even instead of the state. Hence, as its functionality depends less on the unique attributes of the state, legalisation opens the door to the rise of non-state, transnational regulators.[10]

The second and undoubtedly most discussed trigger for transnationalisation is economic globalisation.[11] With goods, services, capital and enterprises moving more freely across the globe, the impact of domestic regulation is no longer a local affair.[12] High levels of domestic regulation are cast as potential barriers to trade; low levels of environmental regulation transform into 'leakage risks' that could siphon off investment and defeat the purpose of stricter standards elsewhere.[13] Economic globalisation thus creates powerful incentives for international harmonisation. Inter-state

[8] Christian Brütsch & Dirk Lehmkuhl, 'Complex Legalization and the Many Moves to Law', in Brütsch & Lehmkuhl, *Law and Legalization*, p. 13.

[9] Eric Windholz & Graeme A. Hodge, 'Conceptualising Social and Economic Regulation: Implications for Modern Regulators and Regulatory Activity' (2012) 38(2) *Monash University Law Review*, pp. 212–237, at 213.

[10] Meidinger, 'Beyond Westphalia', p. 129.

[11] Christoph Knill & Dirk Lehmkuhl, 'Private Actors and the State: Internationalization and Changing Patterns of Governance' (2002) 15(1) *Governance*, pp. 41–63; David Held & Anthony G. McGrew (eds.), *Governing Globalization: Power, Authority and Global Governance* (2002, Polity Press); David Miliband, 'The New Politics of Economics', in Colin Crouch & David Marquand (eds.), *Ethics and Markets: Co-Operation and Competition within Capitalist Economies* (1993, Oxford Blackwell), pp. 21–30.

[12] See, e.g., Joanne Scott, 'From Brussels with Love: The Transatlantic Travels of European Law and the Chemistry of Regulatory Attraction' (2009) 57(4) *American Journal of Comparative Law*, pp. 897–942.

[13] Jonathan Baert Wiener, 'Global Environmental Regulation: Instrument Choice in Legal Context' (1999) 108(4) *The Yale Law Journal*, pp. 677–800, at 693.

negotiation and rule making, however, are a slow and cumbersome mechanism through which to channel this demand.[14] This fosters a call for transnational institutions (such as the European Commission, the World Trade Organization General Council) to manage and expedite harmonisation initiatives, as well as oversee their implementation.[15] In this process, national governments arguably trade off a degree of direct control over the regulatory agenda in exchange for participation in a more expedient transboundary regulatory regime.[16] At the same time, the globalisation of communication greatly facilitates the establishment of transnational networks of commercial enterprises, civil society organisations, epistemic communities, national public sector administrators, and so on.[17] At times, initiatives that start as 'like-minded communities' desirous to share common experiences, interests and expertise, gradually transform into bodies with transnational regulatory responsibilities.[18] In other cases, networks are established with the express purpose to develop new, shared standards of behaviour. The combination of a vibrant demand for transboundary rule making, the inability of state regulators effectively to meet this demand through international co-operation and agreement and the proliferation of transnational networks with the means and motives to fill in the regulatory gap, constitutes an environment in which TER flourishes.

The ascent of global environmental risks, such as climate change, ozone depletion and marine pollution add more fuel to the demand for regulatory responses that transcend the national level.[19] In determining climate change policies, for example, individual governments face a debilitating prisoner's dilemma: if state A opts for proactive and thorough climate change control measures but states B, C and D no not, or fail to make good on earlier statements of intent, A may place itself at a competitive disadvantage and risks incurring the ire of its domestic fossil fuel producing and dependent sectors. What is more, in the absence of globally

[14] Wade Jacoby & Sophie Meunier, 'Europe and the Management of Globalization' (2010) 17(3) *Journal of European Public Policy*, pp. 299–317.

[15] Jessica F. Green, *Rethinking Private Authority. Agents and Entrepreneurs in Global Environmental Governance* (2014, Princeton University Press), pp. 54–77.

[16] Eyal Benvenisti, 'The Conception of Law as a Legal System' (2008) Tel Aviv University Law School Faculty Papers 83/2008, p. 12.

[17] Manuel Castells, *The Rise of the Network Society: The Information Age*, 2nd edn. (2010, Wiley Blackwell); Lars H. Gulbrandsen, *Transnational Environmental Governance: The Emergence and Effects of the Certification of Forests and Fisheries* (2010, Edward Elgar), p. 7.

[18] See e.g., Rieneke Slager, Jean-Pascal Gond & Jeremy Moon, 'Standardization as Institutional Work: The Regulatory Power of a Responsible Investment Standard' (2012) 33 (5–6) *Organization Studies*, pp. 763–790, at 768, regarding the FTSE4GOOD Responsible Investment standard, which started as a financial index to facilitate measurement of investment behaviour, but evolved into a de facto standard for investment behaviour.

[19] Wiener, 'Global Environmental Regulation', p. 686.

shared mitigation efforts, A's costly and unpopular mitigation efforts will be utterly in vain.[20] The stock answer to the 'state as prisoner' dilemma is international treaty making. In the case of climate change, this resulted in the adoption of world's best-known and, arguably, most influential multilateral environmental agreement (MEA), the 1992 United Nations Framework Convention on Climate Change (UNFCCC).[21] The UNFCCC is an international agreement, but it is also a vivid illustration of how internationalisation and transnationalisation feed off each other.[22] The implementation and day-to-day management of the UNFCCC regime has sparked an explosion in transnational committees, working groups, expert advisers, standing bodies and countless networks that assume an ever-expanding array of facilitating, administrative and (quasi) regulatory functions.[23] Moreover, the UNFCCC is much more than a collection of general climate stabilisation targets, environmental principles and (fairly minimal) commitments to which the member countries have signed up. It is also the world's busiest meeting place for a wealth of public and private actors and networks that seek to share ideas and launch initiatives on particular aspects of the climate change complex. Some of the initiatives that bubble up around the 'coral reef' of the UNFCCC are carried out within the framework of the Convention, but others develop outside the UNFCCC compact. The argument has been made that offering such a coral reef for the germination of thematically linked initiatives is an overlooked but crucial function of contemporary international environmental law.[24]

An alternative account of the relation between inter-state treaty negotiation and the emergence of transnational environmental regulators focuses less on the synergistic and more on the complementary aspects of the relationship. With the possible exception of the Vienna Convention for the Protection of the Ozone Layer,[25] MEAs have not exactly established a reputation as nimble instruments for managing complex environmental problems. Arguably, the 'high politics' format, the rigid infrastructure and the consensus-based model of treaty decision making are

[20] Cf. Aynsley Kellow & Anthony R. Zito, 'Steering through Complexity: EU Environmental Regulation in the International Context' (2002) 50(1) *Political Studies*, pp. 43–60, at 45.

[21] New York (US), 9 May 1992, in force 21 Mar. 1994, available at: http://unfccc.int.

[22] Kal Raustiala, 'The Architecture of International Cooperation: Transgovernmental Networks and the Future of International Law' (2002) 43(1) *Virginia Journal of International Law*, pp. 1–92.

[23] Robert O. Keohane & David G. Victor, 'The Regime Complex for Climate Change' (2011) 9(1) *Perspectives on Politics*, pp. 7–23.

[24] Jessica F. Green, 'Order Out of Chaos: Public and Private Rules for Managing Carbon' (2013) 13(2) *Global Environmental Politics*, pp. 1–25, at 15 & 22.

[25] Vienna (Austria), 22 Mar. 1985, in force 22 Sept. 1988, available at: http://ozone.unep.org/en/handbook-vienna-convention-protection-ozone-layer/2205.

anathema to the rapidly evolving nature of global environmental challenges.[26] With regard to climate change, for instance, Liliana Andonova and others observe that

> climate change is characterized by unenviable complexity and the need for policy coordination vertically, horizontally, and across sectors. Unlike many other environmental policies that often focus on one industry or several sets of actors, climate governance has to involve multiple sectors, often with divergent interests and roles. As a result, interests are more likely to be disaggregated around narrowly defined climate-related issues (e.g., adaptation, carbon markets, renewable energy, reporting), which in turn facilitates collective action across borders within specific governance niches.[27]

Climate change has come to represent the epitome of a complex problem which, even if political willingness abounded, cannot be sufficiently governed by any one regime at any level of governance, but instead clamours for a multitude of governance initiatives, unfolding across the private-to-public, local-to-global spectrum.[28] But the case can equally be made for problems ranging from biodiversity depletion to environmental waste control. The inadequacy or perceived failure of national and international regulatory responses spurs a quest for alternative, transnational responses.

A final factor for consideration concerns the relation between risk regulation and transnationalisation. Risk regulation has become the dominant regulatory paradigm for environmental protection, which represents a shift from the previously prevailing model of welfare regulation.[29] Arguably, the pursuit of risk control objectives lends itself better to transnational organisation than the pursuit of welfare. The latter is an explicitly political concept; its meaning is contested and the consequences of attributing a different meaning to what constitutes aggregate welfare, and how it should be achieved, have a direct, visceral impact on the distribution of wealth. Risk, by contrast, is perceived to belong to the world of economics. It presents itself as relatively neutral since risks can be identified according to universalisable criteria; risks are measurable and lend themselves to ranking and rational prioritisation regardless of scale. To be sure, risk's pretensions to objectivity and neutrality have been comprehensively skewered in a torrent of sociological, socio-legal and

[26] Joost Pauwelyn, Ramses A. Wessel & Jan Wouters, 'When Structures Become Shackles: Stagnation and Dynamics in International Lawmaking' (2014) 25(3) *European Journal of International Law*, pp. 733–763, at 734–735.

[27] Liliana Andonova, Michele Betsill & Harriet Bulkeley, 'Transnational Climate Governance' (2009) 9(2) *Global Environmental Politics*, pp. 52–73, at 57–58.

[28] Jacqueline Peel, Lee Godden & Rodney J. Keenan, 'Climate Law in an Era of Multi-Level Governance' (2012) 1(2) *Transnational Environmental Law*, pp. 245–280.

[29] Julia Black, 'The Role of Risk in Regulatory Processes' in Robert Baldwin, Martin Cave & Martin Lodge (eds.), *The Oxford Handbook of Regulation* (2010, Oxford University Press), pp. 302–307; Veerle Heyvaert, 'Governing Climate Change: Towards a New Paradigm for Risk Regulation' (2011) 74(6) *The Modern Law Review*, pp. 817–844, at 822–827.

governance studies,[30] but it is nonetheless a representation that holds sway in governmental, regulatory and also judicial circles. Claims to neutrality and universality, however ill-founded they may be, help to legitimise decision making by actors who would not have the required representational credentials or gravitas to make political decisions. To the extent that risk regulation de-politicises decision making, it enables transnational regulators, whose weak ties to domestic democratic processes and weak representative accountability no longer stand in the way of their ambitions for governance.

In sum, legalisation, globalisation, the prominence of global environmental risks and the consolidation of risk governance as a regulatory objective all play a part in creating an environment conducive to the emergence of TER. Greater awareness of the phenomenon moreover increases the likelihood that a broader range of non-state initiatives are recognised as transnational and regulatory in nature.

The image of TER rising and flourishing across the regulatory landscape is highly evocative, but it is also open to criticism. The framing of environmental regulation as an increasingly transnational phenomenon has an admittedly Eurocentric bent. From a postcolonial perspective, particularly, the emphasis on the transnational raises difficult political questions, as it arguably downplays the importance of national sovereignty just at a time when many former colonies are coming into their own as regulatory states. Compared to European Union (EU) countries, the proportion of, for instance, Indian law that directly interacts with or derives from international or regional law is considerably smaller. Indian lawmakers, policy makers, researchers and practitioners are far more likely to characterise environmental law as a primarily national discipline, and to qualify transnational developments as ancillary to the main event.

Moreover, even in the EU, which represents the most advanced model of environmental regulation beyond the state, national regulation retains a key role in the pursuit of environmental protection goals. Indeed, there is a strong argument to be made that, just as internationalisation and transnationalisation feed off each other, TER is at least as likely to shore up state regulation as to displace it. For example, the Forest Law Enforcement, Governance and Trade Facility (FLEGT) is a transnational initiative for the prevention of illegal logging.[31] The reference to illegality assumes the existence of national and international laws that regulate the harvesting, processing, transporting, buying or selling of timber. The FLEGT Voluntary Partnership Agreements (VPAs) incorporate acceptable logging standards that result from multi-partite negotiations between the Commission, developing countries and stakeholders, but these negotiations happen against the backdrop of domestic and European conceptions of illegality. Indeed, a broad range of TER regimes treat compliance with national environmental regulation as a minimum criterion for

[30] For a succinct overview, see Black, 'The Role of Risk', pp. 309–314.

[31] See also Chapter 2.4.1.

accession. The existence of overlapping national and transnational regulation arguably lowers the threshold for accession to TER, since it represents a small marginal increase in effort in exchange for potentially significant benefits. These examples call into question the displacement effect of TER and instead corroborate the theory that traditional and alternative forms of regulation are mutually supportive.[32]

Hence, even in a study dedicated to TER, it remains important not to lose sight of the continued relevance of 'state-based' environmental regulation.[33] By the same token, however, it would be a serious mistake to underestimate the scale or profundity of the changes brought about by TER. They are not limited to the emergence of a new level of governance that partly overlaps, partly complements and partly displaces national regulation. They are also a driving force in the ongoing development of a new regulatory ethos and praxis across all levels of government, including the domestic level.

The changes rung by TER are unlikely to unravel in the foreseeable future. That TER is here to stay remains the most plausible prediction even as the current geopolitical mood reflects a vivid discontent with globalisation, and a reversal in some countries to nationalism and protectionism. While specific institutions inevitably evolve and some will founder, TER has reached a level of penetration and maturity that bestows upon it a considerable degree of resilience in the short and medium term. Moreover, the range and variety of transnational initiatives makes them adaptive in the face of geopolitical shifts. For example, it is indeed profoundly unlikely that the United States (US) Trump administration will be interacting intensely with intergovernmental environmental organisations in the pursuit of internationally agreed environmental targets, let alone provide impetus for the adoption of additional multilateral agreements. Yet this does not necessarily imply that American corporations or civil society organisations will be equally reluctant to contribute to the development of environmental governance regimes across borders. In fact, it might incentivise non-state actors to strengthen their involvement in transnational initiatives. In the EU context, Brexit will alter the terms of engagement between the United Kingdom (UK) and the EU on issues such as environmental standardisation, but it is highly unlikely to dampen British manufacturers' interest in legal approximation, either within the EU sphere or beyond. Moreover, even in the unlikely occurrence of a downturn in global trade overall, environmental threats remain inescapably transboundary. For these reasons, it is difficult to conceive of a future in environmental law and governance without a strong role for transnational regulation. Hence, TER is not a fleeting phenomenon; it will continue to affect and even determine environmental governance for decades and centuries to come.

32 Cf. Raustiala, 'The Architecture of International Cooperation'.

33 Cf. Craig Scott, '"Transnational Law" as Proto-Concept: Three Conceptions' (2009) 10(7) *German Law Journal*, pp. 859–876, at 875.

1.3 AN INTRODUCTION TO TER: THE CASE OF CHEMICALS CONTROL

This section offers a rough first sketch of the transnational dimension of chemicals risk regulation. TER covers environmental issues from sustainable palm oil production[34] to oil rig safety,[35] but the chemicals sector is a good place to start because it is a highly regulated field that is densely populated by different variants of regulation beyond the state.

In Europe, chemicals regulation was one of the first key product regulation fields to undergo thorough transnationalisation soon after the establishment of the (then) European Economic Community (EEC) in 1958. Because of the dominant role of the chemicals sector in the EU economy and the intensity of intra-EU trade in chemicals, there was a strong push to harmonise national product regulations for chemical substances and preparations under the EEC common market project. The first European Directive on the classification, packaging and labelling of dangerous substances dates back to 1967. It introduced an initially very modest degree of environmental standardisation, but its main function was overwhelmingly to streamline national regulations and thereby facilitate trade. Over time and after various bouts of regulatory reform, the health, safety and environmental risk control aspects of the EU regulatory regime acquired greater prominence, and are now arguably of equivalent importance to the trade liberation goal. However, whether TER can be genuinely 'dual purpose' or whether, instead, the trade imperative inescapably hampers any green aspirations remains a controversial question.[36] This offers an early illustration of the new opportunities, but also the dilemmas that beset environmental regulation in a transnational context.

Over the span of four decades, EU chemicals regulation expanded into a dense – some claimed impenetrable – patchwork of regulations, directives and endless amendments that covered classification, packaging and labelling of dangerous substances and preparations; data reporting rules for new substances; risk evaluation of old chemicals and restrictions on marketing and use. The regime was thoroughly revamped and partly consolidated in the landmark 2007 REACH Regulation.[37] REACH requires the registration of any chemical substance, preparation or

34 See the Roundtable on Sustainable Palm Oil at www.rspo.org.

35 'EU Seeks Industry Assurance Over Oil Rig Safety' *ENDS Europe Daily*, 11 May 2010.

36 Suzanne Kingston, Veerle Heyvaert & Aleksandra Čavoški, *European Environmental Law* (2017, Cambridge University Press), pp. 450–453.

37 Regulation (EC) No 1907/2006 concerning the Registration, Evaluation, Authorisation and Restriction of Chemicals (REACH), establishing a European Chemicals Agency, amending Directive 1999/45/EC and repealing Council Regulation (EEC) No 793/93 and Commission Regulation (EC) No 1488/94 as well as Council Directive 76/769/EEC and Commission Directives 91/155/EEC, 93/67/EEC, 93/105/EC and 2000/21/EC [2007] OJ L136/3.

chemical in an article[38] that is produced or marketed in a quantity of at least one ton per manufacturer and per year. Private parties submit registration requests directly to an EU entity, the European Chemicals Agency (ECHA), and typically team together in substance groups to limit duplication. The data gathered through the registration process enables priority setting of substances that flag up concern, which are then subjected to evaluation, a process during which member state rapporteurs conduct a thorough risk assessment and produce risk management recommendations. Substances of very high concern are placed on a candidate list and must obtain authorisation by a sunset date, or they can no longer lawfully be used within the EU. Furthermore, the REACH Regulation incorporates pre-existing restrictions on marketing and use, and sets out a procedure for the European Commission to adopt alternative restrictions where authorisation is not indicated.

The REACH Regulation offers a very first glimpse of the depth and variety of environmental regulatory strategies at the transnational level. Registration is a chiefly information-oriented tool; authorisation is significantly more intrusive and follows a permitting strategy; and the adoption of marketing and use restrictions involves extensive technical standardisation. The scope for team work offers an example of facilitation, which is a pronounced characteristic of many TER initiatives.[39] Conversely, a feature which is less widespread in TER yet prominent in REACH is its high level of centralisation: private regulatory addressees engage directly with EU authorities in the fulfilment of regulatory requirements rather than through the intermediacy of national authorities. However, even REACH still depends heavily on state cooperation, particularly in the enforcement of its 'no data, no market' rule, which requires local authorities to prevent the circulation of chemicals unless they duly display an ECHA registration number. Generally, the relatively greater distance between rule making and enforcement is a key feature of TER regimes. Its impact on regulatory effectiveness, and the development of strategies to bridge the distance or secure regulatory effectiveness through alternative means, are some of the abiding themes in the transnational regulation literature.

Institutional complexity, too, is a key feature of both REACH and TER generally. In REACH, manufacturers and importers cooperate in transnational Substance Information Exchange Forums (SIEFs) for the production of registration dossiers. The dossiers are submitted directly to the ECHA, an EU regulatory institution. Substance evaluation happens at the national level but the process is orchestrated by the European Commission. The Commission also decides on the authorisation of

[38] An article is 'an object which during production is given a special shape, surface or design which determines its function to a greater degree than does its chemical composition' (REACH Article 2[3]). This includes most common household objects such as toys, clothes, vehicles etc. See ECHA, Requirements for Substances in Articles, Doc. ECHA-11-B-05-EN, 2011, available at: https://echa.europa.eu/documents/10162/13632/nutshell_guidance_articles2_en.pdf.

[39] See Chapter 4.3.3.

use of substances of very high concern and adopts marketing and use restrictions. Both sets of measures have EU-wide application. However, national regulatory authorities still play an important part in the implementation of the REACH framework and are co-opted within the regulatory regime through committees, through rapportage on evaluation dossiers, help desking and enforcement responsibilities. Within REACH, regulatory authority is neither national nor strictly EU-based but is the product of highly structured cooperation between domestic, European and private actors. Like many transnational regulatory regimes, REACH challenges traditional demarcations between regulators, advisers, stakeholders and regulatees, and highlights instead their interdependency.

Moreover, the picture would be incomplete without consideration of the role of international regulatory standards within the REACH regime. A number of the exposure and use restrictions incorporated in REACH are taken in compliance not with national or EU decision making, but in accordance with the regulatory requirements adopted under the 1998 Stockholm Convention on Persistent Organic Pollutants (the Stockholm Convention or the POPs Convention).[40] The aim of the Stockholm Convention is to ban or tightly restrict the use of a range of highly toxic, bioaccumulating and non-biodegradable chemicals, which bear the group name of 'persistent organic pollutants' and include substances such as DDT, dioxin and bichlorinated biphenyls. The initial list of twelve POPs was agreed to by all member countries signatories to the POPs Convention, and later additions must be adopted by the POPs Conference of the Parties (COP).[41]

At first sight, we might question whether regulatory standards such as those in the POPs Convention qualify as genuine regulation 'beyond the state'. National regulatory authorities do, after all, maintain a firm grip on decision making via representation in national negotiating delegations and in the COP. This assumption, however, seriously underestimates the intricacy of the arrangements that enable regulatory action in a multilateral environmental treaty context and the extent to which it creates opportunities for non-state actors to acquire agency in the regulatory enterprise. For instance, Article 8 of the POPs Convention provides that the member states may put forward proposals for inclusion of additional substances in the POPs list. An overview of the procedure for inclusion quickly confirms, however, that the key actor in this process is the POPs Review Committee, which consists of government-designated experts in chemical assessment or management. The Committee reviews proposals and can either push them forward or set them aside. For those proposals that are favourably received, it is the Committee that drafts the risk profile and on this basis decides that, either, the chemical is likely as a result of its

[40] Stockholm (Sweden), 22 May 2001, in force 17 May 2004; available at: http://chm.pops.int/TheConvention/Overview/TextoftheConvention/tabid/2232/Default.aspx.

[41] Thus far, sixteen new POPs have been added to the original list. 'The New Pops under the Stockholm Convention', available at: http://chm.pops.int/TheConvention/ThePOPs/TheNewPOPs/tabid/2511/Default.aspx.

long-range environmental transport to lead to significant adverse human health and/or environmental effects such that global action is warranted, or that the proposal should not proceed. In the former case, the Committee is tasked with preparing the risk management evaluation and an analysis of possible control measures. It also formulates the recommendation for inclusion of the substance on the POPs list. Member countries can challenge Committee decisions, but the slow and unwieldy mechanisms for interpellations are likely to stifle all but the most pressing of protests. Effectively, decisions on which additional POPs will continue to circulate across the globe, and which will be phased out, are in the hands of a compact, technocratic expert body. In fact, the decision making that unfolds under the auspices of the POPs Convention is more centralised and less supervised than any comparable process under the EU Treaties.

REACH and the POPs Convention are solid examples of transnational regulatory activity, but they still retain a strong link with traditional conceptions of regulation in that decision making is dominated by public authorities. The Globally Harmonised System of Classification and Labelling of Chemicals (GHS), by comparison, is further removed from the traditional understanding of regulation as the exercise of state authority.[42] Drawing up the GHS was a formally voluntary exercise, orchestrated under the auspices of the United Nations Conference on Environment and Development (UNCED). Diverse actors participated in both the organisation of GHS meetings and the negotiation of classification and labelling criteria. They included the Organisation of Economic Cooperation and Development (OECD), the International Labour Organisation (ILO), the Inter-Organisational Program for the Sound Management of Chemicals (IOMC), delegates from national administrations, trade representatives, industry representatives, public interest groups, members from academia, etc. In her discussion of the GHS negotiation process, Mary Frances Lowe observes that: 'No single organization had the resources or expertise to develop the GHS'.[43] The GHS is a formally voluntary set of standards, but it is the most widely subscribed to chemicals classification system in the world, and deviation from its prescriptions can have a serious impact on the worldwide marketability of non-conforming chemicals. Since its adoption, the GHS has moreover been incorporated into various national and regional regulatory instruments, including EU Regulation 1272/2008/EC on classification, labelling and packaging of substances and mixtures.[44]

[42] Cf. Gerd Winter, 'Transnational Administrative Comitology: The Global Harmonisation of Chemicals Classification and Labelling' in Olaf Dilling, Martin Herberg & Gerd Winter (eds), *Transnational Administrative Rule-Making* (2011, Hart Publishing), pp. 111–150.

[43] Mary Frances Lowe, 'Toward a Globally Harmonized System: Negotiating to Promote Public Health, Environmental Protection, and International Trade', (2003) 27 *Fletcher Forum of World Affairs*, pp. 195–208, at 199.

[44] EU Regulation 1272/2008/EC on classification, labelling and packaging of substances and mixtures, amending and repealing Directives 67/548/EEC and 1999/45/EC, and amending Regulation (EC) No 1907/2006 [2008] OJ L353/1.

The unconventional authorship of the GHS raises difficult questions regarding its legal status and that of the standards it produces. It is unclear whether the GHS constitutes a public institution that should abide by the prescriptions of public law and, if so, which public law system governs GHS decision making. This question has a more straightforward answer at the EU level, since Commission decisions on, for instance, chemical authorisation unquestionably fall within the remit of EU administrative law and the jurisdiction of the Courts of Justice of the European Union (CJEU). Yet this does not make the EU case unproblematic. It has been called into question whether the recent and mostly reactive layer of EU administrative law is up to the challenge of disciplining the ever-expanding regulatory capacity of EU institutions.[45] In fact, it is debatable whether administrative law beyond the state even intends to discipline transnational regulation, and whether its true goal is not rather to legitimise it.

Chemical risk management is also the subject of one of the first world-wide private regulatory enterprises. Since 1985, Responsible Care® has been a major producer of chemical safety standards, performance indicators and verification procedures. The initiative was launched by the American Chemicals Council and, to date, counts nearly sixty national chemical manufacturing associations among its members. Together, they constitute the International Council of Chemicals Associations (ICCA), which governs Responsible Care®. Although overtly a private sector organisation, the ICCA emphasises the role of stakeholder involvement in its programme development, including state representatives, intergovernmental organisations and civil society organisations. Moreover, it has partnerships and alliances with a number of global public organisations, such as United Nations Environment (UNEP) and the United Nations Training and Research Programme (UNITAR). Part of UNITAR's mission is to offer training to UN member country governments for the development of their chemical safety programmes. In this manner, the influence of Responsible Care® gets indirectly conveyed to the state level with the potential to affect the course of domestic chemicals regulation.

As with the GHS, there is no preordained legal regime to instruct and review Responsible Care®'s decision making. It is moreover questionable whether this non-profit organisation, composed overwhelmingly of private companies that seek to further their private business interests by joining, should be governed by public law. On the other hand, Responsible Care®'s prestige and its privileged relation with high profile intergovernmental organisations (IGOs) sets it apart from garden variety

[45] E.g., Päivi Leino, 'Efficiency, Citizens and Administrative Culture: The Politics of Good Administration in the EU' (2014) 20(4) *European Public Law*, pp. 681–710; Deirdre Curtin, 'Holding (Quasi-)Autonomous EU Administrative Actors to Public Account' (2007) 13(4) *European Law Journal*, pp. 523–541.

contractual arrangements. Arguably, the appropriate interface between Responsible Care® and the law is located in the grey zone between public and private law.

The overview of transnational chemicals regulation is by no means exhaustive, but it is sufficient to illustrate the variety of regulatory regimes that governs one and the same industrial sector, as well as the multiplicity of actors with regulatory responsibilities involved. Moreover, even this bare-bones overview already flags up a number of important challenges that characterise chemicals regulation as a transnational regime. The aim of REACH and the GHS is to lay down minimum expectations for chemicals safety, but trade facilitation is an equally important driver. Responsible Care® members may have the best interests of their workers and environment at heart, but they are at least as keen to preserve their reputation. Transnational chemicals regulation therefore seems to fulfil different or additional functions from those traditionally associated with environmental, health and safety regulation. The establishment of SIEFs under the REACH framework, and the heavy reliance on information-based tools such as classification and labelling by the GHS and Responsible Care®, suggests that transnational regulators need to think carefully about how to allocate regulatory burdens and choose engagement mechanisms that will find acceptance among the addressees. This is all the more the case for regulators which, like Responsible Care®, depend on voluntary accession and compliance by their members. As to regulatory effectiveness, the entanglements between international, regional and local regimes as well as the combination of public and private actors involved, profoundly complicate assessments of how effectively regulatory messages are received and responded to. The legal governance of bodies such as the POPs Review Committee, GHS Working Groups and the Responsible Care® executive board is an equally challenging affair: it is unclear which legal regime their actions fall under and their decisions contribute to. The aim of this book is to explore these and related challenges across a broader range of transnational environmental regimes so as to develop a richer understanding of TER as an institutional design and practice with a distinctive set of opportunities, challenges and consequences.

1.4 EXPLANATION OF THE CHOSEN APPROACH

Different paths can be followed to study the distinctiveness of transnational regulation. One possibility is to perform a thorough analysis of one or a select few cases of TER, and to extrapolate on the basis of the case study to arrive at general conclusions about TER's nature and dynamics. This approach has much going for it: it generates in-depth expertise regarding a particular regime and is bound to contribute to the knowledge base on the environmental challenge and the examined regulatory response. The confined parameters enable a comprehensive study of the subject matter and significantly reduce the risk that key features of the regulatory regime will be overlooked or misinterpreted. Because of the high degree of control fostered by in-depth and comprehensive analysis, any conclusions from the study are likely to be firmly corroborated and, hence, reliable. Many excellent pieces of legal and regulatory scholarship exemplify the case study approach. Studies range from examinations of various aspects of climate change policy,[46] the contractualisation of nature conservation[47] and private governance of health and safety in the mining sector,[48] to non-state regulation of forests and fisheries[49] and transnational regimes for the control of chemical risks.[50] The chief limitation of a single or select case study approach, conversely, is that either the scope of the conclusions inferred from the study is contained to a single transnational regime, which significantly limits their theoretical reach, or the results of the study are assumed to have more universal application, which significantly increases the vulnerability of the conclusions. Those familiar with the trials and tribulations of science-based risk assessment know that extrapolation is a fraught enterprise; the assumption that cause-and-effect relations observed in the artificial microcosm of a research lab will similarly occur outside of it all too often proves incorrect. It is no different for social science studies.

The second approach is to sample from a much broader range of transnational regimes, covering a variety of environmental issues. The appeal is obvious: the work will speak to a broader audience, and any conclusions regarding the nature of TER and its relation to law will be founded on a much broader, and therefore more representative, range of transnational regulatory activity. The most obvious limitation resonates in the choice of the term 'sampling' to describe the selection process: it is practically impossible to conduct an exhaustive study of the rapidly growing body of transnational environmental regulatory regimes and still produce a manuscript of manageable scale for the reader – let alone the researcher. As a consequence, the second approach comes with an undeniably broader margin of error risk than the first. Nonetheless, this is the approach chosen for my study. The main reasons are that, first, many excellent studies focus on single regimes. In contrast, studies that engage with the phenomenon of TER in a broad sense are considerably less prevalent. Most of the existing studies that do espouse a wide-angle approach are situated in the field of climate change studies, which has come to encompass such a variety of policies and regulatory regimes that it would be misleading to still qualify

46 Karin Bäckstrand, 'Accountability of Networked Climate Governance: The Rise of Transnational Climate Partnerships' (2008) 8(3) *Global Environmental Politics*, pp. 74–102.

47 Natasha Affolder, 'Transnational Conservation Contracts' (2012) 25(2) *Leiden Journal of International Law*, pp. 443–460.

48 Hevina S. Dashwood, 'Canadian Mining Companies and Corporate Social Responsibility: Weighing the Impact of Global Norms' (2007) 40(1) *Canadian Journal of Political Science*, pp. 129–156.

49 Gulbrandsen, *Transnational Environmental Governance*; Errol E. Meidinger, 'The New Environmental Law: Forest Certification' (2003) 10 *Buffalo Environmental Law Journal*, pp. 211–300.

50 Noah M. Sachs, 'Jumping the Pond. Transnational Law and the Future of Chemical Regulation', (2009) 62 *Vanderbilt Law Review* pp. 1815–1869.

them as single case studies. However, studies that discuss environmental policy fields across regulatory regimes are genuinely rare, which enhances the potential for contribution of this study. Secondly, single case studies tend to support mapping exercises that differentiate environmental regulatory regimes depending on authorship. Often, they will self-identify as studies on 'private governance', or 'network regulation', or 'multi-level governance'. This is very useful. In fact, Chapter 2 of this book deploys actor-based distinctions to offer a first approach towards a meaningful categorisation of TER. However, the ultimate motivation of the study is to go beyond actor-based distinctions, which inexorably shepherd us back to the state/non-state divide and its related, predominantly oppositional understanding of TER as 'not state regulation'. Therefore, the examinations need to focus on what unites TER rather than on what separates it in terms of policy area and authorship. An inclusive or 'wide-angle' approach is indispensable to this end.

The risks that accompany a wide-angle approach, particularly those of concluding on the basis of incomplete information, cannot be ignored away, but they are to an extent controllable. A first and straightforward way of harnessing the representativeness of the examples used in support of the study is to select on the basis of salience. This ensures that the 'big issues' and the high profile regimes of the day, in particular climate change regulation, but also new developments in biodiversity protection, pollution and product regulation, are included in the scope of the analysis. Secondly, Chapter 2 develops and uses different actor-based categories of regulation that aim to capture the gamut of possible public, private and 'hybrid' public/private combinations. The categories function as a checklist, assembled to ensure that the ensuing exploration of the nature and attributes of TER cover examples from each different category. Like salience-based selection, this device seeks to bolster the representativeness of the selected examples. Then, there are simply the added safeguards of years of professional experience which, I trust, place me in a good position to make reasonable and responsible selections of issues and materials. Particularly relevant in this context is my editorship over the past seven years of *Transnational Environmental Law* (*TEL*). I am greatly indebted to *TEL*'s growing family of authors, whose intellectual curiosity and forays into areas as diverse as long-range transboundary air pollution and new developments in environmental constitutionalism have helped me keep a finger on the pulse of a rapidly evolving discipline.

The final risk management strategy is the simplest – although perhaps not the easiest. It consist of the acknowledgement that the analyses in this work, the discussions of the key attributes of TER and its relation to law, are based on expansive but non-exhaustive reading and study. Consequently, the conclusions in this work are not of a nature to be chiselled on stone tablets. Yet they do constitute well-informed and plausible reflections. They are building blocks that are open to challenge as well as corroboration. The goal of the research is not to establish an absolute truth, but a workable model of TER as a regulatory domain with its own agenda, its own set of regulatory and legal challenges and its own ethos.

It will be clear from the preceding statements that the aspirations of this study are analytical more than normative. The catalyst is a quest to understand what constitutes TER, what its key attributes are, and how the transnational exercise of regulatory authority challenges law as an instrument for regulatory governance. However, even studies with a pronounced analytical bent tend to embody certain normative assumptions and beliefs.[51] This work is no exception and, therefore, should be open about its assumptions and critical beliefs. First, the research is supported by the conviction that obtaining better and more systematic insights into the nature and operation of TER is a vital precondition for productive discussions about its desirability. In particular, I propose that discussions about the legitimacy of TER, and the accountability of transnational regulators, are of limited use unless discussants have a good grasp on why TER works as it does, in what circumstances it is likely to emerge and how it is likely to affect state regulation, and unless they have an articulated understanding about the standards against which transnational regulatory behaviour should be measured. The second and related normative perspective that this study embraces is that we *should* query the legitimacy and accountability of TER. This may seem obvious, but it is by no means an uncontroversial viewpoint. The shortcomings of 'traditional' domestic environmental regulation, the snail's pace of international negotiations, and the ticking time bombs of global environmental risks such as climate change and biodiversity depletion all too easily foster a climate in which critical discussion of whichever alternative response is being mooted – whether through private regulation, network regulation or any other channel – is treated as tantamount to looking a gift horse in the mouth. This study reflects the view that a desperate need for action does not remove our responsibility to think critically about the choices and consequences of intervention. TER, it is submitted, is not intrinsically 'better' or 'worse' than the most likely alternatives of state regulation or no regulation, but it comes with a different combination of strengths and weaknesses. Covering any 'unfortunate by-products' of the rise of TER with the mantle of grateful ignorance for fear of a backlash underestimates our ability to appreciate that any response – state-based or transnational, market-driven or regulatory – has its limitations, and deprives us of the tools with which to diagnose and make some attempts to better our always disappointing, imperfect, frustrating but ever-changing reality.

[51] On the partisan nature of interpretations of authority, see generally Joseph Raz, *The Morality of Freedom* (1986, Clarendon Press), as discussed in Scott, 'Proto-Concept', pp. 861–862.

1.5 THE TRANSFORMATION OF ENVIRONMENTAL REGULATION: AN OVERVIEW

This book consists of three main segments, anchored by a conceptual discussion in Chapter 2 and followed by a conclusion in Chapter 9. The conceptual discussion in Chapter 2 defines key terminology for the study and, in doing so, explains the book's approach to regulation, the relation between regulation and law, and the concept of transnational regulation. The chapter develops the argument that the rise of transnational regulation, as a physical as well as perceived phenomenon, has had a fundamental impact on scholarly conceptualisations of regulation. These, in turn, may influence public expectations about how different actors in society organise and behave towards each other and the outside world. Whereas, formerly, regulation was typically equated to commands voiced by state authorities, the growing diversification of regulatory authority has shifted attention to alternative attributes by which acts of regulation can be identified. The chapter reviews and discusses these attributes with specific regard to environmental governance. It also emphasises the relevance of labelling a transnational structure as either regulatory or not. In its second part, the chapter maps a broad range of TER initiatives with reference to the public or private status of their actor base, identifying two groups of public TER (public/public and public/private), two categories of private TER (private/private and private public) and a fifth hybrid category. The map illustrates the broad range and variety in TER, and its categorisations are used as points of reference throughout the text.

Chapter 3 addresses the first of the book's three central themes, and investigates the various intentions of transnational regulators. I argue that actors engage in TER either to overcome collective action problems that thwart the effective national regulation of global public goods; to facilitate trade; to make up for state inaction; to manage risks of under-regulation; or to enhance the effectiveness of existing regulation. The different forms of TER adopted in pursuit of these goals are, correspondingly, (a) collective action TER; (b) trade facilitation TER; (c) substitute TER; (d) risk management TER; and (e) enhancement TER. The analysis uncovers a strong correlation between actor-based categorisations and organisation on the basis of intentionality. The chapter explores how the regulatory purpose is likely to affect the design and the evolution of established regimes and concludes that, although specific causes differ depending on the category of TER, the most prominent and troublesome shared feature is a propensity towards permissive or even lowest common denominator environmental regulation.

Chapters 4 to 6 are dedicated to the question of TER strategies and examine the various ways in which environmental regulatory goals are formulated and operationalised at the transnational level. In contrast to the preceding theme of transnational regulatory intentionality, the impact of transnationalisation on regulatory strategies is the subject of a rich literature. Chapter 4 takes this literature as its point of departure but strives to go beyond established conceptualisations by developing a new analytical model which organises regulation into five recursive stages of activity: goal setting; normalisation; engagement; learning; and response. The need for this new, activity-based model of regulation is explained by the perceived limitations of the standard representation of environmental regulatory strategies as either 'command-and-control' or 'alternative' approaches, such as incentive-based regulation, responsive regulation, or risk-based regulation. I argue that, although this 'standard account' has contributed greatly to the maturing of environmental regulation as a discipline, it tends to simultaneously obscure and overplay the differences between different regulatory strategies. The activity-based model of regulation can help to correct these weaknesses by enabling a more granular and targeted identification of where and how TER strategies differ. Improved identification skills, in turn, enhance the ability for critical assessment and the scope for effective reform. Chapter 4 develops the activity-based model and Chapter 5 tests its analytical potential by applying it to five TER frameworks in the field of climate change: the Paris Agreement, the European Union Fuel Quality Directive, the Carbon Neutral Protocol, the Compact of Mayors and the Regional Greenhouse Gas Initiative. The five case studies illustrate the variety as well as the distinctive, repeated patterns in TER strategies. On the foundation of the case studies, Chapter 6 offers an overall critical assessment of the main features and challenges of TER strategies. Key lessons from the analysis are that, while TER strategies are impressively diverse at every stage of activity, TER is essentially networked in organisation, with each studied variant displaying moderate to pronounced levels of regulatory interdependence. Equally prominent is TER's complexity: TER regimes generally rely on an intricate mix of goal setting, normalisation, engagement, learning and response methods to convey regulatory content and pursue compliance. TER regimes are particularly striking in terms of their investment into securing the engagement of regulatory addressees through communication, bonding and facilitation strategies. The combination of operational complexity with the networked character of TER necessitates a reassessment of popular assumptions regarding TER strategies, particularly those regarding regulatory compliance and deterrence. Deterrence options are relatively scarce at the transnational level, but it would be mistaken automatically to equate this scarcity with a lack of enforceability or, relatedly, with regulatory ineffectiveness. The advanced engagement strategies that characterise many TER initiatives could open alternative pathways towards compliance and effectiveness, which may compensate for a lower level of deterrence. Further research into the relation between TER engagement mechanisms, target audiences, and willingness to comply is essential in order to obtain a fuller picture of the power dynamics between transnational regulators, cohorts of regulatory addressees, and the public at large.

The third part of the book tackles the normative dimension of TER. Chapter 7 offers a conceptual discussion and explores the impact of transnational regulation, and TER in particular, on the way in which we understand the organisation, workings and functions of law. I argue that TER's proliferation challenges the continued appropriateness of ubiquitous representations of law as territorial, emanating from the state, composed of a public and private sphere, constitutive and regulatory in function, and cohesive and regimented. Instead, law is increasingly perceived as de-localised, flowing from a plurality of sources, organisationally inchoate, reflexive and coordinating in function, and polycentric. Together, these shifts in perception amount to a transformation that the chapter identifies as a transnationalisation of law. Responses to transnationalisation fall into three main categories and are either motivated by a desire to reclaim the traditional attributes of law, to reconstruct law at the transnational level or to reconceptualise law. Each response, it will be shown, creates a different set of opportunities for and challenges to the relevance of law for TER.

Chapter 8 delves into the specific normative content of TER in a search for TER's governance principles. Responding to the conceptual challenges unearthed in Chapter 7, it combines a deductive and an inductive approach to discover TER principles, drawing information both from external legal sources and from the content generated by TER regimes themselves. The resulting analysis reveals that, first, deduced and induced conceptualisations of TER governance principles significantly overlap. Many of the good governance ideals championed by transnational environmental regulators echo legal principles featuring in international environmental law, human rights law, and public law disciplines concerning the exercise of public authority (such as constitutional and administrative law). Secondly, procedural rights feature prominently as governance principles: a wealth of TER regimes subscribe to a rendition of the Aarhus triptych of access to environmental information, participation in decision making, and access to justice.[52] However, whereas transparency and inclusiveness are well-established, contestability tends to be work in progress. Moreover, TER regimes tend to fulfil transparency and inclusiveness commitments through managed dissemination and consultation rather than through guarantees of access. Beyond procedural guarantees, TER widely subscribes to principles of sound science and sustainable development and displays an arguably surprisingly widespread commitment to precaution. Moreover, there is a growing commitment to a new and potentially transformative principle of progression among TER regimes. In sum, TER governance principles present as both familiar and different, incorporating many well-established principles of public, environmental and human rights law, but applying them in a new, more managerialised manner.

Finally, Chapter 9 draws the threads of the three investigations together and offers overarching reflections. Most importantly, I conclude that notwithstanding the great diversity in TER, it is possible to identify shared and overlapping characteristics that

[52] Aarhus (Denmark), 25 June 1998, in force 30 Oct. 2001, available at: www.unece.org/env/pp/welcome.html.

imbue TER with a positive identity and validate its treatment as a distinctive model of regulation. Some of TER's most prominent features are a networked structure, complexity, vulnerability to environmentally weak normalisation, strong investment in bonding and facilitation strategies, and a widespread embrace of procedural governance principles coupled with a managerial approach to implementing procedural guarantees. In its closing sections, the conclusion moreover reflects on the potential lessons from the study of TER for state environmental regulation, and explores its scope for contributions to ongoing debates about regulatory authority, legitimacy, and effectiveness.

2

The Concept of Transnational Environmental Regulation

The earliest days of conceptual infancy may be behind us, but TER is still rightly qualified as an emerging field of study. Definitional underdeterminacy can be intellectually productive, but in excess it obstructs meaningful debate. This chapter therefore develops a workable understanding of the concept of TER that will be used as a reference point in subsequent chapters. It also maps out the spectrum of transnational environmental regulatory activity with an expansive range of concrete examples. TER is organised on the basis of two parameters: the public or private status of the regulating authority, and the public or private status of the regulatory addressees. This constitutes an initial, actor-based lens through which to conceptualise transnational environmental regulatory activity. Subsequent chapters will build up the knowledge base by analysing TER with reference to regulatory purpose, strategy and its impact on law and legal principles.

2.1 LAW AND REGULATION

This book offers a study of regulation rather than a legal analysis, but inevitably law features prominently in that discussion. This makes it essential to stop and reflect briefly on the respective meanings of the terms 'law' and 'regulation', and to try to make sense of the overlaps and differences between them. From the outset, this is quite a challenging assignment because, unsurprisingly, the meaning of both terms is subject to perennial discussion. Moreover, an added complication is that the processes of transnationalisation, which constitute the very focal point of this book, are one of the key triggers for definitional contestation. Indeed, it will be argued that the transnationalisation of regulation has caused a sea change in the way regulation is identified and conceptualised. Later on, in Chapter 7, we will explore the ways in which the emergence of transnational regulation, in turn, problematises and urges renewed reflection on the concept and meaning of law. Hence, what is offered in this introductory section cannot be a definitive account, but needs to be understood as a set of 'working definitions' reflecting broadly held yet contestable views on the meaning of law and regulation, which will be nuanced and enriched throughout the inquiries in this book.

Law refers to a particular type of authoritative communication. One of the most influential premises in legal thinking, which implicitly underlies most legal academic reflection, is that societies have stable conventions that enable them to distinguish those communications that count as 'law' from those that do not.[1] In fact, authors such as H. L. A. Hart attribute such stability to these conventions that they present them as rules, or more precisely 'rules of recognition', which allow the user to distinguish law from non-law, and to determine whether the law in question imposes an obligation or instead empowers.[2] In contemporary constitutional democracies, a dominant iteration of these stable conventions is that law consists of communications that are either incorporated in the constitution or derive their legal authority directly or indirectly from the constitution. Practically, this entails that law is created exclusively by a select group of constitutionally recognised sources (typically comprising, as a minimum, the legislative and judicial branches of government) or their delegates, to the extent that such delegation is constitutionally permitted. Recognised authorities can make law provided that they adhere to prescribed procedures (e.g., voting, adjudication, ratification) and, in some cases, provided that the normative content of their communications is compatible with a number of constitutionally enshrined criteria.[3]

It bears repeating that, first, there are alternative ways of conceptualising law[4] and, secondly, if we embrace the notion of a rule of recognition, we must take into account that different societies operate different rules of recognition; there is no single set of 'markers' that will work regardless of era or circumstance. The purpose of the discussion in this chapter, however, is not to parse the finer points of legal theory, but to offer a workable and working definition of the concept of law implicit in mainstream legal literature.

Regulation, in turn, refers to the act of steering behaviour, deliberately, towards a goal which the steering entity, or regulator, deems desirable.[5] Very frequently, this steering will be undertaken by a public authority that has a specific mandate to that effect and carries out its mission by means of prescriptive rules. In fact, there has long been such a close correlation between the process of steering behaviour, the steering entity and the instrument, that the terms 'regulation' and 'rule', or

1 Andrei Marmor, 'Legal Conventionalism' (1998) 4(4) *Legal Theory*, pp. 509–531.
2 H. L. A. Hart, *The Concept of Law*, 2nd edn. (1994, Oxford University Press), pp. 94–95.
3 Such as the proportionality principle in EU law.
4 See, e.g., John Finnis, *Natural Law and Natural Rights*, 2nd edn. (2011, Oxford University Press) and Lon Fuller, whose critique is succinctly summarised in James C. Ketchen, 'Revisiting Fuller's Critique of Hart: Managerial Control and the Pathology of Legal Systems: The Hart-Weber Nexus' (2003) 53 *University of Toronto Law Journal*, pp. 1–35, at 2–4.
5 See also Section 2.3 in this chapter.

'regulator' and 'public authority', were and often still are used interchangeably.[6] However, as will be discussed in the next sections, the proliferation of TER is a key cause of the recent unravelling of this close conceptual connotation.

A comparison of the working definitions of law and regulation elucidates why the two terms are easily conflated, particularly when the process of regulation is equated with the prescriptive rules through which regulation is still most often operationalised. Indeed, many laws are adopted with an explicitly regulatory intent: to steer a target group's behaviour to serve a goal which is deemed in the public interest. However, not every law is regulatory in nature, and not every regulation is expressed through law. Article 193 of the Belgian Constitution declares that the colours of the Belgian flag are red, yellow and black. It would take an heroically creative interpretation to read a regulatory intent into this authoritative communication. The same goes for Article 23(3), which provides that everyone has a right to a life of human dignity, which includes the right to a healthy environment. Conversely, regulators frequently resort to non-legal means to steer behaviour, either because, for example, an alternative approach is deemed more (cost) effective,[7] or because the regulator does not have lawmaking authority. Returning briefly to the low countries, the Belgian order of physicians regulates the profession, yet its rules and standards are not part of Belgian law.[8]

In sum, there is a close affinity between law and regulation, but although their spheres of meaning overlap, they remain different concepts. That is most emphatically the case for the many laws that do not aim to steer behaviour, and for the many regulations that operate through non-legal means. However, even for those regulations which are encapsulated in legal form, it is argued that the terms are fundamentally distinct because they refer to two different aspects of authority. Regulation is a dynamic notion which focuses on the *exercise* of authority towards a particular goal. Law, in contrast, is an essentialist concept that seeks to convey *what* is being created.[9] To express the distinction in slightly oversimplified but accessible terms: for those cases within the zone of overlap, when the discussion focuses on the *act* of communicating norms, and all that this entails, it focuses on regulation. When it engages with the *content* of the communication, it engages with law.

6 See, e.g., Hood, Rothstein and Baldwin, defining risk regulation as '*governmental* interference with market or social processes to control potential adverse consequences to health' (emphasis added), in Christopher Hood, Henry Rothstein & Robert Baldwin, *The Government of Risk. Understanding Risk Regulation Regimes* (2001, Oxford University Press), p. 3.

7 E.g., 'don't drink-and-drive' campaigns and more frequent policing might be favoured over tightening the maximum allowable limit.

8 P. Vankrunkelsven, K. Merckx, M. De Meyere & J. J. Amy, 'De Orde van geneesheren op een keerpunt: hervormen of verdwijnen' (2012) 68(2) *Tijdschrift voor Geneeskunde*, pp. 57–65, at 59.

9 Cf. Franz von Benda-Beckmann & Keebet von Benda-Beckmann, 'The Dynamics of Change and Continuity in Plural Legal Orders' (2006) 53(4) *Journal of Legal Pluralism & Unofficial Law*, pp. 1–44, at 12.

2.2 WHEN ARE LAW AND REGULATION TRANSNATIONAL?

The terms transnational law and transnational regulation have become mainstays of scholarly and professional discussions. Yet a brief contemplation of the meaning of 'transnational' remains useful, particularly since one of the most prominent characteristics of the term is that it signifies different things to different people.[10] This is partly a consequence of the explosive popularity of the term – ubiquity and precision are poor bedfellows. Moreover, the definition that is conventionally recognised as the bedrock of transnational law,[11] developed by Philip Jessup in 1956, casts its net extremely wide:

> I shall use, instead of 'international law', the term transnational law to include all law which regulates actions or events that transcend national frontiers. Both public and private international law are included, as are other rules which do not wholly fit into such standard categories.[12]

Jessup's definition welcomes a staggering range of provisions under the heading of transnational law, from the *lex mercatoria* to the European Arrest Warrant. It can be read to include every single bilateral and multilateral treaty, as well as any national rule that has a direct or indirect impact on actors located outside the home jurisdiction.

There is much to be said for broad definitions.[13] Jessup's formulation draws our attention to the fact that law can cross boundaries by consequence as well as by design. It reminds us that, even if nationally conceived and implemented, laws echo across borders and that, from the perspective of the addressee, the effects of legal provisions are far more relevant than their provenance. However, for the purpose of case-based exploration, the Jessup formula can be unwieldy. Over time, various refinements have entered the debate, which help distinguish between transnational law in the broad, Jessup sense, and more compact, functionally differentiated readings of transnational law and regulation. The following paragraphs survey some of the most prominent distinctions and explain the approach adopted in this book.

A first distinction separates transnational from international law. The latter is taken to mean treaties made between sovereign states, customary international law and the body of case law issued by international courts; the former covers all legal

[10] Roger Cotterrell, 'What Is Transnational Law' (2012) 37(2) *Law & Social Inquiry*, pp. 500–524, at 501; Craig Scott, '"Transnational Law" as Proto-Concept: Three Conceptions' (2009) 19(7) *German Law Journal*, pp. 859–876, at 862.

[11] Scott, 'Proto-Concept', p. 859.

[12] Philip Jessup, *Transnational Law* (1956, Yale University Press), p. 2.

[13] Veerle Heyvaert & Thijs Etty, 'Introducing Transnational Environmental Law' (2012) 1(1) *Transnational Environmental Law*, pp. 1–11, at 3–7.

arrangements transcending national boundaries that are not captured by these three categories.[14] This is not the distinction adopted in this book. Although it offers a beguilingly straightforward solution to the challenge of locating transnational law, and recognises the importance of varying modes of institutionalisation of law, it is heavily formalistic. The distinction arguably ignores the complexity of lawmaking under the auspices of international conventions, and it underestimates the degree of interpretative autonomy of international adjudication bodies, whose authority is tied to but not wholly reducible to the state.[15] Moreover, from the vantage point of international lawyers, casting transnational law as 'all that is not international law' could be perceived as a regressive exercise. In the past decades, international law professionals and scholars have displayed a marked sensitivity to the role of non-state actors both in the gestation and application of international law.[16] Many of those involved in or commenting on international negotiations have come to see the inclusion of epistemic communities, civil society organisations, indigenous groups and other stakeholders as not only a necessary but also a desirable and constitutive element of international lawmaking. To box international law back into a rigid inter-state confinement could be viewed as a denial of progress in international legal thought and practice.

Related but different from international law, global law refers to cohorts of norms that are unconstrained by jurisdiction or geography. Contemporary scholarship on global law directs our attention to the universalistic, transcendental qualities of law, and typically seeks to abstract a shared, collective core of normativity from myriad localised laws, principles and practices.[17] These abstracted, de-localised global norms, such as the proposed norm of 'publicness' in global administrative law,[18] then become a primary reference point against which to assess the legality of transboundary behaviour, particularly when this behaviour defies straightforward classification under a well-defined jurisdiction. There is, clearly, a great synergy between the concepts of global and transnational law.[19] They share an engagement

[14] Cf. Christoph Schreuer, 'The Waning of the Sovereign State: Towards a New Paradigm for International Law?' (1993) 6(4) *European Journal of International Law*, pp. 447–471, at 447–449; Antonio Cassesse, 'States: Rise and Decline of the Primary Subjects of the International Community' in Bardo Fassbender & Anne Peters, *The Oxford Handbook of the History of International Law* (2012, Oxford University Press), pp. 49–70.

[15] Cf. Anne-Marie Slaughter, 'International Law in a World of Liberal States' (1995) 6(3) *European Journal of International Law*, pp. 503–538, at 517.

[16] Schreuer, 'The Waning of the Sovereign State', pp. 449–453; Math Noortmann, August Reinisch & Cedric Ryngaert (eds.), *Non-State Actors in International Law* (2015, Hart Publishing).

[17] Rafael Domingo, *The New Global Law* (2010, Cambridge University Press); Gunther Teubner (ed.), *Global Law Without a State* (Ashgate, 1997).

[18] Benedict Kingsbury, 'The Concept of "Law" in Global Administrative Law' (2009) 20(1) *European Journal of International Law*, pp. 23–57.

[19] See. e.g., Peer Zumbansen's discussion in 'Transnational Legal Pluralism' (2010) 1(2) *Transnational Legal Theory*, pp. 141–189.

with the challenge of governing transboundary situations, and both embrace the assumption that the norms governing such situations are not and ought not to be wholly reducible to state or inter-state law. It has been claimed that the difference between global and transnational law is chiefly one of perspective: global law is mostly concerned with the construction from the bottom up of an overarching normativity. Transnational legal scholarship, it is argued, is more focused on understanding the interplay between transboundary regimes and the bodies of law and regulation that surround them.[20] It is less preoccupied with the identification of universalisable principles and more willing to find the distinctiveness of transnational law within the plurality of normativity that governs transboundary contexts. This book does not adhere to a strict global law/transnational law divide. Instead it engages with both the interstitial and the transcendental aspects of environmental law and regulation.

In 'Transnational Legal Ordering and State Change', Gregory Shaffer adopts a pragmatic approach towards organising the sprawling world of Jessup's transnational law.[21] He conceptually distinguishes transnational law as 'law applying to transnational situations', from transnational law as 'transnational construction and flow of legal norms'. The former refers to law that targets transnational events and activities. The latter is narrower and consists of legal norms that are exported and imported across borders, with the involvement of international and regional institutions and transnational networks that define and convey the legal norm. The latter condition adds an important institutional dimension to the recognition of transnational law. Yet it is flexible enough to avoid erecting an artificial boundary between transnational and international law and, for this reason, remains open to a productive engagement with the hybridity and complexity of various forms of lawmaking beyond the state, whether they are filed under the rubric of 'private', 'regional', 'supranational' or 'international' law.

The understanding of transnational law and regulation that undergirds this book is akin to 'transnational law as transnational construction and the flow of legal norms' in the Shaffer sense. For regulation to be qualified as transnational within the remit of this work, it has to be *produced* rather than merely *applied* in a transnational setting, with the involvement of actors that are not state authorities.[22] What is attractive about this approach is that it focuses on one of the most game-changing aspects of transnationalisation, namely, the permutation of the institutional

[20] Cf. Veerle Heyvaert, 'What's in a Name? The Covenant of Mayors as Transnational Environmental Regulation' (2013) 22(1) *Review of European, Comparative & International Environmental Law*, pp. 78–90, at 81.

[21] Gregory Shaffer (ed.), *Transnational Legal Ordering and State Change* (2012, Cambridge University Press), p. 5.

[22] It is acknowledged that, from a reflexive perspective, a strict distinction between norm production and application is open to question. This perspective, and its potential consequences for the relation between TER and law, is included in the discussion in Chapter 7.

arrangements and processes through which regulation is generated. It is inclusive yet makes it possible to exclude from the scope of the investigation the countless scenarios in which rules are wholly domestically conceived and applied, but resonate across borders by dint of the economic and technological dominance of the state in question.[23]

2.3 REGULATION IN AN ERA OF TRANSNATIONAL GOVERNANCE

Every year, the Environmental Working Group (EWG) publishes a list of produce sold in the US with the most and the least pesticide contamination. The EWG is a US-based non-profit organisation, and its annual lists are widely known as 'the Dirty Dozen' and 'the Clean Fifteen'.[24] EWG's self-professed aspiration is to use 'the power of information to protect human health and the environment'. The EWG started producing the lists in 2007, when the US Environmental Protection Agency (EPA) discontinued its own annual brochure that informed the public about pesticide residues in food.[25] One of EWG's board members, Drummond Pike, is also a principal with Equilibrium Capital, an intercontinental asset management enterprise that focuses on sustainability-driven investment. Equilibrium Capital's vision is to 'transform the planet through capital markets'; its mission is to 'create and operate a market driven investment platform that catalyzes a significant part of the planet into sustainable prosperity'.[26]

EWG and Equilibrium Capital are both conventionally categorised as private actors, yet they profess not to act – or at least not to act primarily – in the private interest. The information produced by EWG is freely accessible, for the benefit of consumers everywhere, and conveyed in the hope that it will inform consumer choice and, in this manner, transmit incentives through the food marketing chain to switch to pesticide-free produce. Equilibrium Capital channels capital towards sustainable investments in order to strengthen the competitiveness of sustainable enterprises on the market. Its investment behaviour is aimed to incentivise entrepreneurs to adopt sustainable practices and technologies and gradually drive underperforming firms out of the market. The hoped-for conversion to sustainable practices is a public good rather than a private benefit accruing chiefly to the investors.

These kinds of orchestrated steering activities are nowadays often captured under the collective name of 'governance', which in contemporary literature tends to be broadly understood to include 'all processes and institutions, both

[23] As described in Joanne Scott, 'From Brussels with Love: The Transatlantic Travels of European Law and the Chemistry of Regulatory Attraction' (2009) 57(4) *American Journal of Comparative Law*, pp. 897–942.

[24] www.ewg.org/foodnews/.

[25] www.ewg.org/foodnews/summary.php.

[26] www.eq-cap.com/defining-sustainable-alpha/.

formal and informal, that guide and restrain the collective activities of a group'.[27] In fact, the term 'governance' is often reserved for precisely those 'non-hierarchical forms of steering' characterised by the participation of a diverse group of public and private actors, differentiating them from top-down, mandatory forms of public intervention.[28] A more contentious question is whether the actions of EWG and Equilibrium Capital also belong in the subset of governance activities that qualify as 'regulation'. They appear leagues removed from the classical, archetypical image of regulation, which is that of a written rule that prescribes or prohibits certain kinds of behaviour, and that is developed, implemented and, if necessary, enforced by a public authority. The public authority typically will have received a special mandate and commensurate special competencies from the state government, enabling it to fulfil its rule-making and -enforcing functions.[29]

Neither the EWG nor the Equilibrium Capital scenarios previously discussed comfortably fit the bill. Most glaringly, neither are public authorities that operate under a legislative mandate. Increasingly, however, commentators agree that this is not a determinative feature.[30] The presence of a state authority may still be an important marker of regulatory activity, but it is certainly no longer treated as a prerequisite. For instance, as anyone with an even rudimentary knowledge of the European Union will confirm, a significant proportion of the output of EU institutions is, incontrovertibly, classified as regulation. Indeed, the regulatory prowess of the European Union as a level of governance beyond the state is so pronounced that

[27] Douglas Kysar, 'Sustainable Development and Private Global Governance' (2005) 83(7) *Texas Law Review*, pp. 2109–2166, at 2145. Kellow and Zito deploy a narrower definition of governance, one that emphasises a less direct, more steering-oriented mode of engagement but still assumes the central position of a public authority focused on public authority: 'Governance is the capacity of governments or designated public actors to steer their economy and society in a goal-oriented way that differs from what the spontaneous cooperation of actors in the markets and society might achieve'. See Aynsley Kellow & Anthony R. Zito, 'Steering through Complexity: EU Environmental Regulation in the International Context' (2002) 50(1) *Political Studies*, pp. 43–60, at 43. Möllers treats 'governance' as the institutional perspective on the conduct of public institutions that focuses particularly on their externality from the state; their public/private hybridity; their high degree of informality; their efficiency and output; and their sectorality. See Christoph Möllers, 'European Governance: Meaning and Value of a Concept' (2006) 43(2) *Common Market Law Review*, pp. 313–336, at 314–318. Pauwelyn, Wessel and Wouters, in turn, relate 'governance' particularly to policy coordination between public and private actors. See Joost Pauwelyn, Ramses A. Wessel & Jan Wouters, *Informal International Lawmaking* (2012, Oxford University Press), p. 2.

[28] Liliana Andonova, Michele Betsill & Harriet Bulkeley, 'Transnational Climate Governance' (2009) 9(2) *Global Environmental Politics*, pp. 52–73, at 55.

[29] Cf. Julia Black, 'Critical Reflections on Regulation' (2002) 27(1) *Australian Journal of Legal Philosophy*, pp. 1–35, at 2.

[30] Ibid.; Heyvaert, 'What's in A Name', p. 81.

Giandomenico Majone, one of the leading scholars in EU political studies, famously labelled the EU a 'regulatory state'.[31] Evidently, there is regulation outside the institutional trappings of the state.[32]

A second drawback is that neither EWG nor Equilibrium Capital are explicitly engaged in making written, prescriptive rules that can be enforced by public authorities. However, experience has also taught that prescriptive, 'command-and-control' or 'direct' rules constitute an important but not the only technique through which regulation is effectuated. Few would dispute that alternative approaches such as standard setting coupled with certification and accreditation, market-based instruments, disclosure and exemplary codes of conduct have a rightful place in the regulatory panorama. In fact, these approaches have become part and parcel of the regulatory arsenal not only of 'non-traditional' transnational bodies, but of good old-fashioned national regulators as well.[33] As a case in point, we recall that when EWG started its annual release of information on pesticide residues in produce, it took over this role from a body with an undisputed regulatory mandate, the US EPA.[34]

In sum, regulation is no longer identified purely on the basis of authorship (national competent authority) or mode of communication (prescriptive rule). Having unshackled the concept of regulation from its institutional and instrumental chains, a pressing need emerges for an alternative set of definitional boundaries that will prevent this newly liberated notion from becoming too overstretched to remain meaningful.[35] Various attempts have been made at redefining regulation,[36] one of the most successful of which is found in Julia Black's discussion of 'decentred' regulation, which defines regulation as 'the sustained and focused attempt to alter the behaviour of others according to defined standards or purposes with the intention of producing a broadly identified outcome or outcomes, which may involve mechanisms of standard-setting, information-gathering and behaviour-modification'.[37] Another influential approach to developing a de-institutionalised meaning of regulation features in the work of Colin Scott, who focuses on the authoritative nature of regulatory communications and calls regulation 'any process or set of processes by

[31] Giandomenico Majone, 'The Rise of the Regulatory State in Europe' (1994) 17(3) *West European Politics*, pp. 77–101.

[32] Cf. Bronwen Morgan & Karen Yeung, *An Introduction to Law and Regulation* (2007, Cambridge University Press), pp. 303–338.

[33] See Chapter 4.

[34] Cf. Andonova et al., 'Transnational Climate Governance', p. 65.

[35] See Christel Koop & Martin Lodge, 'What Is Regulation? An Interdisciplinary Concept Analysis' (2017) 11(1) *Regulation & Governance*, pp. 85–101.

[36] For an overview, see Black, 'Critical Reflections', p. 8.

[37] Ibid., p. 26.

which norms are established, the behaviour of those subject to the norms monitored or fed back into the regime, and for which there are mechanisms for holding the behaviour of regulated actors within the acceptable limits of the regime (whether by enforcement action or by some other mechanism)'.[38] Building on this rich body of thought, I propose a related but slightly different and, to some extent, more pared-down understanding of regulation: the deliberate exercise of influence on a target's behaviour (designed either to stabilise or modify this behaviour) performed with a certain degree of authority and persistence. In contrast to Black's definition, this formulation recognises that the goal of regulation can be to stabilise rather than modify behaviour and focuses less on a non-exhaustive list of mechanisms that is subject to change. In contrast to Scott's framework, this approach pays more attention to the intent of the regulator, and relatively less to the existence of specific compliance mechanisms.

The proposed definition introduces a new set of interpretative challenges, as neither 'deliberateness' nor 'degree of authority' can be easily ascertained. It is, however, possible to infer the purposive nature and authority from information about an entity or group's behaviour with a reasonable degree of reliability. If an actor or group of actors adopts particular instruments and practices that entrench or modify behaviour (such as standards, guidance documents, tax relief schemes, inspection practices, audit routines) and explicitly identifies the objectives in pursuit of which action is undertaken (e.g., giving more information to consumers, facilitating trade, making bankers more accountable to shareholders, restoring biodiversity), there are clear indications that this actor's behaviour is deliberate. The status of the author can help to inform determinations of authority. However, information about the likely consequences of non-accession or non-compliance, and about the external impacts of adopted instruments (effects on those outside the circle of direct addressees) can also play an important part. If decisions to cooperate or not have serious consequences for candidate addressees, and if the governance regime discernibly affects the experience and choices of third parties, then the regime has a strong claim to authority. Together, these features and attributes may not be sufficient to draw a crystal-clear line between subtly different variants of regulatory and non-regulatory behaviour, but they offer a good starting point for discussion and, ultimately, determination of regulatory action beyond the traditional scope of state-sanctioned intervention.

[38] Colin Scott, 'Analysing Regulatory Space: Fragmented Resources and Institutional Design' (2001) *Public Law*, pp. 329–353, at 331.

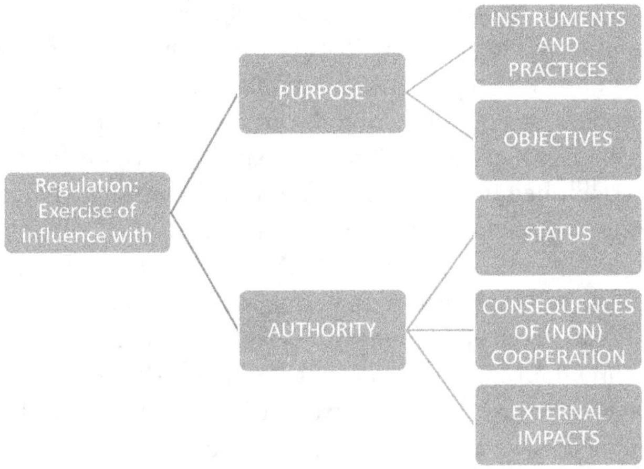

FIGURE 2.1 Key Attributes of Regulation

Armed with this more flexible definition of regulation, and an understanding of the attributes that are indicative of regulatory purpose and authority, a world of transnational regulatory activity beckons. Supranational institutions such as the European Union – whether acting through the Council and Parliament or via the European Commission – regularly and explicitly seek to stabilise or modify a target group's behaviour. Frequently, their target will be one or several Member States, but the latter's behaviour is bound to have a compelling impact on their inhabitants. Moreover, in areas such as complex risk regulation, EU institutions regularly exert a direct influence on the behaviour of private parties. For instance, to market a new pharmaceutical that incorporates biotechnology in the European Union, manufacturers and importers must submit an application to the European Medicines Agency (EMA), which will review and advise the European Commission on whether to grant authorisation.[39] Whether addressing Member States or private parties, EU institutions act with a high degree of deliberation, authority and persistence; their behaviour displays all the attributes indicative of regulation.

EU environmental regulation offers a rich vein of cases for students of transnational regulation to explore. However, the realm of TER and, correspondingly, the scope of this book reach considerably beyond the by now well-established remit of EU regulatory authority. As a transnational regulator, the EU is joined by a constellation of intergovernmental organisations, international associations and networks, ranging from the Association of Southeast Asian Nations (ASEAN) to

[39] Regulation (EC) No 726/2004 laying down Community procedures for the authorisation and supervision of medicinal products for human and veterinary use and establishing a European Medicines Agency [2004] OJ L136/1.

the Organisation for Economic Cooperation and Development (OECD) and the International Maritime Organisation (IMO), which display a growing interest in influencing environmental behaviour and to this end assume regulatory functions. An even more noticeable development is the arrival on the scene of private actors.[40] Standardisation bodies such as the International Organisation for Standardisation (ISO) have an established track record as producers of transnational environmental norms.[41] While their output is not legally binding, ISO standards enjoy a high level of informal authority. Incorporation of ISO standards can even be a proxy for compliance with binding regulatory prescriptions such as compatibility with best available techniques. Non-governmental bodies such as the Forest Stewardship Council (FSC) and the Marine Stewardship Council (MSC) have as their mission the enhancement of environmental protection in the forestry and fisheries sectors respectively, and both have adopted particular instruments and practices (including labelling, certification, inspection, disclosure) towards this end. Neither body can compel the participation of private companies in the forestry or fisheries sector, but the esteem in which they are held, and the positive consumer response their certification elicits, do draw many towards accession and compliance. Such entities are far removed from the official sphere of governmental authority but unquestionably seek to exercise influence towards the achievement of environmental goals, and do so with persistence and a degree of authority.[42]

A major benefit of developing a 'de-governmentalised' or 'de-centred' understanding of regulation is that it injects a degree of flexibility and dynamism into conversations about regulation. Authority and purpose are evolving concepts, the interpretation of which can be adapted depending on the circumstances. However, they are not only evolving but also evaluative: people can reasonably disagree about whether enough indicators are present to qualify a particular exercise of influence as sufficiently deliberate and authoritative to be classified as 'regulation'.[43] For example, is a WTO panel opinion that causes national food safety regulation to be amended a deliberate exercise of behaviour-modifying influence, or are the amendments an unintended side effect of the dispute settlement that is the main purpose of the communication? Is EWG sufficiently high-profile and does it have enough

40 Jessica F. Green, *Rethinking Private Authority. Agents and Entrepreneurs in Global Environmental Governance* (2014, Princeton University Press).

41 Kristina Tamm Hallström & Magnus Boström, *Transnational Multi-Stakeholder Standardization. Organizing Fragile Non-State Authority* (2010, Edward Elgar).

42 Errol Meidinger, 'Beyond Westphalia. Competitive Legalization in Emerging Transnational Regulatory Systems', in Christian Brütsch & Dirk Lehmkuhl (eds.), *Law and Legalization in Transnational Relations* (2007, Routledge), pp. 121–143; Neil Gunningham, 'Environmental Law, Regulation and Governance: Shifting Architectures' (2009) 21(2) *Journal of Environmental Law*, pp. 179–212, at 197. See also David F. Murphy & Jem Bendell, *In the Company of Partners: Environmental Groups and Sustainable Development Post-Rio* (1997, Polity Press), who coin the term 'civil regulation' to refer to instances where organisations of civil society such as NGOs set the standards for business behaviour.

43 Cf. Cotterrell, 'What Is Transnational Law', p. 508.

gravitas for people to actually change their consumer behaviour in response to the Dirty Dozen and Clean Fifteen lists?

On whether to favour a narrow or a wide definition of regulation, the position adopted in this book is that it depends on the nature of the exercise. To investigate whether different variants of TER have a sufficient degree of commonality to constitute a model of regulation, the more cautious approach is to espouse an inclusive perspective. If a large group of subjects is found to share significant features, then this will *a fortiori* be the case for a subset within this group. Drawing the circle too narrowly, in contrast, exposes the analysis to a risk of false-positive identification. Since the search of shared distinctive features is an overarching theme of this work, it is appropriate to adopt an inclusive approach. However, where causal claims are made about the impact of TER on other phenomena, as in the study of TER's impact on law in Chapter 7, I have taken care not to derive conclusions solely from examples located at the periphery of the regulatory landscape. Borderline cases are not avoided, but the analysis does not to attribute characteristics to TER exclusively on the basis of examples that would only fit within a very liberal conceptualisation of regulation.

Finally, I should acknowledge that the adoption of a wide-angled viewpoint, with safeguards where needed, is also in line with a personal, normative choice that, when in doubt, the possibility of authority should not be easily dismissed. For putative regulatory addressees, decisions to join so-called governance networks may have foregone conclusions even if they are formally 'free'. Or, the real choice may not reside in *whether* to accede to an environmental governance scheme, but *which one* to join. Most importantly, after accession the costs of non-compliance or withdrawal can be significantly higher than the optional or consensual nature of the arrangement suggests. Sunk costs, reputational costs, the loss of opportunity to recoup on investment in compliance, loss of access to facilitation, and the prospect of public or private dispute resolution can conspire to create an environment in which freedom is experienced in name only. For these reasons, this books errs on the side of inclusion.

2.4 FIVE CONTINENTS OF TER

Reflections on the meaning of both the 'transnational' and 'regulatory' components of TER help to bring into focus a more cohesive picture of the subject of analysis. The following section aims to stabilise the field of TER further by mapping different spaces of transnational environmental regulatory activity and enriching them with concrete examples. The spaces are constructed with reference to the type of regulatory authority involved, which generates the following three categories: public TER, private TER and a mixed category of hybrid TER. Within the public and private TER groups, it is furthermore possible to distinguish between those regulatory initiatives that are primarily addressed to public authorities, and those that chiefly engage with the private sector. In total, therefore, the TER map consists of five continents of regulation: public/public TER, public/private TER, private/private TER, private/public TER and hybrid TER.

There is an admittedly old-fashioned tinge to an approach that seeks to organise a field of authoritative communication by looking at the formal status of the authors and the addressees. It might even seem an unfortunate choice for a study premised on the observation that regulation is no longer the prerogative of one privileged actor. The main reason why this study does initially draw on public and private categorisations is that much of contemporary scholarship on regulation uses the public/private distinction as a delineating and organisational tool. Echoing this approach here, at least at the introductory stage, helps to anchor the study within a broader context of existing scholarship, and thus facilitates knowledge building.[44] The strategy is to start with a more familiar approach to analytical organisation, and then build up a layered, thicker understanding of TER in subsequent chapters, which approach TER from an alternative range of vantage points such as intentionality (Chapter 3), strategy (Chapters 4–6) and normativity (Chapters 7 and 8).

It should also be clear that the following TER categories serve as an organisational tool but are not meant to drive rigid wedges between fields of transnational regulatory activity. One compelling consequence of embracing a decentred understanding of regulation is that it challenges the image of the regulator as a monolithic entity.[45] Let us take the example of the European Commission. On the one hand, this institution is unquestionably a public body with wide-ranging regulatory competencies. On the other, our appreciation of the European Commission as a regulatory authority would be anaemic if it disregarded the vital contributions made by Member States, agencies and even stakeholders to the smooth running of the EU regulatory machinery.[46] If we see the latter as external inputs to regulation, the categorisation of the European Commission under the public regulator heading stands. If, however, we embrace the alternative but equally plausible view that Member States, epistemic communities, stakeholders and so on play a constitutive part in the consolidation of regulatory authority, we might treat Commission rules as an example of hybrid regulation. In sum, the reconceptualisation of regulation comes with a realisation that regulatory authorship is always, to an extent, composite.[47] The difference between public, private and hybrid regulation is therefore one of degree rather than essence.

44 Cf. Gralf-Peter Calliess & Peer Zumbansen, *Rough Consensus and Running Code: A Theory of Transnational Private Law* (2010, Bloomsbury Publishing).

45 Rieneke Slager, Jean-Pascal Gond & Jeremy Moon, 'Standardization as Institutional Work: The Regulatory Power of a Responsible Investment Standard' (2012) 33(5/6) *Organization Studies*, pp. 763–790, at 764.

46 Heyvaert, 'What's in a Name', p. 81.

47 Cf. Meidinger, 'Beyond Westphalia', p. 128; Andonova et al., 'Transnational Climate Governance', p. 67.

2.4.1 *Public TER*

TER that emanates from public authorities often regulates public authorities. However, there is also a rich vein of TER initiatives governed by public actors that directly address private parties. The following sections discuss each in turn.

Public/Public TER

The public/public category houses TER that is both developed by and addressed to public authorities. This includes cases in which states feature as the main governing and governed entities, and TER managed by or addressed to public authorities other than national governments.

A first and very prominent group of examples of public/public TER is MEAs. For instance, Article IV of the Convention on the Prevention of Marine Pollution by Dumping of Wastes and Other Matters (London Convention)[48] addresses its signatory states with a demand to prohibit the dumping at sea of 'any wastes or other matter in whatever form'. Article 4(1) of the Minamata Convention on Mercury[49] orders its member countries to ban the manufacture and trade in mercury-added products. Often, international agreements will call for the establishment of transnational commissions or committees that assume regulatory powers to implement the general treaty-based environmental objectives. Article 6 of the Southern Bluefin Tuna Convention (SBT Convention)[50] establishes the Commission for the Conservation of SBT, which annually sets the Total Allowable Catch for each signatory state.[51] Students of EU environmental law, too, are thoroughly familiar with the public/public variant of TER. EU environmental directives, covering issues from ambient air quality to wild birds,[52] typically contain a high quotient of prescription directed at the Member States, which are charged with either maintaining or, much more frequently, modifying their regulatory regimes to achieve the directive's environmental protection targets.

International conventions and EU law yield the most familiar examples of public/public TER, but there are many others. In the past two decades, several non-European regional associations have expanded their remit to include environmental protection, and they increasingly expect their member states to achieve collectively

48 London (UK), 29 Dec. 1972, in force 30 August 1975, available at www.imo.org/en/OurWork/Environment/LCLP/Documents/LC1972.pdf.

49 Geneva (Switzerland), 19 Jan 2013, in force 16 August 2017, available at www.mercuryconvention.org/.

50 Canberra (Australia), 10 May 1993, in force 20 May 1994 (SBT Convention), available at www.ccsbt.org/userfiles/file/docs_english/basic_documents/convention.pdf.

51 Howard S. Schiffman & Briony Patricia MacPhee, 'The Southern Bluefin Tuna Dispute Revisited: How Far Have We Come?' (2014) 3(2) *Transnational Environmental Law*, pp. 395–396.

52 Directive 2008/50/EC on ambient air quality and cleaner air for Europe [2008] OJ L152/1; Directive 2009/147/EC on the conservation of wild birds (codified version) [2010] OJ L20/7.

agreed environmental targets. ASEAN, for one, has significantly expanded its environmental agenda. It has developed a range of instruments in the areas of biodiversity, wildlife protection and climate change that will promote regulatory reform and convergence within the region.[53] Within the Asia-Pacific Economic Cooperation Mechanism (APEC), too, awareness is growing that its attempts at economic integration must be complemented by enhanced cooperation on environmental policy.[54] In Africa, cooperative networks such as the Southern African Development Community (SADC) foster the adoption of cooperative frameworks to further environmental protection and sustainable management of collective natural resources.[55] One such framework is the Revised Protocol on Shared Watercourses which, inter alia, introduces requirements of notification and consultation between countries in the southern African region on measures that may affect the condition of a shared watercourse.[56] Given the predicted intensification of regional cooperation and agreement,[57] it is important to be aware of this growth sector in TER.

Moreover, states are not the only public entities that pursue environmental governance through transnational initiatives. The EU environmental legal regime, for one, is co-determined by at least two public entities that are non-state actors: the European Commission, and the European Parliament. Other public/public networks with a more 'mixed' character include initiatives such as the Forest Law Enforcement, Governance and Trade (FLEGT) Facility.[58] FLEGT's mission is to prevent exports of illegally logged wood. To this end, the European Commission negotiates Voluntary Partnership Agreements (VPAs) with developing countries to create export-licensing regimes. Licensing operates on the basis of jointly defined standards, requirements for monitoring and performance review, and third-party verification. In exchange for developing countries' VPA commitments, the FLEGT Facility offers capacity-building and development assistance.[59]

[53] Koh Kheng Lian, 'Transboundary and Global Environmental Issues: The Role of ASEAN' (2012) 1(1) *Transnational Environmental Law*, pp. 67–82.

[54] Antonina Ivanova & Manuel Angeles, 'Trade and Environment Issues in APEC' (2006) 43(4) *The Social Science Journal*, pp. 629–642.

[55] Aldo Chircop et al., 'Governance of Marine Protected Areas in East Africa: A Comparative Study of Mozambique, South Africa, and Tanzania' (2010) 41(1) *Ocean Development & International Law*, pp. 1–33, at 7.

[56] Windhoek (South Africa), 7 Aug. 200, in force 22 Sept. 2003, available at www.sadc.int/files/3413/6698/6218/Revised_Protocol_on_Shared_Watercourses_-_2000_-_English.pdf.

[57] Gabriele Suder, 'Regional Trade Agreements and Regionalisation: Motivations and Limits of a Global Phenomenon' (2013) 4 (1) *ANU Centre for European Studies Briefing Paper Series*, available at http://ces.anu.edu.au/research/publications/regional-trade-agreements-and-regionalisation-motivations-and-limits-global-ph.

[58] www.euflegt.efi.int/about-flegt.

[59] Christine Overdevest & Jonathan Zeitlin, 'Assembling an Experimentalist Regime: Transnational Governance Interactions in the Forest Sector' (2014) 4(1) *Regulation & Governance*, pp. 22–48, at 28.

The Covenant of Mayors for Energy and Climate Change offers yet another example of complex public/public TER involving authorities other than national governments. The signatories to the Covenant are cities and towns that, by virtue of their accession, commit to increasing energy efficiency and use of renewable energy sources on their territories.[60] In practical terms, this requires the signatories to develop a baseline emission inventory (with 1990 as the recommended but not compulsory baseline). Within one year of accession, signatories are expected to submit a Strategic Energy Action Plan, or 'SEAP', which maps out the different approaches and policies that the town or city intends to implement to achieve its minimum 20% reduction target. Additionally, participating towns and cities are expected to submit regular implementation reports. The European Commission developed and now administers the programme.[61] It is in charge of facilitating, supervising and policing compliance with the Covenant's prescriptions. In exchange for participation, cities and towns gain access to expertise and funding opportunities, they become part of an extensive information exchange and support network, and they are able to give their green credentials a substantial boost.[62]

Public/public TER also flourishes outside the EU context. In the field of climate change, particularly, initiatives such as the Regional Greenhouse Gas Initiative (RGGI), the Western Climate Initiative (WCI), Local Governments for Sustainability (ICLEI) and World Cities Network are steadily expanding their agenda to include a broader range of steering and standard-setting activities. This is overtly the case for RGGI, which developed a mandatory cap-and-trade programme for greenhouse gas (GHG) emissions.[63] At present, participation in the RGGI emissions trading system is limited to nine US-based states, but several Canadian provinces have observer status.[64] WCI is a non-profit and, hence, strictly speaking it is a private organisation.[65] However, its board members are officials from Quebec, British Columbia and the state of California, and its mission is to support the implementation of state and provincial GHG emissions trading programmes. WCI is responsible for the management of allowance auctioning and for compliance monitoring. It thus plays a key role in securing the effectiveness of climate change regulation in parts of Canada and the US.

60 Information available at www.eumayors.eu/index_en.html.

61 Pedro Ballesteros Torres & Roman Doubrava, 'The Covenant of Mayors: Cities Leading the Fight against the Climate Change' in Maryke Van Staden & Francesco Musco (eds.), *Local Governments and Climate Change* (2010, Springer), pp. 91–98.

62 Heyvaert, 'What's in a Name', p. 82.

63 Andonova et al., 'Transnational Climate Governance', p. 65.

64 www.rggi.org/.

65 www.wci-inc.org/.

Public/Private TER

A second category of TER is public/private TER. In contrast to the previous cohort, public/private TER eschews the intermediary of the state, region or city and speaks directly to the private sector. In recent years, public/private arrangements have become increasingly prominent in EU product risk regulation. The EU REACH Regulation, for example, addresses itself immediately to manufactures and importers of chemicals and instructs them to register traded substances and products with ECHA.[66] National regulatory authorities retain facilitating and policing roles in this arrangement, which are certainly significant but do not change the fact that channels of communication now flow directly between a transnational regulator and the private addressee. Similarly, the 2012 EU Biocides Regulation puts the European Commission in charge of approving the use of active ingredients in biocidal products.[67] Authorisations and refusals are directly addressed to the private company that produces or imports the biocide in question, and are challengeable before the CJEU, rather than before domestic courts.[68] The application process moreover fosters the development of network structures that require a novel degree of coordination between transnational regulators, state authorities and private regulatees. Pursuant to Article 9 of the Biocides Regulation, the applicant submits the request for approval to ECHA, accompanied by, first, a proposal for a candidate national competent authority to evaluate the application and, secondly, written proof that the competent authority has agreed to perform the evaluation. This aptly illustrates how relations between the public and private are constantly being reconfigured in the transnational legal sphere.

At the United Nations (UN) level, too, a number of programmes interact directly with the private sector. The Global Compact, for example, is a UN-led initiative that encourages businesses to adopt sustainable and corporate-responsible practices.[69] Acceding to the Compact signals an enterprise's commitment to abide by the standards and sustainability targets of the Compact, and to comply with associated

[66] Regulation (EC) No 1907/2006 concerning the Registration, Evaluation, Authorisation and Restriction of Chemicals (REACH), establishing a European Chemicals Agency, amending Directive 1999/45/EC and repealing Council Regulation (EEC) No 793/93 and Commission Regulation (EC) No 1488/94 as well as Council Directive 76/769/EEC and Commission Directives 91/155/EEC, 93/67/EEC, 93/105/EC and 2000/21/EC [2007] OJ L136/3.

[67] Regulation (EU) No 528/2012 concerning the making available on the market and use of biocidal products [2012] OJ L167/1.

[68] See, e.g., Case C-190/13P *Rütgers Germany GmbH and Others* v *European Chemicals Agency (ECHA)* ECLI: EU: C: 2014: 2174; C-287/13P *Bilbaína de Alquitranes SA and Others* v *ECHA* ECLI: EU: C: 2014: 599; and C-199/13P *Polyelectrolyte Producers Group and Others* v *European Commission* ECLI: EU: C: 2014: 205.

[69] www.unglobalcompact.org.uk/. See 'More Firms Join UN Sustainability Initiative' *ENDS Europe Daily*, 6 June 2012.

information-disclosure requirements.[70] The Compact's structure is similar to that of the Covenant of Mayors for Energy and Climate Change, in that it is a voluntary membership scheme orchestrated and administered by a supranational public entity at the behest of its signatories. A notable difference is that the Covenant is addressed to public actors (towns and cities), whereas the Compact has private businesses for signatories. As a final example, one of the most prominent exponents of government-led OECD measures directed at the private sector is the OECD Guidelines for Multinational Enterprises (OECD MNE Guidelines). The Guidelines are

> far-reaching recommendations addressed by governments to multinational enterprises operating in or from adhering countries. They provide voluntary principles and standards for responsible business conduct in areas such as employment and industrial relations, human rights, environment, information disclosure, combating bribery, consumer interests, science and technology, competition, and taxation.[71]

2.4.2 *Private TER*

The past decades have witnessed an explosive growth of private environmental regulation. This regulation tends to rely heavily on standard-setting and certification methodologies, its membership is typically sectorally rather than jurisdictionally defined and it trades on a high degree of informal authority. The boom in private TER is one of the most important factors propelling the transformation of environmental regulation and necessitating the development of a new model of TER.

Private/Private TER

Nearly all private TER is designed by (or with heavy involvement of) the private sector for the private sector. Prominent among private/private TER are schemes that essentially function as self-regulatory regimes within an industrial or service sector. Responsible Care® in the chemicals sector is one such scheme.[72] Its key role is to standardise health, safety and environmental practices for chemicals manufacturing and professional use. The Global Sustainable Tourism Council (GSTC) is an example from the service sector. Its members are travel associations, tourism boards and large operators, and its overarching mission is to arrive at a common understanding of sustainable tourism and develop a set of minimum criteria that every tourism business should uphold.[73] Business-driven participation in sectoral self-regulation

70 Kenneth W. Abbott & Duncan Snidal, 'Strengthening International Regulation through Transnational New Governance: Overcoming the Orchestration Deficit' (2009) 42 *Vanderbilt Journal of Transnational Law*, pp. 501–578, at 506.

71 http://mneguidelines.oecd.org/about/.

72 Cary Coglianese & Evan Mendelson, 'Meta-Regulation and Self-Regulation' in Robert Baldwin, Martin Cave & Martin Lodge (eds.), *The Oxford Handbook of Regulation* (2010, Oxford University Press), pp. 146–168, at 154–155.

73 www.gstcouncil.org/.

can be seen as an expression of corporate social responsibility (CSR), which generally refers to companies taking responsibility for their impact on society.[74]

Private/private TER has flourished particularly in 'heavy industry' sectors with a history of environmental disasters and, correspondingly, a vulnerable public reputation. Self-regulation initiatives in extractive industries and in construction are cases in point. For example, the Initiative for Responsible Mining Assurance (IRMA) was set up to deliver a multi-stakeholder and independently verifiable responsible mining assurance system that purports to improve the social and environmental performance of the ever-controversial mining sector.[75] Of a newer generation but equally controversial is shale gas extraction. Given the strong business interest in fracking, the myriad uncertainties surrounding its long-term impact and the pressure from well-organised civil society campaigning groups, it is unsurprising that the sector is deeply invested in developing private/private governance networks. The Centre for Sustainable Shale Development (CSSD) is an interesting example: its strategic partners include environmental organisations,[76] philanthropic foundations,[77] energy companies[78] and other stakeholders.[79] This multi-party collaboration's professed aim is to develop and maintain sustainable shale gas exploitation standards. Increasingly, like-minded organisations in different countries are linking and developing networks. This multiplies opportunities for the transnational generation of environmental prescriptions and standards.

The food industry, too, is known for its heavy environmental impact and its vulnerability to consumer opinion. Private/private TER in this sector ranges from large cross-sectoral programmes to governance regimes that focus on particular food groups. In the former category, the International Federation of Organic Agriculture Movements (IFOAM) targets private operators that want to use the IFOAM Global Organic Mark label. However, most of its activity concentrates on offering guidance to other private certification programmes, streamlining certification practices and pursuing the harmonisation and equivalence of both private and publicly developed food standards.[80] In the latter category, the MSC develops sustainable fishing standards and offers certification and labelling services to its members.[81]

Private/private TER is also revolutionising conservation law. Forestry programmes such as the FSC, the Programme for the Endorsement of Forest Certification

[74] Adrian Cadbury, 'Corporate Social Responsibility' (2006) 1(1) *Twenty-First Century Society: Journal of the Academy of Social Sciences*, pp. 5–21.

[75] www.responsiblemining.net/.

[76] E.g., the Environmental Defense Fund (EDF) and Group Against Smog Pollution (GASP)

[77] E.g., Citizens for Pennsylvania's Future (PennFuture); the Benedum Foundation.

[78] E.g., Chevron, Shell.

[79] E.g., the Pennsylvania Environmental Council. Like many transnational networks, multi-stakeholder organisations such as CSSD are rarely 'purely' public or private in either authorship or audience. CSSD could therefore also be classified under the hybrid category.

[80] www.ifoam.org/en/node.

[81] www.msc.org/.

(PEFC) and the Sustainable Forestry Initiative (SFI) offer similar, even competing schemes for sustainable forest management and wood harvesting, as well as widely recognised certification and labelling services.[82] The previously mentioned MSC is modelled on the FSC and seeks to do for seas and oceanic ecosystems what the FSC does for forests. The Rainforest Alliance targets the conservation of Brazilian rainforest biodiversity through the implementation of a combination of environmental, social and fair-trade standards to establish and maintain sustainable rainforest-management practices. Its development of these multi-resource, holistic ecosystem-oriented meta-standards partly happens through in-house standardisation, but the Alliance also recognises and incorporates other privately developed environmental standards, such as the FSC standards.[83] The proliferation of private environmental standard setting, certification and labelling thus also stimulates the development of private regimes for the mutual recognition of externally produced private regulation. With it emerge new transnational legal conventions for the treatment and review of claims to equivalence.[84]

A last, very significant group of private/private TER concerns those programmes that address the financial and investment sector and seek to harness the regulatory potential of capital flows as communication devices between the public and the economy. Assuming pride of place among these are the Equator Principles, which are currently in their third iteration (EP III). EP III is a credit risk management framework for determining, assessing and managing environmental and social risk in project finance transactions. Equator Principles Financial Institutions (EPFIs), which number eighty organisations located in thirty-four countries, commit to not providing loans to projects where the borrower will not or is unable to comply with their respective social and environmental policies and procedures.[85] The Equator Principles are probably the best-known example of a banking- and investment-focused TER initiative, but there are many others, such as the Banking Environment Initiative,[86] the FTSE4Good index,[87] and the 2050 Criteria for Sustainable Commodities Investment.[88] These organisations have different membership and operating procedures, but they all share a mission to promote and even compel

82 www.fsc-uk.org/; www.pefc.co.uk/; www.sfiprogram.org/; Veerle Heyvaert, 'Regulatory Competition – Accounting for the Transnational Dimension of Environmental Regulation' (2012) 25(1) *Journal of Environmental Law*, pp. 1–31, at 21.

83 www.rainforest-alliance.org/.

84 Kalypso Nicolaidis & Gregory Shaffer, 'Transnational Mutual Recognition Regimes: Governance without Global Government' (2005) 68(3/4) *Law & Contemporary Problems*, pp. 263–317.

85 www.equator-principles.com/.

86 www.cisl.cam.ac.uk/Business-Platforms/Banking-Environment-Initiative.aspx.

87 www.ftse.co.uk/Indices/FTSE4Good_Index_Series/.

88 www.worldwildlife.org/publications/the-2050-criteria-guide-to-responsible-investment-in-agri cultural-forest-and-seafood-commodities.

environmentally sustainable industry and service provision by channelling investment and banking services.[89]

Private/Public TER

Just as examples of public/private TER are less plentiful than the nearly countless number of public/public regulatory regimes, we find far fewer instances of private/public TER than of private/private ones. Transnational environmental regulators, it transpires, chiefly communicate with similarly situated addressees. Nevertheless, in some cases private governance regimes do steer the behaviour of public authorities. This happens when private environmental standards become so successful that public authorities decide to formally join in or *de facto* abide by them. Errol Meidinger discusses this phenomenon with respect to the FSC. He observes that several municipalities and countries have adopted procurement policies that track FSC requirements. Some have had publicly owned forests FSC certified; others have made certification a condition for lawfully conducting forestry in the country, and others still have essentially cut and pasted the FSC standards into national legislation.[90]

In a similar vein, the work of European (private) standardisation bodies became a legally relevant benchmark under the EU's New Approach to Harmonisation.[91] Products and services conforming to standards issued by the European Committee for Standardization (CEN), the European Committee for Electrotechnical Standardization (CENELEC) or ETSI[92] are presumed to be in conformity with EU law, which shifts the burden of proof to any entity questioning their lawfulness to be traded on the EU internal market.[93] The case of the GHS goes one step further as the EU formally incorporated this set of voluntary standards, developed under the auspices of the OECD by a combination of private- and public-sector representatives, in EU law.[94]

Finally, an intriguing development in the sphere of private/public TER involves the indirect regulation of public authorities via private certification. In a recent analysis of transnational fisheries regulation, Markus Karavias discusses the case of the Maldives Seafood Processors and Exporters Association (MSPEA), which aimed

89 Cf. Slager et al., 'Standardization as Institutional Work'.

90 Errol Meidinger, 'Beyond Westphalia', p. 131.

91 Council Resolution 85/C 136/01 of 7 May 1985 on a new approach to technical harmonisation and standards [1985] OJ C136/1.

92 ETSI standardises information and communications technologies (ICT). Its name used to be an acronym of 'European Telecommunications Standardization Institute', but the long name has fallen into disuse in light of the expansion of ETSI's remit. See www.etsi.org/about.

93 Jacques Pelkmans, 'The New Approach to Technical Harmonization and Standardization' (1987) 25(3) *Journal of Common Market Studies*, pp. 249–269.

94 Regulation (EC) No 1272/2008 on Classification, Labelling and Packaging of substances and mixtures, amending and repealing Directives 67/548/EEC and 1999/45/EC, and amending Regulation (EC) No 1907/2006 [2008] OJ L353/1.

to have its pole-and-line skipjack tuna fishery certified by the MSC. The MSC conditionalised certification on compliance with a number of requirements, some of which were addressed to the MSPEA but including others that could only be met by the Maldives state authorities. In particular, the MSC conditions included a requirement that, within five years of certification, the Maldives state would have successfully promoted the adoption of harvest-control rules by the intergovernmental Indian Ocean Tuna Commission (IOTC).[95] This MSC requirement ultimately led to the adoption of IOTC Resolution 16/02.[96]

In sum, private/public TER happens when public authorities incorporate, accede to or are indirectly annexed in private/private TER. The examples aptly illustrate a widespread phenomenon affecting transnational networks: as they mature, their membership diversifies and their organisation structure becomes more elaborate and complex. In some cases, the qualities of diversification and complexity become so pronounced that they arguably constitute the network's most defining characteristic. The final category discussed in the next paragraphs offers illustrations of such complex, hybrid networks.

2.4.3 *Hybrid TER*

Governance networks inevitably depend on some combination of public and private engagement to acquire the content, traction and credibility that are necessary to claim regulatory authority. Moreover, arrangements evolve. What starts as a private initiative may catch the attention of government officials. Over time, transnational public authorities may get more opportunities to skip the national regulatory middleman and address themselves directly to the private sector. It is therefore likely that, over time, hybrid regulatory networks will become the norm rather than the exception in the environmental landscape. Several earlier examples of transnational networks have clear hybrid features, such as FLEGT, the Covenant of Mayors for Climate and Energy,[97] the FSC and the CSSD. For example, local civil society stakeholders are heavily involved in developing mutually workable definitions of 'legally harvested wood' in FLEGT VPAs. They are also instrumental in monitoring local certification practices.[98] The Covenant of Mayors, in turn, relies extensively on

[95] Markos Karavias, 'Interactions between International Law and Private Fisheries Certification', (2018) 7(1) *Transnational Environmental Law*, pp. 165–184.

[96] Resolution 16/02, 'On Harvest Control Rules for Skipjack Tuna in the IOTC Area of Competence, IOTC, 26 Nov. 2016, available at www.iotc.org/cmm/resolution-1602-harvest-control-rules-skipjack-tuna-iotc-area-competence.

[97] The Covenant of Mayors relies extensively on the involvement of private funding organisations. Non-governmental bodies, such as the Italian Fondazione Cariplo, condition the award of grants to towns and cities upon compliance with the Covenant's requirements. Heyvaert, 'What's in a Name', p. 82.

[98] Overdevest & Zeitlin, 'Assembling an Experimentalist Regime'.

the involvement of private funding organisations. Non-governmental bodies, such as the Italian Fondazione Cariplo, condition the award of grants to towns and cities upon compliance with the Covenant's requirements. The prospect of access to funding is one of the key consequences of cooperation that affirms the authority of the Covenant and, hence, draws it closer to the regulatory sphere.[99] In fact, in certain networks public and private actors have become so entangled that they defy categorisation under either a 'public' or 'private' heading. These are referred to as hybrid networks, or as constituting a 'regime complex'.[100]

The European Union is involved in various hybrid networks to pursue environmental goals. EU oil-rig-safety regulation, for example, effectively relies on a mixture of EU legislation and industry initiatives to function.[101] Corporate and social responsibility, which started as a private-led initiative, is now sanctioned and undergirded by a European Commission policy.[102] Beyond the EU, hybrid network structures are highly prominent in climate change governance. The Chicago Climate Exchange, for instance, is a voluntary cap-and-trade programme that counts states, provinces and countries, as well as businesses, banks and non-governmental organisations (NGOs) among its signatories.[103] In the field of food safety, the Codex Alimentarius Commission (CAC) has seen both its authorship and its audience evolve. At its inception, the CAC was organised as public/private regulation. Its membership was (and continues to be) open to Member Nations and Associate Members of the UN Food and Agriculture Organization and the World Health Organisation, as well as to regional economic integration organisations.[104] Initially, CAC food standards were targeted at the private sector. Yet over time, both the participation in CAC standard setting and the use of resulting CAC standards have diversified. Private interest groups affected by a standard in development will often submit information to the CAC expert committees, and may be consulted by their national governments on the resulting draft standard. A number of member governments include civil society and business representatives in their delegations, and some NGOs have been granted observer status. On the addressees' side, not only food producers but also national governments as well as international organisations, such as the WTO, increasingly deploy CAC standards as benchmarks for compatibility with domestic or international food safety law.[105] Hence, the CAC has transformed from a public/private arrangement into a hybrid transnational network.

99 Heyvaert, 'What's in a Name', p. 82.

100 Overdevest & Zeitlin, 'Assembling an Experimentalist Regime', p. 28.

101 'EU seeks industry assurances over oil rig safety', *ENDS Europe Daily*, 11 May 2010.

102 http://ec.europa.eu/enterprise/policies/sustainable-business/corporate-social-responsibility/index_en.htm.

103 www.theice.com/ccx. See Andonova et al., 'Transnational Climate Governance', p. 62.

104 www.codexalimentarius.org/members-observers/en/.

105 Alexia Herwig, 'The Contribution of Global Administrative Law to Enhancing the Legitimacy of the Codex Alimentarius Commission' in Olaf Dilling, Martin Herberg & Gerd Winter (eds.), *Transnational Administrative Rule-Making. Performance, Legal Effects and Legitimacy* (2011, Hart Publishing), p. 171.

The advantage of designating TER as 'hybrid' is that this effectively conveys the complexity of the network structure. Less felicitously, since every instance or regulation at least informally requires some degree of cooperation by public as well as private actors, the term can easily become a generic default, which undermines the very purpose of the mapping exercise. The approach taken in this book, therefore, is to designate regulatory initiatives as public or private wherever possible, and only fall back on the hybrid category in instances where the former categories fail to convey an aspect of the TER initiative under discussion that is important for the analysis.

2.5 TOWARDS A MODEL OF TRANSNATIONAL ENVIRONMENTAL REGULATION

This chapter has shown that TER covers a broad spectrum of projects and measures. The aim of the following chapters is to build on this framework in order to flesh out the identity of TER. To this end, Chapters 3 to 6 go beyond the common denominator of their non-traditional (non-state) authorship and explore the essential features and qualities of TER through a systematic analysis of, first, the various intentions of transnational environmental regulators and, secondly, the range of regulatory strategies TER deploys. Chapters 7 and 8, in turn, investigate TER through the lens of normativity, examining both the relation between TER and law and the content of TER's key guiding principles.

3

Why Regulate beyond the State?

This chapter examines TER through the lens of regulatory intention. The driving questions are why do actors decide to engage in transnational rule making and what do they seek to achieve through the establishment of transnational environmental regulatory initiatives?

Notwithstanding the burgeoning literature on transnational regulation and governance, the intentions of transnational regulators are rarely subjected to sustained inquiry. Presumably, the answer is considered self-evident: environmental regulators regulate in order to protect the environment. An examination of the underlying reasons why transnational regulators embrace this cause is either considered superfluous, or confined exclusively to the sphere of private TER.[1] However, a thorough exploration of the intentions of transnational environmental regulators has much to contribute. It reorders the expansive field of TER according to different fault lines and thereby creates opportunities to discover thus far submerged commonalities between forms of regulation not usually discussed within the same context. By the same token, it highlights significant differences between regulatory frameworks that are often lumped together for the purpose of analysis. Moreover, the discussion will show that, in the field of TER, intentionality is a useful proxy for a range of regulatory attributes. Different types of actors tend to engage in regulation for different reasons. Conversely, actors with similar intentions tend to deploy similar regulatory strategies and develop regulatory initiatives that display similar strengths and weaknesses. Hence, a thorough understanding of the intentions of regulators can help to predict key features of the regulatory environment in which they operate. Finally, a better understanding of the intentions of the regulator is essential for the development of a meaningful critique of TER. This is, in the first place, because intentions matter in gauging the effectiveness of regulatory regimes: transnational initiatives undertaken to, for example, boost the efficiency of market-based

[1] See Sections 3.3.3 and 3.3.4.

TABLE 3.1 *TER Categorised with Reference to Intentionality*

Purpose	Dominant form	Key features
Collective action TER	Public/public	Consensualism Lowest common denominator risk
Trade facilitation TER	Public/public Public/private	Some 'trading up'; more 'bargaining down' Stagnation risk
Substitute TER	Private/private Private/public	Optional Dependent on cooperation
Risk management TER	Private/private	Club features Aimed at satisficing
Enhancement TER	Hybrid	Linked regimes *or* 'soft' governance networks

instruments should not be measured by the same benchmarks as regulation adopted to stave off state intervention.[2] Secondly, better information on regulatory intentionality, and its impact on the operation and evolution of TER, can help to explain why regulation underdelivers. Moreover, it can show that, even if various TER initiatives display similar strengths and weaknesses, the reasons for their occurrence may be different in each case. Hence, an understanding of intentionality and its effects can result in a better diagnosis of the causes of regulatory deficiencies, which in turn may strengthen our ability to identify paths towards productive change.

The analysis starts with a brief survey of conventionally proffered reasons for the emergence of environmental regulation, and then quickly moves on to the field of TER. It identifies five different types of purpose pursued by transnational regulators. TER may be established: (1) to overcome the challenges to effective governance which jeopardise the protection and delivery of global public goods at a national level; (2) to facilitate trade; (3) to make up a deficit in state or inter-state environmental regulation; (4) to manage the regulator's institutional risks; or (5) to boost the impact of environmental governance. Correspondingly, TER adopted in pursuit of these objectives can be understood as, respectively, (1) collective action TER; (2) trade facilitation TER; (3) substitute TER; (4) risk management TER; and (5) enhancement TER. The analysis offers examples of each variant, and discusses the likely characteristics, strengths and weaknesses that the five types of TER will display.

3.1 WHY REGULATE?

Regulation theory offers three standard accounts for the emergence of regulation: to correct market failure and thereby restore the efficient self-organisation of

[2] Cf. Harro van Asselt, *The Fragmentation of Global Climate Governance: Consequences and Management of Regime Interactions* (2014, Edward Elgar), pp. 89–90.

society; to pursue public interest goals in response to public demand; and to secure an efficient allocation of risk between different social actors.[3] Which view commentators espouse, depends primarily on their conceptualisation of the state as either a sophisticated but morally neutral clearing house for society's diverse political and economic interests; a supplier of social goods with its own understanding of what the good of society means and entails; or a fixer of 'social bads' whose chief role consists of keeping the negative side-effects of private choices within acceptable limits. Applied to the field of environmental protection, measures governing, say, industrial waste disposal may thus be explained as either designed to internalise the costs of industrial production in a context where transaction costs prevent industries and those exposed to industrial waste from striking efficient bargains (market failure paradigm);[4] a reallocation of the risks attached to waste dumping from the public to the enterprise (risk paradigm); or as an intervention to protect biodiversity and the landscape, sustainability or, potentially, human rights through safeguarding the peaceful enjoyment of the home (public interest paradigm).[5]

The market, risk and public interest explanations are an invaluable cornerstone in the expanding edifice of regulation theory, but they barely touch on the intentions of the regulator. In their focus on the particular deficits or wants within society to which regulation responds, the explanations are overwhelmingly demand-focused. Society may want waste disposal regulation, but this does not directly explain why regulators respond and deliver it. When we approach the question from the supply side, we underline alternative aspects of the regulatory complex. Moreover, and importantly in the context of this discussion, the answers work out quite differently depending on whether the regulator in question is operating at the level of the state, or beyond.

Within a conventional national context, the most immediate instigator of environmental regulatory activity, from formulating waste disposal standards and administering environmental licensing schemes to reviewing development applications, inspecting industrial premises and orchestrating flood defence, is the existence of a legislative mandate. The mandate, in turn, is articulated by the legislative and executive branches of government which, in democratic societies, respond to the

[3] Cf. Eric Windholz & Graeme A. Hodge, 'Conceptualising Social and Economic Regulation: Implications for Modern Regulators and Regulatory Activity' (2012) 38(2) *Monash University Law Review*, pp. 212–237, at 213–215.

[4] Robert Baldwin, Martin Cave & Martin Lodge, *Understanding Regulation. Theory, Strategy, and Practice*, 2nd edn. (2012, Oxford University Press), p. 18.

[5] Tony Prosser, *The Regulatory Enterprise: Government Regulation and Legitimacy* (2010, Oxford University Press), pp. 13–17; Tony Prosser, 'Regulation and Social Solidarity' (2006) 33(3) *Journal of Law and Society*, pp. 364–387.

electorate.[6] Environmental regulation beyond the state, however, rarely happens because of a legal mandate. In the case of private regulation, actors assume a regulatory role without being required (or in many cases even invited) to do so. In the public sphere, while national legal and constitutional provisions may not prevent authorities from pursuing public interest goals at a transnational level, they will typically not demand it either. The choice to regulate at a level beyond the state is therefore one that needs to be explained.

3.2 WHY REGULATE TRANSNATIONALLY?

It has become commonplace in the transnational regulation and governance literature to attribute the rise of regulation beyond the state to globalisation.[7] Key globalisation phenomena such as the multinational scale of corporations, the intensification of trans-border investment and trade, the proliferation of trans-boundary health and environmental risks, and the increasingly transnational character of scientific and technological research, represent as many challenges to effective governance at an exclusively national level.[8] The globalisation of trade, enterprise, the workforce, finance and knowledge fuels a demand for institutions and interventions that can reach beyond the boundaries of national jurisdiction.

Fascinating though the globalisation perspective is, it too is a demand-focused account which offers little insight into the reasons why public authorities, organisations and individuals answer the call for transnational regulation and become transnational regulators. The aim of this chapter is to bridge this knowledge gap to understand in greater detail the variety or reasons why actors – ranging from state authorities, regional entities and intergovernmental organisations to private commercial enterprises and civil society organisations – decide to engage in transnational environmental regulatory behaviour.

One challenge to the identification of regulatory purpose is that transnational environmental regulators may not be explicit about their intentions. Ostensibly, all TER is adopted to improve environmental protection, and this is the justification most frequently expressed in the mission statements of transnational regulators. Article 191(1) of the Treaty on the Functioning of the European Union (TFEU) stipulates that EU policy on the environment shall contribute to the pursuit of environmental and human health objectives and the protection of natural resources, and that it shall promote measures to further such goals at the international level, in

6 Veerle Heyvaert, 'Regulatory Competition – Accounting For the Transnational Dimension of Environmental Regulation' (2013) 25(1) *Journal of Environmental Law*, pp. 1–31, at 5.

7 See Section 1.2; Christoph Knill & Dirk Lehmkuhl, 'Private Actors and the State: Internationalization and Changing Patterns of Governance' (2002) 15(1) *Governance*, pp. 41–63.

8 David Held & Anthony McGrew (eds.), *Governing Globalization: Power, Authority and Global Governance* (2002, Polity Press).

particular to combat climate change. The preamble to the Paris Agreement declares itself in pursuit of 'the objective of the [UNFCCC] Convention' which is the 'stabilization of greenhouse gas concentrations in the atmosphere at a level that would prevent dangerous anthropogenic interference with the climate system'.[9] The overarching agenda of Local Governments for Sustainability is the creation of sustainable cities, which support and deliver low-emission, nature-based, circular, resilient, equitable and people-centred development.[10] The MSC mission is to 'use our ecolabel and fishery certification program to contribute to the health of the world's oceans by recognising and rewarding sustainable fishing practices, influencing the choices people make when buying seafood, and working with our partners to transform the seafood market to a sustainable basis'.[11] Yet, again, such statements reveal little about why transnational regulators want to organise around this goal. In the absence of a public mandate,[12] it is not obvious why public or private transnational actors would set themselves the difficult and often thankless task of safeguarding general interest objectives such as having the oceans 'teeming with life'.[13]

It is, however, possible to infer different intentions behind TER from texts and documentation released by transnational regulators, particularly when read in combination with discussions in the literature about the rationale for regulation generally and transnational regulation in particular. On some occasions, explicit confirmations of regulatory intent are available. For instance, the Equator Principles self-define as a 'risk management framework, adopted by financial institutions, for determining, assessing and managing environmental and social risk in projects ... *primarily intended to provide a minimum standard for due diligence to support responsible risk decision-making*' (emphasis added).[14] In other cases, allusions to regulatory intent are less direct. Responsible Care®, a chemical health and safety regime established and managed by the chemicals sector, indicates in its mission statement that its aim is 'to drive continuous improvement in chemical product safety, as part of the industry's signature environmental, health, safety and security program'.[15] The noteworthy term, here, is 'signature': environmental objectives are pursued, but the mission statement heavily hints at a preoccupation with the

[9] Paris (France), 12 Dec. 2015, in force 4 Nov. 2016, available at http://unfccc.int/paris_agreement/items/9485.phph.

[10] ICLEI – Local Governments for Sustainability, 2018. ICLEI in the urban era. Bonn, Germany (available at https://worldcongress2018.iclei.org/wp-content/uploads/World%20Congress%202018%20booklet.pdf).

[11] https://20.msc.org/about-the-msc/what-is-the-msc.

[12] Exceptionally, the EU could be said to have a mandate for TER as expressed in Article 191 TFEU. However, the EU (formerly the European Community) had already adopted an impressive range of environmental measures before the incorporation of an environmental policy mandate during the 1987 Treaty amendments.

[13] https://20.msc.org/about-the-msc/what-is-the-msc.

[14] www.equator-principles.com/.

[15] www.icca-chem.org/responsible-care/.

creation of a distinctive identity. It alludes to environmental self-regulation as part of a corporate branding strategy and a reputational management tool.

The remainder of this chapter identifies and discusses five reasons why state or non-state actors engage in the development or support of TER. As usual, the analytical parsimony expressed in five categories is distilled from a considerably messier reality. In practice, regulators often hope to kill several birds with one stone; one set of measures may be adopted both to, say, facilitate trade and to manage risks confronted by the regulator. The likelihood of multi-purpose regulation is all the more pronounced in the context of TER, which is often founded on composite rather than singular regulatory authority. Hence, actors may cooperate in the same transnational regulatory endeavour for different reasons. However, in a significant number of cases, it is nonetheless possible to discern a primary or dominant motivation which drives the regulatory scheme. Moreover, for those examples that do not lend themselves to straightforward categorisation, the ability to identify a combination of intentions, and to reflect on the ways in which they are likely to influence the resulting framework and its key features, is all the more helpful to lend a modicum of predictability to what would alternatively be a collection of ramshackle, *sui generis* environmental governance regimes. Arguably, complexity in practice elevates rather than reduces the importance of analytical simplification.

3.3 THE INTENTIONS OF TRANSNATIONAL ENVIRONMENTAL REGULATORS

Based on an analysis of international agreements, preambles, explanatory memoranda, mission statements and scholarship, it is possible to distinguish five main reasons why either state or non-state actors engage in TER: to confront environmental problems that cannot effectively be governed at a local level; to facilitate trade; to make up for absent or insufficient state regulation; to manage private sector risks; and to enhance the effectiveness of national environmental regulation.

3.3.1 *Overcoming Governance Challenges of National Environmental Regulation*

Regulators engage in TER to overcome the obstacles that obstruct the effective achievement of environmental protection through national regulation.[16] Most objects of environmental protection – clean air, healthy water, a viable climate, abundant biodiversity – are global public goods, which means they are largely non-rivalrous (one person's enjoyment of clean air does not diminish its availability to

[16] Katharina Holzinger, Christoph Knill & Thomas Sommerer, 'Environmental Policy Convergence: The Impact of International Harmonization, Transnational Communication, and Regulatory Competition' (2008) 62(4) *International Organization*, pp. 553–587, at 557.

others) and non-excludable (it is not possible to restrict enjoyment of a benign climate to a select group), both within and among different countries.[17] The protection of global public goods poses a number of serious governance problems for the state. First, the impacts of environmental pollution may be experienced far beyond their place of origin. This is the case, for example, for persistent organic pollutants, which cause health damage in populations that are leagues removed from their place of production, use and disposal.[18] Secondly, the effectiveness of national environmental regulation is easily jeopardised by incompatible policy and regulatory choices made elsewhere. National migratory bird protection rules may have a very limited impact if the same animals are fair game across the border.[19] National environmental regulation furthermore creates a 'leakage' risk: if regulatory interventions are not matched by the same or similar initiatives in other countries, environmentally harmful production and enterprise could migrate to less regulated regions.[20] In such scenarios, the overall result could be a rise instead of a reduction in global environmental pollution. Finally, if, obstacles notwithstanding, national environmental regulation is successful in safeguarding a global public good, third countries can freeride and may enjoy the same environmental quality at lower cost.[21] This combination of challenges forms a powerful disincentive for national governments to pursue environmental regulation for the protection of global public goods. The transboundary nature of environmental risks and the corresponding transboundary impact of regulatory responses constitute governance challenges that cannot be met effectively by unilateral action.[22]

To overcome the governance challenges faced by national environmental regulation, public authorities can seek to take collective action and cooperate in the establishment of transboundary environmental regimes, which only enter into effect

17 Inge Kaul, Isabelle Grunberg & Marc A. Stern (eds.), *Global Public Goods: International Cooperation in the 21st Century* (1999, published for the United Nations Development Programme by Oxford University Press); Elisa Morgera, 'Bilateralism at the Service of Community Interests? Non-Judicial Enforcement of Global Public Goods in the Context of Global Environmental Law' (2012) 23(3) *European Journal of International Law*, pp. 743–767.

18 'Toxic Traces Found in Arctic mothers-to-be', *ENDS Europe Daily*, 21 June 2005. See Kirsten Hillman, 'International Control of Persistent Organic Pollutants: the UN Economic Commission for Europe Convention on Long-range Transboundary Air Pollution, and Beyond' (1999) 8(22) *Review of European Community and International Environmental Law*, pp. 105–112, at 105.

19 Colin T. Reid, 'Between Priceless and Worthless: Challenges in Using Market Mechanisms for Conserving Biodiversity' (2013) 2(2) *Transnational Environmental Law*, pp. 217–233, at 225.

20 Johannes Ebeling, 'Risks and Criticisms of Forestry-Based Climate Change Mitigation and Carbon Trading' in Charlotte Streck et al. (eds.), *Climate Change and Forests: Emerging Policy and Market Opportunities* (2008, Chatham House) pp. 43–58, at 49–51.

21 Elinor Ostrom, 'Polycentric Systems for Coping with Collective Action and Global Environmental Change' (2010) 20(4) *Global Environmental Change*, pp. 550–557, at 555.

22 Holzinger et al., 'Environmental Policy Convergence', p. 557; Kenneth W. Abbott & Duncan Snidal, 'Taking Responsive Regulation Transnational. Strategies for International Organizations' (2013) 7(1) *Regulation & Governance*, pp. 95–113, at 96.

once a critical mass of governments commits. In addition to reducing leakage and freeriding risks, such 'collective action TER' creates opportunities for inter-jurisdictional bargaining: areas that are well-positioned to protect certain global public goods, but lack the interest or resources to do so, may be prodded into action by the availability of external support or by the prospect of package deals. For example, developing country governments may commit to regulate offshore toxic waste disposal in exchange for investment in regulatory capacity building and financial support.

Collective Action TER

Regulatory cooperation to overcome national environmental governance challenges is the foundation of many of the most iconic transnational environmental regimes. The mid 1970s to late 1990s, particularly, were an era of intensive multilateral environmental negotiation and regime building, and ushered in an extensive set of international environmental agreements under the auspices of which collective action TER could flourish.[23]

Among the many MEAs adopted at the time are the landmark Convention on International Trade in Endangered Species of Wild Fauna and Flora (CITES, 1973)[24]; the International Convention for the Prevention of Pollution from Ships (MARPOL 73/78)[25]; the Convention on Long-Range Transboundary Air Pollution (CLRTAP, 1979)[26]; the Vienna Convention for the Protection of the Ozone Layer (1985)[27]; the Basel Convention on the Control of Transboundary Movement of Hazardous Waste and their Disposal (1989);[28] the Convention on Biological Diversity (CBD, 1992)[29] and the United Nations Framework Convention on Climate Change (UNFCCC, 1992). The need for international coordination and cooperation as a precondition of effective environmental protection against threats that surpass the national remit is a frequently recurring theme in the preambles of these treaties.[30] The Conventions, and their implementing protocols, fuelled the

[23] Holzinger et al., "Environmental Policy Convergence', p. 554.

[24] Washington, DC (US), 3 Mar. 1973, in force 1 July 1975, available at www.cites.org.

[25] London (UK), 2 Nov. 1973, in force 2 Oct. 1983, available at www.imo.org/en/about/conventions/listofconventions/pages/international-convention-for-the-prevention-of-pollution-from-ships-(marpol).aspx.

[26] Geneva (Switzerland), 13 Nov. 1979, in force 16 Mar. 1983, available at www.unece.org/env/lrtap/lrtap_h1.html.

[27] Vienna (Austria), 22 Mar. 1985, in force 22 Sept. 1988, available at http://ozone.unep.org/en/handbook-vienna-convention-protection-ozone-layer/2205.

[28] Basel (Switzerland), 22 Mar. 1989, in force 4 May 1992, available at www.basel.int/TheConvention/Overview/TextoftheConvention/tabid/1275/Default.aspx.

[29] Rio de Janeiro (Brazil), 5 June 1992, in force 29 Dec. 1993, available at www.cbd.int/doc/legal/cbd-en.pdf.

[30] See, e.g., the preambles to CITES ('Recognizing, in addition, that international co-operation is essential for the protection of certain species of wild fauna and flora against over-exploitation through international trade'); MARPOL ('DESIRING to achieve the complete elimination of

development of an expansive and connected (if not always coherent) body of environmental regulation at multiple governance levels.

Transnational regulation developed with the intention to overcome national environmental governance challenges is most readily associated with the adoption of MEAs, but equally occurs at the regional level. The ASEAN Agreement on Transboundary Haze Pollution, for example, emphasises the need for ASEAN members to act collectively in order to devise effective solutions to regional haze pollution.[31] In the same vein, the subsidiarity principle in EU law, which was originally inserted in the environmental protection provision of the (then) European Economic Community Treaty and stipulated that '[the] Community shall take action relating to the environment to the extent to which the objectives . . . can be attained better at Community level than at the level of the individual Member States',[32] contains an implicit acknowledgement that certain environmental goals cannot be achieved effectively at the national level and, therefore, require EU action.

Collective action TER is overwhelmingly public/public in nature. National governments tend to have a determinative say on the design, the organisation and the legal status of the transnational regime, as well as on the type and stringency of transnational regulatory standards developed in pursuit of the regime's environmental goals. The typical instrument of choice is a binding international agreement, which either mandates the member countries to adopt regulation commensurate with the general objectives set out in the agreement, or prescribes regulation for member countries to transpose and implement.

Characteristics of Collective Action TER: Consensualism and a Bias Towards Lowest Common Denominator Decision Making

Collective action TER has a number of distinctive features and faces particular challenges. To have a chance at success, regime accession must be sufficiently broad to contain the risks of leakage and freeriding. Interested governments must also secure the cooperation of those parties who are best positioned to protect global public goods. A biodiversity protection instrument secured without the involvement of the world's mega-diverse countries may have some regional impact, but it will

intentional pollution of the marine environment by oil and other harmful substances and the minimization of accidental discharge of such substances, CONSIDERING that this object may best be achieved by establishing rules not limited to oil pollution having a universal purport'); the Vienna Convention ('Aware that measures to protect the ozone layer from modifications due to human activities require international cooperation and action'); and the CBD ('Affirming that the conservation of biological diversity is a common concern of humankind' in combination with 'Stressing the importance of, and the need to promote, international, regional and global cooperation among States and intergovernmental organizations and the non-governmental sector for the conservation of biological diversity').

[31] See information at http://haze.asean.org/?wpfb_dl=32.

[32] Article 130r(4) of the Single European Act (SEA).

barely make a dent in global extinction rates. This need for a broad uptake creates a bias in favour of consensual decision making, which is less likely to deter hesitant participants than majoritarian approaches.

Consensual decision-making structures lower the threshold for participation and can foster a culture of deliberation. They also introduce a bias towards lowest common denominator decision making, and create a risk of regulatory paralysis.[33] There tends to be an inverse relation between scale and regulatory ambition: the broader the remit of an international environmental agreement, the weaker its regulatory provisions. The history of international climate change law powerfully illustrates this dynamic. The UNFCCC enjoys near-universal accession. Yet for all its sweeping preambular statements and its lofty aspirational language, it contains very little regulatory 'bite'; the openness of its regulatory provisions is such that virtually any participant's climate change policy, however modest or advanced, could be said to fall within the parameters of UNFCCC obligations. The Kyoto Protocol took a comparatively more prescriptive approach and introduced quantified GHG emissions reduction targets for developed countries, as well as a functioning compliance mechanism.[34] The targets were hardly draconian, yet this firming up of the regulatory approach was enough to deter a number of key players from signing up or from remaining committed to the Protocol.[35]

A few MEAs arguably escape the rule that broad accession equals weak ambition. The Vienna Convention and its Montreal Protocol on Ozone Depleting Substances[36] are generally considered to lay down environmental protection goals that are, if not exactly pioneering, at least credible as instruments towards the protection of global public goods.[37] Yet such examples are feted for being exceptional. Moreover, a select membership is no guarantee of regulatory ambition, as illustrated

33 Cary Coglianese, 'Is Consensus an Appropriate Basis for Regulatory Policy?' in Eric W. Orts & Kurt Deketelaere (eds.), *Environmental Contracts: Comparative Approaches to Regulatory Innovation in the United States and Europe* (2001, Kluwer Law International); Nico Krisch, 'The Decay of Consent: International Law in an Age of Global Public Goods' (2014) 108(1) *American Journal of International Law*, pp. 1–40, at 4.

34 Kyoto (Japan), 11 Dec. 1997, in force 16 Feb. 2005, available at http://unfccc.int/kyoto_protocol/items/2830.php. See Anna Huggins, 'The Desirability of Depoliticization: Compliance in the International Climate Regime' (2015) 4(1) *Transnational Environmental Law*, pp. 101–124, at 102.

35 Scott Barrett, 'The Political Economy of the Kyoto Protocol' (1998) 14(4) *Oxford Review of Economic Policy*, pp. 20–39; Cinnamon Carlarne, *Climate Change Law and Policy. EU and US Approaches* (2010, Oxford University Press), pp. 7–11; Amanda M. Rosen, 'The Wrong Solution at the Right Time: The Failure of the Kyoto Protocol on Climate Change' (2015) 43(1) *Politics & Policy*, pp. 30–58, at 43.

36 Montreal (Canada), 16 Sept. 1987, in force 1 Jan. 1989, available at http: //ozone.unep.org/en/handbook-montreal-protocol-substances-deplete-ozone-layer/5.

37 Suzanne Kingston, Veerle Heyvaert & Aleksandra Čavoški, *European Environmental Law* (2017, Cambridge University Press), pp. 302–304.

by the SBT Convention,[38] which is marked by ongoing struggles to determine credible, sustainable total allowable catches (TACs) for its three participating countries.[39] In many cases, collective action TER is broadly circumscribed, targets the lowest common denominator and does not push the overwhelming majority of member countries beyond their regulatory comfort zone.

In sum, MEAs and their implementing protocols are large, prestigious and slow-moving creatures in the regulatory landscape. Respected rather than feared, they display a grandness of purpose that rarely matches their ability to deliver. Arguably, a degree of sluggishness may be inevitable in the context of multilateral, intergovernmental cooperation. Yet transnational regimes can and do develop strategies to reduce their vulnerability to transnational regulatory stagnation and paralysis. Such adaptation often happens in two ways: through increased reliance on expertise and technocratic decision making and through increased reliance on non-binding instruments in the regulatory framework.

Overcoming Consensualism in Collective Action TER: Institutionalisation, Managerialism and Hybridisation

A first strategy to overcome the sluggishness and conservativism of large-scale intergovernmental decision making is to increasingly delegate and bureaucratise decision making. This option is available to most MEAs since environmental treaties and their implementing instruments typically engage in an impressive degree of institution building. In addition to a conference of the parties (COP), environmental treaties usually provide for the establishment of a permanent secretariat and a range of implementing and expert advisory bodies. As MEAs mature, do does the institutional infrastructure, as exemplified by the near-dizzying numbers of committees, mechanisms, groups and arrangements that have sprung to life under the UNFCCC.[40]

Delegation to implementing and expert bodies usually relates to the extensive preparatory work that goes into transnational regulation. In the vast majority of cases, the intergovernmental level retains final decision-making power and new regulatory provisions adopted in furtherance of MEAs still need the approval of the member country governments to become binding. Yet this does not dull the impact of delegation as a transnational decision-making management strategy. Arguably, the most powerful aspect of delegation lies in its de-politicising force: regulation prepared and drafted by bodies that are distinguished primarily by their scientific and

[38] Canberra (Australia), 10 May 1993, in force 20 May 1994, available at www.ccsbt.org/en/content/origins-convention.

[39] Howard S. Shiffman & Briony Patricia MacPhee, 'The Southern Bluefin Tuna Dispute Revisited: How Far Have We Come' (2014) 3(2) *Transnational Environmental Law*, pp. 391–406.

[40] See overview of UNFCCC bodies at https://unfccc.int/process/bodies/the-big-picture/what-are-bodies.

technical expertise, and that reflect a predominantly bureaucratic ethos, enjoy a different kind of legitimacy from that of interest-based, political decisions.[41] The technocratic nature of the preparatory process may spill over into the political process and lead the COP to recast its own role as one of problem-solving rather than bargaining which may, in turn, help to overcome decision-making deadlocks. We discern this dynamic at work in the SBT Convention, as documented in Howard Shiffman and Briony MacPhee's research.

The SBT Convention was hamstrung by regulatory stagnation as its three signatory states (New Zealand, Australia and Japan) failed to agree on TAC limits beyond the initially agreed quota, which were widely considered too generous to ensure sustainable fishing of bluefin tuna.[42] Ultimately, a solution was found in institutional reorganisation. Although the TAC still needs to be vetted by the CSBT Commission, which decides by consensus, TAC numbers are now prepared through a management procedure in which the TAC is calculated on the basis of scientific models instead of negotiated.[43] The regime has also strengthened its reliance on independent expertise. In addition to the Scientific Committee, which consists of signatory party representatives and operates consensually, an Advisory Panel and Independent Chairperson are mandated to support the scientific work of the CSBT. The panel is entirely made up of non-members to the CSBT and includes nationals from the United States, Argentina and the United Kingdom. Its establishment has been described as 'clearly an outgrowth of the negotiations to break the governance deadlock' and 'an obvious attempt to constructively . . . involve outsiders to improve a process that had been dysfunctional up to that point'.[44] The governance structure of the SBT Convention thus deliberately turned towards managerialism to fix regulatory paralysis.

An alternative strategy to overcome stagnation within collective action TER is to lower the stakes by developing non-binding instruments in furtherance of treaty objectives.[45] The explicitly voluntary character of exemplary, advisory documents, guidelines, blueprints and recommendations lowers the threshold for their intergovernmental endorsement. Moreover, the adoption of non-binding documents typically does not hinge on unanimous approval. This second strategy results in the emergence of TER hybrid regimes that combine formally binding and optional

[41] Matthew Flinders & Jim Buller, 'Depoliticization, Democracy and Arena Shifting' in Tom Christensen & Per Lægreid (eds.), *Autonomy and Regulation. Coping with Agencies in the Modern State* (2006, Edward Elgar), pp. 53–69.

[42] Shiffman & MacPhee, 'Southern Bluefin Tuna Dispute', pp. 394 & 396. CSBT membership has since grown to include the Republic of Korea (2001), Taiwan (2002) and Indonesia (2008).

[43] See CSBT Commission, Report of the Fifteenth Meeting of the Scientific Committee, 11 Sept. 2010 (Narita, Japan), available at http://www.ccsbt.org/sites/default/files/userfiles/file/docs_english/meetings/meeting_reports/ccsbt_17/report_of_SC15.pdf.

[44] Shiffman & MacPhee, 'Southern Bluefin Tuna Dispute', p. 398.

[45] Armin Shäfer, 'Resolving Deadlock: Why International Organisations Introduce Soft Law' (2006) 12(2) *European Journal of International Law*, pp. 194–208.

regulatory content.[46] The CBD and the Ramsar Convention on Wetlands[47] are two regimes that are vulnerable to regulatory stagnation and that rely increasingly on informal regulation to detail and steer the implementation of broadly framed Treaty objectives. At the 10th COP in Aichi, Japan, the CBD members adopted the Strategic Plan for Biodiversity 2011–2020. The COP Decision represents the Plan as a 'useful flexible framework' and *urges*, rather than mandates, participating governments to take the necessary steps towards its implementation. The decision further *invites* 'Parties and other Governments at the forthcoming meetings of the decision-making bodies of the other biodiversity-related conventions and other relevant agreements to consider appropriate contributions to the collaborative implementation of the Strategic Plan for Biodiversity 2011–2020 and its Aichi Targets'.[48]

The dual impact of managerialism and hybridisation can help to energise collective action TER to a degree, although it is fair to say that treaty-based regimes, from the UNFCCC, the Stockholm Convention and the SBT Convention to the European Union, will never be regulatory gazelles. Even the Montreal Protocol on Ozone Depleting Substances, environmental law's poster child for effective environmental collective action, has seen its reputation challenged by studies asserting that it has generated negligible added protection above and beyond what state and market would have supplied in the absence of international agreement.[49] Moreover, it is important to appreciate that both developments present a new suite of challenges. Increased managerialism, for instance, exposes transnational regulatory decision making to notoriously persistent accusations of democratic deficiency and rule by technocracy. Hybridisation, in turn, exacerbates the complexity and opacity of transnational regimes.

Profile

Collective action TER is mostly public/public and is developed with the purpose of regulating global public goods effectively. The regulatory standards it sets forth tend to be wide but shallow; the regulatory output is typically normatively modest and slow to change. Decision making within collective action TER often evolves in the direction of greater managerialism and expertise-dependence to contain the risk of regulatory stagnation. At the same time, collective action TER tends to hybridise over time and introduce a combination of binding and voluntary instruments. These developments may help to maintain momentum within large-scale transnational

[46] Veerle Heyvaert, 'Levelling Down, Levelling Up, and Governing Across: Three Responses to Hybridization in International Law' (2009) 20(3) *European Journal of International Law*, pp. 647–674, at 650.

[47] Ramsar (Iran), 3 Feb. 1971, in force 21 Dec. 1975, available at www.ramsar.org/.

[48] See COP decision at www.cbd.int/decision/cop/?id=12268h.

[49] David L. Levy, 'Business and International Environmental Treaties: Ozone Depletion and Climate Change' (1997) 39(3) *California Management Review*, pp. 53–71, at 61.

regimes, but they simultaneously open up collective action TER to a host of alternative legitimacy challenges of democratic deficiency and intransparency.

3.3.2 *Trade Facilitation*

Regulation is rarely undertaken exclusively for the sake of protecting the natural environment. Humanity's dependence on the environment for its own survival and progress is a powerful part of the equation and a key justification for regulatory intervention in support of the non-human members of the ecosystem. This awareness resonates, for instance, in the popular representation of environmental processes as ecosystem *services*, a concept which emphasises people's reliance on their natural surroundings and overtly refers to the economic contribution that ecosystems make to human society.[50] The anthropocentric inclination of this approach to ecosystem valuation, which understands environmental value, however liberally inferred, with reference to human utility, is the subject of lively discussion and critique. The intention here is not to delve into an assessment of the strengths and ills of a utilitarian approach to environmental valuation,[51] but to acknowledge that the awareness of the environment as a resource and asset also percolates in most collective action TER. Ultimately, the southern bluefin tuna that constitute the object of the SBT Convention are not just fish in the sea; they are also a global commodity which needs supportive habitats and sustainable management to maintain its yield. The bias towards under-regulation for global public goods jeopardises the market in natural resources and derived products and services, ultimately threatening to bring 'ruin to all'.[52] The pursuit of environmental quality targets and resource management standards at transnational level seeks to counter this threat. In this vein, the final preamble to the SBT Convention underlines the need for the parties to cooperate 'to ensure the conservation *and optimum utilisation* of southern bluefin tuna' (emphasis added). Similarly, the CBD supports and actively promotes a representation of species as genetic resources which can contribute greatly to human welfare if sensibly and sustainably exploited.[53]

50 See Thoko Kaime, 'Symposium Foreword: Framing the Law and Policy for Ecosystem Services' (2013) 2(2) *Transnational Environmental Law*, pp. 211–216.

51 See, e.g., Millennium Ecosystem Assessment, *Ecosystems and Human Well-Being: The Assessment Series* (2005, Island Press); Gretchen C Daily, Stephen Polasky, Joshua Goldstein, Peter M. Kareiva, Harold A. Mooney, Liba Pejchar, Taylor H. Ricketts, James Salzman & Robert Shallenberger, 'Ecosystem Services in Decision Making: Time to Deliver' (2009) 7 *Frontiers in Ecology and the Environment*, pp. 21–28; Jerneja Penca, 'Marketing the Market: the Ideology of Market Mechanisms for Biodiversity Conservation' (2013) 2(2) *Transnational Environmental Law*, pp. 235–257; Nicolás Kosoy & Esteve Corbera, 'Payments for Ecosystem Services as Commodity Fetishism' (2010) 69 *Ecological Economics*, pp. 1228–1236.

52 Garret Hardin, 'The Tragedy of the Commons' (1968) 162(3859) *Science*, pp. 1243–1248, at 1244.

53 Andreas Kotsakis, 'Change and Subjectivity in International Environmental Law: The Micro-Politics of the Transformation of Biodiversity into Genetic Gold' (2014) 3(1) *Transnational Environmental Law*, pp. 127–147, at 130–132.

Economic and ecologic considerations thus are intimately entangled in environmental regulation. In some cases however, the threat to sustainable economic growth which TER seeks to address is not caused by insufficient domestic environmental regulation (to be overcome through transnational cooperation), but rather by *incompatible* national environmental regulation which obstructs the free trade flow of products and services across borders.[54] Goods and, occasionally, services produced in accordance with the environmental prescriptions of one country may fall foul of another's and, consequently, see their access to foreign markets blocked.[55] The potential for environmental protection standards to function as a barrier to trade is affirmed in decades of WTO dispute resolution and EU internal market case law.[56] To unblock trade flows, decision makers typically have a choice of, either, disapplying trade-obstructing national regulation with respect to imported goods and services, or cooperating in the development of harmonised and compatible environmental prescriptions.[57] The latter avenue results in the adoption of TER.[58]

Trade facilitation TER has a dual purpose since it aims to directly affect both market and environmental conditions.[59] Like collective action TER, a large proportion of trade facilitation TER is developed through intergovernmental negotiation and adopted through multilateral agreement. Hence, several features that distinguish collective action TER are also present in trade facilitation environmental regimes. Yet at the same time, the trade liberalisation object imbues transnational regimes of this nature with an added dimension, explored in the following paragraphs.

Trade Facilitation TER

Environmental regulation is most likely to act as a trade barrier when it blocks the importation of goods and, occasionally, services into the domestic market. Consequently, trade facilitation TER is predominantly product-oriented and only exceptionally governs processes or production methods (PPMs).[60] Given the need to align

54 Samuel Bleicher, 'An Overview of International Environmental Regulation' (1972) 2(1) *Ecology Law Quarterly*, pp. 1–90, at 75.

55 C. Ford Runge, 'Trade Protectionism and Environmental Regulations: The New Nontariff Barriers' (1990) 11 *Northwestern Journal of International Law and Business*, pp. 47–61.

56 E.g., Kati Kulovesi, *The WTO Dispute Settlement System. Challenges of the Environment, Legitimacy and Fragmentation* (2011, Kluwer Law International); Nicolas De Sadeleer, *EU Environmental Law and the Internal Market* (2014, Oxford University Press), pp. 229–348.

57 Fritz Scharpf, 'Negative and Positive Integration in the Political Economy of European Welfare States' in Martin Rhodes & Yves Mény (eds.), *The Future of European Welfare* (1996, Springer), pp. 157–177.

58 Daniel C. Esty & Damien Geradin, *Regulatory Competition and Economic Integration: Comparative Perspectives* (2001, Oxford University Press).

59 Kingston et al., *European Environmental Law*, pp. 450–453.

60 But see Agreement on International Humane Trapping Standards and Inter-American Convention for the Protection and Conservation of Sea Turtles below. Daniel C. Esty & Damien Geradin, 'Market Access, Competitiveness, and Harmonization: Environmental Protection in

products to a compatible set of environmental criteria which enables their free circulation, trade facilitation TER heavily relies on standard setting as a regulatory strategy.

Trade facilitation TER can be public/public if the harmonised standards are imposed upon state authorities, but much of the regulatory content is public/private in nature. A large proportion of EU product regulation qualifies as trade facilitation TER. The EU REACH Regulation on chemicals control, which directly addresses chemicals manufacturers, importers and downstream users, affirms the twin objectives of ensuring a 'high level of protection of health and the environment as well as the free movement of substances' in a single breath in its very first preamble. So does the 2008 Regulation on the Classification, Labelling and Packaging of Chemicals (the CLP Regulation).[61] These two preoccupations equally drive EU legislation governing the commercialisation of pesticides and GMOs.[62] In the sphere of consumer goods, EU Regulation 443/2009 on passenger car emissions sets 'emission performance standards for new passenger cars registered in the [European Union], which forms part of the [EU's] integrated approach to reducing CO_2 emissions from light-duty vehicles while ensuring the proper functioning of the internal market'.[63] The EU Ecolabel Regulation, in turn, presents the ecolabel scheme for domestic appliances as 'part of the sustainable consumption and production policy of the [Union], which aims at reducing the negative impact of consumption and production on the environment, health, climate and natural resources', and further emphasises that 'to facilitate the marketing of products bearing environmental labels at national and [EU] levels ... it is also necessary to enhance the coherence and promote harmonisation between the EU Ecolabel scheme and national ecolabelling schemes'.[64] In each of these examples, market and environmental rationales feature side-by-side in seemingly peaceful coexistence.

Trade facilitation TER is thinner on the ground outside the EU regulatory sphere,[65] but it does occur. The International Agreement on Humane Trapping

Regional Trade Agreements' (1997) 21(2) *Harvard Environmental Law* Review, pp. 265–336, at 268.

61 Regulation (EC) No. 1272/2008 on classification, labelling and packaging of substances and mixtures, amending and repealing Directives 67/548/EEC and amending Regulation (EC) No. 1907/2006 [2008] OJ L353/1.

62 Regulation (EC) No 1107/2009 concerning the placing of plant protection products on the market and repealing Council Directives 79/117/EEC and 91/414/EEC [2009] OJ L309/1; Regulation (EC) No 1829/2003 on genetically modified food and feed [2003] OJ L268/1.

63 Regulation (EC) No 443/2009 setting emission performance standards for new passenger cars as part of the Community's integrated approach to reduce CO 2 emissions from light-duty vehicles [2009] OJ L140/1.

64 Regulation (EC) No 66/2010 on the EU Ecolabel [2010] OJ L27/1.

65 Regional and international trade agreements typically mediate the tension between the free flow of goods and services on the one hand, and national environmental regulation on the other, through a strategy of conditional exemption: national environmental provisions are deemed lawful in spite of their trade-suppressing impact if certain criteria are met. In the

Standards (IAHTS), for example, purports to target animal welfare and wildlife sustainability in combination with an easier trade flow between the member countries.[66] Similarly, signatories of the Inter-American Convention for the Protection and Conservation of Sea Turtles (IOC), which mandates, inter alia, the installation of turtle-excluding devices in fishing and shrimping nets, are required to 'endeavor to facilitate trade in fish and fishery products associated with this Convention'.[67] Much of the product standardisation work undertaken by private organisations such as the ISO constitutes trade facilitation TER. Article 2(1) of the ISO Statutes defines the Organisation's object as follows:

> [T]o promote the development of standardization and related activities in the world with a view to facilitating international exchange of goods and services and to developing cooperation in the spheres of intellectual, scientific, technological and economic activity.[68]

Where an ISO standard covers the environmental performance and impact of goods, services or processes – as is the case, for example, for the ISO 17422: 2002 standard which regulates environmental aspects of plastics[69] – it effectively generates dual purpose regulation. Trade facilitation is also behind the development of environmental standards as part of the GHS under the auspices of the OECD. Hence, although dual purpose regulation is strongly associated with the EU, it is not exclusive to the regime. Instead, trade facilitation TER occurs at different levels of governance and is pursued within private and hybrid as well as public transnational regulatory structures.

WTO context, for example, national measures to safeguard exhaustible natural resources are compatible with the General Agreement on Tariffs and Trade (GATT) provided they are not applied in a manner which would constitute arbitrary and unjustifiable discrimination between domestic and imported goods. The GATT thus acknowledges the legitimacy of environmental regulation, but does not itself provide positive environmental regulatory content. See Daniel Bodansky & Jessica C. Lawrence, 'Trade and Environment', in Daniel Bethlehem, Isabelle Van Damme, Donald McRae & Rodney Neufeld (eds.), *The Oxford Handbook of International Trade Law* (2009, Oxford University Press), pp. 506–538, at 530–537. Conversely, some international agreements such as CITES and the PIC Convention (Rotterdam Convention on the Prior Informed Consent Procedure for Certain Hazardous Chemicals and Pesticides in International Trade, Rotterdam [The Netherlands], 10 Sept. 1998, in force 24 Feb. 2004, available at www.pic.int/TheConvention/Overview/TextoftheConvention/tabid/1048/language/en-US/Default.aspx) do set environmental standards that undeniably affect trade, but they are not designed to facilitate trade flows. For these reasons, neither group qualifies as trade facilitation TER.

66 Brussels (Belgium), 15 December 1997, in force 22 July 2008, in [1998] OJ L42/43.

67 Caracas (Venezuela), 1 December 1996, in force 2 May 2001, available at www.iacseaturtle.org/eng-docs/Texto-CIT-ENG.pdf.

68 See www.iso.org/iso/statutes.pdf.

69 See www.iso.org/standard/33053.html.

Characteristics of Trade Facilitation TER: Trading Up or Compromising?

The liberalisation objective of trade facilitation TER is achieved through regulatory harmonisation: national regulators adopt prescriptions that are either uniform or sufficiently compatible to be recognised as equivalent by the customs and import authorities of participating countries.[70] In principle, the precise content of the environmental standards involved should have no bearing on the process of liberalisation: a cross-border agreement on tough environmental standards equalises market conditions between cooperating parties to the same extent as a consensus on permissive criteria. Yet upon closer study, it transpires that the objective of trade liberalisation is likely to affect the quality of environmental regulation. Under certain conditions, the presence of a free trade perspective can drive up the level of ambition of harmonised environmental targets and thus help international agreements overcome the pull towards the lowest common denominator. In other cases, however, the trade facilitation rationale is likely to exert a chilling influence on the environmental ambition of harmonised standards. Moreover, regardless of whether the initial harmonised standards are demanding or weak, once agreed they are difficult to change.

Whether trade facilitation TER contains permissive or strict environmental standards depends chiefly on the bargaining power of the cooperating parties. If the state party with the strictest environmental standards also represents the most desirable export market, other parties to the agreement may be willing to 'trade up' their environmental regulation in exchange for market access.[71] This dynamic explains the willingness of countries such as Honduras, Guatemala and Chile to adopt US-promoted sea turtle conservation standards in the context of the IOC. The introduction of turtle exclusion devices (TEDs) is the price for access to the US fish and fish products market on favourable terms.

The 'trading up' dynamic offers an appealing perspective on globalisation as an engine for progressive environmental regulation, yet empirical evidence of trading up is sparse.[72] In many cases, the negotiating conditions will not be conducive to trading up: if the bargaining power between the parties cooperating in the development of trade facilitation TER is evenly spread, or if parties that favour weaker environmental standards have the upper hand, the pull towards trading up does not materialise. On the contrary, under such circumstances the need for

[70] Humberto Zúñiga Schroder, *Harmonization, Equivalence and Mutual Recognition of Standards in WTO Law* (2011, Kluwer Law International).

[71] David Vogel, *Trading Up: Consumer and Environmental Regulation in a Global Economy* (1997, Harvard University Press).

[72] Per G. Fredriksson & Daniel L. Millimet, 'Is There a "California Effect" in US Environmental Policymaking?' (2002) 32(6) *Regional Science and Urban Economics*, pp. 737–764; Dirk A. Heyen, 'Influence of the EU Chemicals Regulation on the US Policy Reform Debate: Is a "California Effect" within REACH?' (2013) 2(1) *Transnational Environmental Law*, pp. 95–115.

consensus among parties is more likely to push the environmental content of the harmonisation measure towards the permissive end of the regulatory scale.

The push towards weak environmental standards, moreover, may be further propelled by the particular mindset and actor involvement that characterise harmonisation initiatives. In the context of trade facilitation TER, the risks that accompany the adoption of sub-standard environmental targets may be traded off against the benefit of delivering market access. Parties may compromise on environmental quality for the sake of market access.[73] Even if such tradeoffs are not explicitly mooted, the free trade objective implicitly caps the stringency of environmental regulation. Ultimately, environmental standards may shape the market, but they should not come at the expense of the viability of the market itself as this, again, would defeat the goal of trade facilitation.[74] Harmonised standards that are attainable for most manufacturers and producers will be considered to foster a more vibrant and competitive global market than exacting ones, and are therefore likely to find favour. The traditionally strong involvement of the private sector in negotiations and decision making surrounding trade facilitation TER, is a further factor pushing towards compromise on the level of stringency of environmental prescriptions. In sum, in the absence of a clear 'trading up' impetus enabled by the presence of a dominant player who favours high environmental standards, trade facilitation TER is likely to embrace a goal of satisficing rather than optimising with regard to the environmental content of harmonised standards.

Trade Facilitation TER and the Challenge of Stagnation

Once agreed, the environmental standards in trade facilitation TER leave little scope for differentiation. In contrast to collective action TER, which typically permits participating members individually to go beyond the environmental targets in the collective agreement, trade facilitation TER generally disallows parties from opting up, as this would defeat the trade liberalisation goal of the agreement. In EU regulation, for instance, the conditions under which Member States are allowed to opt up from environmental standards adopted in the framework of internal market legislation (under Article 114 TFEU) are far more restrictive than those governing opt ups from 'pure' environmental provisions (Article 192 TFEU).[75] Ultimately, a proportion of actors participating in trade facilitation TER therefore may need to

[73] Stuart R. Harrop, 'The International Regulation of Animal Welfare and Conservation Issues Through Standards Dealing with the Trapping of Wild Mammals' (2000) 21(3) *Journal of Environmental Law*, pp. 333–360, at 360.

[74] Cf. Paulette Kurtzer & Alice Cooper, 'Consumer Activism, EU Institutions and Global Markets: The Struggle over Biotech Foods' (2007) 27(2) *Journal of Public Policy*, pp. 103–128.

[75] Kingston et al., *European Environmental Law*, pp. 451–453; Case T-366/03 and 235/04 *Land Oberosterreich and Austria* v *Commission* ECLI: EU: T: 2005: 347; confirmed on appeal in Case C-439/05 and 454/05 *Land Oberosterreich and Austria* v *Commission* ECLI: EU: C: 2007: 510. Floor Fleurke, 'What Use for Article 95(5) EC? An Analysis of *Land Oberosterreich and Austria* v *Commission*' (2008) 20(2) *Journal of Environmental Law*, pp. 267–278.

accept lower environmental standards than they would in the absence of transnational cooperation. Stuart Harrop commented on the potential chilling effect of harmonisation in his discussion of the IAHTS between the EU, Canada, and the Russian Federation:

> If the standards are rigourously developed, these principles should create a radical regime enabling enforcement of norms which advance animal welfare and conservation issues in a practical manner. However, if the standards prescribed by this agreement consist of undeveloped, lowest common denominators that perpetuate and, effectively, promote suffering; then the effect of the Agreement's creation of a multilateral level playing field is to force in time an erosion – rather than an improvement – of the standards of welfare extended to trapped animals.[76]

Harrop's discussion of the IAHTS emphasises the weakness of the harmonised trapping standards in terms of delivering on animal welfare, a weakness which is unlikely to satisfy the public demand for wildlife protection in Europe. Left to its own devices, the EU might conceivably raise the standards, but it finds itself effectively trapped at the level that its negotiating partners, Russia and Canada, can agree on.[77]

The absence of opportunities for ex-post self-differentiation exacerbates the risk of regulatory stagnation and paralysis which characterises transnational regulatory regimes that operate on the basis of consensual decision making. Like collective action TER, trade facilitation regimes can seek to manage such risks by, for example, delegating standardisation to professional bodies or expert task forces, and/or by shifting from a consensual to a majoritarian mode of decision making. However, the impact of such interventions should not be overstated. Even the EU, which among transnational governance regimes has gone farthest in modifying decision-making structures and processes to counter the risk of regulatory paralysis, struggles to adopt timely amendments to environmental standards embedded in internal market legislation.[78]

Profile

Trade facilitation TER pursues a dual purpose of environmental protection and market liberalisation through harmonisation. Its regulatory output is characterised by a preponderance of product standards. The prospect of enhanced market access may push transnational actors towards the more environmentally ambitious side of the regulatory scale, but it is more likely to incentivise actors to compromise for the

76 Harrop, 'The International Regulation of Animal Welfare', p. 356.

77 Ibid.

78 The EU's ongoing failure to effectively regulate the risks of endocrine disruption illustrate the difficulties in harmonising environmental criteria, see Sarantis Michalopoulos, 'EU Member States Still Divided over Endocrine Disruptor Regulation' 22 Dec. 2016, *EURACTIV*, available at www.euractiv.com/section/health-consumers/news/eu-member-states-still-divided-over-endocrine-disruptor-regulation/.

sake of free trade. Trade facilitation TER rarely leaves participants an option for self-differentiation. Consequently, environmental standards in trade facilitation TER easily become entrenched and are at least as, if not more, vulnerable to regulatory stagnation and paralysis as collective action TER.

3.3.3 *Addressing the State's Failure to Regulate*

A third reason for actors to become engaged in TER is to correct a perceived failure of the state to deliver a publicly acceptable level of environmental regulation.[79] States fail to introduce environmental regulation, whether domestically or in cooperation with other governments, for a number of different reasons. Failure may be deliberate when, for example, the state pushes an aggressive, short-term economic growth agenda that seeks to attract enterprise and investment with a business-friendly, non-interventionist climate.[80] Previously mentioned concerns regarding leakage and freeriding risks, too, may suppress the state's willingness to protect global public goods through national regulation. In some instances, obstacles can be overcome through collective action TER, but such initiatives are not always successful and international agreements moreover have their own considerable effectiveness challenges to contend with.[81]

Deficits in environmental regulation may also reflect the state's diminished capacity to respond. Even under optimal conditions, environmental regulators tend to be strapped for resources, personnel and expertise. In developing countries, national budgets for environmental regulation are often dwarfed by the scale and severity of environmental pollution problems that clamour for regulatory attention. Environmental regulators may operate in a volatile political climate, which further undermines attempts at effective environmental rule setting, implementation and enforcement. Additionally, jurisidictional borders may impair the state's ability to regulate effectively, particularly since its primary target audience are global enterprises that far outstrip state authorities in scale, size and economic heft.[82]

79 Gereffi and Mayer have termed this a 'governance deficit'. See Gary Gereffi & Frederick Mayer, 'Globalization and the Demand for Governance', in Gereffi, *The New Offshoring of Jobs and Global Development* (2006, IILS), pp. 48–49; Kai Purnhagen, 'Mapping Private Regulation – Classification, Market Access and Market Closure Policy and Law's Response' (2015) 49(2) *Journal of World Trade*, pp. 309–324, at 311.

80 Arthur P. J. Mol, 'Environmental Deinstitutionalization in Russia' (2009) 11(3) *Journal of Environmental Policy and Planning*, pp. 223–241; Onyeka K. Osuji, 'Corporate Social Responsibility, Juridification and Globalisation: "Inventive Interventionism" for a "Paradox"' (2015) 11(3) *International Journal of Law in Context*, pp. 265–298, at 280.

81 Tim Bartley, 'Certifying Forests and Factories: States, Social Movements, and the Rise of Private Regulation in the Apparel and Forest Products Fields' (2003) 31(3) *Politics and Society*, pp. 433–464, at 451–453.

82 Dennis Patterson & Ari Afilalo, *The New Global Trading Order: The Evolving State and the Future of Trade* (2008, Cambridge University Press), pp. 35–37; Abbott & Snidal, 'Taking Responsive Regulation Transnational', p. 96.

Differences between regulators and regulatees in terms of respective resources and expertise are felt particularly acutely in developing countries, but they equally colour the interactions between large enterprises and environmental regulators in more affluent regions. Well-organised and well-resourced global firms are eminently equipped to resist environmental regulation via political as well as legal avenues.[83] Moreover, the multi-jurisdictional nature of industrial operations creates opportunities for global firms to shift their most harmful activities to 'weakest link' jurisdictions and still present themselves as formally in compliance with environmental regulation in all the countries where they conduct business.[84]

In sum, whether through unwillingness, lack of capacity, or a combination of both, states may end up undersupplying environmental regulation. This deficit opens a space for non-state actors with a mission to represent public and, particularly, environmental interests to step forward and fill the regulatory void.[85] Their endeavours are not necessarily transnational in scope, but overwhelmingly the substitute environmental regulation developed by non-state actors transcends national borders.[86] This is all the more the case when such substitute regulation seeks to make up for the failure of states effectively to regulate the environmental behaviour of global firms.[87]

Substitute TER

Much of what is referred to as 'private regulation'[88], 'civil regulation'[89] or 'non-state market-driven' regulation (NSMD)[90] is developed with the intention of filling a regulatory deficit. The sustainable forestry standards and procedures adopted by the FSC,[91] as well as the sustainable fishing standards of the MSC,[92] are prominent examples of substitute TER. So are the model codes and guidance documents

83 Cf. Matthias Koenig-Archibugi, 'Transnational Corporations and Global Accountability' (2004) 39(2) *Government and Opposition*, pp. 234–259, at 241–245.

84 Chilenye Nwapi, 'Jurisdiction by Necessity and the Regulation of the Transnational Corporate Actor' (2013) 30(78) *Utrecht Journal of International and European Law*, pp. 24–43, at 25–27.

85 David Vogel, 'The Private Regulation of Global Corporate Conduct' (2010) 49(1) *Business & Society*, pp. 68–87, at 71; Knill & Lehmkuhl, 'Private Actors and the State', p. 42.

86 Sarah Giest & Michael Howlett, 'Comparative Climate Change Governance: Lessons from European Transnational Municipal Network Management Efforts' (2013) 23 *Environmental Policy & Governance*, pp. 341–353, at 346.

87 Koenig-Archibugi, 'Transnational Corporations'.

88 Fabrizio Cafaggi, 'New Foundations of Transnational Private Regulation' (2001) 38(1) *Journal of Law and Society*, pp. 20–49.

89 Vogel, 'Private Regulation', p. 69.

90 Benjamin Cashore, 'Legitimacy and the Privatization of Environmental Governance: How Non-State Market-Driven (NSMD) Governance Systems Gain Rule–Making Authority' (2002) 15(4) *Governance*, pp. 503–529.

91 Catherine E. Rudder, 'Private Governance as Public Policy: A Paradigmatic Shift' (2008) 70(4) *The Journal of Politics*, pp. 899–913, at 902.

92 Lars H. Gulbrandsen, 'The Emergence and Effectiveness of the Marine Stewardship Council' (2009) 33(4) *Marine Policy*, pp. 654–660, at 655.

sponsored by intergovernmental organisations such as the UN, the Food and Agriculture Organisation (FAO), the World Health Organisation (WHO) and the OECD. To highlight but a few, Chapter V of the OECD Guidelines for Multinational Enterprises, relating to environmental matters, 'encourages multinational enterprises (MNEs) to raise their environmental performance through improved internal environmental management and better contingency planning for environmental impacts'.[93] The FAO has issued a voluntary Code for Responsible Fisheries, which is purportedly targeted at 'everyone working in, and involved with, fisheries and aquaculture, irrespective of whether they are located in inland areas or in the oceans'.[94] The UN Global Compact, in turn, represents a UN-led voluntary initiative to steer the private sector towards corporate sustainability. Its directives cover a wide range of public interest issues: human rights, labour and anti-corruption feature alongside environmental protection.

Substitute TER falls chiefly within the private/private category, although some initiatives count public authorities among their regulators and/or regulatory addressees. Attempts to develop substitute TER are generally led by environmental NGOs or IGOs, which either autonomously take charge of a regulatory initiative or work in cooperation with other stakeholders. The MSC, for example, developed largely owing to collaboration between the NGO WWF and the multinational Unilever.[95] Alternatively, public entities such as cities or subnational regions may collaborate in the establishment of transnational networks in order to bypass reluctant or ineffective states, as witnessed in the context of some transnational climate change networks.[96] The addressees of substitute TER, in turn, are often but not exclusively private organisations. For example, a number of national governments, including Croatia and Ireland, have signed up to the FSC for the management of publicly owned forests.[97] On both the regulator's and addressee's side, the institutional arrangements supporting successful attempts at substitute TER often become more multi-faceted and complex over time.[98]

Substitute TER is pursued through different regulatory strategies. Various schemes regulate through standard setting, third-party audits and/or (self) certification.[99] Others, including many of the IGO-driven variants of substitute TER, favour relatively more flexible and procedural approaches such as codes of conduct, principle-based regulation and guidance. There is also a rich tradition among

93 Available at www.oecd.org/env/34992954.pdf, p. 6.

94 Available at www.fao.org/docrep/005/v9878e/v9878e00.HTM.

95 Gulbrandsen, 'The Emergence and Effectiveness of the MSC', p. 655.

96 Kenneth W. Abbott, 'Strengthening the Transnational Regime Complex for Climate Change' (2014) 3(1) *Transnational Environmental Law*, pp. 57–88, at 61.

97 Axel Marx & Dieter Cuypers, 'Forest Certification as a Global Environmental Governance Tool: What is the Macro-effectiveness of the Forest Stewardship Council?' (2010) 4(4) *Regulation & Governance*, pp. 408–434, at 421.

98 Ibid.

99 Purnhagen, 'Mapping Private Regulation', p. 318.

substitute regulators of governing through contract. For example, the Conservation Stewards Program of Conservation International deploys conservation contracting as a means to prescribe environmental behaviour and curtail polluting activities in at-risk regions unprotected by effective state regulation.[100]

Substitute TER and the Challenge of Vulnerability

Strategies diverge, yet what unites all variants of substitute TER is their inability to rely on the apparatus of the state to secure regulatory implementation and enforcement.[101] States may be sympathetic to NGOs that aim to regulate environmental behaviour, but evidently will not and cannot legally deploy policing powers in support of private initiatives.[102] In other instances, states may be indifferent, apprehensive or even hostile to substitute regulators,[103] as illustrated in Ekaterina Sofronova, Cameron Holley and Vijaya Nagarajan's study of the role of NGOs in Russian environmental governance.[104] Substitute environmental regulators therefore cannot legally compel their addressees to submit to privately sponsored frameworks. The FSC can invite yet it cannot coerce timber companies into FSC membership; cities can exert peer pressure on trans-border counterparts to join transnational networks, but cannot compel. Adherence to substitute TER and compliance with its environmental prescriptions or, alternatively, accession to an environmental performance contract, are a matter of choice for the regulatory addressee.

The formally optional nature of substitute TER constitutes a source of vulnerability because it lowers the accession and compliance pull of regulatory initiatives which, on a narrow reading of regulatory authority, locates them towards the periphery of TER.[105] It also makes substitute TER more vulnerable to competition: in a commentary on the FSC, Gary Gereffi, Ronie Garcia-Johnson and Erika Sasser observed: 'Arguing that FSC guidelines are onerous and unwieldy, the timber industries in the US, Canada and Europe quickly countered with their own templates for appropriate forestry practices. Today, more than 40 forest certification programs exist worldwide'.[106] Substitute environmental regulators have developed a range of institutional strategies to mitigate the authority deficit and vulnerability to competition that marks substitute TER. To boost the institutional strength of

[100] See www.conservation.org/projects/Pages/conservation-stewards-program.aspx.
[101] Vogel, 'Private Regulation', p. 69.
[102] Cf. Abbott & Snidal, 'Taking Responsive Regulation Transnational', pp. 97–98.
[103] Gulbrandsen, 'The Emergence and Effectiveness of the MSC', p. 656.
[104] Ekaterina Sofronova, Cameron Holley & Vijaya Nagaran, 'Environmental Non-governmental Organizations and Russian Environmental Governance: Accountability, Participation and Collaboration' (2014) 3(2) *Transnational Environmental Law*, pp. 341–371, at 366.
[105] See Chapter 2.3.
[106] Gary Gereffi, Ronie Garcia-Johnson & Erika Sasser, 'The NGO-Industrial Complex' (2001) 125 *Foreign Policy*, pp. 56–65, at 61. See also Errol E. Meidinger, 'Forest Certification as a Global Civil Society Regulatory Institution' in Errol Meidinger, Chris Elliot & Gerhard Oesten (eds.), *The Social and Political Dimensions of Forest Certification* (2003, Remagen-Oberwinter), pp. 265–289, at 276.

substitute TER, regulators build bridges between the voluntary sphere of substitute TER and the binding, authoritative spheres of public and private law. Additionally, substitute transnational regulators may focus on coalition building and aim to shore up the authority of substitute TER through the support of parties that are directly or indirectly implicated in the substitute regulatory initiative. The two strategies, and their impact on substitute TER, are explored next.

Responding to Vulnerability Through Bridging and Coalition-Building Strategies

In addition to formulating their own regulatory content through standard setting, codes of practice, declarations of principles and other behaviour-steering communications, many instances of substitute TER build in a requirement that participants abide by the applicable laws and regulations of the host country.[107] As the very first of its general principles, the FSC programme pronounces that: 'Forest management shall respect all applicable laws of the country in which they occur, and international treaties and agreements to which the country is a signatory'.[108] National law and international commitments are thus pressed into service as a baseline below which environmental performance may not drop. Yet the establishment of a regulatory floor – of varying stringency depending on the laws applicable in the jurisdiction in which the substitute TER member conducts its business – is not the sole and arguably not even the main reason why substitute regulators incorporate mandatory rules. Locating substitute TER within the same regulatory sphere as national law and international commitments, and emphasising its compatibility with mandatory standards, equally constitutes an attempt to boost the credibility of voluntary initiatives; to bask in the periphery of legal authority.[109] In a similar vein, substitute TER initiatives may seek mutual reinforcement by endorsing each other's regulatory content.[110]

A further avenue through which substitute TER buttresses its authority is through reliance on private law and the opportunities for enforcement that contractual agreements create. Participation in substitute TER is often premised on club membership and adherence to membership rules. Non-compliance with club rules by, for example, misrepresenting fish as sustainably farmed, may constitute a breach of the membership contract and serve as the basis for claims in compensation. Substitute TER programmes also rely on intellectual property law and trademarks to

[107] Vogel, 'Private Regulation', p. 69.

[108] Errol Meidinger, 'Beyond Westphalia. Competitive Legalization in Emerging Transnational Regulatory Systems', in Christian Brütsch & Dirk Lehmkuhl (eds.), *Law and Legalization in Transnational Relations* (2007, Routledge), p. 130; FSC website: https://us.fsc.org/en-us/what-we-do/mission-and-vision.

[109] Markos Karavias, 'Interactions between International Law and Private Fisheries Certification' (2018) 7(1) *Transnational Environmental Law*, pp. 165–184, at 181.

[110] Vogel, 'Private Regulation', p. 69.

insulate voluntary regulatory programmes from freerider risks and help to incentivise membership in the absence of coercion.[111] In the sphere of biodiversity protection, NGOs and IGOs resort to conservation contracting with local communities, private actors or states that are reluctant environmental regulators in order to shadow the binding force of international regulation.[112] Hence, substitute regulators deploy private law mechanisms, backed up by the threat of arbitration or litigation, in lieu of public enforcement.

A third and related strategy to bolster the authority of substitute TER is institutional coalition building.[113] Many successful private environmental governance regimes, including the FSC and MSC, were established in cooperation between environmental NGOs, IGOs, major corporations and sympathetic states.[114] Austria was a major supporter of the FSC initiative and helped to finance its certification scheme. In this manner, the Austrian state sought to compensate for the loss of its own ability to regulate when it decided to withdraw a national import ban on unsustainably harvested timber in order to stave off an impending GATT challenge.[115] The WWF teamed up with manufacturing giant Unilever, the world's largest trader in frozen fish, to set up the MSC.[116] Unilever's championing of MSC certification and its pivotal position in the market for food and consumables helped to spread the MSC label rapidly through the global supply and retail chain. Many substitute regulators also deploy informational tools, including public campaigns and labelling practices, to harness consumer power as a market disciplining force in the absence of policing power.[117]

The need for coalition building steers substitute regulators towards championing particular environmental causes and towards a specific approach to framing

[111] Fabrizio Cafaggi, 'Transnational Private Regulation and the Production of Global Public Goods and Private "Bads"' (2012) 23(3) *European Journal of International Law*, pp. 695–717, at 698.

[112] Natasha Affolder, 'Transnational Conservation Contracts' (2012) 25(2) *Leiden Journal of International Law*, pp. 443–460; Tammy L. Lewis, 'Transnational Conservation Movement Organizations: Shaping the Protected Area Systems of Less Developed Countries' (2000) 5(1) *Mobilization: An International Journal*, pp. 103–121, at 107.

[113] Cf. Abbott & Snidal, 'Taking Responsive Regulation Transnational', pp. 97–98 (on collaboration and orchestration strategies). Marc Allen Eisner, 'Private Environmental Governance in Hard Times: Markets for Virtue and the Dynamics of Regulatory Change' (2011) 12(2) *Theoretical Inquiries in Law*, pp. 489–515, at 495.

[114] Lewis, 'Transnational Conservation Movement Organizations', p. 103.

[115] Gregory Shaffer, 'How the WTO Shapes Regulatory Governance' (2015) 9(1) *Regulation & Governance*, pp. 1–15, at 6. See also Razzaque's discussion of the cooperation on the greening of dikes via the certification of shrimping companies that operate in Bangladesh. The project is organised between the German government-funded NGO 'Sustainable Development and Biodiversity Conservation in Coastal Protection Forests' and private shrimping companies. Jona Razzaque, 'Payments for Ecosystem Services in Sustainable Mangrove Forest Management in Bangladesh' (2017) 6(2) *Transnational Environmental Law*, pp. 309–333, at 332.

[116] Gulbrandsen, 'The Emergence and Effectiveness of the MSC', p. 655.

[117] Abbott & Snidal, 'Taking Responsive Regulation Transnational', pp. 97–98.

environmental problems. For consumers to engage, environmental impacts which occur throughout the industrial cycle need to be connected to and reflected in the representation of the product or service at the point of consumption. This may be achieved through the introduction of indicators such as 'carbon footprint', 'dirty' or 'brown' commodities and, on the flip side, labels such as 'green', 'sustainably harvested' or 'organically produced'. The dependence on consumer policing makes substitute TER most effective in cases where the causal chain between production, consumption and environmental impact is relatively easy to discern; consumers have actual choice; and consumer behaviour conveys a clear message to manufacturers and suppliers. These conditions apply in sectors such as farming, fishing and natural resource exploitation, which correspondingly feature prominently among examples of sectors governed by substitute or private regulation.[118]

To enhance a substitute TER regime's chances of successful uptake and effectiveness, substitute regulators will typically seek the support of other public interest groups, IGOs, states, and, last but not least, the intended regulatory addressees themselves. Substitute TER therefore must be responsive to a broad range of different stakeholders, many of whom have a sharply different agenda and diverging concerns. Pragmatically, substitute TER needs to signal credibility and resoluteness in order to keep the confidence of consumers, public interest groups and supporting states, while at the same time appear sufficiently accommodating and flexible so as not to deter private sector participation. One way to accommodate opposing messages and pull poachers and gamekeepers into the same regulatory fold, is through an increased emphasis on procedural guarantees and stakeholder participation in regulatory decision making.[119] An alleged second way is by deploying market-based approaches, which are reputed to achieve environmental objectives at a lower cost than across-the-board standard-setting approaches.[120]

Profile

Substitute TER responds to a deficit in state and international environmental regulation. In the absence of adequate public provision, voluntary regulatory frameworks are developed by non-state actors, among whom NGOs and IGOs are particularly prominent. Substitute TER comprises a range of different regulatory techniques, including standard setting, certification, codes of conduct and principle-based directives. The voluntary status of substitute TER constitutes a vulnerability which non-state regulators may seek to correct through bridging and

[118] See, for example, Vogel, 'Private Regulation', pp. 71–72: 'Private regulations that define standards for "responsible" business practices now exist for virtually every global industry and internationally traded commodity, including forestry, fisheries, chemicals, computers and electronic equipment, apparel, rugs, coffee, cocoa, palm, oil, diamonds, gold, toys, minerals and mining, energy, tourism, financial services, and athletic equipment'.

[119] Gulbrandsen, 'The Emergence and Effectiveness of the MSC', p. 656. See further Chapter 8.

[120] Cashore, 'NSMD'. See further Chapter 4.

coalition-building strategies. Bridging strategies connect substitute TER to law and seek to harness public and private legal authority in support of voluntary mechanisms. Coalition-building strategies pursue cooperation in the substitute TER endeavour with other non-state actors, including public interest groups, private enterprises and consumers, as well as with sympathetic states. Coalition building may enhance the likelihood of adherence to and compliance with substitute TER, but is also likely to influence its ambition, the choice of regulatory strategies and their implementation.

3.3.4 *Risk Management*

A fourth reason for the development of TER is risk management. Non-state actors may choose to self-regulate, or to cooperate in a transnational governance initiative, in order to avert the potentially negative consequences of under-regulation.[121] From the regulatory addressee's perspective, environmental under-regulation represents a potentially significant reputational and legal risk as it leaves companies vulnerable to workplace accidents, pollution and environmental disaster. Even from the narrowest of wealth-maximising perspectives, such scenarios are to be avoided since the costs of remedying pollution and compensating for health and environmental damage typically outweigh the costs of regulation.[122] Furthermore, accidents and spillage expose companies to the long-term damage of public condemnation and potentially ruinous liability claims.[123] Well-designed and appropriately pitched environmental regulation, in contrast, can steer companies towards greater efficiency and, hence, profitability.[124] For example, more energy-efficient production processes following the adoption of state-of-the-art industrial standards may lower companies' fuel consumption costs, reduce their CO_2 emissions and thereby cushion the impact of any binding CO_2 emissions targets. They can also reduce the volume of production-generated waste which, in turn, lowers the costs of waste treatment and disposal.

[121] Heather C. Lovell, 'Governing the Carbon Offset Market' 2010(1) *WIRES Climate Change*, pp. 353–362, at 358; Julia Black, '"Which Arrow?": Rule Type and Regulatory Policy' (1995) *Public Law*, pp. 94–117, at 95.

[122] Marc Orlitzky, Frank L. Schmidt & Sara L. Rynes, 'Corporate Social and Financial Performance: A Meta-analysis' (2003) 24(3) *Organization Studies*, pp. 403–441, at 423.

[123] Gereffi et al., 'The NGO-Industrial Complex', p. 56; Bartley, 'Certifying Forests and Factories', p. 434.

[124] Simon Deakin & Richard Hobbs, 'False Dawn for CSR? Shifts in Regulatory Policy and the Response of the Corporate and Financial Sectors in Britain' (2007) 15(1) *Corporate Governance: An International Review*, pp. 68–76, at 69–71; T. H. Tietenberg, 'Economic Instruments for Environmental Regulation' (1990) 6(1) *Oxford Review of Economic Policy*, pp. 17–33, at 17; Isabelle Maignan & David A. Ralston, 'Corporate Social Responsibility in Europe and the U.S.: Insights from Businesses' Self-Presentations' (2002) 33(3) *Journal of International Business Studies*, pp. 497–514; Eisner, 'Private Environmental Governance in Hard Times', pp. 490 & 493.

Some instances of risk management TER have blossomed in the wake of environmental scandals. Self-regulation can be a strategy to restore public and, by extension, investor confidence in the sector and to ward off the introduction of more exacting and potentially punitive binding regulation.[125] Major environmental incidents will typically make some form of binding regulatory response inevitable, all the more since state regulators, too, face public rebuke if they are seen not to react quickly or forcefully to traumatic events. Yet even if an increase of state regulation is inevitable, the adoption of self-regulating practices may help to soften the blow of mandatory prescriptions and to limit the scope and intensity of public intervention. The existence of a privately developed regulatory model may successfully nudge state regulators towards regulatory strategies that are most favoured within the sector, and may reposition the affected sector as a proactive cooperating partner in public interest regulation instead of the truculent target of top-down mandatory intervention.

Risk Management TER

Risk management TER and substitute TER mirror each other in many ways. Neither is necessarily transnational in scope. In practice, however, private sector-run initiatives are rarely designed as jurisdictionally limited and many examples of both substitute TER and risk management TER have a clear transboundary reach. Both substitute and risk management TER produce voluntary requirements, depend on the willingness of regulatory addressees to submit to the scheme for their credibility and effectiveness, and rely heavily on standardisation, audit and certification techniques for the implementation of regulatory targets. Their voluntary status leaves substitute and risk management TER similarly vulnerable to risks such as a potential lack of credibility, uncertainty as to whether the self-regulatory regime will be maintained or instead supplanted by a binding framework, the risk of free riders exploiting the reputational gains in the sector without adhering to the regime's prescriptions, and the risk of compliance deficits in the absence of state-sanctioned enforcement. Like substitute TER, risk management TER initiatives often resort to bridging and coalition building strategies to manage such risks.[126] Extensive coalition building may even blur the distinction between both types of regulatory action: what is substitute TER from the perspective of one partner in the regulatory endeavour, may be risk management TER through the eyes of another.

The most iconic example of risk management TER is the Responsible Care® initiative. After a string of industrial accidents in the 1970s and 1980s, causing deaths and environmental destruction at chemical plants in Flixborough (UK), Seveso (Italy) and Bhopal (India), the reputation of the chemical industry was in tatters.

[125] Cf. Tanja A. Börzel & Thomas Risse, 'Governance Without a State: Can It Work?' (2010) 4(1) *Regulation & Governance*, pp. 113–134, at 115–118.

[126] Vogel, 'Private Regulation', p. 74.

The Bhopal tragedy, a chemical explosion which caused the release of a poisonous gas that claimed anywhere between 3,000 and 10,000 victims on the day and which has blighted the life and environment of an estimated 500,000 people in the region since, fuelled a global public outcry for governments to adopt stringent chemical safety regulation with punitive sanctions and criminal liability for CEOs and company directors. Confronted with public outrage and the threat of tough new rules, the Public Perception Committee of the Chemicals Manufacturers Association (since then renamed the American Chemistry Council) called for pre-emptive action and urged the Association to adopt a self-regulatory regime for health, safety, security and environmental performance with regard to toxic contamination, based on an existing Canadian model. This resulted in the establishment of Responsible Care®, a self-regulation scheme that concentrates on health, environmental and safety performance with regard to toxic contamination.[127] Responsible Care® is developed by and for the chemicals sector. Membership is voluntary and the organisation relies heavily on self-assessment and self-accreditation as compliance instruments.[128] Other examples of risk management TER include various Corporate Social Responsibility (CSR) frameworks; the Equator Principles which, according to the EP Association, constitute 'a risk management framework, adopted by financial institutions, for determining, assessing and managing environmental and social risk in projects';[129] and a broad range of self-regulation frameworks in the commodities sector, relating to products ranging from minerals to palm oil.[130]

Like substitute TER, risk management TER falls primarily within the private/private category. It shares with substitute TER a heavily reliance on regulation strategies of standardisation, assessment, audit and certification practices, has similar strengths and weaknesses to those of substitute TER, and deploys similar coping strategies.[131] However, risk management TER also displays some more idiosyncratic features. Risk management TER is arguably more vulnerable to a bias towards permissive standardisation. Its regulatory practices run a relatively higher risk of constituting anti-competitive behaviour than the actions of other transnational environmental regulators. Thirdly, although both substitute and risk management TER face compliance challenges, these challenges may manifest in a different way in the case of risk management TER. The following section discusses the three challenges in turn.

[127] Cary Coglianese & Evan Mendelson, 'Meta-Regulation and Self-Regulation' in Robert Baldwin, Martin Cave & Martin Lodge (eds.), *The Oxford Handbook of Regulation* (2010, Oxford University Press), pp. 146–168.

[128] Nicholas Cheremisinoff; Paul Rosenfield & Anton Davletshin, *Responsible Care. A New Strategy for Pollution Prevention and Waste Reduction Through Environment* (2008, Elsevier Science).

[129] See www.equator-principles.com/.

[130] Vogel, 'Private Regulation', p. 74.

[131] Cf. Osuji, 'Corporate Social Responsibility', p. 268.

The Challenges of Risk Management TER: Lax Standard Setting; Managing Opportunities for Anti-Competitive Behaviour; and Compliance-Related Challenges

Risk management TER is vulnerable to acute credibility challenges. With a primary focus on reputation and profitability enhancement, and an aspiration to pre-empt or moderate public intervention in the sector, the environmental effectiveness of industry-led self-regulation easily appears suspect. Arguably, ulterior motives tempt self-regulating entities towards the adoption of standards and practices that create a semblance of enhanced environmental performance while achieving little real change.[132] At worst, risk management TER may be no more than a glorified delaying tactic designed to defer the costs of environmental risk internalisation for as long as companies can get away with it.[133] CSR schemes may be nothing but callous marketing tools; sustainability labels a crass rebranding of business-as-usual.[134]

Bridging and coalition-building strategies can help to correct the bias and, correspondingly, to curb suspicions and bolster credibility. However, empirical data suggests that, for many initiatives, concerns about the environmental quality of the regulatory framework are all too real. The study conducted by Gereffi and others indicates that risk management TER in the forestry sector had produced far laxer standards and approaches to certification than substitute TER in the same field.[135] On CSR, in 2015 Amnesty and Global Witness reports asserted that over 80% of company filings offer 'little useful information' and do not meet due diligence expectations.[136] Recently conducted investigations into palm oil certification schemes indicate that more than 400 companies have made a total of 700 pledges to reduce their impacts on the world's forests, with palm oil and timber dominating the commitments thanks to the availability of certification schemes. Yet

[132] Neil Gunningham & Joseph Rees, 'Industry Self-Regulation: An Institutional Perspective' (1997) 19(4) *Law & Policy*, pp. 363–414, at 366–370.

[133] See Olivier De Schutter, 'Corporate Social Responsibility European Style' (2008) 14(2) *European Law Journal*, pp. 203–236, at 204, addressing the risk for CSR to become '*a codeword for abandoning to market mechanisms certain questions which might otherwise be the target of regulatory approaches*'. See also Gereffi et al., 'The NGO-Industrial Complex', p. 57.

[134] Kingston et al., *European Environmental Law*, pp. 145–146.

[135] Gereffi et al., 'The NGO-Industrial Complex', p. 61.

[136] Reported in Osuji, 'Corporate Social Responsibility', p. 265. See also Abbott & Snidal, 'Taking Responsive Regulation Transnational', p. 99: '[A] few path-breaking firms, such as the Body Shop (1991), pioneered self-regulation, adopting codes of conduct for their own operations and for suppliers. Today, virtually all major firms have self-regulatory codes that include varied monitoring and implementation procedures, often extending to suppliers; many also issue public reports on social responsibility and sustainability. Like other forms of corporate self-regulation, however, many others exist more on paper than in practice'. See also Rieneke Slager, Jean-Pascal Gond & Jeremy Moon, 'Standardization as Institutional Work: The Regulatory Power of a Responsible Investment Standard' (2012) 33(5/6) *Organization Studies*, pp. 763–790, at 768.

deforestation continues unabated as existing schemes do not deter participating companies from converting rainforests or peatlands into palm plantations.[137]

Secondly, risk management TER can raise concerns of anti-competitive behaviour. Since regulator and regulatory addressee coincide, and as risk management TER is overwhelmingly private/private, the lines may blur between regulation, which steers behaviour in the public interest, and cartelisation, which orchestrates behaviour in the private interest.[138] Self-regulation offers tantalising opportunities for large players to orchestrate business practices under the guise of environmental standardisation and impose those same conditions on other scheme participants. In cohesive and well-organised sectors, the voluntary nature of risk management TER easily masks the iron grip of peer pressure.

The club nature of much risk management TER may also trigger unique compliance challenges. Loss of membership seems but a soft penalty for non-compliance compared to the enforcement arsenal at the disposal of public authorities, but the prospect of being ousted from the club may if fact constitute a far greater threat than a civil, administrative or even criminal sanction.[139] Regulation evidently needs a reasonable level of compliance to survive, but non-compliance, too, has a productive role to play as a means of contestation of regulatory decision making. It also performs a valuable diagnostic function as an indicator of shortcomings in regulatory design or implementation and may result in adaptations that more effectively respond to the needs and capacities of a broader range of regulatory addressees. These functions may be lost under conditions when a powerful group of peers sets the tone. Hence, whereas its voluntary status may expose risk management TER to compliance deficits similar to those experienced in the context of substitute TER, there is equally scope for the reverse risk to materialise.

Profile

Risk management TER seeks to reduce the risks associated with under-regulation, such as loss of reputation, legal and financial risks and the prospect of invasive mandatory regulation. As a predominantly private/private form of regulation, risk management TER shares many features with substitute TER, and deploys similar bridging and coalition-building strategies to enhance legitimacy and harness regulatory resilience. Additionally, risk management TER tends to raise elevated concerns of lax environmental standardisation and its club-like structure may foster anti-competitive behaviour. Its voluntary status can create compliance deficits, but by the same token the scope for peer pressure may restrict opportunities for productive non-compliance.

137 Susanna Ala-Kurikka, 'MEP Calls for EU trade to Tackle Palm Oil Driven Deforestation', *ENDS*, 16 Nov. 2016.

138 Cafaggi, 'Transnational Private Regulation', p. 700.

139 Cf. Roger Cotterrell, 'What Is Transnational Law' (2012) 37(2) *Law & Social Inquiry*, pp. 500–524, at 520–521.

3.3.5 *Enhancing the Effectiveness of Environmental Regulation and Governance*

Finally, actors engage in the establishment of transnational schemes to enhance the effectiveness of existing environmental regulation. 'Enhancement TER' develops when regulators join forces, for instance, to increase the market size across which environmental allowances can be traded, so that overall emission caps can be achieved more cost-effectively.[140] Alternatively, environmental regulators may opt to work together in transnational networks in order to share the expense of regulation; to pool the expertise required for key regulatory functions such as standard setting and compliance control; and to exchange information and know-how.[141] Or, actors who are under either a legal or self-imposed obligation to meet certain environmental targets may opt to collaborate in a transnational scheme that bolsters their ability to meet and even transcend domestic expectations.

The identification of 'enhancement TER' as a separate category of regulation, with a different intentionality from the four preceding ones, is admittedly open to some contestation. For enhancement initiatives that are pushed by national regulators wanting to further the effectiveness of domestic environmental regulation, the dividing line between enhancement TER and collective action TER is arguably thin. There is no fixed cut-off point between regulatory collaboration by choice, which would designate the resulting efforts as enhancement TER, and collaboration by necessity, which qualifies them as collective action TER. By the same token, in some cases it is difficult to distinguish private actors who engage in self-regulation to make up for a failing state from those who have risk management or the enhancement of their ability to meet and exceed legal expectations in mind. Nevertheless, the discussion of enhancement TER as a self-standing category is warranted because a growing proportion of transnational environmental regulatory activity cannot be explained satisfactorily as either an attempt to overcome collective action problems, to facilitate trade, to supplant the state, or to manage the risks associated with under-regulation. This is most glaringly the case for many of the rapidly expanding transnational networks dedicated to climate governance. Transnational networks of this type generate distinctive regulatory content, create distinctive opportunities and face distinctive challenges.

[140] Eric Haites, 'Harmonisation Between National and International Tradeable Permit Schemes', in OECD, *Greenhouse Gas Emissions Trading and Project-Based Mechanisms* (OECD, 2004), pp. 105–118; Celeste M. Black, 'Taxation of Cross-Border Transfers of Carbon Emission Allowances under Linked Emissions Trading Schemes' (2017) 6(2) *Transnational Environmental Law*, pp. 335–361, at 339–340.

[141] Giest & Howlett, 'Comparative Climate Change Governance', p. 137; Kenneth W. Abbott & Duncan Snidal, 'Strengthening International Regulation Through Transnational New Governance: Overcoming the Orchestration Deficit' (2009) 42 *Vanderbilt Journal of Transnational Law*, pp. 501–578, at 512–520.

Enhancement TER

In the past decade, the field of climate change governance has proven a uniquely fertile soil for the introduction of transnational regulatory enhancement initiatives. The establishment of a pan-European emissions allowance market under the EU Emissions Trading Directive (ETD),[142] and its compatibility with the Kyoto Joint Implementation and Clean Development Mechanism (CDM) mechanism under the EU Linking Directive,[143] constitute attempts to maximise the potential for efficiency of regulatory, market-based instruments.[144] Beyond the EU, too, environmental regulators either unilaterally connect to other trading schemes or agree with foreign counterparts to harmonise regulatory strategies so as to integrate carbon markets and maximise opportunities for cost-effective emissions reductions.[145] California (US), for example, has joined its cap-and-trade programme to that of Quebec (Canada), and in 2010 signed a Memorandum of Understanding with the states of Chiapa (Mexico) and Acre (Brazil) to make Reductions in Environmental Deforestation and Forest Degradation (REDD) offsets from the latter countries tradeable across borders.[146] Generally, Ranson and Stavins's research affirms that many jurisdictions which have introduced emissions trading regimes are keen on transnational linking. They report that, among the thirty-six cap-and-trade systems that were either active or ready for launch by May 2014, most had 'established or proposed at least one linkage with another cap-and-trade or credit system'.[147]

Linking regulation happens either when a regulator unilaterally decides to recognise allowances generated under a different emissions trading system (ETS), or through bilateral agreement between emissions trading regimes. Most linking regulation therefore falls within the public/private sphere. Linking measures aim to create sufficient convergence to enable the interchangeability of offsets and allowances generated through different ETSs, while preserving the environmental credibility of the regime. Hence, regulatory strategies tend to focus on the harmonisation of market conditions, for instance, through the development of common approaches to carbon pricing, and the development of criteria for mutual recognition.[148]

[142] Directive 2003/87/EC establishing a scheme for greenhouse gas emission allowance trading within the Community [2003] OJ L275/32 (as amended).

[143] Directive 2004/101/EC establishing a scheme for greenhouse gas emission allowance trading within the Community, in respect of the Kyoto Protocol's project mechanisms [2004] OJ L338/18.

[144] Michael Mehling & Erik Haites, 'Mechanisms for Linking Emissions Trading Schemes' (2009) 9(2) *Climate Policy*, pp. 169–184.

[145] Ostrom, 'Polycentric Systems', p. 553.

[146] Ernesto Roessing Neto, 'Linking Subnational Climate Change Policies: A Commentary on the California-Acre Process' (2015) 4(2) *Transnational Environmental Law*, pp. 425–437, at 426.

[147] Matthew Ranson & Robert N. Stavins, 'Linkage of Greenhouse Gas Emissions Trading Systems: Learning from Experience' (2016) 16(3) *Climate Policy*, pp. 284–300, at 286.

[148] Partnership for Market Readiness; International Carbon Action Partnership, *Emissions Trading in Practice: A Handbook on Design and Implementation* (2006, World Bank), pp. 151–168.

A second form of enhancement TER emanates from transnational networks that connect a variety of stakeholders to offer mutual support in the pursuit and implementation of environmental objectives. Such networks typically develop around a specific environmental challenge and draw on the involvement of actors ranging from governmental delegations, subnational authorities and regulatory agencies to intergovernmental organisations, civil society bodies, private sector actors and charities. Expectedly, the preponderance of networking activity for environmental governance concerns the field of climate change.[149] Particularly prominent among transnational climate change networks are city-focused initiatives, such as Eurocities; the Climate Alliance; the Covenant of Mayors for Climate and Energy; the C40 Cities Climate Leadership group; the Compact of Mayors; the Asian Cities Climate Change Resilience Network (ACCCRN); Cities for Climate Protection (ICLEI) and Energie-cités.

Initiatives to launch transnational networks are either member-driven, as in the case of the C40 group[150] and the Climate Alliance, or spearheaded by transnational policy entrepreneurs such as UN or EU institutions, large philanthropic organisations or coalitions of state governments. For example, the ACCCRN was kickstarted by the Rockefeller Foundation; the European Commission was a key organising force behind the Covenant of Mayors for Climate and Energy; and the establishment of Compact of Mayors was championed by the UN Secretary General with support from UN Habitats and in collaboration with other transnational city networks. Generally, the primary aim of the network is to form a governance hub to facilitate information exchange and transnational learning between public and private stakeholders with environmental responsibilities.[151] Networks also create opportunities for policymakers, regulators and energy-intensive enterprises to liaise with international, public and private funding bodies. Moreover, transnational networks enable similarly situated stakeholders, such as rapidly growing cities or renewable energy regulators, to orchestrate positions and organise more effective interest representation in local and international negotiations.[152] Beyond facilitation, some networks explicitly aim to transcend the goals of binding international or domestic climate change regulation. For example, the Climate Alliance of European Cities with Indigenous Rainforest Peoples subscribes to a GHG

[149] Michele M. Betsill & Harriet Bulkeley, 'Cities and the Multilevel Governance of Global Climate Change' (2006) 12(2) *Global Governance*, pp. 141–159. For an example beyond the sphere of climate change, see Radoslav S. Dimitrov, 'International Coral Reef Initiative' in Thomas Hale & David Held (eds.), *Handbook of Transnational Governance. Institutions & Innovations* (2011, Polity Press), pp. 182–189.

[150] www.c40.org/history.

[151] Giest & Howlett, 'Comparative Climate Change Governance', pp. 342–343; Ostrom, 'Polycentric Systems', p. 553.

[152] Ostrom, 'Polycentric Systems', p. 553; Paula Castro, 'Common But Differentiated Responsibilities Beyond the Nation State: How is Differential Treatment Addressed in Transnational Climate Governance Initiatives?' (2016) 5(2) *Transnational Environmental Law*, pp. 379–400, at 386.

emissions reduction of by 50% by 2030;[153] this target surpasses the mitigation goals articulated in the overwhelming majority of countries from which the network participants hail.

Given their diverse membership, most transnational networks fall into the hybrid category. Their regulatory output, too, is extremely varied. Regulation generated through transnational networks such as city climate change alliances is often pronouncedly procedural: participating members may be expected to generate indicators to measure the state of the environment within their sphere of operation; to inventorise emissions; to draw up action plans for environmental improvement; and to report on their progress.[154] Networks may adopt an overall aspirational target of, say, cutting down GHG emissions 10% below legally allowable levels, but such targets tend not to be translated into specific performance or technical standards. Instead, participating members retain a high level of discretion in designing their contribution strategy towards the overall goal. An often used strategy to shore up commitment among network members is through the adoption of declarations, which tend to be heavy on aspirational language, light on quantifiable targets and reflect a principle-based approach to regulation.[155]

In addition to procedural standardisation, many of the coordinating activities within transnational networks informally steer participants' behaviour towards regulatory convergence. Information exchange on best regulatory practice can foster the development of codes of conduct, which may subsequently foster an expectation of adherence by network participants.[156] Expense- and expertise-pooling may fuel an interest in the adoption of harmonised environmental standards so that decision-making resources are more easily transferable from one regulatory environment to the next. Adherence to best practice and reporting requirements may be a prerequisite to access funding opportunities within the network.

Enhancement TER: The Challenges of Amplification, Complexity and Opacity

Enhancement TER offers significant potential benefits to its participants. Through linking, shared research, information exchange and greater access to public and private funding opportunities, environmental regulators are able to fulfil their mandate more (cost-)effectively and strengthen the legitimacy of their regulatory

[153] See www.climatealliance.org/home.html.

[154] See further Chapter 5.4.2.

[155] E.g., the 2016 ICLEI summit led to the adoption of the Basque Declaration, which embraces broadly drawn goals such as the promotion of sustainable urban mobility patterns and the protection of water resources, and formulates equally broad commitments to, inter alia, develop a 'culture of sustainability' and 'wisely select new and smart technologies', to which the ICLEI member cities are invited to subscribe. See http://conferences.sustainablecities.eu/fileadmin/user_upload/_imported/uploads/DOCUMENTS/Basque-Declaration-ENGLISH-WWW.pdf.

[156] Chiara Armeni, 'Global Experimentalist Governance, International Law and Climate Change Technologies' (2015) 64(4) *International & Comparative Law Quarterly*, pp. 875–904, at 882.

actions. Transnational networks support participants in the implementation and compliance with regulatory requirements.[157] Network actors who are themselves targets of national environmental regulation can take greater ownership of their commitments and may therefore prove more willing to go beyond mandatory minimum requirements. This could in turn ease the path for a corresponding ratcheting up of environmental standards in national regulation. The governance structures and procedural requirements generated through the network also constitute a guarantee for funding organisations as they afford more effective supervision and reduce the risks of non-compliance with the terms of funding agreements.

Yet, unsurprisingly, enhancement TER comes with its own range of vulnerabilities. Linking initiatives confront a clear amplification risk.[158] Where there is linking, there is a weakest link. Just as the efficiencies of trading between allowances buyers and sellers can be amplified across emissions markets, so too can the diseconomies caused by regulatory failure. A miscalibrated cap, resulting in allowance price volatility in one jurisdiction, will have knock-on effects across markets. A failure to secure genuine additionality of offsetting activities, or to police fraud in the issuance of allowances, may jeopardise the credibility of every ETS in the chain.

The risk of amplifying vulnerability is also present at a structural level: because of its efficiency-maximising and facilitating potential, enhancement TER may end up entrenching sub-optimal regulatory strategies and obstructing reform.[159] Experience with emissions trading and linking suggests that this risk is not just hypothetical. Considering the heady promises made regarding the superior efficiency of market-based regulation in the academic literature of the 1980s–2000s,[160] practical experience with, for example, the EU ETS has been comparatively sobering. While workable, emissions trading strategies so far have proved less dynamic, democratic and self-enforcing than anticipated, and their maintenance requires much heavier administrative intervention than assumed.[161] Yet emissions trading regimes continue to proliferate across the globe. The choice of regulatory strategy is typically the product of a combination of considerations, but it is highly plausible that the prospect of linking plays a role in steering regulators towards market-based over alternative regulatory approaches. Hence, amplification may be sustaining the popularity of emissions trading beyond its pareto-optimal point, and thus stifle experimentation with alternative, potentially superior regulatory strategies.

157 Ostrom, 'Polycentric Systems', p. 552.
158 Cf. Veerle Heyvaert, 'Globalizing Regulation: Reaching Beyond the Borders of Chemical Safety' 36(1) *Journal of Law and Society*, pp. 110–128, at 122–123.
159 Ibid.
160 E.g., Robert W. Hahn & Robert N. Stavins, 'Incentive-Based Environmental Regulation: A New Era from an Old Idea?' (1991) 18(1) *Ecology Law Quarterly*, pp. 1–41; Richard B. Stewart, 'Models for Environmental Regulation: Central Planning Versus Market-Based Approaches' (1992) 19(3) *Boston College Environmental Affairs Law Review*, pp. 547–562.
161 Kingston et al., *European Environmental Law*, pp. 289–296.

As to enhancement TER generated through cooperative transnational networks, its most obvious drawback relates to the added degree of institutional complexity it injects into the regulatory sphere. This is emphatically illustrated in the tangle of city-based alliances for climate change. Berlin (Germany) is a member of the Climate Alliance;[162] the Covenant of Mayors for Climate and Energy;[163] the environmental chapter of Eurocities;[164] the C40 Cities Climate Leadership Group;[165] the Compact/Global Covenant of Mayors;[166] and ICLEI.[167] There are numerous linkages between networks (e.g., Covenant of Mayors is supported by the Climate Alliance), which have overlapping although not identical membership. Similarly overlapping yet different are the missions and targets that the various networks embrace. Energie-cités focuses on capacity building in the field of sustainable energy, and heavily emphasises the representative role of the network vis-à-vis EU decision-making bodies. The Mexico City Pact, which is supported by ICLEI and connects a relatively smaller group of approximately 200 cities across the world, most of which – although not Berlin – are also members of the Compact/Global Covenant of Mayors, places greater emphasis on voluntary commitments to develop mitigation and adaptation strategies, on awareness raising and the promotion of civil society involvement in climate policy. The Covenant of Mayors for Climate and Energy shares with the Mexico City Pact a mission to foster emissions reduction initiatives, but in contrast to the latter expresses this in a numerical target of a minimum 40% reduction by 2030,[168] and focuses less on the promotion of public participation.

Complexity obviously problematises comprehension. It also exacerbates the opacity of regulation. Even if individual networks resolutely embrace transparency, the institutional complexity of intersecting and overlapping networks threatens to erode its usefulness. When a clutch of governance frameworks, commitments and action plans cover roughly similar ground, it becomes supremely difficult to gauge the respective contribution of each. Correspondingly, any attribution of accountability may be compromised. This challenge is all the more pressing in the context of enhancement TER when we consider the very particular form of regulation that transnational networks produce. With a primary focus on facilitation and orchestration, enhancement TER rarely comes in the guise of top-down, binary, prescriptive

[162] www.climatealliance.org/municipalities/the-network.html.

[163] www.covenantofmayors.eu/about/about/signatories_en.html?commitments2=1&commitments3=1&commitments1=1.

[164] www.eurocities.eu/eurocities/members&category=envi.

[165] www.c40.org/cities.

[166] www.compactofmayors.org/cities/berlin/.

[167] www.iclei-europe.org/members/who-are-our-members/.

[168] www.covenantofmayors.eu/about/covenant-of-mayors_en.html. By comparison, Article 2 of the Mexico City Pact stipulates: 'If we have set targets for reducing GHG emissions, we will adopt and implement measures to achieve them'. See www.worldmayorscouncil.org/fileadmin/Materials/GlobalCitiesCovenantonClimate_MXCP_20110315.pdf.

standards typically associated with conventional command-and-control regulation.[169] Instead, regulatory content is more likely to develop informally and incrementally, for instance, through the practice of information sharing and the accumulation of implementation plans from which standard practice is gradually inferred. The disciplining force within transnational networks, too, emanates from sources that are difficult to pinpoint or measure, such as peer pressure and competition for funding within the network. Regulatory authority within a network therefore is not easily attributable to one particular participating institution, one particular type of instrument or sanction, but builds through combination and interaction. This makes the coercive force of enhancement TER difficult to assess, and, again, complicates the establishment of lines of accountability.

Profile

Enhancement TER is adopted to boost the effectiveness of environmental regulation, either through linking or through facilitation and orchestration. Linking initiatives are mostly public/public, and focus on regulatory convergence to support the transferability of tradeable offsets and allowances. Linking can boost the cost-effectiveness of regulation, but it equally amplifies its vulnerabilities and may entrench it, which could stifle regulatory innovation. A second strand of enhancement TER concerns the regulatory activities within hybrid, transnational networks, which are particularly prominent in the field of climate change. Transnational networks are primarily conceived as capacity-building entities with a mission of knowledge production and exchange, representation and resourcing. As a source of environmental regulation, transnational networks typically produce broad and principle-based targets, and focus on procedural standardisation. Much of their regulatory content matures through informal, iterative processes: through the accumulation and exchange of regulatory practice information within the network. Network participation may enhance participants' ability to determine, meet and go beyond mandatory minimum standards, but the ensuing institutional complexity may jeopardise transparency.

3.4 LEARNING FROM THE REGULATOR'S INTENTIONS

The regulator's intentions are often taken for granted in law and policy analyses, yet a closer examination of the different reasons why actors set up or lend their support to transnational regulatory regimes is extremely instructive. It reveals a degree of commonality between regimes that are rarely considered within the same analytical context, such as EU passenger car regulation and animal trapping standards, or ETS linking and city networks, which fosters opportunities for mutual learning. Conversely, but at least as importantly, the analysis indicates that there may be reasons to

[169] See further Chapter 5.4.

differentiate between sets of instruments that are often grouped together. Discussions of international environmental agreements do not often distinguish measures adopted to overcome collective action problems and regimes to facilitate trade, yet this difference may explain why an agreement between exactly the same countries results in lowest common denominator standards in one case, and 'trading up' in the other. Similarly, research on private regulation rarely differentiates between substitute TER and risk management TER. Yet the discussion revealed that, while they do share overlapping features, each variant has particular strengths and vulnerabilities that are less pronounced in their counterpart.

Secondly, the analysis reveals a high level of overlap between the actor-based categories of TER drawn in Chapter 2, and the intentionality-based organisation developed in this chapter. It is not a full match, but by the same token it is difficult to ignore the prevalence of public/public measures among collective action TER; public/private regulation among trade facilitation TER; private/public and private/private arrangements in substitute and risk management TER, and hybrid measures in enhancement TER. The overlap injects a degree of predictability into regulatory conversations about the likely intentions of different cohorts of regulators and addressees, and, conversely, about the type of actor that is most likely to organise in pursuit of a particular regulatory goal.

The third lesson from the intentionality-based-analysis is, from an environmental perspective, much more concerning. In the world of TER, much conspires against the likelihood of tough and ambitious environmental regulation materialising. Whether because of consensualism, the presence of a dual purpose, the need to get regulatory addressees to buy into the regulatory scheme, or the regulator's own desire to stave off stringent regulation, in nearly every case the conditions in which TER happens are likely to push environmental requirements towards the permissive end of the scale. It is vital to be aware of this frequent bias towards low environmental ambition, and equally important to understand the different factors producing the bias in each case. This chapter has provided a key first step towards such understanding.

4

Strategies for Environmental Regulation

The Recursive Activities of Regulation

All regulation seeks to influence behaviour, but there are many different strategies through which this goal can be achieved. Environmental regulation offers the quintessential illustration of the strategic diversity of regulation, as permitting regimes operate alongside market mechanisms, disclosure requirements, negotiated agreements and so on. The aim of the next three chapters is to examine and explain the key strategies that characterise TER. Such analysis is essential in order to achieve a thorough understanding of the scope and scale of transformation that environmental regulation has undergone in the past decades. It also constitutes vital groundwork for informed critical assessments and debates about the qualities, drawbacks and legitimacy of TER.

The study of TER strategies can build on a rich body of literature that critically examines different instruments and approaches through which environmental regulators seek to achieve their goals. Chief among the categories used in scholarship and in practice are 'command-and-control' regulation as well as alternative strategies such as 'market instruments', 'self-regulation', 'meta-regulation' and 'responsive regulation'. The organisation of the field of environmental strategies on the basis of a 'command-and-control versus alternatives' divide has helped to conceptualise environmental regulation as a distinctive area of theory and practice, but it is argued in this chapter that the entrenchment of the 'command-and-control *versus* alternatives' narrative also has obfuscatory consequences and inhibits the development of a more granular, detailed analysis of range and variety in environmental regulatory strategy. Moreover, it has resulted in the consolidation of a number of widespread but rarely examined assumptions about the differences between 'traditional' and 'alternative' regulatory strategies, which hinder critical examination and stunt our ability to learn.

To enable a more granular examination of the range and variety in environmental regulatory strategy, this chapter develops an alternative, activity-based model of regulatory work. I argue that a primary focus on activities, rather than on the style of regulation, meaningfully adds to our knowledge about environmental regulatory strategies, the differences between them and the significance of these differences. The activity-based model is organised in five interconnected stages, which are explained and illustrated with reference to environmental regulation generally. By unpacking regulatory strategies into a sequence of interconnected activities, the model better equips us to identify the multiple choices that go into the design of regulatory instruments and control mechanisms, and to pinpoint the impact of those choices on reception and responses to regulation. It is also more effective at highlighting not just the differences but also the many points of overlap between command-and-control and its alternatives. Thus, it helps to generate more reliable insights into what a shift from one style to another will and will not deliver.

4.1 THE TRANSFORMATION OF ENVIRONMENTAL REGULATORY STRATEGIES

When asked to identify the most significant transformation in environmental regulation in the past three decades, it is a safe bet that most commentators would point towards the diversification of regulatory strategies. The last thirty years have witnessed an exploding interest in what are, essentially, regulatory instrumentalisation choices. The relative merits of various alternative approaches to regulation (command-and-control versus market-based instruments versus nudging versus meta-regulation), scrutinised from a vantage point that might alternatively focus on efficiency, effectiveness, justice or legitimacy, constitute one of the most intensely debated themes in the environmental law and governance literature.[1]

Many aspects of this debate are still in flux, but other conversations have acquired familiar beats over time. In particular, understandings about the early development of environmental regulatory strategies have crystallised into a standard account which is now frequently taken as read. It functions as an unspoken backdrop against which contemporary debates on regulatory strategy unfold.[2]

1 See, e.g., Robert Baldwin, 'Regulation: After Command and Control' in Keith Hawkins (ed.), *The Human Face of* Law (1997, Oxford University Press); Nathaniel O. Keohane, Richard L. Revesz & Robert O. Stavins, 'The Choice of Regulatory Instruments in Environmental Policy' (1998) 22(2) *Harvard Environmental Law Review*, pp. 313–367; Daniel H. Cole & Peter Z. Grossman, 'When Is Command-and-Control Efficient? Institutions, Technology, and the Comparative Efficiency of Alternative Regulatory Regimes for Environmental Protection' (1999) *Wisconsin Law Review*, pp. 887–983; Rena I. Steinzor, 'Reinventing Environmental Regulation: The Dangerous Journey from Command to Self-Control' (1998) 22(1) *Harvard Environmental Law Review*, pp. 103–202; Brian Galle, 'Tax, Command . . . or Nudge? Evaluating the New Regulation' (2014) 92(4) *Texas Law Review*, pp. 837–894; Mia Mahmudur Rahim, 'Meta-Regulation Approach of Law: A Potential Legal Strategy to Develop Socially Responsible Business Self-Regulation in Least Developed Common Law Countries' (2011) 40(2) *Common Law World Review*, pp. 174–206.

2 See Neil Gunningham, 'Environment Law, Regulation and Governance: Shifting Architectures' (2009) 21(2) *Journal of Environmental Law*, pp. 179–212.

The following sections review the standard account and explore its particular relevance in a context of transnationalisation.

4.1.1 *The Transformation of Regulatory Strategies: Development of the Standard Account*

The standard account goes as follows: in the beginning, there was command-and-control regulation which constituted, if not the sole, then at least the dominant strategy through which environmental regulators pursued public interest objectives. In line with this strategy, regulators determined the technical details of the kind of behaviour that regulatory addressees should adopt, for example, through the formulation of technology-based standards or maximum emission limits. They imposed the resulting prescriptions on all parties engaged in the targeted behaviour, to the same degree. Compliance with the imposed prescriptions was secured through inspections and a system of penalties for breach, which was again applied across-the-board and uniformly.[3]

Command-and-control is credited as the vehicle through which a first major wave of deliberate change in industrial environmental behaviour was effectuated during the 1970s and 1980s.[4] Policy makers and commentators from the world's most active regions in environmental regulation at the time, with the United States at the forefront, tended to agree that, by and large, command-and-control regulation was key in curbing some of the most prominent environmental problems of the time, such as air pollution, water pollution and land contamination.[5] Yet at the same time, discontent grew among regulators, stakeholders and commentators alike about certain features of command-and-control which were deemed to suppress the effectiveness of the instrument.[6]

One line of critique, buoyed by the Reaganite and Thatcherite turn to neoliberalism in the 1980s, challenged command-and-control for being an overbearing, micro-managerial approach which counterproductively and unnecessarily stifled private enterprise.[7] Environmental regulators' heavy reliance on technical standards,

[3] Richard B. Stewart, 'Models for Environmental Regulation: Central Planning versus Market-Based Approaches' (1992) 19(3) *Boston College Environmental Affairs Law Review*, pp. 547–562, at 550–552.

[4] Steinzor, 'Reinventing Environmental Regulation'; Howard Latin, 'Ideal versus Real Regulatory Efficiency: Implementation of Uniform Standards and "Fine-Tuning" Regulatory Reforms' (1985) 37(5) *Stanford Law* Review, pp. 1267–1332.

[5] Alvin L. Alm, 'A Need For New Approaches. Command-and-Control Is No Longer a Cure All' (1992) 18(2) *EPA Journal*, pp. 7–11, at 7.

[6] Robert Baldwin, Martin Cave & Martin Lodge, *Understanding Regulation. Theory, Strategy, and Practice*, 2nd edn. (2012, Oxford University Press), pp. 106–111.

[7] Ibid.; Bruce A. Ackerman & Richard B. Stewart, 'Reforming Environmental Law' (1985) 37(5) *Stanford Law* Review, pp. 1333–1365; Marc Allen Eisner, 'Private Environmental Governance in Hard Times: Markets for Virtue and the Dynamics of Regulatory Change' (2011) 12(2) *Theoretical Inquiries in Law*, pp. 489–515, at 490.

developed with extensive expert input, was seen to result in the imposition of regulatory prescriptions that excessively curtail private choice. Moreover, since regulators need to acquire the expertise necessary to formulate the appropriate technical standards, command-and-control tended to be slow in development, resource-intensive and therefore inefficient.[8] Also potentially inefficient was the uniform application of requirements across the regulated sector. The imposition of, say, a maximum sulphur dioxide emissions level on every site where the substance is released, regardless of the abatement costs involved, resulted in society arguably paying too much for too little environmental improvement. Similarly, the requirement that every industrial installation adopt the best available techniques in the sector, irrespective of the cost or associated environmental gain this represents for the individual installation, generated outcomes that were both economically and environmentally sub-optimal.[9]

In addition to its alleged poor performance against a benchmark of allocative efficiency, the 'controlling' and enforcement-oriented aspects of command-and-control, too, were considered a possible obstruction to effectiveness. Command-and-control, commentators asserted, treats its primary target audience as an adversary which must be made to submit and should be penalised for non-compliance.[10] The antagonistic stance inherent in command-and-control was seen to erode the willingness of the private sector to cooperate in the pursuit of public interest goals. Instead, industry would direct its energy and resources towards fending off attempts at regulation.[11] Antagonism was moreover untenable because, given their strong need for expertise in the design of detailed regulatory prescriptions, command-and-control regulators were chronically dependent on the very sectors they policed.[12] Command-and-control therefore needed to rely on a combination of close cooperative and arms' length approaches, which thwarted the adoption of a clear and consistent vision for the relationship between public authorities and the private sector. Moreover, if regulatory addressees failed to comply with commands because of a lack of capacity, the imposition of a penalty under a command-and-control strategy would, if anything, reduce the party's ability to meet its environmental obligations. In either case, the regime was likely to underperform in terms of achieving its regulatory objectives.

These are but some highlights of the much more detailed and extensive critique which, over time, has permeated into the standard account of the evolution of

8 Julia Black, 'Critical Reflections on Regulation' (2002) 27(1) *Australian Journal of Legal Philosophy*, pp. 1–35, at 2.

9 Ackerman & Stewart, 'Reforming Environmental Law', p. 1335.

10 Darren Sinclair, 'Self-Regulation versus Command and Control? Beyond False Dichotomies', (1997) 19(4) *Law & Policy*, pp. 529–559, at 531.

11 Ian Ayres & John Braithwaite, *Responsive Regulation: Transcending the Deregulation Debate* (1992, Oxford University Press), pp. 49–51.

12 Baldwin et al., *Understanding Regulation*, pp. 107–108.

environmental regulation, but they suffice to convey the key demerits which command-and-control has become associated with: laborious, excessively technical, adversarial, inflexible and inefficient. In response, decision makers and commentators turned their attention towards alternative strategies that promised greater efficiency, flexibility and a lighter touch.[13] Chief among discussed alternatives are incentive-based regulation, which prices rather than prescribes behaviour and leaves regulatory addressees the choice between paying for the status quo and implementing change,[14] and disclosure-based regulation, which requires addressees to be transparent about their choices and relies on the policing power of market forces.[15] Also covered are responsive regulation, which incorporates a starting assumption of compliance and deploys an escalating range of control mechanisms rather than a single set of penalties to police non-compliance[16] and a range of self-regulating strategies that devolve the task of regulation back to the regulatory addressees,[17] while equipping them with varying levels of instruction.[18] Under a meta-regulation approach, regulating bodies stipulate the procedural conditions which self-regulating entities must observe in decision making, but leave the actual process of standard setting and the organisation of compliance control to self-regulation.[19] Principle-based approaches articulate the main qualities that regulatory strategies must reflect, such as fairness and sustainability, and leave it up to the regulatory addressee to work out and report back on how these qualities are incorporated within the standards, decision-making procedures and operating practices adhered to within the sector.[20]

[13] Cf. Tim Bartley, 'Certifying Forests and Factories: States, Social Movements, and the Rise of Private Regulation in the Apparel and Forest Products Fields' (2003) 31(3) *Politics and Society*, pp. 433–464, at 433–434; Ulrich Beyerlin & Thilo Marauhn, *International Environmental Law* (2011, Hart Publishing), p. 303.

[14] Stewart, 'Models for Environmental Regulation'; T. H. Tietenberg, 'Economic Instruments for Environmental Regulation' (1990) 6(1) *Oxford Review of Economic Policy*, pp. 17–33, at 17.

[15] Baldwin et al., *Understanding Regulation*, pp. 119–121.

[16] Ayres & Braithwaite, *Responsive Regulation*, p. 3.

[17] Julia Black, 'Constitutionalising Self-Regulation' (1996) 59(1) *The Modern Law Review*, pp. 24–55; Cary Coglianese & Evan Mendelson, 'Meta-Regulation and Self-Regulation' in Robert Baldwin, Martin Cave & Martin Lodge (eds.), *The Oxford Handbook of Regulation* (2010, Oxford University Press), pp. 146–168.

[18] Depending on the degree of public authority involvement, approaches may be either described as instances of self-regulation or co-regulation. See Laura Albareda, 'Corporate Responsibility, Governance and Accountability: From Self-Regulation to Co-Regulation' (2008) 8(4) *Corporate Governance: The International Journal of Business in Society*, pp. 430–439.

[19] Sharon Gilad, 'It Runs in the Family: Meta-Regulation and Its Siblings' (2010) 4(4) *Regulation & Governance*, pp. 485–506; Christine Parker, *The Open Corporation: Effective Self-Regulation and Democracy* (2002, Cambridge University Press), pp. 245–291.

[20] Julia Black, 'Forms and Paradoxes of Principles-Based Regulation' (2008) 3(4) *Capital Markets Law Journal*, pp. 425–457

Or, regulators may develop an optional framework to which addressees can accede if they so choose, rather than impose a set of binding requirements.[21]

The understanding of alternative, incentive-based or meta-regulatory strategies as, essentially, a set of solutions to the experienced failings of command-and-control shaped much of the scholarship on environmental regulation throughout the late 1980s and 1990s.[22] The image of environmental regulation as progressing from the 'base model' towards superior alternatives remains deeply influential today, but from the late 1990s onwards the standard account was enriched with a burgeoning stream of scholarship on the impacts of economic globalisation on regulation generally, and environmental regulation in particular. Here, the diversification of regulatory strategies was cast not primarily as a deliberate response to regulatory failure, but rather as the inevitable consequence of the changing nature of regulatory authority.[23]

There are persuasive reasons to conceive of the growth of regulation beyond the state and the diversification of regulatory strategies as connected and mutually reinforcing. Thinking of regulation as decentred, no longer necessarily tethered to the institutional trappings of state authority, infuses the debate with a degree of conceptual liberalisation that simultaneously invites renewed reflection not only on the institutions of regulation, but also on the realm of the possible in the field of regulatory strategy. As Colin Scott put it: 'The concept of regulatory space "decentres the state as a source of regulation and points to the role that can be played by a whole host of regulatory schemes". It suggests alternative ways to shape regulatory regimes with the potential to affect outcomes indirectly, both through the sensitive deployment of oversight regulation, and through the use of other mechanisms which regulate without the classic public institutional focus'.[24] Moreover, rethinking regulatory strategy is not only possible; it is a necessary adaptation to an environment populated by a much broader variety of regulating institutions.

[21] Antero Honkasalo, 'The EMAS Scheme: A Management Tool and Instrument of Environmental Policy' (1998) 6(2) *Journal of Cleaner Production*, pp. 119–182, at 119–120.

[22] See, e.g., Rüdiger K. W. Wurzel, Anthony R. Zito & Andrew J. Jordan, *Environmental Governance in Europe* (2013, Edward Elgar), p. 206: 'Clearly, EU and member state environmental regulations have become more flexible and innovative. In other words, European environmental regulations have become smarter'. See also David M. Trubek & Louise G. Trubek, 'New Governance and Legal Regulation: Complementarity, Rivalry, and Transformation' (2007) 13(3) *Columbia Journal of European Law*, pp. 539–564.

[23] Andrew J. Jordan, Rüdiger K. W. Wurzel & Anthony R. Zito, 'Still the Century of "New" Environmental Policy Instruments? Exploring Patterns of Innovation and Continuity' (2013) 22 (1) *Environmental Politics*, pp. 155–173, at 159.

[24] Colin Scott, 'Analysing Regulatory Space: Fragmented Resources and Institutional Design' (2001) *Public Law*, pp. 329–353, at 344.

Indeed, it is commonly contended that several key features of command-and-control are poorly suited to a transnational context.[25] Transnational regulatory regimes such as collective action TER and enhancement TER can have an extremely wide field of application, with regulatory addressees scattered across continents.[26] Great diversity in location and circumstance arguably complicates the task of developing technical specifications that are appropriate and achievable for all. Hence, command-and-control's strong reliance on technical standardisation is a potential hindrance for its application on a transnational scale. Moreover, in the sphere of transnational governance, regulatory authority is often less secure and more conditional than at the domestic level. Transnational regulators may therefore lack the required credibility to impose and secure compliance with detailed prescriptive measures which overtly curtail the addressees' freedom.[27] Furthermore, they generally do not have access to the type and range of penalties that prop up the controlling aspects of command-and-control strategies. In the absence of the regulatee's consent, a dawn raid organised by a private regulator might amount to trespass, breach of privacy and theft; the imposition of a fine for non-compliance with private standards could constitute extortionate behaviour. Hence, the very different circumstances in which TER takes shape necessitate the development of different regulatory strategies.

The upshot is that, in the past 30 years, the environmental regulatory landscape is said to have transformed and extended from a virtual monoculture of command-and-control into a sprawling ecosystem rooted in and sustained by a diversity of regulatory authority and regulatory strategy.[28] It is a landscape in which regulatory addressees may find themselves less frequently pushed by the blunt force of binding prescriptions, but are just as inexorably steered through the guiding power of myriad public and private communications.

4.1.2 *The Standard Account and Its Consequences*

Standard accounts perform a highly valuable function in academic disciplines. They create a sense of a shared history among the participants to the debate, and thus nourish the identity and autonomy of newly forming disciplines and sub-disciplines, such as 'the field of environmental regulation and governance'. They offer a stable point of departure for new research endeavours and a yardstick against which to

[25] Onyeka K. Osuji, 'Corporate Social Responsibility, Juridification and Globalisation: "Inventive Interventionism" for a "Paradox"' (2015) 11(3) *International Journal of Law in Context*, pp. 265–298, at 275.

[26] See Chapter 3.3.1 and 3.3.5.

[27] See Abbott & Snidal, 'Taking Responsive Regulation Transnational', p. 97.

[28] Cf. David Levi-Faur & Jacint Jordana, 'The Rise of Regulatory Capitalism: The Global Diffusion of a New Order' (2005) 598(1) *The ANNALS of the American Academy of Political and Social Science*, pp. 200–217.

measure the originality of new contributions. Yet the process of streamlining unruly masses of daily events into general trends and manageable narratives also creates casualties. Most obviously, there is the loss of detail and nuance to consider. Standardisation — whether in the service of environmental rule making or the development of a shared history and identity – is by design a reductionist exercise in which ill-fitting and minority features are deliberately marginalised. Thus, allusion to an environmental regulatory past populated exclusively, or nearly so, with command-and-control measures invites us to overlook or discount past initiatives which, although not tailored along command-and-control lines, nonetheless sought to regulate the environmental behaviour of particular categories of social actors.[29] The history of regulation is unquestionably richer in strategic variety than the standard account allows.[30]

Moreover, this particular standard account poses a number of normative and analytical challenges. In the first place, the standard account of the evolution of environmental regulation enshrines the compelling normative assumption that alternative regulatory strategies are superior to command-and-control. This assumption is supported both structurally and narratively. Structurally, the representation of the trajectory of environmental regulation as evolving from command-and-control towards alternatives taps into a deeply rooted cultural practice of equating evolution with progress.[31] Narratively, the standard account is built on the explicit premise that alternative strategies have developed in response to the deficiencies experienced with command-and-control regulation. The problem this creates is not that the normative assumption is necessarily wrong, but that the combination of structure, narrative and entrenchment through repetition of the standard account create a Latourian 'black box'[32] which has arguably become too well insulated for its own good. Normative assumptions can be powerful engines for inquiry and hypothesis testing, but when they are fully absorbed into the 'official version of events', they may instead obstruct further learning. Rather than a rebuttable assumption, the superiority of alternative regulatory strategies to command-and-control risks to become an article of faith. This may dissuade decision makers and commentators alike from examining the quality of alternative regulatory strategies on their own merits and, ultimately, reduce the value of the contribution made by environmental regulation and governance studies.

A second and related difficulty with the standard account of the evolution of environmental regulation is that it combines two explanations for strategic

29 Veerle Heyvaert, 'Codification and Centralisation of Environmental Law: A UK Perspective' (2005) 5 *Rivista Italiana di Diritto Pubblico Comunitario*, pp. 1329–1343, at 1336.

30 Jordan et al., 'Still the Century', p. 156.

31 John M. Gowdy, 'Progress and Environmental Sustainability' (1994) 16(1) *Environmental Ethics*, pp. 41–55.

32 Bruno Latour, *Science in Action: How to Follow Scientists and Engineers through Society* (1987, Harvard University Press).

diversification that are, if not directly conflicting, then at least ill-matched. The progressive explanation portrays strategic diversification as the result of a trial-and-error process in which the base model of command-and-control was tested, found wanting in certain regards, and is therefore increasingly supplanted by alternative, more efficient, less bureaucratic, more responsive approaches. Yet the standard account also supplies a globalisation explanation, which represents diversification as primarily borne out of necessity, because non-traditional regulatory regimes tend to lack the authority, infrastructure or resources needed to deploy command-and-control strategies. Necessity is the proverbial mother of invention, and we should certainly not discount the possibility of win-win scenarios, but it is nonetheless puzzling that alternatives to command-and-control strategies would always be both the *only* available option and the *best* available option. This tension is rarely explicitly addressed, but its influence is certainly felt in the literature, which displays a confusing tendency to equate command-and-control with poor regulation on the one hand, but still use it as the gold standard against which alternatives are measured and critiqued on the other.[33]

A third challenge to the standard account relates to the very complexity of the concept at its core. In the standard account, command-and-control is treated as a singular approach, the archetype or base model for environmental regulation. Yet as its name signals, command-and-control is a composite notion consisting of two discrete operations which are, themselves, the product of an extensive set of framing, design and instrumentalisation choices. The composite nature of command-and-control explains a prominent peculiarity of the regulation and governance literature, namely, the existence of its multiple opposites. In academic and policy writing, command-and-control is routinely contrasted to such widely differing notions as incentive-based regulation, self-regulation, risk-based regulation, smart regulation, responsive regulation and private regulation.[34] Each is a plausible foil for command-and-control regulation, depending on which aspect of the latter regime is subject to examination. If command-and-control's reliance on detailed technical prescriptions is taken as its defining feature, then its opposite are price-based mechanisms as incorporated in, for instance, emissions trading regimes and environmental taxes. If researchers focus on the organised inspection aspects of command-and-control, then approaches which summon market forces and organisational learning for the

[33] See nn. 6–12 in this chapter.

[34] Robert W. Hahn & Robert N. Stavins, 'Incentive-Based Environmental Regulation: A New Era from an Old Idea?' (1991) 18(1) *Ecology Law Quarterly*, pp. 1–41; Sinclair, 'Self-Regulation versus Command and Control?'; Michael Power, 'The Risk Management of Everything' (2004) 5(3) *The Journal of Risk Finance*, pp. 58–65, at 61; Neil Gunningham, Peter Grabosky & Darren Sinclair, *Smart Regulation: Designing Environmental Policy* (1998, Oxford University Press); Jenny Job, Andrew Stout & Rachael Smith, 'Culture Change in Three Taxation Administrations: From Command-and-Control to Responsive Regulation' (2007) 29(1) *Law & Policy*, pp. 84–101 and Bartley, 'Certifying Forests and Factories'.

purposes of policing, such as pollutant release registers, offer a contrast.[35] If the emphasis falls on the formalist sanctioning regimes, which are characteristic of command-and-control's enforcement strategy,[36] then responsive regulation and risk-based regulation present themselves as alternatives.[37] Since the particular aspects of command-and-control that serve as reference points in compare-and-contrast discussions are rarely made explicit, and more often subsumed under the general caption 'command-and-control', the literature on the subject exposes its readers to a significant risk of confusion and misinterpretation. It can lead researchers to assume a priori that all alternative approaches to regulation are similar, or that the commonality between different alternatives must be greater than that between any alternative and command-and-control regulation. It can foment mistaken beliefs that, for instance, incentive-based regulation will not only deliver greater efficiency, but is also necessarily less expertise-dependent, bureaucratic, and more responsive in its compliance mechanisms than command-and-control. None of these unexamined assumptions are conducive to developing an unbiased, well-informed critique of regulatory strategy.

The status of command-and-control as a mature term of art arguably also deters researchers from paying closer attention to the different operations, institutions and choices that, together, make up the approach. Considering the wealth of writing on the subject of regulatory instrument choice, there is a surprising paucity of analysis of, particularly, the 'command' side of the command-and-control equation.[38] An interesting, if compact, body of literature exists on the phenomenon of standardisation,[39] but many aspects of the full trajectory, from the formulation of a regulatory mandate to the reception of a command (or set of commands) by a target audience,

35 Michael Sauder & Wendy Nelson Espeland, 'The Discipline of Rankings: Tight Coupling and Organizational Change' (2009) 74(1) *American Sociological Review*, pp. 62–82.

36 Doreen McBarnet & Christopher Whelan, 'The Elusive Spirit of the Law: Formalism and the Struggle for Legal Control' (1991) 54(6) *The Modern Law Review*, pp. 848–873.

37 Job et al., 'Culture Change'; Power, 'The Risk Management of Everything'.

38 Insightful contributions include Sarah E. Light & Eric Orts, 'Parallels in Public and Private Environmental Governance' (2015) 5(1) *Michigan Journal of Environmental & Administrative Law*, pp. 1–72; James Salzman & Buzz Thomson, 'Teaching Policy Instrument Choice in Environmental Law: The Five P's' (2013) 23(3) *Duke Environmental Law & Policy Forum*, pp. 363–376; Jonathan Baert Wiener, 'Global Environmental Regulation: Instrument Choice in Legal Context' (1999) 108(4) *Yale Law Journal*, pp. 667–800, at 675–680. While these works offer a greater level of detail on some of the strategic choices that inform the environmental regulatory process than reflected in the standard account, they are all heavily instrument-focused.

39 E.g., Ross E. Cheit, *Setting Safety Standards: Regulation in the Public and Private Sectors* (1990, University of California Press); Harm Schepel, *The Constitution of Private Governance: Product Standards in the Regulation of Integrating Markets* (2005, Hart Publishing); Panagiotis Delimatsis, *The Law, Economics and Politics of International Standardisation* (2015, Cambridge University Press).

remain relatively under-analysed.[40] To a degree, the very concept of 'command-and-control' blankets complexity and insulates the multitude of activities underneath from further inquiry. As a result, not only do we know less about command-and-control than the ubiquitous use of the term suggests, we are underinformed about regulatory strategy generally, whether devised in a national or a transnational context.

Finally, although the standard account engages with the impacts of globalisation, it is less attuned to scenarios of multilevel governance.[41] The model of regulatory interaction that shapes the standard account is that of a single regulator communicating with a group or several communities of regulatory addressees. If this regulator communicates in a very prescriptive way, by means of detailed technical commands which leave the addressees limited interpretive discretion, the interaction is considered to conform to a 'command-and-control' style. By contrast, if the regulator issues broadly framed, procedural or principle-based instructions, the interaction is considered flexible. Consequently, the presence of either detailed technical standards or broad, open-ended standards becomes a proxy for either rigid or flexible regulation. In a multilevel governance context, this association easily results in misdiagnosis. The communications received by the regulatory addressee do not necessarily emanate from a single source, but may be the product of connected or sequential decision making by a network of regulatory authorities. If an MEA provision issues broad, principle-based standards, this does not necessarily mean the regulatory addressee retains a high level of self-determination; broad standards may be translated into more detailed prescriptions by national competent authorities, or through the intermediacy of standardisation bodies or other regulatory actors.[42] The 'command-and-control versus alternatives' model does not adequately respond to the mixed character of multilevel or network regulation and pushes commentators to suppress either their more flexible or more commanding features.

4.2 AN ACTIVITY-BASED MODEL OF REGULATORY STRATEGY

Building on the contributions of the environmental regulation and governance literature, as synthesised in the standard account, the aim of this inquiry is to move beyond the basic characterisation of transnational environmental strategies as a form of 'new governance' which is generally more flexible and less coercive than command-and-control, and to develop a methodology that supports a more granular

[40] Rieneke Slager, Jean-Pascal Gond & Jeremy Moon, 'Standardization as Institutional Work: The Regulatory Power of a Responsible Investment Standard' (2012) 33(5/6) *Organization Studies*, pp. 763–790, at 765.

[41] Cf. Abbott & Snidal, 'Taking Responsive Regulation Transnational'.

[42] See, e.g., EU regulation of industrial emissions, Suzanne Kingston, Veerle Heyvaert & Aleksandra Čavoški, *European Environmental Law* (2017, Cambridge University Press), pp. 321–328.

analysis of regulatory strategies in TER. The key to doing so, I propose, is moving from a regulatory style-centred analysis of regulation (commanding/incentivising/responsive/risk-based/meta) to one that focuses on the different activities that need to come together for authoritative and purposive behaviour-steering to materialise. The aim is to operationalise a model of regulatory strategy that comes with fewer preconceived notions about the relative efficiency, effectiveness and responsiveness attached to different labels, and instead offers a more systematic overview of the range and variety of choice in transnational environmental regulatory strategy than is commonly available in the law and governance literature today.[43] To this end, the complexity of environmental regulation is first broken down into the copious sets of deliberations, framing choices, operational decisions and formulations which together form a regulatory strategy, and then reconstructed into recursive regulatory stages, which are analytically manageable but offer more detail, and more opportunity for distinction, than the standard terminology of 'command-and-control versus alternatives'.

The model will also afford greater precision in determinations of where and how various TER strategies diverge from those processes commonly associated with state-based command-and-control approaches and, crucially, to identify points of commonality that risk to be overlooked in less granular comparisons. Moreover, as the approach treats activities as constitutive of regulation, rather than particular categories of actors, the model responds well to the realities of transnational environmental governance, where state, international, regional and non-state actors operate side by side and in combination to steer environmental behaviour.

The proposition in this chapter is therefore to analyse regulation in terms of the *work* it involves,[44] and to treat the range of choices that shape and direct this work as constitutive of regulatory strategy. Activity-based approaches are quite rare in law and regulation scholarship,[45] although they are more commonly found in policy process

[43] For comparable approaches, see, e.g., Tony Porter & Karsten Ronit, 'Self-Regulation as Policy Process: The Multiple and Criss-Crossing Stages of Private Rule-Making' (2006) 39(41) *Policy Sciences*, pp. 41–72, at 42, which describes the approach as: 'a non-determinist functionalism that treats organizational forms as shaped by sets of generic tasks that must be tied together in particular logical sequences if they are to be carried out successfully, but we recognize that self-regulation can be designed and implemented in ways that allow for at least some flexibility in the sequential order'.

[44] The notion of regulatory work takes inspiration from the writings of Slager et al. on standardisation as institutional work. Their contribution is gratefully acknowledged. See Slager et al., 'Standardization as Institutional Work'.

[45] The closest to an activity-based analysis is probably the analytical framework for transnational business governance interactions developed by Eberlein et al., see Burkhard Eberlein, Kenneth W. Abbott, Julia Black, Errol Meidinger & Stepan Wood, 'Transnational Business Governance Interactions: Conceptualization and Framework for Analysis' (2014) 8(1) *Regulation & Governance*, pp. 1–21. A similar approach is represented in the OECD's 'cycle of regulatory activities', which distinguishes the stages of making, operating and reviewing regulation. See OECD, *The Governance of Regulators, OECD Best Practice Principles for Regulatory Policy* (2014, OECD Publishing), p. 26, available at http://dx.doi.org/10.1787/9789264209015-en.

studies, such as in the work of Harold Lasswell and Peter deLeon.[46] Combining the broad categorisations found in regulation studies with the more detailed stage analysis approaches in policy process studies, I propose to conceptualise regulation as a combination of the following activities: 1) regulatory goal setting; 2) normalisation; 3) engagement; 4) learning and 5) response. Every instance of regulation, I contend, cycles through these stages and involves two sets of determinations at each stage: choices regarding the general principles to be followed in the implementation of regulatory work (choice of approach) and a determination of the technology through which the regulatory work is conducted (choice of instrument). Table 4.1 represents the stages of the model with corresponding approach and instrumentalisation options.

The step-wise representation of regulatory work is admittedly somewhat artificial since, in practice, regulatory decisions and activities are recursive:[47] they constantly intersect and influence each other.[48] Environmental objectives, which are determined in the first stage of the regulatory activity model, are often at least partly reverse-engineered, as new advances in technology shift the conceptualisation of standard practices within the sector which, in turn, invites a reconsideration of attainable and acceptable environmental objectives.[49] In a similar vein, the boundaries between normalisation and engagement are porous, since the very act of communicating standards, rules, entitlements or prices is inevitably dialectic and interpretative, and creatively contributes to the normative content of the communication. When deploying an activity-based model of regulation in analysis, it is therefore important to be attuned to its recursive nature and take into account the many interfaces and feedback loops that fuel the dynamics of regulatory work.[50]

[46] Harold Lasswell, *The Decision Process: Seven Categories of Functional Analysis* (1956, University of Maryland Press); Peter deLeon, 'The Stages Approach to the Policy Process: What Has It Done? Where Is It Going?' in Paul A. Sabatier (ed.), *Theories of the Policy Process* (1999, Westview Press) and, more recently, Kenneth J. Knappa, R. Franklin Morris, Jr., Thomas E. Marshall & Terry Anthony Byrd, 'Information Security Policy: An Organizational-Level Process Model' (2009) 28 *Computers & Security*, pp. 493–508, at 496–499.

[47] Hajime Sato, 'The Advocacy Coalition Framework and the Policy Process Analysis: The Case of Smoking Control in Japan' (1999) 27(1) *Policy Studies Journal*, pp. 28–44, at 31. Cf., in the EU context, Ingmar von Homeyer, 'Emerging Experimentalism in EU Environmental Governance' in Charles F. Sabel & Jonathan Zeitlin, *Experimentalist Governance in the European Union* (2010, OUP), pp. 121–150, at 136–141 and 144–147.

[48] For a theory which emphasises the composite and fluid nature of public decision making, see, e.g., the garbage can model, as developed by Cohen, March and Olsen. Michael D. Cohen, James G. March & Johan P. Olsen, 'A Garbage Can Model of Organizational Choice' (1972) 17 (1) *Administrative Science Quarterly*, pp. 1–25.

[49] Cf. Slager et al., 'Standardization as Institutional Work', p. 774, on 'commensuration'.

[50] Cf. Paul Verbruggen, 'Gorillas in the Closet? Public and Private Actors in the Enforcement of Transnational Private Regulation' (2013) 7(4) *Regulation & Governance*, pp. 512–532, at 514.

TABLE 4.1 *An Activity-Based Model of Regulation*

Stage			Approach	Instruments
1	Goal setting		Broad or specific; Integrated or sectoral; Outcome or performance-oriented	Legislation; Policy declaration; NGO mission statement; Treaty preamble & provisions; (Internal) strategy document
2	Normalisation		Flexible or prescriptive; Centralised or devolved	Rules; Standards (technical/performance-based/quality-based/ procedural/ principle-based/methodological); Prices; Entitlements; Allowances
3	Engagement	Communication Bonding	Mandatory or persuasive; General or differentiated; Unilateral or dialectic	Information publication Reporting; Negotiation; Permitting; Licensing; Certification; Labelling; Distribution/Auctioning; Taxation
		Facilitation		Example; Guidance; Derogation; Transition; Opt-up provision; Capacity building;

(*continued*)

TABLE 4.1 (*continued*)

Stage			Approach	Instruments
				Trading; Offsetting; Financing; Facilitation 'mechanisms'
4	Learning	Feedback	Active or passive; Systematic or incidental; Restrictive or inclusive	Helpdesk Notification & Logging of feedback Mandatory reporting
		Assessment	Compliance- or effectiveness-focused	Investigation Monitoring Profiling Third-party reporting Audit Inspection
5	Response	Individual	Compliance- or deterrence-focused; Corrective or adaptive; Universalistic versus or graduated	Information; Support; Differentiation/Exception; Mediation; Publication/Listing/Delisting/Shaming; Sanctions (fine, repeal of entitlements, mandated suspension of activities) Dispute settlement; Arbitration; Judicial enforcement; Blocking, Exclusion
		Systemic		Repeal Redefinition Reform

4.3 THE RECURSIVE ACTIVITIES OF REGULATION

The following sections discuss the model's five stages of regulation, with particular reference to environmental regulation.

4.3.1 *Defining Regulatory Goals*

The first cohort of actions and decisions involved in regulatory work is geared towards the definition of regulatory goals. Regulatory goals here refer to the outcomes, behaviour and behavioural change which the regulator seeks to effectuate. Environmental regulation pursues a broad diversity of regulatory targets including, to give but a few examples, halting biodiversity loss; developing and adopting CSR strategies; increasing recycling rates; lowering emissions of hazardous substances into air, water and soil; changing logging practices to reduce forest degradation; enhancing health and environmental safety protocols in the workplace; reducing fisheries' by-catch; lowering GHG emissions, introducing rapid response systems for environmental accidents; increasing the proportion of renewable energy use and so on.

As evident from the illustrative list, regulatory goals can either be defined in more encompassing, integrated or holistic terms ('halting biodiversity loss') or in a more sectoral and discrete manner ('halting the decline in the sea turtle population'). Goals may be outcome-oriented ('halting the decline in the sea turtle population') or performance-oriented ('reducing by-catch in commercial fishing'). The choice of approach is determined by a range of factors, including the regulator's interests, competence and mandate, the presence or absence of other regulators with whom the regulator can or must cooperate, technical and economic constraints, and the type of audience to whom the goals are communicated. If regulatory work is to progress to the stage of normalisation, however, then more holistic and integrated targets at some stage will need to be elaborated into sectoral targets. By the same token, different performances that, together, put regulatory addressees in a position to achieve desirable outcomes, will need to be determined to give greater direction to qualitative targets. From an activity-based perspective, a representation of regulation that only generates integrated, outcome-based approaches is therefore incomplete.

In terms of instrumentalisation, regulatory goals are usually consolidated through official, declarative acts. In the public sphere, such acts are typically adopted through legislative channels in the form of laws, decrees, directives, regulations, statutes, statutory instruments and, in the case of international law, conventions, treaties, protocols and other implementing measures. Alternative channels, more pertinent to regulation in the private and hybrid sphere, include policy declarations, mission statements, strategy papers and so on. Theoretically, it is possible for a regulator not to formulate its goals in writing, in which case the information on goals needs to be inferred from data regarding the subsequent stages of regulation. In contemporary environmental regulatory practice, however, reliance on an unwritten understanding regarding the goals of regulatory intervention is bound to be exceedingly rare, and no such instances were identified in the research underlying this work.

4.3.2 *Normalisation*

A pivotal stage of regulatory activity involves the translation of regulatory goals into information that enables the regulatory addressee to conceptualise the behaviour which is identified as desirable by the regulator, to check this against the prevailing principles, practices and routines within the addressee's organisation, and to introduce the necessary adaptations. I call this translation process 'normalisation'.

Rules and Standards

Two iconic instruments through which norms are conveyed, are rules and standards.[51] In general terms, rules prescribe a particular set of reactions to identified events; standards are more teleologically informative and afford a greater degree of discretion in individual application.[52] The 'five second rule' tells me it is acceptable to pick a carrot stick off the floor within five seconds of it landing there and still eat it; the standard is that I can continue to use edibles without additional treatment provided there is only a negligible risk that their hygiene has been compromised.[53] In some instances, the results of either following the five second rule or the food hygiene standard will be identical. However, if I am dealing with a newly scrubbed, squeaky-clean floor, or if I find myself in a student dorm, results might differ.[54]

Rules and standards are representative of two main approaches to normalisation: regulators have the choice between prescriptive and flexible approaches to norm setting.[55] The former centralise a greater proportion of decision-making work at the level of the regulator; the latter devolve more decision-making work to the regulatory addressee. Each approach offers advantages and shortcomings: the five second rule is easy to communicate, requires little additional intellectual effort on the part of the addressee and enables straightforward compliance assessments. The food hygiene standard lacks the simplicity of the five second rule, makes greater demands of the

[51] Pierre Schlag, 'Rules and Standards' (1985) 33(2) *UCLA Law Review*, pp. 379–430.

[52] Franziska Weber, 'European Integration Assessed in the Light of the "Rules vs Standards Debate"' (2013) 35(2) *European Journal of Law & Economics*, pp. 187–210, at 189.

[53] See Schlag's discussion of the different approaches favoured by Justices Holmes and Cardozo. In *Baltimore & Ohio R. R. v. Goodman*, 275 U. S. 66 (1927), Holmes posited that, at railroad crossings, drivers need to stop and look (rule). In *Pokora v. Wabash Ry.*, 292 U. S. 98 (1934), Justice Cardozo determined that drivers must exercise reasonable caution (standard). Schlag, 'Rules and Standards'.

[54] Please note that the 'five second rule' and its standardised counterpart are used for the purpose of illustration only, and are not to be read as an endorsement of this particular rule or standard.

[55] Light & Orts, 'Parallels', pp. 24–25.

addressee's interpretive capacity and its observance is harder to gauge. However, because of its scope for judicious application, it is less likely to result in over-regulation or under-regulation and therefore promises greater efficiency than the five second rule. Moreover, standards are better didactic tools than rules; they harness the addressee's capacity for learning and self-correction, which may enhance their effectiveness over time and gradually reduce dependence on regulatory intervention and enforcement.

The different strengths and weaknesses of each approach indicate that neither is preferable in absolute terms.[56] Ideally, the regulator's choice between rules and standards ought to be guided by whether the regulatory goals in question will most likely be achieved through prescription or flexibility. This, in turn, is influenced by a variety of factors, including the composition of the cohort(s) of regulatory addressees and their processing capacity; the likelihood of exceptional situations occurring; the estimated damage from flawed interpretation of the standard compared to the estimated damage from rigid application of the rule; the regulator's capacity to gather and process compliance information and the expectations for regulatory enforcement.[57] If the likelihood of either squeaky-clean floors or germ-ridden death traps is remote because of long-established traditions of bi-weekly floor cleaning adhered to in all segments of the population, the five second rule will perform better than if it is applied in circumstances reflecting vastly differing hygiene practices. If the regulatory body in charge of normalisation is also tasked with policing compliance, it might favour an approach which makes non-compliance formally easy to detect over one in which effective implementation must be assessed on a case-by-case basis.

Reflections on the pros and cons of prescription versus flexibility in the normalisation of regulation cast a revealing light on the assumptions underlying the debate on instrument choice in environmental regulation. First, the juxtaposition of command-and-control with flexible approaches, and the equation of the latter with the superior choice, confirm the prioritisation of efficiency over other qualities, such as the ease of compliance checking. Secondly, they indicate that the concept of the regulatory addressee in environmental regulatory thinking is heavily modelled on the prototype of a well-informed and well-resourced institution, capable of effectively interpreting standards and, thus, of capitalising on the greater efficiency potential of flexible approaches.[58] By the same token, the

[56] Cf. McBarnet & Whelan, 'The Elusive Spirit of the Law'. Also Weber, 'European Integration', p. 191–193 and 203–206, in which the author identifies six factors that influence the effectiveness of rules and standards respectively: volatility; judges' specialisation; frequency of application; the complexity of reality; the costs of switching from one to the other approach and information costs.

[57] John Braithwaite, 'Rules and Principles. A Theory of Legal Certainty' (2002) 27 *Australian Journal of Legal Philosophy*, pp. 47–82.

[58] Cf. Black, 'Forms and Paradoxes', p. 432.

correlation between flexibility and efficiency assumes significant differentiation in the environment in which the regulatory instrument is received. If all floors are alike, there is little value added by the flexibility inherent in the food hygiene standard.

Variety in Standardisation Approaches

The distinction between rules and standards is a useful point of departure to explore normalisation strategies, but it does not offer a full picture. Preliminarily, it should be noted that the terms do not have a universally fixed meaning. Robert Baldwin, for example, uses the term 'rule' to refer to 'a general norm guiding conduct or action in a given type of situation' which can have varying degrees of specificity.[59] Such norms cover both rules and standards in the context of this discussion. Conversely, writings in environmental regulation routinely distinguish between technical standards, performance-based standards and environmental quality standards.[60] In the field of air pollution regulation, for instance, a technical standard would prescribe the use of specific equipment or processes, such as the installation of wet scrubbers to lower the amount of sulphur dioxide (SO_2) emitted into the air from industrial chimneys and exhausts. A performance standard focuses on the results that regulatory addressees must achieve within their installation, as in the case of a maximum emissions standard for SO_2. A quality standard, finally, specifies the maximum acceptable level of SO_2 in the ambient atmosphere. Following Schlag, Holmes and Cardozo, a technical standard by any other name would be a rule.[61]

Whereas quality standards typically still relate to a concrete and often quantifiable regulatory outcome (such as a maximum concentration of SO_2 in ambient air), regulators may also develop standards that primarily regulate the addressee's decision-making procedures (procedural standards), or that emphasise the principles to which the addressee's behaviour should conform (e.g., compliance with sustainable development; fairness; transparency). Moreover, environmental regulatory normalisation often involves extensive methodological standardisation, aimed at, for instance, ensuring that compatible measurement techniques are used to implement and check maximum emissions levels. As is the case for regulatory goal setting, the introduction of broadly framed, flexible or methodological standards does not obviate the need to engage with the nitty-gritty of technical standardisation, but the regulatory work may be shared among a range of different parties, including the regulatory addressee.

[59] Robert Baldwin, 'Why Rules Don't Work' (1990) 53(3) *The Modern Law Review*, pp. 321–337, at 321.

[60] Cf. Kingston et al., *European Environmental Law*, pp. 309–312; Light & Orts, 'Parallels', p. 24

[61] Schlag, 'Rules and Standards'.

Beyond Rules and Standards: Alternative Approaches to Standardisation; Entitlements; Allowances and Prices

It is impossible to escape some degree of standardisation activity in regulatory work,[62] but the final instrument in which the regulatory targets are expressed is not necessarily a standard. Alternative instruments include entitlements, which attach a premium to particular types of regulatory addressees' behaviour; allowances, which typically relate to an acceptable amount or volume of activity; and prices, which attach a direct or indirect cost to certain types of behaviour. Experimentation with entitlements, allowances and prices as regulatory instruments has been particularly lively in the field of environmental regulation. On the entitlement side, various regulatory regimes have introduced enticements such as subsidies for green innovation, tax breaks for investment in cleaner technology, feed-in-tariffs for renewable energy access to the grid and so on.[63] The best-known form of allowances, in turn, are emissions allowances, such as EU GHG emissions allowances which entitle the holder to one ton of CO_2 per allowance.[64] On the pricing side of the equation are instruments such as environmental taxes, recycling deposit-and-return schemes and carbon prices.[65]

Entitlements, allowances and prices – also named 'incentive-based' instruments – are commonly associated with a higher degree of flexibility than rules and technical or performance standards, but in fact their specificity varies. Emissions allowances do not dictate *how* the match between overall emissions and total allowances should be reached within an industrial installation; only *that* it should be reached.[66] In case of a shortfall of allowances, entrepreneurs could decide either to buy more or to cut down emissions and, if so, they might devise alternative strategies to achieve this reduction. Similarly, taxes can be paid or avoided through a variety of behavioural changes (e.g., downscaling production; changing energy suppliers or modernisation to increase production efficiency). Recycling deposit-and-return schemes, on the other hand, or a tax rebate for the installation of solar panels, dictate highly specific forms of behaviour. The sole choice left to the regulatory addressee, is whether or not to participate.

62 As reflected in Black's decentred definition of regulation, which explicitly refers to 'mechanisms of standard-setting, information-gathering and behaviour-modification', see Black, 'Critical', p. 8.

63 See, e.g., Egyptian feed-in-tariffs for renewable energy, Mohamed Farag, 'Three Companies Win in First Phase of Solar Feed-In Tariff Project' 27 Feb. 2017, *Daily News Egypt*, available at https://dailynewsegypt.com/2017/02/27/three-companies-win-first-phase-solar-feed-tariff-project/.

64 EU ETD.

65 See, e.g., carbon taxation in Canada, initially levied at state level, and recently introduced at the federal level. Mia Rabson, 'Federal Carbon Tax Plan to Follow Alberta Program, Include Individual Rebates', 9 May 2017, *The Globe and Mail*, available at www.theglobeandmail.com/news/politics/federal-carbon-tax-plan-to-follow-alberta-program-include-individual-rebates/article34939245/

66 Light & Orts, 'Parallels', pp. 33–34.

4.3.3 *Engagement: Communication, Bonding and Facilitation*

To gain effect, rules, standards, entitlements and prices must engage with the outside world. This implies that, at the very least, they must be communicated to the target addressees whose behaviour the regulator intends to steer.

Communication

Regulators have various communication strategies at their disposal and can convey the results of their regulatory work in either a unilateral or more dialectic manner. Unilateral communications are generally more inclusive in scope in that they tend to be addressed to an undifferentiated audience composed of direct regulatory addressees, stakeholders and third parties, whereas dialectic communications are more selective. Regulators may opt to generate different versions of regulatory communications for different audiences and circulate, for example, the details of technical standards to the regulatory addressees while a non-technical summary is produced for the benefit of stakeholders and interested members of the public. Regulatory regimes also embrace different communication styles, with some adopting mandatory formulations and others favouring exhortatory or persuasive language.

It is possible for regulators to engage with addressees and other affected parties purely through the publication of rules or standards, but in practice the engagement of a regulatory regime with its target audience(s) tends to be effectuated through a much more extensive and sophisticated range of instruments or, for the purpose of this discussion, 'engagement technologies'. In addition to communication, engagement technologies seek to create a connection, to *bind* the regulatory addressees to the regime. Additionally, many regulatory regimes develop technologies that aim to lower the threshold for addressees to engage with the rules, standards or alternative norms produced by the regime. Hence, the engagement stage of regulatory work covers at the very least communication, but will in most cases also include bonding and facilitation activities.

Bonding

Bonding technologies are widely used in environmental regulation and are embedded in a range of different regulatory requirements. In addition to the sheer conveyance of regulatory content, bonding technologies develop infrastructures to enhance the likelihood that regulatory addressees will take ownership of the regulatory requirements.[67] For example, regulatory addressees may be asked to report on their implementation of rules and standards, which helps regulators to assess

[67] Cf. Slager et al., 'Standardization as Institutional Work', p. 779, on 'valorising' activities; Abbott & Snidal, 'Taking Responsive Regulation Transnational', pp. 97–98, on 'enrolment'.

compliance but, equally importantly, is designed to increase the chances that addressees reflect more thoroughly on the appropriate implementation of the norms within their organisation and, hence, engage effectively with the regulatory regime.[68] Alternatively, regulators may structure the communication of regulatory content not as a one-directional act of publication, but instead as a negotiation with individual parties or groups of addressees. Communication through negotiation creates the opportunity to fine-tune normalisation, and simultaneously fosters closer understanding of and involvement between the addressees and the regulatory enterprise.[69] Or, regulators may seek to bind addressees to the regulatory endeavour via the establishment of a market which incentivises addressees to engage with the regulatory framework as a business opportunity as well as a regulatory requirement. Each of these examples is, essentially, an advanced mode of regulatory communication that aims to bind the addressees to the endeavour of regulation.

Other engagement technologies include registration,[70] permitting and licensing schemes[71] and certification requirements. The certification requirements imposed upon FSC members clearly illustrate the importance of certification as the primary mode of fostering engagement with FSC goals and norms.[72] FSC environmental forestry standards are described in general terms in FSC public communications.[73] This information gives a first steer to, for instance, a logging company and helps it to make an initial determination whether FSC adherence is in its interests and feasible. If so, the logging firm might pursue FSC certification, which starts with it contacting an FSC accredited certification authority. The applicant will then be requested to document its working processes, which enables the certification body to communicate the applicable FSC standards and enter into a discussion about any required changes for the applicant to meet the certification threshold. Upon implementation of the FSC standard, the logging firm must submit to an audit conducted by an accredited, independent auditor, and a positive report will result in the logging firm obtaining certification from the certification authority.[74]

Facilitation

All communication and bonding technologies have a facilitative streak in that regulatory compliance is impossible in the absence of at least basic communication.

68 See Jürgen Friedrich, *International Environmental 'Soft Law'* (2013, Springer Verlag), p. 39, on reporting requirements as 'subtle pressure tools' deployed in the context of the International Atomic Energy Agency (IAEA) and the International Civil Aviation Organisation (ICAO).

69 Daniel J. Fiorino, 'Regulatory Negotiation as a Policy Process' (1988) 48(4) *Public Administration Review*, pp. 764–772.

70 See, e.g., EU REACH Regulation Arts 5–19.

71 E.g., hunting and fishing are activities that are permit- or license-based in most countries.

72 Graeme Auld & Lars H. Gulbrandsen, 'Certification Schemes and the Impacts on Forests and Forestry' (2008) 33 *Annual Review of Environment and Resources*, pp. 187–211.

73 See www.fsc-uk.org/en-uk/business-area/become-certified.

74 Ibid.

Nevertheless, it is useful to single out facilitation as an additional, third pillar of engagement activities because environmental regulation regimes increasingly incorporate engagement technologies that are not strictly necessary to convey regulatory content or tie the addressees to the framework, but that are specifically developed to make it easier for regulated parties to comply.[75]

Foremost among facilitation technologies are the extensive supporting documents and guidance notes that accompany the binding provisions of environmental regulation, which are now a staple of environmental regulatory strategy across levels of governance. Additionally, regulators increasingly publish implementation reports submitted by the addressees of regulation, and thus contribute to the informal development of a body of best practice to be shared among and further developed by the addressees.[76] Regulators may stimulate information and resource sharing between regulatory addressees through the institutionalisation of platforms and forums, such as the Substance Information Exchange Forums (SIEFs) under the EU REACH Regulation, which group together manufacturers and importers of the same chemicals and compounds so that they can collaborate on the development of the technical dossiers which are the key requirement for compliance with REACH's registration provisions.[77] In the context of international environmental conventions, which engage primarily with states as regulatory addressees (public/public TER), facilitation technologies are often embedded within so-called mechanisms, such as the financial mechanism under the Stockholm Convention on Persistent Organic Pollutants (POPs Convention). The POPs financial mechanism essentially facilitates compliance with the requirements of the POPs Convention through the establishment of a funding structure that helps developed country parties to implement their financial obligations pursuant to the Convention, and helps developing countries comply with the POPs reduction targets in the Convention by channelling funding towards convention-compatible projects.[78]

4.3.4 *Learning*

Functional regulators must be in a position to learn and to assess the impact of their regulatory communications. In the first instance, they must gather feedback about how these communications are received and responded to by the target audience.

[75] Cf. Christopher Taylor, Simon Pollard, Sophie Rocks & Andy Angus, 'Selecting Policy Instruments for Better Environmental Regulation: A Critique and Future Research Agenda' (2012) 22(4) *Environmental Policy and Governance*, pp. 268–292, at 281.

[76] Black, 'Forms and Paradoxes', p. 443.

[77] Kingston et al., *European Environmental Law*, p. 455.

[78] See Veerle Heyvaert, 'Levelling Down, Levelling Up, and Governing Across: Three Responses to Hybridization in International Law' (2009) 20(3) *European Journal of International Law*, pp. 647–674, at 656–658.

Feedback

Conceivably, regulators might adopt an entirely passive stance and place the onus of feeding back fully on the addressees' and third parties' shoulders, but such an approach would severely dent the credibility of the process, and it would dramatically erode the regulatory capacity to pursue compliance. It would also theoretically be possible for a regulatory feedback strategy not to involve any form of direct reporting, and simply to rely on spontaneously relayed feedback, originating either from the addressees or third parties, or on in-house or independent research. Such research would most likely focus on the state of the regulated sector generally (for example, research on recent CO_2 emissions trends among the carbon majors) rather than on the specific impact of a regulatory regime.

In practice, however, the lion's share of regulatory regimes in the environmental field and beyond do include as a minimum the expectation that the addressee will report on implementation, an expectation which is typically expressed in mandatory terms. Often, reporting will be organised to occur at fixed intervals. Among the data to be conveyed will be reports on the decisions made and practices introduced in compliance with the normalisation instruments, but the range of information relayed may also run to impact studies, such as statistical analyses of the state of the environment in affected regions. Core reporting duties are often bolstered by monitoring and verification requirements. The former expect regulatory addressees to track and document responses to the application of regulatory requirements. For example, the EU Regulation on GMO Food and Feed provides that authorisation holders entitled to trade genetically modified food products may be required to organise post-market monitoring regarding use of the food for human consumption, and must report on monitoring to the European Commission.[79] Verification requirements call for documentation processes and outcomes to be externally vetted. Every three years, companies registered under the voluntary eco-management and audit scheme (EMAS), for instance, must have their full environmental management system and audit programme and its implementation verified by a licensed environmental verifier.[80] Evidently, the implementation of such requirement presumes the regulation of verification practices. As with the regulatory engagement activities, even the briefest reflection on the infrastructure to facilitate feedback reveals the enormous labour-intensity and complexity of the regulatory enterprise.

Two prominent alternatives to reporting merit some further attention. First, as a substitute or a complement to reporting, regulatory authorities may collect feedback and assess the impact of regulation through audits and inspections. Such learning demands a high level of involvement on the part of the regulator and typically

[79] Arts 5 and 9 of Regulation (EC) No 1829/2003 on genetically modified food and feed [2003] OJ L268/1.

[80] Arts 1 and 6 of Regulation (EC) No 1221/2009 on the voluntary participation by organisations in a community eco-management and audit scheme (EMAS), repealing regulation (EC) No 761/2001 and Commission Decisions 2001/681/EC and 2006/193/EC [2009] OJ L342/1.

requires special powers to intervene in the day-to-day conduct of regulated firms and gather information. It is therefore primarily associated with public and state-based regulatory agencies. That said, regulatory schemes with voluntary adherence, which are prominent in the cohort of private/private TER, may conditionalise membership of the scheme on an agreement to submit to auditing, which may moreover be financed by the regulatory addressee. Secondly, regimes which deploy allowances or prices as norms can derive additional feedback from market and financial data. For example, assuming stable trading conditions, a gradual rise in the market price of emission allowances followed by a drop suggests that, in response to the rising cost of emissions, regulatory addressees have introduced innovation to cut down CO_2 emissions and have consequently released allowances onto the market. Hence, the analysis of price fluctuations on the market can serve as a proxy for assessing regulatory effectiveness.[81] By the same token, green tax revenues give an indication of whether and the extent to which tax payers are modifying their behaviour to avoid higher tax rates. Hence, regulatory learning may be based on a varied range of feedback.

Finally, regulatory regimes may include strategies to obtain feedback for assessment from outside the circle of directly implicated regulatory addressees. Mechanisms for third party feedback can assume different guises. Regulatory engagement processes, such as the licensing and certification frameworks discussed in the previous section, may invite or afford the opportunity for third party comments, which is commonly referred to as enabling 'public participation' or 'citizen participation' in regulatory decision making.[82] Alternatively, regulatory regimes may provide for third parties to report instances of non-compliance via notification and complaint procedures.[83]

Assessment

The purpose of the collection of feedback is to enable the regulator to assess and evaluate the impact of the regulatory regime on, primarily, the target audience of regulatory addressees and, in second order, on other stakeholders and the public generally. Assessment may be compliance-focused if regulators strictly concentrate on whether the rules and standards generated through regulation are observed and implemented, or outcome-focused when attempts are made to determine whether the shifts in the addressees' behaviour are capable of achieving the regulatory objectives.[84] For example, the impact of a carbon tax could be measured on the

[81] Kingston et al., *European Environmental* Law, p. 292.

[82] Cary Coglianese, 'Citizen Participation in Regulatory Rulemaking: Past, Present and Future' (2006) 55(5) *Duke Law Journal*, pp. 943–968.

[83] See, e.g., regulatory learning through citizen complaints, also known as 'fire alarm oversight' in EU environmental regulation: Mogens Hobolth & Dorte Sindbjerg Martinsen, 'Transgovernmental Networks in the European Union: Improving Compliance Effectively?' (2013) 20(10) *Journal of European Public Policy*, pp. 1406–1424, at 1409.

[84] Daniel Bodansky, *The Art and Craft of International Environmental Law* (2010, Harvard University Press), pp. 252–258.

basis of the affected parties' tax returns, or by tracking over time the correlation between the carbon tax rate and carbon emissions from affected parties.

Conceivably, the assessment of, say, a carbon tax might indicate that the measure generally functions well and effectively facilitates the achievement of the regulatory goals. As in other stages of regulatory activity, the performance and conclusion of such assessment requires a significant amount of supporting work. It involves consensus building and decision making about acceptable interpretations of received feedback with reference to the regulation's norms and goals. Determinations of compliance presuppose the development of benchmarks and practices to enable regulators and third party assessors to distinguish compliant from transgressive behaviour.[85] Determinations of effectiveness are even more complex as they additionally require the adoption of (contestable) assumptions regarding the relation between the addressees' behaviour and environmental outcomes. An environmental regulatory regime may enjoy a fair level of compliance yet low effectiveness,[86] a condition which many would argue afflicted the Kyoto Protocol.[87] Conversely, effectiveness may not hinge on full, across-the-board compliance by every single regulatory addressee. The odd tax dodger will not incapacitate a carbon tax initiative. As a rule of thumb, however, regulators operate on the premise that effectiveness generally requires a robust level of compliance.

4.3.5 *Response*

The fifth and final essential regulatory activity involves the formulation of regulatory responses on the basis of what has been learned. This stage is often equated with the 'control' or 'enforcement' stage of regulation, but the regulator's choices span a much wider field of action.

Individualised Responses

Where regulation is viewed as largely effective, regulators are likely to maintain the regime through the periodical renewal of regulatory communications. Over time, the regulatory goals, normalisation, engagement and assessment methods may be revisited to adapt to changing external circumstances. As to individual instances of non-compliance, regulators may adopt a more or less permissive attitude, and either

[85] Cf. Anthony Heyes, 'Implementing Environmental Regulation: Enforcement and Compliance' (2000) 17(2) *Journal of Regulatory Economics*, pp. 107–129, at 107–108; on the contestability of non-compliance determinations, John Kambhu, 'Regulatory Standards, Noncompliance and Enforcement' (1989) 6(1) *Journal of Regulatory Economics*, pp. 103–114.

[86] Cf. Bodansky, *Art and Craft*, p. 254.

[87] Although Japan and Canada did not meet their emissions reduction targets, the EU did overall achieve an 8% reduction from 1990 levels. However, the effectiveness of the Protocol as a global emissions abatement mechanism is considered extremely low. Amanda M. Rosen, 'The Wrong Solution at the Right Time: The Failure of the Kyoto Protocol on Climate Change' (2015) 43(1) *Politics & Policy*, pp. 30–58, at 35–40.

condone or police low-level non-compliance. Regulators can condone non-compliance by choosing not to gather feedback on individual regulatees' behaviour and instead rely on aggregate data. For example, an environmental regulator could consider itself satisfied with the effectiveness of air pollution regulation on the basis of indications of improving air quality, and not review individual installation emissions data. Alternatively, the regulator could turn a blind eye to reported instances of non-compliance, or formalise the condoning strategy by crafting and granting exemptions to regulatees who fail to meet the regulatory requirements.

For policing, regulators face the familiar choice between carrot and stick approaches, also referred to as compliance and deterrence strategies.[88] They either support the target addressees towards achieving full compliance, or penalise them for non-compliance. Deterrence strategies harness powers external to the regulatory regime, or the threat of powers external to the regime, as a way of achieving compliance. This may be the power vested in the legal system, which is invoked when a regulatory agency issues a remedial order, imposes a fine or issues a suspension order backed up by the threat of judicial enforcement. Alternatively, enforcement strategies may rely on the disciplining force of market power, peer pressure or public opprobrium, for example, when regulators name and shame poorly performing regulatees or threaten them with suspension of membership or exclusion.[89] Or, the pressure may stem from the threat of replacement by an alternative, more coercive structure unless a high level of compliance with the incumbent arrangements is maintained.[90] Compliance strategies, in turn, seek to enhance the regulatory addressees' performance through instruments of facilitation and positive incentives. We see such strategies in action when regulators offer training and advice; when they renegotiate compliance deadlines and introduce graduated compliance targets to facilitate the transition; and when assessments of compliance are linked to measurements of improvement rather than, or in addition to, a binary compliance/non-compliance evaluation. In many cases, regulators deploy a combination of compliance and deterrence techniques in their exchanges with regulatory addressees.

Systemic Responses

Regulatory responses may focus on the behaviour of individual addressees and seek to bring this behaviour into line with regulatory expectations. Alternatively or additionally, regulators may react to feedback about the workings of the regulatory

[88] Baldwin et al., *Understanding Regulation*, pp. 238–243; Scott, 'Analysing Regulatory Space', p. 343; Bridget M. Hutter, *Compliance: Regulation and Environment* (1997, Oxford University Press).

[89] Judith Van Erp, Toine Spapens & Karin van Wingerde, 'Legal and Extralegal Enforcement of Pollution by Seagoing Vessels' in Tanya Wyatt, *Hazardous Waste and Pollution. Preventing Green Crimes* (2016, Springer International).

[90] Verbruggen, 'Gorillas in the Closet?', p. 513.

regime by making changes to the regime itself. If the feedback indicates widespread and persistent non-compliance, a focus on individualised responses alone may be insufficient or inappropriate. Or, feedback may reveal a mismatch between different stages of regulatory activity. For example, markets in emissions allowances may be nominally functional and feedback may show that, by and large, participants comply with the registration and verification processes put in place to enable emissions trading, but the regime could still fail to deliver the industrial innovation that the scheme aspires to generate. The EU Emissions Trading System is a case in point: available data indicate that GHG emissions from regulated sectors are on a downward trajectory and will hit the 20% GHG emission reduction target by 2020, but the market price of emission allowances is too low[91] to incentivise enterprises to innovate with an eye to releasing and selling excess allowances.[92] In response, the EU has approved backloading to reduce the number of allowances currently in circulation and, hence, prop up their value, and has authorised the establishment of a Market Stability Reserve to avoid excessive market fluctuation and, especially, price drops in future years.[93]

Alternatively, feedback may indicate an insufficient uptake of the regulation to secure the achievement of its goals. If certification requirements in, for instance, voluntary commodities regulation schemes are demanding and time-consuming, and if there is a shortage of accredited certification bodies, enterprises will be deterred from signing up. In any of these scenarios, the regulator may choose not, or not solely, to respond to instances of non-compliance, but instead to revisit and revise the stages of goal setting, normalisation, engagement or, even, the organisation of feedback itself.

Individualised and Systemic Responses as Strategic Alternatives

There is a rich body of literature on individualised regulatory responses, and on systemic regulatory responses. However, both streams have developed largely separately: works on individualised responses tend to be housed under 'compliance', 'enforcement' or 'effectiveness' studies;[94] whereas systemic responses typically are examined in literature on regulatory change.[95] The activity-based model developed in this chapter, in contrast, groups them together as, respectively, corrective and

[91] At the time of writing, EU ETS emission allowances trade for approximately €5 per allowance.

[92] Kingston et al., *European Environmental Law*, p. 292.

[93] Ibid., p. 296.

[94] E.g., Keith Hawkins, *Environment and Enforcement* (1984, Oxford University Press); Hutter, *Compliance*; Ayres & Braithwaite, *Responsive Regulation*; Fabrizio Cafaggi (ed.), *Enforcement of Transnational Regulation: Ensuring Compliance in a Global World* (2012, Edward Elgar).

[95] E.g., Christopher Hood, *Explaining Economic Policy Reversals* (1984, Open University Press); Julia Black, Martin Lodge & Mark Thatcher, *Regulatory Innovation: A Comparative Analysis* (2005, Edward Elgar); Robert Baldwin, Julia Black & Gerard O'Leary, 'Risk Regulation and Transnationality: Institutional Accountability as a Driver of Innovation' (2014) 3(2) *Transnational Environmental Law*, pp. 373–390.

adaptive variants of regulatory responses. A downside of this approach is that combines a broad variety of different decisions and activities within one category, which to a degree counteracts the aim of developing a more granular account of regulatory strategies. However, the approach does offer two important countervailing advantages: it effectively illustrates the wealth of regulatory choice in responding to feedback, and it serves as an important reminder that regulatory reform can be deployed as a strategic alternative to either compliance-building or deterrence strategies.[96] The strategic use of regulatory reform was eloquently illustrated in the UK in early 2017, after a record number of Accident and Emergency (A&E) medical facilities failed to meet the standard requirement of treating patients within a four-hour period. Instead of enabling or enforcing higher levels of compliance at A&E units, health secretary Jeremy Hunt changed the scope of the requirement to mean that only emergency cases need to be seen within the four-hour timeframe. In an arguably breath-taking interpretation of the term 'protection', the health secretary asserted that: 'if we are to protect our four-hour standard, we need to be clear it is a promise to sort out all urgent health problems within four hours, but not all health problems, however minor'.[97]

4.4 THE STANDARD ACCOUNT RETOLD

The argument of this chapter is that the development and application of an activity-based model of regulation productively enhances our knowledge about regulatory strategies beyond the distinctions drawn between, respectively, command-and-control and its alternatives. Its greater degree of granularity enables more precise determinations of the ways in which various regulatory strategies differ and, at least as importantly, the ways in which they do not. For example, if we filter the features associated with command-and-control through an activity-based model, we see that the term is unspecific as to goal setting, although often associated with the articulation of narrow and performance-oriented goals in legislative or binding regulatory acts. Command-and-control's normalisation strategy relies on rules and detailed standards, which are communicated through publication. Bonding strategies, if present, typically involve the establishment of permitting, licensing or authorisation procedures, and investment in facilitation is limited. Learning happens through inspection, and the response phase is focused on deterrence, with an emphasis on penalties, threat of suspension and judicial enforcement.

This brief characterisation is already more informative on its own terms than the relatively opaque label of 'command-and-control', but its greater descriptive force

[96] Scott, 'Analysing Regulatory Space', p. 344.

[97] Denis Campbell & Rowena Mason, 'Jeremy Hunt Ditches Four-Hour Target as A&E Crisis Deepens' 9 Jan. 2017, *The Guardian*, available at www.theguardian.com/society/2017/jan/09/labour-party-jeremy-hunt-nhs-waiting-time.

TABLE 4.2 *Regulatory Strategies Compared*

Stages	Command-and-control	Incentive-based regulation	Responsive regulation	Risk-based regulation
Goal setting	Unspecified, but mostly associated with narrow, performance-based goals in legally binding acts	Unspecified	Unspecified	Risk management goal; identifying actionable from tolerable risks and responding to the actionable ones
Normalisation	Rules and predominantly technical and performance-based standards	Entitlements, allowances, prices	Unspecified	Unspecified
Engagement	Publication Bonding through permitting/ licensing/authorisation	Tender procedures/ application for grants (subsidies); distribution or auctioning; tax levy	Strong investment in facilitation	Unspecified
Learning	Inspection	Unspecified	Extensive feedback and assessment	Selective Focus on individual and overall regime performance
Response	Deterrence-focused, reliance on penalties, threat of suspension, judicial enforcement	Unspecified	Tailored response approaches, from compliance to deterrence	Selective individualised responses; strong investment in systemic responses

becomes all the more apparent when the same activity-based filter is applied to alternative regulatory strategies and the different groups are compared. Thus, the activity-base analysis brings to the fore that incentive-based regulation differs from command-and-control in the normalisation and engagement stages, but is unspecific with regard to learning and response. Responsive regulation, in turn, differs from command-and-control in the response stage, is likely to invest more in learning and facilitation than the average command-and-control instrument, and is unspecific when it comes to goal setting and normalisation. In this manner, the activity-based model gives us a firmer grip on the standard account's reach and its limitations.

4.5 THE STRENGTHS OF THE ACTIVITY-BASED MODEL OF REGULATION

The organisation of regulatory work in sequential activities can further our understanding of environmental regulatory strategies because it better articulates the range of choices that regulators make in the design of regulatory instruments and control mechanisms. The model allows for an account of the regulatory process in terms that are more informative of the variety of decisions to be made, and activities to be undertaken, than broader terminology such as 'command-and-control', 'incentive-based', 'responsive', 'meta' or 'self' regulation. For example, by distinguishing normalisation and engagement, the model draws attention to the fact that certification schemes, which are a defining feature of many self-regulatory regimes (or private/private regimes) do not obviate the need for rule making or standard setting within the self-regulation enterprise. They are not an alternative to standard setting but a particular, highly developed technology through which rules and standards are communicated to the regulatory addressee. By the same token, the model underscores that market-based approaches, notwithstanding their self-enforcing qualities, still require the establishment of assessment and response mechanisms to function as regulatory regimes. This quality can help to correct some of the earlier discussed oversimplifications which have been absorbed into the standard account, and may help to explain some of the prominent disconnects between contemporary environmental regulatory theory and practice, such as the abiding popularity of command-and-control in spite of its portrayal as inferior to more efficient approaches, and the difficult adolescence and relative underperformance of emissions trading regimes notwithstanding their theoretical edge.

An activity-based analysis underlines that the adoption of environmental targets and performance standards, which tends to be the focal point in discussions on environmental regulation, is but the tip of the iceberg: the operationalisation of standards, rules or other normative instruments requires vast amounts of supporting regulatory work. This is most prominently the case for data gathering, the need for which permeates every single step in the regulatory cycle. Every stage of regulatory activity, from goal setting to the formulation of individual and systemic regulatory responses, is information-intensive.[98] In many cases, this information will not be readily available and must be purposely produced, often by the very entities whose behaviour the regulator seeks to steer. Consequently, data production itself becomes a supporting regulatory objective, subject to its own modes of normalisation, engagement, assessment and response. Similarly, the deployment of engagement technologies necessitates intensive supporting regulatory activity. The communication of FSC standards, for example, not only requires the adoption of streamlined processes and conditions for application and information exchange, it also gives rise to several cottage industries of regulation of certification, accreditation and auditing practices. The regulatory infrastructure that supports the communication of rules, standards or alternative forms of regulatory operationalisation to the regulatory addressees may be so extensive as to overshadow the actual normative aspects of the regulatory enterprise. In the European Union, the organisation of the market mechanism through which emission allowances are allocated, redistributed and periodically recalled and renewed, has proved more labour- and rule-intensive and, in recent years, more controversial than the actual determination of the overall emissions cap.[99] Hence, the activity-based model strengthens our awareness of the vast and varied range of work that goes into authoritative behaviour-steering. At the same time, it reminds us that many regulatory frameworks, which are often thought of in the singular, are more productively understood as combinations of regulation, some of which may be more stringent and ambitious, and others more permissive. The model cautions against drawing reductionist conclusions about the overall quality of a regulatory regime on the basis of, say, its data provision requirements, its standards, or its registration requirements alone.

Thirdly, an activity-based presentation of regulation helps to convey the deeply recursive nature of the regulatory process. For instance, bonding activities foster engagement and at the same time serve as a strategy to embed mechanisms for supervision and compliance control. In a similar vein, the engagement stage of regulation can contribute to normalisation, as exemplified when regulators and addressees negotiate about the scope, reach or stringency of environmental rules and standards. The different stages of regulatory activity are therefore not primarily to be thought of as chronologically sequential, but rather as different modes of activity that need to come together for regulation to function.

Moreover, because the activity-based model focuses on the work that needs to be performed for regulation to happen, instead of the actions of one particular regulating entity, it urges renewed reflection on the meaning and relevance of commonly

98 Cf. Bradley C. Karkkainen, 'Information as Environmental Regulation: TRI and Performance Benchmarking, Precursor to a New Paradigm' (2001) 89(2) *Georgetown Law Journal*, pp. 257–370, at 263–268.

99 Kingston et al., *European Environmental Law*, pp. 294–296; Sanja Bogojević, 'Ending the Honeymoon: Deconstructing Emissions Trading Discourses' (2009) 21(3) *Journal of Environmental Law*, pp. 443–468, at 460–467.

used dividing lines in regulatory scholarship. Standards are more flexible than rules, but the imposition of a standard does not do away with the need for more detailed normalisation; it simply means that a different entity is in charge of the specification work. In the state-centric model of regulation, this division of responsibilities is between the regulator and the regulatory addressee, which indeed justifies a qualification of standardisation as the more flexible approach. In a transnational context, however, both types of work may be performed by different actors in a regulatory network who are, themselves, distinct from the regulatory addressees.[100] Hence, the presence of open, broadly formulated standards does not necessarily signal a greater degree of flexibility. In a similar vein, an activity-based analysis cautions against confusing the devolutionary traits of meta- and self-regulatory regimes with flexibility for the regulatory addressee. Just like command-and-control, self-regulatory schemes may opt for prescriptive rather than flexible approaches to operationalisation; mandatory rather than persuasive language in communication; an active rather than passive stance on feedback; and deterrence- rather than compliance-based response strategies.

Furthermore, the activity-based model vividly illustrates that compliance is not a reaction that is sought *after* the regulatory framework has been established. Instead, considerations of compliance permeate regulatory choices from the stages of goal setting to response. By focusing on engagement and engagement technologies, including bonding strategies, the model emphasises that compliance strategies are built into the design of the regulatory regime. This may invite renewed reflection on the meaning of and responsibility for compliance failures, which could, in turn, foster different and more productive individualised as well as systemic responses.

Finally, it should be acknowledged that the activity-based model as developed in this chapter is open to critique. It might be argued that, if supporting activities constitute such an important aspect of the operationalisation of regulation, then perhaps a model should be developed that puts their role central rather than one that simply enables their detection. Or, given the deeply recursive nature of regulatory activities, the wisdom of still deploying a five-step representation of regulatory activity might be called into question.[101] However, such alternative approaches

[100] Cf. Scott, 'Analysing Regulatory Space', p. 330, on regulatory space as a concept that illuminates the variable distance within and between rule formation and enforcement: 'The dispersed nature of resources between organisations in the same regulatory space means regulators lack a monopoly both over formal and informal authority. This observation draws our attention to the need to conceive of strategies of regulation as consisting of a wide range of negotiated processes, of which rule formation and enforcement are but two'. See also Slager et al., 'Standardization as Institutional Work', p. 777, on 'convening work', which refers to the 'loose alliances with external third party experts'.

[101] Cf. Critiques of policy process modelling, see Sato, 'Advocacy Coalition Framework', p. 31. For a theory which emphasises the composite and fluid nature of public decision making, see, e.g., the garbage can model, as developed by Cohen, March and Olsen. Cohen et al., 'Garbage Can Model'.

would have countervailing weaknesses which, in my opinion, outweigh any limitations of the activity-based model. An approach that puts supporting strategies central risks to lose sight of the ultimate changes which regulation seeks to effectuate, and thus fosters an understanding of regulation that is exclusively and narrowly bureaucratic. A model which foregoes any form of sequencing in its representation of regulatory activity, in turn, does not provide sufficient structure or organisation to support consistent, case-based analysis. On balance, the activity-based model of regulation offers a greater degree of granularity than the opaque, broad categorisations of 'command-and-control', 'incentive-based regulation', 'responsive regulation' and other fixtures of the environmental regulation literature, but it retains sufficient parsimony to enable analysis, comparison, and theory building. The next chapter therefore uses the activity-based model to analyse and identify key features of TER strategies.

5

The Activity-Based Model for TER Strategies Illustrated in Five Easy Pieces

The present chapter examines five prominent examples of TER through the lens of the activity-based model. To retain a degree of thematic coherence, and to avoid that particular strategic choices would be correlated with specific policy fields, the examples have all been drawn from the field of climate change. They are: the Paris Agreement to enhance and implement the UNFCCC (PA), the European Union Fuel Quality Directive (FQD), the Carbon Neutral Protocol (CNP), the Compact of Mayors (which is scheduled to be subsumed by the Global Covenant of Mayors for Climate and Energy by the end of 2018)[1] and the Regional Greenhouse Gas Initiative (RGGI). The analysis is conducted largely on the basis of the original documents issued by the regulator to explain its regulatory strategy, including both binding instruments and supporting documents such as preambles, guidance documents and other explanatory memoranda. The inclusion of the latter is justified because the aim of the analysis is not to simply identify the 'officially binding' content of TER but to understand the way in which goal setting, normalisation, engagement, learning and response are operationalised in various TER settings.

The five case analyses represent many of the different types and cohorts of TER identified in the book so far; they include public/public and public/private TER (PA, RGGI, FQD), private TER (CNP), and hybrid networks (Compact of Mayors), and they were adopted in pursuit of a range of different purposes. The regulatory provisions in the PA chiefly qualify as collective action TER; the FQD has a strong trade facilitation dimension; the CNP is primarily risk management TER; and the RGGI and Compact of Mayors represent two different types of enhancement TER.

[1] The Compact of Mayors is a UN-supported initiative that links cities worldwide in the attempt to optimise conditions for effective climate action at city level (see www.compactofmayors.org/history/). It is distinct from the EU-supported Convenant of Mayors for Energy and Climate Change (see www.covenantofmayors.eu/index_en.html). Both the Compact and Covenant are involved in the organisation of an overarching initiative, the Global Covenant of Mayors for Climate and Energy, which was launched in 2016.

The only actor-based category not explicitly covered by the selected case studies is private/public TER, and the only intentionality cohort not separately included is substitute TER. The reasons for leaving these two groups out of the equation are that, first, exclusively private/public TER is extremely rare; typically, private/public TER regimes are private/private regimes to which public authorities have acceded.[2] Secondly, from a consequentialist perspective, it is important to distinguish between substitute TER and risk management TER because the different intentions generate distinctive sets of challenges that the regulatory regimes must confront. However, from an organisational and instrumental perspective, substitute and risk management TER tend to be largely interchangeable. The way in which regulatory activities of goal setting, normalisation and so on are executed does not significantly vary depending on whether the chief motivation for the establishment of the regime was either to fill a gap in public regulation or to stave off public regulation. Hence, in terms of understanding regulatory strategies, the CNP is representative of both substitute TER and risk management TER.

The five cases have also been selected on the basis of their correspondence to several of the key categories of environmental regulation that populate the standard account. Most prominently, the RGGI is a textbook example of an incentive-based or market-based instrument. Notwithstanding some flexible features, commentators would most likely classify the FQD as a command-and-control measure, the PA as form of meta-regulation and the CNP as a paragon of self-regulation. To the extent it were recognised as environmental regulation from a conventional perspective, the Compact of Mayors would most likely be characterised as either meta-regulation or, more generically, as a flexible, 'new governance' instrument. The analysis of the five regimes will bring into focus the much greater level of information that the activity-based model generates, and the extent to which this supports the identification of points of overlap and difference between alternative regulatory regimes with greater accuracy than the conventional categorisations allow.

Finally, it should be acknowledged that what follows is an unabashedly 'nuts and bolts' examination, which focuses on the technical operations of the five selected TER regimes rather than on critical commentary. Moreover, the repeated pattern of analysis in five cohorts of regulatory activities, applied across five case studies, could induce a slight sense of déjà vu in the discerning reader. However, to demonstrate the effectiveness of the activity-based model as an analytical tool and to identify its contribution towards our understanding of TER strategies, it is essential to apply and reapply it across a sufficiently sizeable sample. Moreover, the technical information uncovered through the activity-based analysis vitally feeds into the overall assessment and critique in Chapter 6, which reviews and concludes the exploration of TER strategies.

2 See Section 2.4.2.

5.1 THE PARIS AGREEMENT

As the long-awaited successor to the Kyoto Protocol in implementation of the UNFCCC, the Paris Agreement (PA) hardly needs an introduction. Much has been written about its most prominent feature, namely, the espousal of a 'bottom-up' approach to transnational regulation, in which member countries, as the PA's chief regulatory addressees, determine their own contributions to the global effort of controlling climate change rather than commit to an internationally agreed GHG emissions reduction target from a standardised benchmark over a fixed period of time.[3] The bottom-up approach is the trademark of the PA's regulatory strategy. It is a flexible strategy that leaves a great deal of discretion to its signatory countries and, consequently, it leaves them responsible to organise and implement extensive regulatory activity at the national or regional level.

The bottom-up structure of the PA could easily support an assumption that the instrument itself must be correspondingly light on regulatory activity. After all, most 'real' activity takes place at a decentralised level with the PA functioning mostly as a glorified repository of state-based climate change regulation. Yet an activity-based analysis of the PA reveals a surprising richness and depth of regulatory content. This suggests that, first, it is mistaken to automatically equate flexible approaches with low-intensity approaches. The adoption of a bottom-up regulatory strategy does not necessarily lighten the workload of the transnational regulator. Secondly, regulatory addressees in a bottom-up arrangement may well be more intensely managed and steered than the absence of fixed targets suggests. The analysis below sheds greater light on both propositions.

5.1.1 *Goal Setting*

The PA states its aim to 'strengthen the global response to the threat of climate change' by enhancing the implementation of the UNFCCC, 'including its objective'.[4] The UNFCCC's objective, in turn, is expressed in the well-known language of Article 2 UNFCCC as the 'stabilization of greenhouse gas concentrations in the atmosphere at a level that would prevent dangerous anthropogenic interference with the climate system', to be achieved 'within a timeframe sufficient to allow ecosystems to adapt naturally to climate change, to ensure food production is not threatened and to enable economic development to proceed in a sustainable manner'. This is a clear example of a sectoral, broadly formulated,

3 Robert Falkner, 'The Paris Agreement and the New Logic of International Climate Politics' (2016) 92(5) *International Affairs*, pp. 1107–1125; Annalisa Savaresi, 'The Paris Agreement: A New Beginning' (2016) 34(1) *Journal of Energy & Natural Resources Law*, pp. 16–26; Charles F. Sabel & David G. Victor, 'Governing Global Problems under Uncertainty: Making Bottom-up Climate Policy Work' (2017) 144(1) *Climatic Change*, pp. 15–27.

4 Art. 2 PA.

outcome-oriented approach to goal setting, instrumentalised via an internationally binding legal provision.

The PA supplements the original goal-setting activity by translating the broadly formulated stabilisation goal into a more specific numerical target: Article 2(A) PA incorporates and tightens the 2° C target agreed at the 2010 Cancún Conference of the Parties[5] and provides that the increase in global average temperatures should be held 'to well below 2° C above pre-industrial levels' and that 'efforts to limit the temperature increase to 1.5° C' should be pursued'. The timeframe, too, has gained in specificity: in accordance with Article 4 PA, member states must achieve global peaking of GHG emissions as soon as possible, and 'undertake rapid reductions thereafter' to achieve zero net emissions in the second half of this century. This more performance-oriented take on goal setting is equally in evidence in Article 2 PA, which refers to 'efforts to limit the temperature increase' and lists additional targets of 'increasing the ability to adapt to the adverse impacts of climate change' and 'making finance flows consistent with a pathway towards low greenhouse gas emissions and climate resilient development'.[6]

5.1.2 *Normalisation*

The PA's best-known feature is that, in manifest contrast to the Kyoto Protocol, it does not impose quantified emissions reduction targets. Instead, member countries commit to submitting nationally determined contributions (NDCs), the content of which is largely within their discretion. Nor does the PA prescribe specific adaptation efforts to be undertaken. Yet these absences by no means imply that the PA is devoid of norms; in fact it delivers a rich variety of standards. The analysis that follows identifies the various standardisation approaches on display in the PA and discusses principle-based, substantive, procedural and methodological standards. Predictably, there is a degree of fluidity in the categorisations. For instance, a requirement to operate transparently is both principle-based and procedural, and PA provisions will typically communicate a combination of behavioural expectations that are tricky to disentangle entirely into separate strands of 'procedural', 'principle-based', 'substantive' and so on. The point of the analysis, however, is not to carve up standardisation into subsets with surgical precision, but rather to convey the range and depth of normalisation activities in the Paris Agreement.

Principle-Based Standards

A number of PA stipulations are principle-based standards as they set out the general directions and considerations that member countries must observe in developing

5 Cancún Agreements, available at http://unfccc.int/meetings/cancun_nov_2010/items/6005.php.

6 Art. 2(b) and (c) PA.

climate change measures in pursuit of the Agreement's objectives. Various provisions in Article 4 require that member countries' climate change policies, as rendered in the NDCs, become more ambitious over time, thereby expressing a principle of *progression*.[7] Financing efforts, too, should comply with the principle of progression beyond previous efforts.[8] All Parties must aspire to develop and communicate long-term low-GHG-emissions development strategies, taking into account their *common but differentiated responsibilities and respective capabilities*, in the light of different national circumstances.[9] Developed countries are expected to assume leadership in mitigation and climate finance, whereas developing countries must continue to enhance their mitigation efforts.[10] Capacity building, in turn, should be country-driven, *responsive* to national needs, and should foster country ownership by parties, particularly developing country parties.[11] Furthermore, a significant number of PA provisions enforce a *cooperation* principle; exhorting countries to work together in, for example, technology development and capacity building.[12]

Substantive Standards

The PA introduces and affirms a number of flexible substantive standards, which broadly describe the kinds of policies that the member countries are expected to develop. For example, the Paris Decision to adopt the PA urges all parties that have not yet done so to make and implement 'a mitigation pledge', and the PA itself requires developed country parties to adopt an emissions reduction target.[13] Developing countries 'are encouraged' to adopt reduction targets, whereas least developed countries (LDCs) and small island developing states (SIDS) may develop strategies for low-GHG-emissions development reflecting their special circumstances.[14] Developed countries are also required to give financial assistance to developing countries to help them in meeting both mitigation and adaptation targets; 'other parties' are encouraged to provide such support voluntarily.[15]

The PA further introduces the expectation that signatory parties take action to conserve and protect carbon sinks and reservoirs[16] and to engage in planning for adaptation and the implementation of adaptation policies 'as appropriate'. It also offers quite some detail on the range of actions that may be carried out in pursuit of

7 Art. 4(3) PA. See also Section 8.3.2.
8 Art. 9(3) PA.
9 Art. 4(19) PA.
10 Arts. 4(4) & 9(3) PA.
11 Art. 11(2) PA.
12 Arts. 10(2) & 11(3) PA.
13 Art. 4(2) PA.
14 Art. 4(6) PA.
15 Art. 9(1) PA.
16 Art. 5(1) PA.

adaptation policies.[17] In a similar vein, the PA expects its member parties to ramp up their initiatives in dealing with climate change loss and damage[18] and details the variety of activities that such initiatives may include.[19]

Procedural Standards

At the heart of the PA is the requirement for all signatory parties to 'prepare, communicate, and maintain' NDCs,[20] the content of which are mostly left to the discretion of individual countries, provided they remain within the broad substantive parameters and accord with the general principles identified previously. In fact, a number of PA principles have a distinctly procedural inclination, such as the principle of cooperation and the requirement of responsiveness to local needs for capacity building. Further examples of procedural standardisation include the Article 4(15) PA requirement for all parties to take the concerns of LDCs into consideration in the implementation of climate change policies, and repeated expectations of information sharing, as well as exchange of good practices, experiences and lessons learned.[21]

Methodological Standards

Finally, a number of behavioural prescriptions in the PA primarily focus on what could be qualified as the methodological aspects of climate change action. For instance, Article 5(2) PA singles out 'results-based payments' as one of the avenues through which member countries might pursue, among others, 'activities relating to reducing emissions from deforestation and forest degradation'. Thus, the PA anticipates action at the member country level and essentially prescribes the engagement strategies that member countries should explore in developing their own regulatory

[17] Art. 7(9) PA: 'Each Party shall, as appropriate, engage in adaptation planning processes and the implementation of actions, including the development or enhancement of relevant plans, policies and/or contributions, which may include: (a) The implementation of adaptation actions, undertakings and/or efforts; (b) The process to formulate and implement national adaptation plans; (c) The assessment of climate change impacts and vulnerability, with a view to formulating nationally determined prioritized actions, taking into account vulnerable people, places and ecosystems; (d) Monitoring and evaluating and learning from adaptation plans, policies, programmes and actions and (e) Building the resilience of socioeconomic and ecological systems, including through economic diversification and sustainable management of natural resources'.

[18] Art. 8(3) PA.

[19] Art. 8(4) PA: 'Accordingly, areas of cooperation and facilitation to enhance understanding, action and support may include: (a) Early warning systems; (b) Emergency preparedness; (c) Slow onset events; (d) Events that may involve irreversible and permanent loss and damage; (e) Comprehensive risk assessment and management; (f) Risk insurance facilities, climate risk pooling and other insurance solutions; (g) Non-economic losses; (h) Resilience of communities, livelihoods and ecosystems'.

[20] Art. 4(2) PA.

[21] Arts. 7(7) and 12(2) PA. The latter provision further suggests that capacity building should be a process that is 'iterative, participatory, cross-cutting and gender-responsive'.

responses. Further examples of methodological standardisation are found in Article 6(2) PA, which requires that signatory parties engaged in transnational carbon offsetting '*shall apply robust accounting to ensure, inter alia, the avoidance of double counting*'[22], and the assurance that mitigation co-benefits flowing from adaptation can be accounted for as part of a country's mitigation outcomes.[23] The Agreement also foresees the development of further methodological standardisation in some of its provisions, such as Article 13(13) PA, which calls for the development of 'common modalities, procedures and guidelines' for maintenance and enhancement of the PA's transparency framework (see the next section for more detail).

5.1.3 *Engagement*

The PA evidently communicates with its addressees through the publication of the Agreement's provisions. Noticeable in this context are the explicit use of differentiated communications towards cohorts of addressees (developed countries, developing countries, LDCs and SIDS) and the frequent reliance on persuasive rather than mandatory language, as signatory parties, and particularly addressees other than developed countries, are often either 'urged' or 'encouraged' rather than instructed to take certain action.

The PA moreover deploys an extensive array of different bonding and, particularly, facilitation technologies to foster member country engagement and to enhance conduciveness to regulatory compliance. In the first place, signatory countries are connected to the regime through the introduction of periodic reporting responsibilities. Member countries must report on NDCs every five years.[24] Additional provisions affirm a requirement for periodic communications on adaptation and capacity building,[25] as well as biennial quantitative and qualitative information on financial resources committed and projected to assist developing countries in implementing the PA's provisions.[26] Further, Article 13(7) PA calls for the submission of annual inventory reports of GHG emissions by sources and removals by sinks, as well as information necessary to track progress in implementing the targets set forth in the countries' respective NDCs.

Secondly, the Agreement introduces a veritable arsenal of supportive measures and structures to facilitate engagement. These include guidance documents, frameworks and mechanisms such as the transparency framework, the financial mechanism, the mitigation and sustainable development support mechanism and the technology mechanism. The transparency framework is explicitly presented as a bonding instrument: pursuant to Article 13(1) PA, it is designed to 'build mutual trust

22 Emphasis added.

23 Art. 4(7) PA.

24 Art. 4(9) PA.

25 Arts. 7(10) (adaptation) and 11(4) (capacity building) PA.

26 Art. 9(5) PA.

and confidence and to promote effective implementation'. It is couched in the persuasive language that characterises many of the PA's provisions, and it emphasises fostering compliance in 'a facilitative, non-intrusive, non-punitive manner'. Demonstrating the interconnected and recursive nature of regulatory activity, the framework functions as both an engagement tool vis-à-vis the member country addressees and as a learning tool on the basis of which regulatory impacts are assessed and responses formulated: 'The purpose of the framework for transparency of action is to provide a clear understanding of climate change action in the light of the objective of the Convention as set out in its Article 2, including clarity and tracking of progress towards achieving Parties' individual nationally determined contributions under Article 4, and Parties' adaptation actions under Article 7'.[27]

Bespoke 'mechanisms' such as the PA's financial, technology, and mitigation and sustainable development support mechanisms,[28] are examples of a bonding and facilitation technology that is typical of multilateral agreements. They are, essentially, satellite regimes, typically managed by a transnational executive committee, which support the implementation of the main agreement's provisions through services such as information collection and dissemination, targeted advice, networking and liaising between signatory parties for the purpose of cooperation, assistance and exchange and clearinghouse functions.[29] In this manner, they provide a functional equivalent for the facilitating and supporting tasks that, at a domestic level and vis-à-vis private regulatory addressees, would be exercised primarily by national administrations and help desks.

5.1.4 *Learning*

The extensive reporting responsibilities, which secure the engagement of the member country addressees with the regulatory regime, simultaneously function as the PA's main feedback mechanisms. The submission of NDCs, additional adaptation data and national inventories of GHG emissions and removals enables both regulated and regulating entities to examine how the broad principle-based, substantive and other standards are being received, understood and translated into performance expectations, rules, policies and supporting measures at the local level. The countless bodies, working groups and committees established under the UNFCCC, including the UNFCCC Secretariat and the recently established Paris Committee on Capacity-building,[30] are also actively involved in extensive

[27] Art. 13(5)(6) PA (excerpts).

[28] Arts. 9(8) (financial mechanism), 6(4) (mitigation and sustainable development support mechanism), and 10(3) (technology mechanism) PA.

[29] Cf Robin R. Churchill & Geir Ulfstein, 'Autonomous Institutional Arrangements in Multilateral Environmental Agreements: A Little-Noticed Phenomenon in International Law' (2000) 94(4) *American Journal of International Law*, pp. 623–659, at 650–651.

[30] For an overview, see http://unfccc.int/bodies/items/6241.php.

information production on matters ranging from up-to-date figures on overall GHG emissions and the functioning of the various mechanisms to the economic, social and environmental impacts of mitigation actions on developing countries.[31] Additionally, regulatory learning is enhanced by the contributions of interested third-party environmental organisations, such as the World Resources Institute, Climate Action Tracker and Civil Society Review, which generate key data on global as well as country-based emissions trends. Robert Falkner notes that as 'the Paris Agreement enters into force, civil society organizations can be expected to continue to scrutinize national policies and their implementation, and to calculate the world's remaining carbon budget and the additional efforts states will need to make to stay within this budget. As in other contexts, civil society can therefore be expected to take on the role of informal monitor of the climate agreement'.[32]

In terms of assessment, the PA calls for a 'technical expert review' of the information submitted by the signatory parties, which consists of a 'consideration of the Party's [financial] support provided' and, importantly, its implementation of its NDCs.[33] The dominant assessment instrument under the PA is the five-yearly global stocktake, which draws on all information submitted by signatory parties as well as data generated by the frameworks, mechanisms, committees and ad-hoc formations operating within the remit of the UNFCCC and its implementing provisions. Its aim is 'to assess the collective progress towards achieving the purpose (of the PA) and its long-term goals'.[34]

5.1.5 *Response*

International frameworks are famously restricted in the extent to which they can compel their member state addressees to implement regulatory requirements,[35] and the PA is no exception to this rule. Correspondingly, the PA's response strategy reflects the cooperative and compliance-oriented approaches that are available to regulators with limited enforcement powers.[36] The key provisions on response are Articles 13 and 14 PA. Article 13 provides that:

> (11) Information submitted by each Party [on the national GHG inventory, on the implementation of NDCs, and on financial assistance] shall undergo a technical

[31] See Paris Decision paras 34, 105, 110(c).

[32] Falkner, 'The Paris Agreement', pp. 1122–1123.

[33] Art. 13(11) PA.

[34] Art. 14 PA.

[35] Daniel Bodansky, *The Art and Craft of International Environmental Law* (2010, Harvard University Press), pp. 245–251; Andrew Watson Samaan, 'Enforcement of International Environmental Treaties: An Analysis' (1993) 5 *Fordham Environmental Law Journal*, pp. 261–283, at 262–268.

[36] Cf. Osamu Yoshida, 'Soft Enforcement of Treaties: The Montreal Protocol's Noncompliance Procedure and the Functions of Internal International Institutions' (1999) 1 *Colorado Journal of International Environmental Law and Policy*, pp. 95–142.

> expert review ... For those developing country Parties that need it in the light of their capacities, the review process shall include assistance in identifying capacity-building needs. In addition, each Party shall participate in a facilitative, multilateral consideration of progress with respect to efforts [in financial assistance] and its respective implementation and achievement of its nationally determined contribution. (12). The technical expert review ... shall consist of a consideration of the Party's support provided, as relevant, and its implementation and achievement of its nationally determined contribution. The review shall also identify areas of improvement for the Party, and include a review of the consistency of the information with the modalities, procedures and guidelines [provided in the PA], taking into account the flexibility accorded to the Party.

Article 14, in turn, addresses the consequences of the global stocktake:

> (3) The outcome of the global stocktake shall inform Parties in updating and enhancing, in a nationally determined manner, their actions and support in accordance with the relevant provisions of this Agreement, as well as in enhancing international cooperation for climate action.

Hence, the PA operates on a core expectation of self-policing by member countries on the basis of the global stocktake. However, this expectation is bolstered by a more centralised compliance mechanism in the shape of the technical review, which offers 'facilitative, multilateral consideration of progress' but does impose mandatory participation. Finally, the PA also foresees the possibility of inter-party policing via its Article 24, which imports into the PA the UNFCCC's provisions on the settlement of disputes regarding the implementation or application of the Convention. In the UNFCCC, as in most MEAs, the dispute settlement provision is dormant, and it is similarly unlikely that it would be triggered within the PA. However, the possibility of dispute may still exert a soft-policing influence on member countries in their implementation of treaty requirements.[37]

The PA does not explicitly provide for systemic responses to learning, but such responses are clearly part of the institution's activities as a regulator. This is reflected, for example, in paragraph 37 of the Paris Decision, which recommends the adoption of rules, modalities and procedures for the GHG-emissions mitigation and sustainable development mechanism. It continues to stipulate that such rules should be based on, among other factors, '[R]eal, measurable, and long-term benefits related to the mitigation of climate', '[S]pecific scopes of activities', '[R]eductions in emissions that are additional to any that would otherwise occur' and '[E]xperience gained with and lessons learned from existing mechanisms and approaches adopted under the Convention and its related legal instruments'. This paragraph alludes to the well-

[37] Barbara Koremenos & Timm Betz, 'The Design of Dispute Settlement Procedures in International Agreements' in Jeffrey L. Dunoff & Mark A. Pollack (eds.), *Interdisciplinary Perspectives on International Law and International Relations: The State of the Art* (2012, Cambridge University Press), pp. 371–393, at 387–390.

documented credibility and effectiveness problems that have beset, particularly, the Clean Development Mechanism under the Kyoto Protocol,[38] and it even explicitly calls upon the Conference of the Parties to take into account this experience in devising implementing regulation.

5.2 THE FUEL QUALITY DIRECTIVE

The FQD is an EU instrument that regulates all petrol, diesel and biofuels used in road transport, as well as gas-oil used in non-road-mobile machinery.[39] It embraces an overall GHG emissions intensity target and lays down conditions for the sustainability of biofuels. The FQD therefore constitutes part of the EU's climate change package, which encompasses law and regulatory measures on emissions reductions, renewable energy and energy efficiency.[40] As a Directive, the FQD primarily regulates the EU Member States, which are responsible for the effective implementation and enforcement of the scheme. However, the FQD's audience is more varied than its format suggests. First, a number of FQD provisions concern the administration of the regulatory scheme and are addressed to the European Commission rather than the Member State. Moreover, if we 'pierce the public veil' we easily discern a range of regulatory communications that, although formally addressed to the Member States, target and immediately impact the behaviour of petrol, diesel and gas-oil suppliers. Hence, the private sector is at the very least implicated. Finally, by referring to and conditionalising EU operators' reliance on external standardisation regimes, the FQD arguably extends its regulatory reach beyond the zone of its direct and indirect addressees and towards both external regulatory frameworks and those who are governed by them.

5.2.1 *Goal Setting*

The FQD refers in its preamble to the general goals of trade facilitation, achieving a high level of environmental protection and meeting the EU's commitments under international climate change law. It also sets much more specific, sectoral and outcome-oriented objectives. The target for the regulation is to gradually achieve a

[38] See, e.g., Christopher Arup & Hao Zhang, 'Lessons From Regulating Carbon Offset Markets' (2015) 4(1) *Transnational Environmental Law*, pp. 69–100; Jacqueline M. Drew & Michael E. Drew, 'Establishing Additionality: Fraud Vulnerabilities in the Clean Development Mechanism' (2010) 23(3) *Accounting Research Journal*, pp. 243–253.

[39] See Directive 2009/30/EC amending Directive 98/70/EC as regards the specification of petrol, diesel and gas-oil and introducing a mechanism to monitor and reduce greenhouse gas emissions and amending Council Directive 1999/32/EC as regards the specification of fuel used by inland waterway vessels and repealing Directive 93/12/EEC [2009] OJ L140/88.

[40] Kati Kulovesi, Elisa Morgera & Miquel Muñoz, 'Environmental Integration and Multi-Faceted International Dimensions of EU Law: Unpacking the EU's 2009 Climate and Energy Package' (2011) 48(3) *Common Market Law Review*, pp. 829–891.

10% reduction in GHG emissions per unit of energy from fuel by end 2020. 6% of this reduction is to be achieved by the use of biofuels, 2% should be gained via carbon capture and storage technology and an additional 2% through carbon offsetting.[41]

5.2.2 *Normalisation*

Like the PA, the FQD reveals an intense level of normalisation activity. However, the majority of the standards incorporated in the FQD are more detailed and prescriptive than anything found in the PA. Articles 3(1) and 5 FDQ, for example, issue uncompromising rules: 'No later than 1 January 2000, Member States shall prohibit the marketing of leaded petrol within their territory' and, conversely, '[no] Member State may prohibit, restrict or prevent the placing on the market of fuels which comply with the requirements of this Directive'. Moreover, the framework is rich in mandatory performance and technical standards, governing matters from the environmental specifications with which petrol must comply to be lawfully marketed[42] and the sourcing of biofuels[43] (performance standards) to the maximum content in petrol of substances such as sulphur, oxygen, ethanol and metallic additives (technical standards).[44]

In addition to the high level of specificity of FQD standards, two features stand out: the framework's reliance on standardisation by reference, and the prominence of methodological standardisation. Standardisation by reference refers to the practice whereby externally developed standards are integrated into a regulatory framework. The FQD's biofuel sustainability criteria, for example, must be developed in coordination with the criteria in the 2009 EU Renewable Energy Directive[45] and should deploy a concept of biodiverse forests that is compatible with the definition used by the UN FAO in its Global Forest Resource Assessment.[46] The work of the

[41] Art. 7A(2) FQD.

[42] Art. 3(2) FQD and Annex I FQD.

[43] See Arts. 7B(3) to (6) FQD, stipulating that, to count towards the 6% quota which constitutes one of the FQD's targets, biofuels should not be made from raw material obtained from land with high biodiversity value (such as primary forests and nature conservation areas), land with high carbon stock (such as wetlands) or peatland, and that their harvesting should meet the requirements and standards contained in (former) Council Regulation 73/2009 establishing common rules for direct support schemes for farmers under the EU Common Agricultural Policy (CAP). The latter regulation has since been replaced by Regulation (EU) No 1307/2013 establishing rules for direct payments to farmers under support schemes within the framework of the common agricultural policy and repealing Council Regulation (EC) No 637/2008 and Council Regulation (EC) No 73/2009[2013] OJ L347/608.

[44] Arts. 3(2), 3(3) and 8A(2) FQD. See also Annex II and Art. 4(1) FQD for further examples of technical fuel specifications.

[45] Directive 2009/28/EC on the promotion of the use of energy from renewable sources [2009] OJ L140/16.

[46] Preamble (11) FQD.

Intergovernmental Panel on Climate Change (IPCC), in turn, is identified as the appropriate basis for the calculation of standard values for carbon stocks in land use and after land-use change.[47] Also, the agricultural raw materials used for the production of biofuels must be obtained 'in accordance with the requirements and standards' set out in a different piece of EU legislation governing common rules for direct support schemes for farmers under the EU's Common Agricultural Policy.[48] For the marking of petrol and biofuels, the FQD refers to the work performed by the European Committee for Standardization (CEN), and moreover exhorts the latter 'to continue working rapidly on a standard allowing the blending of higher levels of biofuel components into diesel'.[49]

The FQD also actively fosters inter-regulatory cooperation. Pursuant to Article 7C(4) FQD, the EU will endeavour to enter into bilateral or multilateral agreements on the standardisation of biofuels-sustainability criteria. Moreover, the Commission 'may decide that voluntary national or international schemes setting standards for the production of biomass products', or 'schemes to measure [GHG] savings', contain accurate data for the purpose of determining sustainability criteria. Finally, in its determination of Member State requests for derogation from some of the FQD's technical standards,[50] the European Commission is to assess such requests against the technical standards contained in EU air quality legislation.[51]

Thus, the FQD pulls normalisation activities performed in different governance settings into its own regulatory orbit. The provisions offer an eloquent illustration of both the recursive and the expansionist nature of regulatory activity. Article 7C(5) FQD provides that:

> The Commission shall adopt decisions [on voluntary or international schemes] only if the agreement or scheme in question meets adequate standards of reliability, transparency and independent auditing. Schemes to measure [GHG] savings shall also comply with the methodological requirements in Annex IV. Lists of areas of high biodiversity value . . . shall meet adequate standards of objectivity and coherence with internationally recognised standards and provide for appropriate appeal procedures.

47 Preamble (12) FQD.

48 Art. 7B(6) FQD refers to Council Regulation (EC) No 73/2009 establishing common rules for direct support schemes for farmers under the common agricultural policy and establishing certain support schemes for farmers, amending Regulations (EC) No 1290/2005, (EC) No 247/2006, (EC) No 378/2007 and repealing Regulation (EC) No 1782/2003 [2009] OJ L30/16. The Regulation currently in force is Regulation (EU) No 1307/2013 [2013] OJ L347/608.

49 Preamble (32) FQD.

50 Provisions on maximum vapour pressure of petrol, see Arts. 3(4) to (5) FQD.

51 Directive 2008/50/EC on ambient air quality and cleaner air for Europe [2008] OJ L152/1; and Directive (EU) 2016/2284 on the reduction of national emissions of certain atmospheric pollutants, amending Directive 2003/35/EC and repealing Directive 2001/81/EC [2016] OJ L344/1.

> The voluntary schemes … shall regularly, and at least once per year, publish a list of their certification bodies used for independent auditing, indicating for each certification body by which entity or national public authority it was recognised and which entity or national public authority is monitoring it.
>
> In order in particular to prevent fraud, the Commission may … specify the standards of independent auditing and require all voluntary schemes to apply those standards.

Hence, while the recognition of standardisation performed elsewhere can reduce the work pressures within the context of the FQD, it simultaneously spawns a new range of normalising and engagement activities, as the conditions for recognition themselves need to be standardised and ascertained.

Finally, the FQD is heavily preoccupied with the standardisation of methodologies to calculate GHG emissions under a variety of circumstances, such as when considering emissions in the case of fuel co-production,[52] emissions resulting from indirect land-use change[53] or emissions from biofuels.[54] With regard to the latter, the FQD goes into the technicalities of calculation,[55] and it additionally provides for subsequent adoption of a detailed common methodology via the 'regulatory procedure with scrutiny', which is one of several EU procedures for enacting implementing measures.[56] The calls for methodological standardisation, too, concern more technical matters, and are more prescriptive, than comparative approaches in the Paris Agreement.

5.2.3 *Engagement*

The FQD incorporates a broad range of engagement tools, some of which are targeted at the Member States, while others seek to connect private sector addressees, such as fuel suppliers, to the regulatory enterprise. Beyond the baseline strategy

[52] Preamble (18) FQD.

[53] Preamble (20) FQD.

[54] Arts. 7A(4) to (5) FQD.

[55] See Art. 7D(1) FQD: 'For the purposes of Article 7a and Article 7b(2), life cycle greenhouse gas emissions from biofuels shall be calculated as follows:

(a) where a default value for greenhouse gas emission savings for the biofuel production pathway is laid down in Part A or B of Annex IV and where the e_l value for those biofuels calculated in accordance with point 7 of Part C of Annex IV is equal to or less than zero, by using that default value;

(b) by using an actual value calculated in accordance with the methodology laid down in Part C of Annex IV; or

(c) by using a value calculated as the sum of the factors of the formula referred to in point 1 of Part C of Annex IV, where disaggregated default values in Part D or E of Annex IV may be used for some factors, and actual values, calculated in accordance with the methodology laid down in Part C of Annex IV, for all other factors'.

[56] Michael Kaeding & Alan Hardacre, 'The European Parliament and the Future of Comitology after Lisbon' (2013) 19(3) *European Law Journal*, pp. 382–403.

of communicating the regulation's normative content through publication in the EU's Official Journal, the FQD foresees the development of a 'positive list' with default savings values for common biofuels production pathways, which economic operators can claim simply by virtue of using the biofuels in question.[57] If the default energy savings are insufficient to meet the efficiency savings thresholds established in the Directive,[58] the burden of proof reverts to the producers, who are 'required to show that actual emissions from their production values are lower than those ... assumed in the calculation of the default values'.[59]

In addition to publication and listing, the FQD relies heavily on reporting, monitoring and verification as a bonding strategy: Member States must designate responsible fuel suppliers that are to monitor and report annually on the GHG intensity of fuel and energy supplied within each Member State,[60] and they must ensure that annual reports are verified.[61] In the same vein, the FQD calls on Member States to require economic operators to show that biofuels fulfil the Directive's sustainability criteria, and that operators' data production and submission processes are independently audited.[62] These requirements evidently spur the development of supporting national frameworks to govern auditors and verification processes, which are, themselves, orchestrated at the transnational level through the issuance of Commission criteria for 'appropriate and relevant information'.[63]

The reporting requirements extend to Member States as well as fuel suppliers: in compliance with Article 8 FQD, Member States must monitor compliance with the Directive's petrol and diesel fuel specifications, in accordance with a standardised monitoring formula.[64] They must supply the Commission with an annual report on national fuel quality data that, again, should be drawn up in accordance with standardised criteria. The information is then aggregated by the Commission and released to the general public.

The FQD's engagement with voluntary schemes for sustainable biofuels, too, is built on reporting, auditing and certification,[65] the minimum criteria for which are set out in a 2010 Commission Communication.[66] The European Commission assesses the compatibility of the voluntary scheme with the FQD's sustainability criteria, and its key points of reference in this exercise are the adequacy of auditing and verification mechanisms that the voluntary scheme prescribes to its members.

[57] Communication from the Commission on voluntary schemes and default values in the EU biofuels and bioliquids sustainability scheme [2010] OJ C160/1.
[58] 35% until end 2017; 50% onwards, see Art. 7B(2) FQD.
[59] Preamble 19 FQD.
[60] Art. 7A(1)(a) FQD.
[61] Art. 7A(1)(b) FQD.
[62] Arts. 7C(1) and (3) FQD.
[63] Art. 7C(3) FQD.
[64] Annex II FQD.
[65] Art. 7C(5) FQD.
[66] N. 57 in this chapter.

To measure the adequacy of verification, the Communication refers to a set of external standards developed under the auspices of the ISO. For example, verifiers need to be accredited against standard ISO Guide 65, which establishes general requirements for bodies operating product-certification systems, as well as the more specific standard ISO 14065, which establishes requirements for GHG validation and verification bodies.[67]

A further bonding strategy deployed in the FQD is labelling, which seeks to secure the commitment of economic operators to the regulatory enterprise by marshalling the vigilance of the public generally, and consumers in particular. In accordance with Article 8A(4) to (6) FQD, fuel containing metallic additives (MMT) must be identified as such at the point of sale to end users. Hence, MMT is subject to both a technical standard that caps its presence in fuel to a maximum of 2mg/l as of 2014,[68] and a labelling requirement for MMT below this level of concentration. Here, a strategy that is typically seen as a textbook example of command-and-control is deployed jointly with one that is typically associated with alternative, flexible regulation.

The FQD is also richly stocked with facilitation mechanisms. Facilitation comes, for instance, in the shape of Commission reporting guidelines, which help fuel suppliers in meeting annual reporting duties.[69] Moreover, in an acknowledgement of the challenges that confront both Member States and private actors in meeting the Directive's targets, the FQD contains a number of flexibility provisions. Article 7A(2) FQD allows Member States to introduce intermediate fuel-efficiency targets in the run-up to the overall '6+2+2' % goal to be achieved by 2020, and the Directive affords a range of exemptions and derogations. In particular, the regulation foresees an exemption for older vehicles, which cannot be run on petrol with a high biofuel content, and it allows temporary deviation from the fuel specifications if Member States face a sudden change in the supply of crude oils or petroleum products.[70] Any Member State request for derogation from the FQD's technical specifications must be notified, substantiated and approved by the European Commission.[71] Conversely, Article 6 FQD allows Member States to opt up from the Directive's prescriptions to protect ecologically and environmental sensitive areas, or to combat specific pollution problems. Like derogations, opt-ups need to be substantiated and approved by the European Commission, which will focus its assessment on the compatibility of the opt-up with the Directive's trade-liberalisation objective.

Finally, an analysis of facilitation mechanisms attached to EU instruments must also take into account the broader regulatory context in which these instruments are deployed. Beyond the remit of the FQD, EU regulation can rely on the support of

67 Ibid.
68 Art. 8A(1) FQD.
69 Art. 7A(1) FQD.
70 Art. 7 FQD.
71 Art. 3(5) FQD.

the EU Network for the Implementation and Enforcement of Environmental Law (IMPEL). IMPEL's central mission is to improve the state of implementation of environmental law in Europe, and a key strategy to this end is the development of special projects that, for example, may organise knowledge sharing and exchange between implementing authorities or offer training to enhance the attainment of regulatory goals with limited resources.[72]

5.2.4 *Learning*

Virtually all EU Directives include a requirement for Member States to supply basic information on transposition and implementation, and the FQD is no exception: 'Member States shall communicate to the Commission the texts of the main provisions of domestic law which they adopt in the field covered by this Directive'.[73] However, the FQD goes to significantly greater lengths to ensure learning under the auspices of the regulatory framework. Learning activities are in the first place facilitated by the reporting obligations of Member States, suppliers and voluntary schemes, which support the development of an extensive compliance data set. Moreover, on the basis of the data reported and own-initiative research, the European Commission produces extensive reports covering all implementation aspects of the Directive, which are typically drawn up for the benefit of the European Parliament and the Council and made publicly available via the Commission's transparency platform. Some reports are focused primarily on compiling feedback from the regulatory addressees, but many explicitly include an assessment of the appropriateness and sufficiency of FQD standards, or of the effectiveness of particular engagement strategies. For example, the first paragraph of Article 7C(6) FQD on voluntary schemes for the recognition of biofuel stipulates:

> By 6 April 2017, the Commission shall submit a report to the European Parliament and to the Council analysing the reports [prepared by the voluntary schemes that have been accredited under the framework of the Directive], reviewing the operation of the … voluntary schemes …, and identifying best practices. The report shall be based on the best information available, including following consultations with stakeholders, and on practical experience in the application of the … [voluntary] schemes concerned.

Also noteworthy in this context are the Directive's arrangements concerning metallic additives in fuel. The concentration of the additive 'MMT'[74] is regulated by a technical standard: 6mg/l up to 2014, and 2mg/l onwards. However, in the light of the scientific uncertainty surrounding the impact of MMT on human health and the environment, Article 8A FQD explicitly mandates the Commission to conduct a

[72] See www.impel.eu/about-impel/strategy/.

[73] Art. 13 FQD.

[74] Methylcyclopentadienyl manganese tricarbonyl.

risk assessment, on the basis of which the European Parliament and Council 'may revise the limit for the MMT content of fuel'.[75]

Moreover, like normalisation and engagement strategies, learning activities as constituent parts of EU regulation are embedded within broader, cross-regulatory learning schemes.[76] The Commission annually compiles and releases large-scale reports and statistics on implementation and compliance with EU environmental rules. The European Environment Agency, in turn, has as a key function the gathering, processing and releasing of data on the state of the environment in Europe. The combination of both sources enables preliminary but important assessments of the overall correlation between regulatory compliance and effectiveness. IMPEL, too, contributes to regulatory learning through data production projects on implementation challenges and solutions in the environmental regulatory sphere.[77]

5.2.5 *Response*

The FQD's engagement with a variety of audiences, most prominently Member States and economic operators, is reflected in its differentiated strategy for individualised responses to compliance breaches. In accordance with the general rules on allocation of competencies between the EU and national level, the task of policing or otherwise responding to private sector non-compliance is left to the Member States. The Directive underlines national responsibility for enforcing the FQD's requirements. Thus, Article 4(1) FQD provides that Member States must ensure that diesel fuel is marketed only if it meets the performance and technical standards set out in the Directive. Article 9A FQD stipulates that 'Member States shall determine the penalties applicable to breaches of the national provisions adopted pursuant to this Directive', and continues that such penalties must be 'effective, proportionate and dissuasive'. Both requirements are supplemented by Article 13 FQD, which requires Member States to adopt and publish the 'laws, regulations and administrative provisions' necessary to comply with the FQD. The expectation that Member States will take all appropriate steps to secure compliance with the FQD's provisions is an expression of the fidelity principle, a foundational EU legal principle enshrined in the Treaty of the European Union (TEU).[78]

When it comes to individualised responses to non-compliant Member States, the FQD itself does not provide detail, but EU law generally is famously well-stocked

75 This provision has been the subject of litigation but was upheld, see C-343/09, *Afton Chemical Limited* v *Secretary of State for Transport* ECLI:EU:C:2010:419.

76 Aleksandra Čavoški, 'Assessment of Compliance Strategies' (2016) *European Law Review*, pp. 254–261.

77 See www.impel.eu/about-impel/strategy/.

78 Art. 4(3) TEU; see Damian Chalmers, Gareth Davies & Giorgio Monti, *European Union Law*, 3rd edn. (2014, Cambridge University Press), p. 214.

with policing and enforcement mechanisms. Articles 258 TFEU authorises the European Commission to initiate infringement proceedings against Member States for non-compliance. The Article 258 mechanism has both a facilitating and disciplining function: the first stages of infringement proceedings are geared towards distinguishing trivial from serious breaches and towards informal problem solving;[79] the latter stages are geared towards formal adjudication.[80] The adjudication stage is further bolstered by Article 260 TFEU, which foresees the possibility of Member States being fined for non-transposition and persistent non-compliance.[81] Moreover, beyond the opportunities for public compliance and enforcement action, the provisions of the FQD may be judicially enforced by private parties in domestic litigation. In accordance with the doctrine of 'direct effect' of EU law, the terms of EU Directives may be directly relied on in domestic court proceedings vis-à-vis state authorities, provided they are sufficiently clear and precise to be justiciable.[82] The detailed normalisation work that undergirds the FQD leaves little doubt that several FQD provisions would be deemed directly effective. Private enforcement of Directives is not available vis-à-vis private parties;[83] however, the prospect of domestic claims vis-à-vis the state for, for example, unlawful accreditation of biofuel sources may have some indirect disciplining force on the economic operators involved in the regulatory regime.

As to systemic responses to compliance and effectiveness challenges, the FQD has an extensive range of review and reform mechanisms built into the regulation, which can be deployed to respond to lessons from feedback and assessment and to seek greater effectiveness of the regulation through regulatory reform. Among the matters that are open to review and amendment, the Directive identifies: FQD performance targets, such as the percentage of fuel emissions reduction to be achieved via increased deployment of biofuels and reliance on the Clean Development Mechanism; the legal status of supporting measures, which may be transformed from voluntary into mandatory; the details of technical standards, which are to be regularly revisited and updated in the light of, among other factors, the latest available scientific data, assessment methodologies and the standardisation of verification mechanisms, and the maximum concentration of MMT. Article 9 FQD, furthermore, requires that the Commission's triannual report to the European Parliament and the Council be accompanied, as appropriate, by a proposal for

79 See Jonas Tallberg, 'Paths to Compliance: Enforcement, Management, and the European Union' (2002) 56(3) *International Organization*, pp. 609–643, at 616–617.

80 Pål Wennerås, *The Enforcement of EC Environmental Law* (2007, Oxford University Press).

81 Brian Jack, 'Article 260(2) TFEU: An Effective Judicial Procedure for the Enforcement of Judgements?' (2013) 19(3) *European Law Journal*, pp. 404–421.

82 See Case C-26/11, *Belgische Petroleum Unie VZW and Others* v *Belgische Staat*, ECLI:EU:C:2013:44.

83 Chalmers et al., *European Union Law*, pp. 308–312.

FQD amendments, taking into account, in particular, 'the potential need for adjustments' in order to reach the 10% GHG reduction target by 2020.

5.3 THE CARBON NEUTRAL PROTOCOL

The CNP is a prime exemplar of private TER. It is run by Natural Capital Partners (formerly the Carbon Neutral Company), a for-profit organisation that specialises in supporting its corporate clients to manage their carbon footprint and to obtain recognised accreditation for doing so.[84] The key instrument through which this is facilitated is the CNP, a standardisation and quality-assurance regime to which the clients of Natural Capital Partners voluntarily submit.

5.3.1 *Goal Setting*

The environmental target for adherents to the CNP is to achieve carbon neutrality (or 'net zero' GHG emissions). Yet this target is alluded to rather than explicitly affirmed in CNP-related documents.[85] The goal of carbon neutrality needs to be inferred from the overtly stated aim of the CNP to enable its clients to achieve CarbonNeutral® *certification* which, in turn, will help them make 'credible, transparent claims anywhere in the world'. Carbon neutrality, in the CNP context, is represented primarily as a secondary goal; a means to an end. The ultimate objective of the scheme is to create certified companies which get 'business value from a strong statement on carbon emissions'.[86] Stated in CNP documents in a very subsidiary order to reputation building, effective and efficient emissions reductions 'stimulated by the presence of a carbon neutral target'[87] can also add to business value.

5.3.2 *Normalisation*

The CNP understands its essential function as delivering a standard that enables a CarbonNeutral® certification that enjoys global recognition. To this end, the normalisation work of the CNP places particular emphasis on two aspects of the standardisation process: the procedural quality of standard setting and the compatibility of CNP standards with other broadly recognised carbon-neutrality standards.

The core prescriptive norm of the CNP is that the GHG emissions of the 'subject', which can either be a corporate entity, a particular product or an activity,

[84] See www.carbonneutral.com/about.

[85] Natural Capital Partners (NCP), *The Carbon Neutral Protocol: The Global Standard for Carbon Neutral Programmes*, Jan. 2017, p. 17, available at https://assets.naturalcapitalpartners.com/downloads/The-CarbonNeutral-Protocol-Jan2017.pdf.

[86] See www.carbonneutral.com/certification/how.

[87] NCP, *The Carbon Neutral Protocol*, p. 27.

must be reduced to net zero for a duration to be determined in the certification. Net-zero emissions may be achieved through a combination of emissions reductions and offsetting.[88] How different entities, products or activities meet the overall net-zero standard is determined on an individual basis, but the process through which determinations are reached is heavily standardised. Thus, the CNP sets out its key principles for technical standardisation, which include requirements for standard setting to be *transparent*; *accurate* through reliance on credible and up-to-date data, methodology and assumptions; *conservative* in its estimations so that progress towards net-zero emissions is not overstated; geared towards *continual improvement*; and based on a *wider context* reflecting the environmental, social and economic context in which the subject is situated.[89]

The CNP also sets across-the-board procedural and methodological standards. Applications for CarbonNeutral® certification must go through a sequential five-step process that starts with an identification of the entity, product or activity to be certified and ends with a communication of the results of implemented emissions reduction and offsetting measures.[90] Post-certification, CNP subscribers are expected to periodically 'assess progress against planned actions and to assess the feasibility for further reductions, taking into account the availability of new technologies, enabling policies and incentives provided by government, and the overall business context. Where applicable, a director or senior manager should be given responsibility for overseeing the development and ensuring the implementation of the plan for reducing emissions'.[91] The CNP therefore operates on a principle of progression similar to the expectation of progressively increasing climate ambition in the PA.

With regard to methodology, the Protocol pursues the standardisation of the requirements and conditions for GHG measurements, ranging from the selection of accounting protocols and chemicals to be included in the calculation of GHG emissions to the acceptability of particular quantification techniques to infer subject-specific emissions from general emissions data. Conditions for carbon credits to be used in offsetting, too, are standardised. Most importantly, any credit used towards the achievement of CarbonNeutral® certification must be *additional*, which means it must be shown that, in the absence of the carbon financing that made the project possible, GHG emissions would have been higher. Furthermore, to count towards carbon neutrality under the CNP, carbon credits must have a clear record of ownership ('*legally attributable*') and also be *measurable*, *permanent*, *unique* and *independently verified*.[92]

88 Ibid., p. 28.
89 Ibid., p. 17.
90 The steps are further mapped in Section 3.3.
91 NCP, *The Carbon Neutral Protocol*, p. 28.
92 Ibid., p. 29.

A second major tenet of the CNP's normalisation work involves standardisation by reference. The Protocol repeatedly asserts its broad compatibility with standards developed by alternative authorities such as national governments or the ISO. For example, on the subject of GHG measurement the CNP confirms that it is

> aligned with the GHG Protocol Corporate Standard, GHG Protocol Product Standard, Environmental Product Declarations and the principles of the PAS2050 for products and services. The Protocol is also suitable as a platform for compliance with a number of other emerging and related national standards, such as UK Guidelines on Carbon Neutrality and Australia's National Carbon Offset Standard. Clients may use internationally recognised management standards including but not limited to ISO14000 and ISO9000 to identify and manage their key impacts.[93]

Compatibility concerns are equally reflected in the provisions on the identification of relevant GHGs, which underline that all substances listed in the Kyoto Protocol must be included in the calculation, and in the incorporation of measurement technologies developed and deployed by alternative regulators into the range of CNP-recognised methodologies. For instance, the CNP refers to the assessment factors used by the (now defunct) UK Department of the Energy and Climate Change (DECC) to quantify specific emissions as examples of the kind of 'close to source' emissions factor the CNP favours.[94]

The analysis of normalisation activity reflected in the CNP indicates that the Protocol's standards are overwhelmingly described in broad and generic terms. What is particularly noticeable is the relative scarcity of information on sectoral standardisation, which further details the technical and performance requirements to achieve zero emissions in different segments of industry and for different products or activities, and which constitutes the middle layer between across-the-board standards and their case-by-case implementation. In this context, it is important to bear in mind the proprietary nature of the CNP standard; it is, essentially, an asset that subscribers unlock upon paid accession to the scheme. Hence, the standardisation that is effectively visible in the CNP is meta-standardisation, while the technical and performance-oriented brass tacks of standard setting remain protected from outside scrutiny and appropriation.

5.3.3 *Engagement*

In contrast to the assortment of communication, bonding and facilitation strategies deployed in the PA and the FQD, the CNP's engagement approach is overwhelmingly focused on a single instrument, namely, certification. Alternative modes of fostering engagement, such as publication, reporting requirements, bespoke

[93] Ibid., p. 18.
[94] Ibid., pp. 56–62.

'mechanisms' and derogation schemes, are in much shorter supply. There is communication through publication of the Protocol's rules and standards, but transparency is muted in order to protect the market value of the CNP's normalisation work. The standards released for public consumption are predominantly principle-based, procedural and broadly formulated; information about the more detailed technical and performance standards that governed entities, products or activities must meet are held behind private-access walls.

The exclusivity of communication between the CNP and its regulatory addressees also resonates in the way in which the clients' data production responsibilities are conceived: the CNP requires all clients to 'develop a GHG reduction plan to deliver internal emission reductions', but there is no call for this plan to be made publicly available. Instead, expectations of public disclosure are limited to the clients' release of GHG-inventory metrics.[95] The key channel through which regulatory addressees advertise their adherence to CNP standards is the CarbonNeutral® certification logo, which must be affixed in accordance with Natural Capital Partners' logo guidelines, issued 'upon achievement of their CarbonNeutral® certification'.[96]

The cornerstone of the relationship between the CNP and its clients is the certification requirement. Natural Capital Partners acts as the primary certifier and appoints secondary certifiers that shepherd the regulatory addressees through the application and compliance process, designed to culminate in the award of the CarbonNeutral® certification and the authorisation to use the CarbonNeutral® logo. The certification process is mapped out in broad terms in the CNP, and starts with a classification of the certification subject as either entity, product or activity. Consecutive steps comprise measuring the subject's emissions, in accordance with the standardised methodologies recognised by the CNP; target setting with the aim of the subject achieving net-zero emissions; the implementation of emissions reduction measures; and communication of the results.[97] The CNP certification process, again, illustrates the recursive nature of regulatory activities, as normalisation practices are both clarified and fine-tuned in the interaction between applicant and certifier.

The CNP's dependence on certification as the dominant vehicle to steer the behaviour of regulatory addressees creates an inevitable subsidiary dependence on the competence and trustworthiness of secondary certifiers. The terms of the CNP indicate that Natural Capital Partners manages the risk of reputational damage as a consequence of unreliable certification primarily through due diligence assessments in its selection of candidate certifiers. Additionally, in its contractual relation with secondary certifiers, the company reserves the right to appoint independent auditors

95 Ibid., p. 31.
96 Ibid., p. 31.
97 Ibid., pp. 23–31.

to review the certifiers' operating procedures.[98] This could be viewed as creating a 'who guards the guardians' dilemma that displaces the regulator's dependence from secondary certifiers towards a tertiary group of independent auditors. However, an alternative account of the bonding that goes on in the context of CNP regulation locates the draw towards regulatory cooperation and compliance not in one or another controlling or verifying entity, but in the network between the CNP, its clients, secondary certifiers and external auditors. Arguably, it is their mutual dependence on each other's reliability, and their corresponding vulnerability to reputational collateral damage should one actor within the network be found in breach of either its regulating or regulated mandate, which generates the overall compliance pull of the certification mechanism. To fully understand CNP certification as an engagement strategy, it is therefore important to factor in the role of inter-institutional dependence.

5.3.4 *Learning*

The CNP is relatively reticent on both its learning and response activities, particularly when compared with the corresponding, well-documented practices of the PA and EU as transnational environmental regulators. That does not mean, however, that learning and response are absent from the CNP's set-up. First, the Protocol introduces a number of mechanisms that explicitly support the regulator's ability to review the regime's effectiveness. Thus, the CNP's learning activities are supported partly through the aforementioned client reporting of GHG inventories, which supplies outcome-oriented data regarding the effectiveness of the scheme.[99] Additionally, the Protocol offers the following information about its broader feedback and assessment practices:

> The CarbonNeutral® Protocol undergoes an annual development cycle which involves input from multiple stakeholders. After each release of a new version, the Advisory Forum is invited to submit comments and feedback to guide development priorities over the following 12 months. The development of the subsequent version takes place over the following year, including rounds of consultation with stakeholders. While all opinions and ideas cannot be included within the Protocol, they will be considered. Suggestions for improvement raised too late to be included within the next version of the Protocol will be put on the list for consideration in subsequent versions. Natural Capital Partners also accepts input from clients and members of the public. Suggestions for development priorities for subsequent

98 Ibid., p. 47. The possibility of independent review at the behest of Natural Capital Partners does not preclude the existence of further contractual provisions designed to deter non-compliance on the part of secondary verifiers; however, any such terms are not publicised in the CNP.

99 Ibid., p. 31.

versions of The CarbonNeutral® Protocol should be sent to Natural Capital Partners using the contact details at: www.naturalcapitalpartners.com/contact-us.[100]

Secondly, as a private entity that effectively markets a regulatory regime to potential addressees, Natural Capital Partners has a strong vested interest in obtaining the best available feedback regarding the regime's functioning and effectiveness. However, in a competitive market for carbon standardisation and certification services, more detailed information about its data-gathering and processing practices may be commercially sensitive and therefore withheld from public scrutiny.

5.3.5 *Response*

The CNP does not list potential individualised responses to non-compliance, whether of a compliance- or deterrence-oriented persuasion. However, as in the case of feedback, this is not because the regime cannot deliver individualised responses. Individual compliance is primarily policed through the contractual arrangements between the regulated entity and its certification body, which conditionalise continued certification and the use of the logo upon continued compliance with the CNP standards. In fact, the contractual nature of the relation between regulatory addressee and certifier creates scope for additional penalties to disincentivise non-compliance that, depending on the popularity of the scheme and the premium attached to adherence, arguably exceed the enforcement mechanisms available to public regulators.[101]

Opportunities for systemic responses, on the other hand, are overtly built into the Protocol's operating procedures: the CNP is annually revised 'in the light of changing requirements of international standards, science and business'.[102]

5.4 THE COMPACT OF MAYORS/GLOBAL COVENANT OF MAYORS FOR CLIMATE AND ENERGY

The Compact of Mayors is a worldwide coalition of mayors and city officials committed to reduce local GHG emissions, to boost climate change resilience and to track progress. The initiative was launched at the 2014 UN Climate Change Summit under the leadership of then – UN Secretary-General Ban Ki-Moon and New York (US) Mayor Michael Bloomberg, and with the support of a range of existing city networks such as ICLEI-Local Governments for Sustainability (ICLEI) and the United Cities and Local Governments (UCLG). In 2016, a decision was reached to merge the Compact of Mayors with the European-based Covenant of

[100] Ibid., p. 18.

[101] Fabrizio Cafaggi, 'Enforcing Transnational Private Regulation: Models and Patterns' in Fabrizio Cafaggi (ed.), *Enforcement of Transnational Regulation: Ensuring Compliance in a Global World* (2012, Edward Elgar), pp. 75–130, at 104–107.

[102] NCP, *The Carbon Neutral Protocol*, p. 18.

Mayors for Climate and Energy in a newly formed 'Global Covenant of Mayors for Climate and Energy' (Global Covenant), a process that should be completed by the end of 2018.[103] Up to that point, the commitments under the Compact remain in vigour for Compact members.

5.4.1 *Goal Setting*

The Compact professes a broad, performance-oriented goal: to reduce GHG emissions from participating cities and enhance their climate resilience. The extent to which reduction and enhancement happen, however, is left entirely unquantified. In this regard, the Compact is different from the PA, which commits to a maximum 2°C global temperature rise (with scope to tighten to 1.5 °C) and intends for its signatories to achieve carbon neutrality by the second half of this century. It also differs from the FQD, with its 10% GHGs from fuel reduction target for 2020, from the CNP's expectation of net-zero emissions, and even from its European counterpart, the Covenant of Mayors. The latter does not deploy a self-determined quantified emissions reduction target, but requires participating towns and cities to adopt the EU's overall target of a 40% GHG-emissions reduction by 2030 as a minimum benchmark.[104] The planned Charter for the Global Covenant, which will apply to Compact members as of 2019, adopts a similar approach to the European model and introduces an expectation that cities under the Global Covenant will 'commit to achieving or surpassing the relevant national commitment(s) regarding climate change mitigation and adaptation and energy access to all, which are made, inter alia, in the context of the United Nations' Paris Agreement through the Nationally Determined Contributions or the Sustainable Development Goals'.[105]

5.4.2 *Normalisation*

The Compact's approach to normalisation is geared towards the introduction of broadly defined, flexible prescriptions that leave participating cities ample discretion in implementation. Substantively, the key requirement for Compact members is simply to *reduce* local GHG emissions and *address* the impacts of climate change, without further qualification of either the extent of reduction or type of adaptation response. After the Compact's absorption into the Global Covenant, the latter will require that, at least, Global Covenant cities achieve their respective national or regional emissions reduction targets, thus introducing a substantive, jurisdictionally differentiated minimum standard.

[103] See www.compactofmayors.org/.
[104] See www.globalcovenantofmayors.org/about/history-compact-of-mayors/.
[105] www.bbhub.io/mayors/sites/14/2016/06/Charter-for-the-Global-Covenant-of-Mayors-for-Climate-and-Energy-FINAL.pdf.

The operating procedures and measurement methods that cities must put in place to achieve the substantive targets are comparatively more fleshed out. Within one year of accession to the Compact, members must create a community-wide GHG inventory which identifies emissions according to source, as well as various climate hazards. The Compact references the inventorisation standard of the Global Protocol for Community Greenhouse Gas Emissions Inventories, a collaborative project between the World Resources Institute and the World Business Council for Sustainable Development,[106] as compulsory for cities to apply in this endeavour. Participating cities must also report on inventorisation via one of two preselected outlets; the Carbon Disclosure Project (CDP) or the carbon*n* climate registry.[107] Hence, while the Compact currently does not normalise the level of mitigation and adaptation ambition pursued by its members, it is intensely focused on standardising measurement and reporting practices.

Beyond inventorisation, the Compact's key prescription is that participating cities put in place credible management systems to deliver (unquantified) emissions reduction and adaptation outcomes. This implies that cities must update and enhance the GHG inventory within two years. Within that same timeframe, Compact cities must set emissions reduction targets, conduct a climate change vulnerability assessment in accordance with Compact guidelines and report on their endeavours. Within three years, cities must produce an evidence-based action plan for both mitigation and adaptation.

5.4.3 *Engagement*

Like many transnational environmental regimes reviewed, the Compact of Mayors seeks to secure engagement through publication and reporting requirements. Cities report climate data and actions either through the CDP or carbon*n* platform. Under the terms of the Compact, this information is made centrally and publicly available 'to highlight commitments and allow for easy searchability'.[108] Moreover, the Compact deploys a soft-touch certification mechanism as a bonding strategy: mayors wishing to join may register either via the reporting platforms or via letter of intent, upon which the Compact issues a badge declaring the city in question as 'Committed' to the scheme. A 'Compliant' badge follows once reports show that all Compact requirements are met and is renewed on an annual basis. The Compact provisions allow participating cities to display the badge in publicity materials online and in print.[109]

[106] Information available at www.ghgprotocol.org/.

[107] See Compact of Mayors Full Guide, July 2015, p. 7, available at https://data.bloomberglp.com/mayors/sites/14/2015/07/Compact-of-Mayors-Full-Guide_July2015.pdf.

[108] Ibid.

[109] Ibid., p. 10.

The Compact's bonding strategies reveal a strong emphasis on facilitation: reporting requirements are justified primarily with reference to the establishment of a comprehensive and 'easily searchable' database for the benefit of Compact members, rather than as a means to inspect and assess compliance. The staggered timeframe towards compliance, too, may help to lower the threshold to participation. Moreover, the Compact offers its members technical support, training and guidance documents, as well as direct email support.[110]

5.4.4 *Learning*

The abundance of reporting and data sharing, which constitutes the core of the Compact's engagement strategy, creates ample opportunity for learning and assessment. However, as with certification, the Compact deploys a pronouncedly light-touch approach to feedback and, particularly, assessment. It is conceived primarily as an autodidactic regime. It arranges for the production and publication of both city profiles, which include key points regarding the city's commitment status, actions taken and mayoral profile, and an overall Compact profile, with shows the collective impact of all Compact commitments. The key entities to whom this information is targeted are the participating cities themselves – the Compact does not establish specific review mechanisms that would help the regime to identify particular compliance practices or compliance breaches. Instead, the Compact functions as an enabler of self-learning and self-assessment, both through the generation of information pertaining to individual members and through review and comparison with fellow members.

5.4.5 *Response*

Given the relatively light-touch approach to bonding and the emphasis on self-learning, it is no surprise that the Compact's individual response strategy, too, is overwhelmingly geared towards self-correction. Since the Compact supports the use of a badge system to identify and thereby distinguish participating cities, a failure to meet the scheme's expectations regarding a city's commitment or participation should, presumably, result in a discontinuation of the certificate. However, the Compact provides no practical measures to enable external policing of the appropriate use of 'Committed' or 'Compliant' badges.

The arguable flimsiness of the Compact's individual response mechanisms stands in marked contrast to its European counterpart, the Covenant of Mayors, which explicitly foresees the suspension of membership as a penalty for failure to meet Covenant requirements, and which in recent years has invested heavily in strengthening its compliance mechanism. Jennifer Bansard, Philipp Pattberg and

[110] Ibid., p. 18.

Oscar Widerberg's research confirms that the Covenant actively investigates compliance, and has tightened the application of its membership suspension and termination procedures.[111] Alongside these enforcement measures, the Covenant has launched a monitoring catalogue, which offers graphs and statistical data on participants' implementation of their strategic action plans and their progress towards the 2020 emissions reduction goal,[112] and which functions as both facilitating information and a 'naming and shaming' tool.

Some questions remain as to how response activities will develop under the newly merged Global Covenant. The 2017 Guidance Document on the Global Covenant does not cover performance monitoring requirements,[113] which suggests the Compact's light-touch approach will prevail over the European Covenant's more deterrence-oriented inclination. On the other hand, it is unlikely that the latter will want to jettison its newly made investment in monitoring infrastructure and requirements, which means the monitoring catalogue will probably stay in effect for former European Covenant members, resulting in an internal differentiation of regulatory strategies depending on the provenance of respective member cities.

Finally, neither the Compact nor its successor regime contains an in-built mechanism for regulatory reform. Evidently, given the current transformation process of the Compact into the Global Covenant, reform does take place, but there is little information regarding the role of regulatory learning as a driver of response. In sum, compared to the individual and systemic response activities under the auspices of the FQD, the CNP and, even, the PA, the Compact of Mayors appears weak on response mechanisms.

5.5 THE REGIONAL GREENHOUSE GAS INITIATIVE

The RGGI is a 'cap-and-trade' programme which covers high-emitting sources from nine different northeastern US states with the aim of achieving CO_2 emissions reductions in a cost-effective manner.[114] Before launching into the analysis, it should be acknowledged that the choice of the RGGI as an example of TER could be contentious. First, all RGGI-regulated sources are currently located within the US. It is therefore, strictly speaking, a subnational or 'trans-statal' rather than a

[111] Jennifer Bansard, Philipp Pattberg & Oscar Widerberg, 'Subnational Climate Networks, Who They Are and What They Do', paper presented at the 2014 Amsterdam Conference 'Beyond 2015: Exploring the Future of Global Climate Governance', available at www.indiaeu-climate governance.org/Reports/Subnational-networks_Bansard.pdf.

[112] www.covenantofmayors.eu/actions/monitoring-action-plans_en.html.

[113] www.bbhub.io/mayors/sites/14/2017/04/CDP_-_Global_Covenant_of_Mayors_2017_Guidance .pdf.

[114] See, e.g., Robert Baldwin, Martin Cave & Martin Lodge, *Understanding Regulation: Theory, Strategy, and Practice*, 2nd edn. (2012, Oxford University Press), p. 196; Lawrence H. Goulder & Andrew R. Schein, 'Carbon Taxes versus Cap and Trade: A Critical Review' (2013) 4(3) *Climate Change Economics* 1350010, pp. 1–28.

transnational environmental regime.[115] Secondly, an examination of RGGI rules and documentation reveals that the initiative does not self-define as regulatory. Indeed, official statements repeatedly affirm that all regulatory power remains vested in the participating nine US states.[116]

Notwithstanding these peculiarities, the RGGI is appropriately included as a TER case study. With regard to its trans-statal rather than strictly transnational composition, the defining feature that qualifies RGGI as a subject of study is its multilevel governance structure as a cooperative venture between different regulatory authorities with an overarching and permanent administration, the nonprofit organisation 'RGGI, Inc.'. Its core function is to enhance the environmental effectiveness of state regulation through the creation of an interstate market. It is also open in principle to non-US states, and two Canadian provinces currently have observer status. Structurally and functionally, the RGGI is therefore more akin to an MEA with an enhancement agenda than a national environmental regulatory framework. Secondly, the formal disavowal of regulatory competence does not fundamentally change the nature of the RGGI as a deliberate attempt at behaviour steering in the public interest, conducted with a reasonable degree of authority and persistence.[117] The RGGI purposely and inescapably affects the decision making of participating states and, through their intermediacy, the behaviour of private emitters. In fact, the analysis will show that the RGGI enjoys a compliance pull that few conventionally domestic regulatory regimes can match. Moreover, while participating states officially retain the regulatory initiative, they do declare themselves bound to adopt the measures necessary for the RGGI's implementation. The RGGI's Memorandum of Understanding (MoU) confirms that 'Each of the Signatory States commits to propose for legislative and/or regulatory approval, the Program substantially as reflected in a Model Rule'.[118] The RGGI Model Rule is an explicitly trans-statal and, by virtue of the MoU, highly authoritative regulatory instrument that governs the key features of the cap-and-trade regime. For these reasons, the RGGI constitutes a fitting and instructive last testing ground for the activity-based analysis of TER.

[115] RGGI participating states are: New York, Maryland, Massachusetts, Connecticut, New Hampshire, Delaware, Maine, Rhode Island and Vermont. Virginia has adopted a parallel cap-and-trade programme and may accede to the RGGI in the coming years. See RGGI Statement on Proposed Virginia Greenhouse Gas Rule, 9 Nov. 2017, at: www.rggi.org/docs/PressReleases/Virginia_Statement_2017_11_9.pdf.

[116] RGGI, Inc. states that its exclusive purpose is to 'provide administrative and technical services to support the development and implementation of each RGGI State's CO_2 Budget Trading Program'. The mission statement underlines that RGGI, Inc. has 'no regulatory or enforcement authority'. See RGGI mission statement at www.rggi.org/rggi.

[117] See Section 2.3.

[118] The RGGI Memorandum of Understanding, 20 December 2005, available at www.rggi.org/docs/mou_final_12_20_05.pdf.

5.5.1 *Goal Setting*

The RGGI's goal is to first stabilise and then reduce carbon emissions from power plants established in the participating states,[119] 'while maintaining energy affordability and reliability and accommodating, to the extent feasible, the diversity in policies and programs in individual states'.[120] To this end, the RGGI relies on a singular regulatory strategy, namely, a 'cap-and-trade' emissions programme, which works with an overall, multi-state CO_2 limit or 'cap' and the creation of a corresponding number of allowances. Here, the introduction of a specific regulatory mechanism, which comes with particular promises of efficiency and flexibility, becomes as much part of the regulator's objective as the achievement of environmental results.

5.5.2 *Normalisation*

The overarching and dominant norm of the Initiative is its multi-state CO_2 emissions cap. In 2014, the nine participating RGGI states agreed upon a cap of 91 million short tons of CO_2,[121] scheduled to decrease by 2.5% every year to 2020. The achievement of the overall cap is secured not through the elaboration of a series of sectoral standards, but instead through the creation of entitlements (emissions allowances). In 2017, the RGGI authorised the issuance of 62,500,000 allowances to be auctioned by the participating US states to the regulated sectors.[122]

Compared to the difficulties and resource-intensity of implementing broad environmental protection targets through myriad performance and technical standards,[123] the alternative strategy of translating an overall emissions cap into individual allowances, to be administered by the participating states according to a pre-established allocation key,[124] is appealingly straightforward. As observed previously, the existence of allowances does not obviate the need for detailed technical standardisation and rule making, but the technical work is carried out by the regulated sources internally rather than the regulator. However, reliance on an entitlement strategy does not eliminate the need for regulatory standardisation altogether. Rather, the RGGI's normalisation work focuses on two major alternative fields: standardisation to harmonise the conditions for the implementation of RGGI's chosen engagement

[119] Art. 1 of the Model Rule, available at www.rggi.org/docs/ProgramReview/_FinalProgramReviewMaterials/Model_Rule_FINAL.pdf.

[120] Claire Carothers, 'United We Stand: The Interstate Compact as a Tool for Effecting Climate Change' (2006) 41(1) *Georgia Law Review*, pp. 229–260, at 234.

[121] A unit of weight equal to 2,000 pounds (907.18474 kg).

[122] 62.5 million tons is the adjusted overall budget calculated from the 2017 84.3 million tons overall budget.

[123] E.g., Richard B. Stewart, 'Controlling Environmental Risks through Economic Incentives' (1988) 13(2) *Columbia Journal of Environmental Law*, pp. 153–170.

[124] New York (39%); Maryland (22%); Massachusetts (16%); Connecticut (6%); New Hampshire (5%); Delaware (4); Maine (4%); Rhode Island (3%); Vermont (1%).

strategy of auctioning and trading and, secondly, the standardisation of compliance assessments to ascertain that one surrendered emissions allowance effectively corresponds with one ton of CO_2 emitted, and that the same yardsticks are applied across participating states.

The lion's share of the RGGI's normalisation work is rendered in its 'Model Rule', a document which runs to 135 pages at last revision and that details all the standardisation and rule-making work that participating US states need to undertake in order to implement the RGGI. The Model Rule is a fount of procedural and methodological standardisation and covers issues ranging from the organisation of auctioning platforms to the allowable destination of proceeds. It details permitting requirements for CO_2-emitting entities subjected to the Budget Trading Program, monitoring requirements in accordance with the RGGI Model Rule, carbon budgeting standards, record-keeping and reporting requirements, compliance certification requirements and state-accreditation procedures. The Model Rule also standardises the allocation of allowances, stipulating that at least 25% must go to a consumer benefit or public energy purpose.[125] It spells out the calculation methodology for 'early reduction allowances' (see below), which enable participating states to reward early investors in green energy; details the conditions for the establishment of a CO_2 Allowance Tracking System (COATS), which constitutes the RGGI's key transparency and compliance-checking mechanism; outlines the registration of allowance transfers and standardises the requirements, processes and maximum allowable reliance on offsetting. The latter are moreover further detailed in the RGGI Offsetting Handbook.[126]

In addition to its extensive coverage and depth, the most distinctive aspect of the RGGI standardisation approach is its semi-optional character. A sizeable number of the Model Rule's articles start with a proviso acknowledging that participating states may have different requirements regarding the issue in question, and that the standards in the Model Rule serve, literally, as a model rather than a mandated approach. Thus, the provisions on permitting commence with:

> [each state's text for this subdivision will likely be different because the states have unique permitting requirements. The text below illustrates how this subdivision could be drafted and does not necessarily represent what an individual RGGI state will propose].

This deferential language is in line with the RGGI's overt disavowal of suprastatal regulatory authority. It is, however, noteworthy that the proviso does not feature

125 Bruce R. Huber, 'How Did RGGI Do It? Political Economy and Emissions Auctions' (2013) 40 (1) *Ecology Law Quarterly*, pp. 59–106, at 87.

126 Offset Handbook for Regional Greenhouse Gas Initiative (RGGI) Model Rule Offset Subpart XX–10 and Model Offset Consistency Applications and Model Monitoring and Verification Reports, available at www.rggi.org/docs/Offsets/2015/Revised_Offset_Handbook_2015_05_13.pdf.

ahead of every regulated issue; provisions on the organisation of COATS, on monitoring and reporting and on offsetting conditions, for example, are not represented as optional or subject to state determination. Moreover, the permissive framing obviously does not preclude the existence of strong, informal authority emanating from the normalisation work undertaken under the RGGI's auspices.

5.5.3 *Engagement*

The RGGI's primary addressees are public authorities, namely, the nine states that participate in the Budget Trading Program. Yet, as in the case of the FQD, a full understanding of engagement strategies in the RGGI requires a contemplation of both the mechanisms that tie the states to the RGGI and those that foster compliance on the part of the CO_2 sources that, ultimately, need to adapt their behaviour for the Initiative to succeed. Moreover, a clear connection exists between state and private engagement, since the presence or absence of effective private sector engagement mechanisms may determine the state's willingness to participate in the scheme.

RGGI addressees are tightly bonded to the Budget Trading Program through an orchestration of engagement mechanisms. Most prominently, bonding happens via the annual auctioning of the allowances that regulated CO_2 sources must surrender to cover their emissions, which is facilitated through the establishment of a regional auctioning platform. The system is further backed up by a state-based permitting requirement to ensure that all allowance holders are known, visible and in regular communication with the state regulatory authorities. Additionally, the RGGI Model Rule is well-stocked with compliance certification, monitoring and reporting provisions that organise and regularise emitters' compliance processes.[127]

Equally essential to foster private sector engagement are the RGGI's key facilitation techniques, which consist of the tradeability of allowances, the scope for offsetting and the provision of early reduction allowances (ERAs). Tradeability is the feature that injects the RGGI with the much-vaunted economic efficiency and flexibility of market-based regimes, as CO_2 reduction actions can be concentrated within those facilities that are able to implement them most cost-effectively.[128] The allowances market is further harnessed through an interstate Cost Containment Reserve (CCR). The CCR creates a fixed additional supply of CO_2 allowances, which only become available for sale if CO_2 allowance prices exceed certain price levels.[129] Offsetting and ERAs, in turn, broaden the avenues through which regulated sources can secure compliance with the scheme. The former offers emitting

[127] See Articles XX–4 and XX–8 of the Model Rule.

[128] E.g., Paul Ekins & Terry Barker, 'Carbon Taxes and Carbon Emissions Trading' (2002) 15(3) *Journal of Economic Surveys*, pp. 326–376, at 329–331.

[129] Note, however, that the RGGI does not provide the reserve option of withdrawing allowances from the market if the price drops below a certain level. Such a mechanism is present in the

sources a degree of choice in whether to reduce emissions locally or invest in emissions reduction or clean technology development elsewhere; the latter avoids penalties for early adopters that have made emissions reductions prior to the entry into effect of the Budget Trading Program, which may limit their ability to introduce further cuts in compliance with the annually shrinking overall cap.

The deployment of choice tools in the organisation of compliance is said to make emissions trading regimes an easier political sell than the more conventional regulatory technique of prescribing particular technologies or imposing non-negotiable emissions limits on individual sectors.[130] Direct facilitation of regulated sources thereby has an indirect facilitating impact on public authorities' commitment towards the scheme. However, the argument has been made that the market mechanism is as much a stick as a carrot. In a 2013 article, Bruce Huber explains the adherence pull of the RGGI with reference to the regional organisation of the energy market.[131] From its inception, the launch of the RGGI was expected to exercise an upward pressure on energy prices because regulated energy companies would seek to recoup the cost of emissions allowances. Moreover, early experience with the EU Emissions Trading System indicated that a price hike would occur regardless of whether allowances were auctioned or grandfathered.[132] Hence, states within the northeastern region such as Maine and Vermont, which were less swayed by the Initiative's potential environmental merits, ultimately felt compelled to join the scheme because, otherwise, they would have shared the burden of higher energy prices but not the RGGI-generated benefits.[133] Chief among these were the creation of a new income stream from the auctioning of allowances, as well as the RRGI provisions on public benefit allocation. Hence, although formally optional, the economic consequences of introducing market-based instruments may imbue such a regime with a coercive force far beyond what is suggested by the deferential, non-committal terms in which the relation between the regulating entity and the addressees are formally cast.

5.5.4 *Learning*

One of the most striking features of the RGGI is its huge investment in regulatory learning. The Model Rule sets out broad reporting obligations, which extend not

EU Emissions Trading System. See Suzanne Kingston, Veerle Heyvaert & Aleksandra Čavoški, *European Environmental Law* (2017, Cambridge University Press), p. 296.

130 Robert Baldwin, 'Regulation Lite: The Rise of Emissions Trading' (2008) 2(2) *Regulation & Governance*, pp. 193–215.

131 Huber, 'How Did RGGI Do It?', pp. 95–96.

132 Timothy Laing, Misato Sato, Michael Grubb & Claudia Comberti, 'The Effects and Side-Effects of the EU Emissions Trading Scheme' 2014 5(4) *Wiley Interdisciplinary Reviews: Climate Change*, pp. 509–519.

133 On the other hand, New Jersey, which joined the scheme after 2005, dropped out again in 2010.

only to the regulated sources but also to the participating states. As well as a bonding technique, private and state reporting obligations enable the regime to create a vast repository of information on the functioning of the RGGI overall and the performance of each participant state and each regulated source. This repository is the RGGI COATS, which has as its core objective to enable the comprehensive tracking of the performance of each participating state and of each regulated entity within each state. To this end, COATS offers an impressive range of reports on matters from the individual emissions of each installation to the overall number of annual market transactions, fluctuations in allowance prices and offset prices and compliance data for regulated sources.

Compared to the strong focus on the organisation of feedback, the RGGI and its Model Rule are relatively quiet on the assessment stage of the learning process. The COATS-related provisions place a heavy emphasis on the public availability of Budget Trading Program data, and foresee the production of various summary reports specifically designed to enhance the accessibility of information. These include summary reports on emissions, on auctions and on compliance. Thus, it appears that the RGGI primarily intends for learning to be organised externally rather than within the framework itself. Its key aim is to equip others — whether private enterprises, citizens, states or NGOs – to make informed assessments about the effectiveness of the regime.

5.5.5 *Response*

Considering the RGGI's externalised approach to regulatory learning, as well as its overt disavowal of formal regulatory competence, it is unsurprising that the Initiative is reticent on individualised responses and treats enforcement primarily as a state responsibility. The Model Rule does, however, affirm that 'Each ton of CO_2 emitted in excess of the CO_2 budget emissions limitation shall constitute a separate violation of this Part and applicable state law'.[134] By the same token, the RGGI does not make formal provision for systemic responses through, say, a periodic review and revision process, but in practice the Model Rule has been revised at several instances. Moreover, the RGGI has a built-in reassessment clock in the shape of its 2020 deadline: if the Initiative is to carry on beyond this date, then its key features — such as the annual overall cap, the allocation per state, the allowable level of offsetting versus on-site reductions – will need to be renegotiated.

5.6 CONCLUDING REMARKS

The aim of this chapter was to test the activity-based model of regulatory strategy as an analytical framework by applying it to five very different examples of TER, and

[134] Section XX.1.5(c)2 Model Rule.

thus to provide the basis for a comprehensive commentary in the next and concluding chapter of this triptych on TER strategies. The reflections in this concluding section will not attempt to preempt the critical discussion to follow, but some general observations on the application of the model are warranted. First, the case analyses show that the model does enable the unpacking of regulatory regimes in a meaningful way. Each of the examined frameworks displays features that can effectively be qualified as the result of either goal setting, normalisation, engagement, learning or response activities. Secondly, while it is possible to find evidence of each of the five stages in each example, the evidence is not always the same and not always as strong, which indicates that the model is capable of distinguishing more developed and authoritative TER regimes from looser and more governance-oriented TER regimes. Additionally, the application of the model affirms the recursive nature of regulatory activity, as identical provisions in a number of the studied regimes proved relevant for discussion under, particularly, normalisation, engagement and learning respectively. However, the conceptual boundaries between the stages proved sufficiently robust to avoid a collapsing of one activity into the other. Finally, the application of the model did not reveal any instances in which activities that are conventionally understood as regulatory were excluded because they did not fit under either a goal setting, normalisation, engagement, learning or response caption. Hence, on a first testing the categories appear sufficiently inclusive to capture all activities that are constitutive of regulation.

6

The Transformation of Environmental Regulatory Strategies

Much has changed in recent decades in the design, the implementation and the enforcement of environmental regulation. Moreover, there is broad agreement that the proliferation of environmental regulation beyond the state was, and remains, an important contributor to change.[1] Highly valuable work has been done to identify key distinctions between the approaches associated with conventional state-based regulation and those more typically espoused by transnational regulators, but the resulting categorisations tend to be simultaneously too complex and too reductionist to capture adequately the range and characteristics of environmental regulatory strategies pursued by transnational actors. This book aims to further what we know about TER strategies by developing an activity-based lens through which to analyse regulatory design and decision making, and putting this lens to the test in a variety of TER case studies.

The activity-based analysis of TER does, indeed, help to uncover important new information about environmental regulatory strategies. It also helps to affirm a number of pre-existing assumptions about how environmental regulation works, and destabilise others. Most importantly, the analysis invites us to look anew at some of regulation's core concepts and debates – such as the choice between rules and standards and the notion of enforcement – and devise alternative framings that are better attuned to the actual content and organisation of TER.

[1] David Levi-Faur & Jacint Jordana, 'The Rise of Regulatory Capitalism: The Global Diffusion of a New Order' (2005) 598(1) *The ANNALS of the American Academy of Political and Social Science*, pp. 200–217; Rüdiger K. W. Wurzel, Anthony R. Zito & Andrew J. Jordan, *Environmental Governance in Europe* (2013, Edward Elgar), p. 159; Onyeka K. Osuji, 'Corporate Social Responsibility, Juridification and Globalisation: "Inventive Interventionism" for a "Paradox"' (2015) 11(3) *International Journal of Law in Context*, pp. 265–298, at 275; Kenneth W. Abbott & Duncan Snidal, 'Taking Responsive Regulation Transnational: Strategies for International Organizations' (2013) 7(1) *Regulation & Governance*, pp. 95–113.

This chapter identifies key lessons that emerge from the case studies in Chapter 5. First, the analysis underscores the importance of appreciating the networked, interdependent nature of TER. This feature characterises not only arrangements commonly referred to in the literature as 'networked regulation' or 'networked governance', including the Compact of Mayors or FLEGT, but also regimes that are typically treated as autonomous, such as the CNP. Secondly, the analysis strongly indicates that TER in action displays a level of complexity that is inadequately captured by terms such as 'flexible', 'principle-based' or 'persuasive'. Most TER regimes rely on a combination of normalisation, engagement, learning and response methods to convey regulatory content and pursue compliance. This operational complexity, particularly when considered in combination with the networked character of TER, necessitates a reassessment of several assumptions regarding transnational environmental regulatory strategies (Section 6.3). This is especially the case for assumptions about compliance and deterrence, which for that reason are committed to a dedicated fourth section in this chapter.

6.1 TRANSNATIONAL ENVIRONMENTAL NETWORKS OF REGULATION

Recent regulation and governance studies have pursued the idea that regulation beyond the state may not be the product of a monolithic authority, but instead emanates from a network. Such networks connect a variety of actors who have some degree of investment in governance, but who might individually struggle to achieve the required capacity or credibility to imbue their communications with regulatory authority. The network structure of contemporary transnational regulation is particularly pronounced in complex policy fields such as climate change, as examined by a range of studies by authors including Michelle Betsill and Harriet Bulkeley, Harro van Asselt, Robert Keohane and David Victor.[2] The activity-based analysis adds to their research by revealing how deeply entrenched network structures are in the TER sphere. Indeed, the five case studies compellingly illustrate the extent to which TER is the product of different organisations interlinking, relying on each other's work and integrating each other's strategies towards the pursuit of shared regulatory goals. TER, it transpires powerfully from the investigation, does not

[2] Michele Betsill & Harriet Bulkeley, 'Transnational Networks and Global Environmental Governance: The Cities for Climate Protection Program' (2004) 48(2) *International Studies Quarterly*, pp. 471–493; Harro van Asselt, *The Fragmentation of Global Climate Governance: Consequences and Management of Regime Interactions* (2014, Edward Elgar); Robert O. Keohane & David G. Victor, 'The Regime Complex for Climate Change' (2011) 9(1) *Perspectives on Politics*, pp. 7–23.

merely *include* networked regulation. The network structure *is* one of TER's essential features.[3]

TER regimes are networked in a variety of ways. The first and best known iteration of the network qualities relates to the multilevel governance structure that supports many transnational regimes.[4] The achievement of the regulatory goals set out in the Paris Agreement, FQD, the RGGI and, indeed, in the overwhelming majority of transnational regulatory regimes that involve a high level of public authority engagement, depends on the primary TER addressees picking up the baton and adopting regulation to implement and enforce transnational norms. In many cases, for example in most EU environmental regulation, TER addressees will be explicitly mandated to deploy regulation in implementation of transnational regulatory objectives.[5] In others, such as in the context of the Compact of Mayors, the transnational provisions do not identify a particular regulatory or alternative pathway which the TER addressees must pursue, but regulation is very likely to be one of the key implementation instruments of choice.

The organisation of private environmental regulatory regimes, in turn, may not formally qualify as multilevel governance; however, the architecture of many such schemes shares significant features with multilevel governance structures. Private TER initiatives, such as the CNP and the MSC, rely heavily on certification as their main engagement strategy.[6] Here, the NGO, private company or IGO at the helm of the regulatory scheme essentially delegates the task of implementing the regime's regulatory requirements to a cohort of certification bodies, which are institutionally independent but accountable to the private regulator, and are typically located in a range of different countries. This delegation process bears many organisational similarities with the regulatory networking which unfolds in a multilevel governance context. Furthermore, as in multilevel governance, the relation between different actors in the regulatory network is more dialectic than the formal division of responsibilities suggests. The recursive nature of regulatory work entails that standards are not merely put into effect but are substantively further developed through processes of domestic implementation or certification, and arrangements for learning and response feed this substantiation back into the transnational regulatory

3 Cf. Maria Carmen Lemos & Arun Agrawal, 'Environmental Governance' (2006) 31 *Annual Review of Environment and Resources*, pp. 297–325, at 301.

4 Robert Baldwin, Martin Cave & Martin Lodge, *Understanding Regulation. Theory, Strategy, and Practice*, 2nd edn. (2012, Oxford University Press), pp. 373–387.

5 See, e.g., Art. 80 of the EU Industrial Emissions Directive, which requires Member States to 'bring into force the laws, regulations and administrative provisions necessary to comply with' the Directive's regulatory provisions. Directive 2010/75/EU on industrial emissions (integrated pollution prevention and control) [2010] OJ L334/17. Cf. Judith A. M. Gollata & Jens Newig, 'Policy Implementation through Multi-Level Governance: Analysing Practical Implementation of EU Air Quality Directives in Germany' (2017) 24(9) *Journal of European Public Policy*, pp. 1308–1327, at 1312.

6 Lars H. Gulbrandsen, 'The Emergence and Effectiveness of the Marine Stewardship Council' (2009) 33(4) *Marine Policy*, pp. 654–660, at 656.

cycle. This dynamic further strengthens the image of TER as network instead of a chain of command.

Additionally, TER regimes are often laterally networked.[7] The FQD, the CNP and the Compact of Mayors all deploy standardisation by reference: they either mandate or recognise the validity of norms developed in a different forum as compliant with general requirements of the regulatory scheme. In many cases, cross-referencing will link the regulatory regime with the work of a regional or international standard-setting body, with the ISO as most prominent example.[8] The normalisation work of the International Social and Environmental Accreditation and Labelling (ISEAL) Alliance, which focuses on the production of sustainability standards, is also highly relevant in the TER context, and features most frequently as a point of reference in private TER regimes.[9] Moreover, private TER regimes very often cross-reference the standards set by public regulators as either the indicated norm or a minimum threshold for the participants to the private scheme to observe.[10] Finally, whereas cross-referencing practices are most easily discernible when the normative content involved is expressed in standards, a similar dynamic unfolds when one regulatory regime recognises the validity of entitlements or allowances generated in a different institutional context.[11] The regulatory choice to link emissions markets or to recognise externally generated emissions reduction certificates as offsets, as illustrated in the context of the CNP, can be treated as a variant of cross-referencing and, therefore, expressive of the networked qualities of TER.

6.2 THE COMPLEXITY OF TRANSNATIONAL ENVIRONMENTAL REGULATION

TER regimes tend to defy easy categorisation. Whether attempting to organise the field on the basis of the public or private status of the parties involved (Chapter 2), or in accordance with the regulatory purpose pursued (Chapter 3), we encounter plenty of hybrid cases that irritate definitional boundaries, that combine traits of different cohorts, or that belong in either group A or B depending on whose perspective counts. This feature becomes even more pronounced when we try to match examples of TER with well-known categories of regulatory strategy, such as

7 Cf. Abbott & Snidal, 'Taking Responsive Regulation Transnational', p. 98.

8 Cf. Sarah E. Light & Eric Orts, 'Parallels in Public and Private Environmental Governance' (2015) 5(1) *Michigan Journal of Environmental & Administrative Law*, pp. 1–72, at 43–44.

9 See www.isealalliance.org/. Kristina Tamm Hallström & Magnus Boström, *Transnational Multi-Stakeholder Standardization: Organizing Fragile Non-State Authority* (2010, Edward Elgar), pp. 86–92. See also Chapter 8.3.1.

10 Markos Karavias, 'Interactions between International Law and Private Fisheries Certification', (2018) 7(1) *Transnational Environmental Law*, pp. 165–184, at 173.

11 See, e.g., Art. 11(a) of the EU Linking Directive, Directive 2004/101/EC amending Directive 2003/87/EC establishing a scheme for greenhouse gas emission allowance trading within the Community, in respect of the Kyoto Protocol's project mechanisms [2004] OJ L338/18.

command-and-control; incentive-based regulation; responsive regulation; meta-regulation and so on. Indeed, the activity-based analysis of every single of the five case studies reveals a richness in goal setting, normalisation, engagement, learning and response strategies that is not adequately reflected but is, on the contrary, obscured by prevailing preconceptions about transnational regulatory design and operationalisation. Thus, the activity-based analysis draws our attention to the multiplicity of regulatory communications within a single setup: all investigated regimes directly and indirectly normalise the behaviour of different cohorts of addressees, which typically include both public authorities and private actors. Transnational regulators do not 'just' use principles, standards or rules, but instead rely on a combination of normalisation techniques. Their approaches to foster the engagement of the regulatory addressees, and mechanisms for learning and response, too, betray a degree of complexity and variation that terms such as 'meta-regulation', 'flexible instruments' or 'new governance' fail to convey. The following paragraphs identify and discuss the complexity of TER strategies in greater detail.

6.2.1 *Rules, Standards, Allowances and Prices in TER*

The complexity of TER emerges powerfully from the analysis of the normalisation strategies in each of the five case studies. Overwhelmingly, TER regulators use combinations of normalisation strategies to achieve their goals. The case studies show a strong reliance by transnational regulators on meta-standardisation and principle-based approaches to standardisation in TER: broadly formulated substantive standards feature prominently, and each of the studied regimes displays a heavy reliance on procedural standards.[12] Among the studied examples, the Paris Agreement and the Compact of Mayors stand out as regimes with the strongest preference for flexible over prescriptive approaches to standardisation, and a preference for setting standards over introducing rules. This is all very much in line with expectations, especially when taking into account that the primary addressees of both instruments are public authorities which are expected to implement general directives through standards, rules or, possibly, entitlements and prices. Yet the analyses equally confirm that there is far more to TER normalisation strategies than broad brushstrokes alone.

First, the TER sphere itself is certainly not devoid of the more detailed and technical approaches to normalisation that are typically associated with state level command-and-control regulation. Within the sample of five, performance-based

[12] Sharon Gilad, 'It Runs in the Family: Meta-Regulation and Its Siblings' (2010) 4(4) *Regulation & Governance*, pp. 485–506; Julia Black, 'Forms and Paradoxes of Principles-Based Regulation' (2008) 3(4) *Capital Markets Law Journal*, pp. 425–457; Christine Parker, *The Open Corporation: Effective Self-Regulation and Democracy* (2002, Cambridge University Press), pp. 245–291.

and technical standards are very prominent in the FQD. Moreover, detailed and prescriptive standardisation strategies are not constrained to the arguably exceptional EU case: the CNP, too, entails the imposition of detailed technical standards upon parties seeking certification. Their precise content is kept confidential so as to safeguard property value and secure club advantages for the participants to the scheme that cannot be accessed by third parties, but they are no less interventionist than the norms which typically accompany national authorisation and licensing schemes. Importantly, the CNP is not an outlier in this regard: many instances of private TER, from Responsible Care® to the FSC, rely on detailed and prescriptive standardisation.[13] Moreover, while the Compact of Mayors and the Paris Agreement are admittedly thin on performance-based and technical standards, such norms do regularly feature in other instances of public TER. Transnational regimes such as the CLRTAP and its protocols, the Montreal Protocol to the Vienna Convention and the POPs Convention are all rich in technical and prescriptive detail.

Secondly, the interpretive freedom left by broadly formulated targets and principle-based standards may be considerably hemmed in by detailed procedural and, particularly, methodological standardisation. The ubiquity of methodological standardisation emerges from the case studies as one of TER's most pronounced features. While regulated parties under the Paris Agreement remain free to choose whether, for instance, to engage in carbon offsetting or pursue emissions reduction targets through alternative means, the way in which the value of offsets must be calculated has a serious, potentially determinative impact on the relative cost and viability of offsetting as an emissions reductions technique. Hence, via the choice of calculation methodology, transnational regulators can steer decisions on substance to a more significant degree than the wording of the provisions suggests. Broad reliance on standardisation by reference, too, tends to have a more prescriptive effect in practice than countenanced in theory. Even in cases where the externally produced body of standards is presented as one of various possible implementation strategies, the threshold for customisation may be prohibitive.[14] Here, regulatory addressees are no longer effectively governed by the principle-based and broad substantive standards which are formally binding upon the parties, but by a potentially far more detailed and constraining set of rules.

The five case studies also include one example of normalisation through entitlement, namely, the RGGI which operates a cap-and-trade system. However, outside the context of enhancement TER to scale up the market for emissions trading, with the EU ETS as best known exemplar, alternative normalisation strategies rarely feature in TER instruments. TER regimes may expect or, more frequently, encourage their regulatory addressees to deploy allowance- or price-based strategies in the

[13] Light & Orts, 'Parallels', p. 29.

[14] See Case C-171/11, *Fra.bo SpA* v *Deutsche Vereinigung des Gas- und Wasserfaches eV (DVGW) – Technisch-Wissenschaftlicher Verein* ECLI:EU:C:2012:453.

implementation of TER requirements,[15] but the transnational regulator itself typically does not normalise by creating allowances or setting prices. A few intriguing examples do exist of price- or allowance-based strategies that operate within large corporate enterprises. Both the Disney and Microsoft companies, for example, set an internal price for GHGs which departments must factor into their budgeting, and the latter even has been known to hold inter-departmental competitions for which unit can cut carbon costs most.[16] As a rule of thumb, however, private TER relies more on 'traditional' normalisation strategies such as performance-based and technical standards than on alternative approaches. Normalisation through taxation, in turn, is practically unheard of at the transnational level.[17] Even the EU, arguably the most developed transnational environmental regulator worldwide with the most extensive and varied regulatory arsenal at its disposal, thus far has refrained from introducing carbon taxes or alternative environmental fiscal measures. In sum, while the transnational level is often associated with a rise in flexible mechanisms,[18] it is important to remember that the actual process of translating norms into allowances and prices usually takes place at the national level, and that TER typically encourages but only very exceptionally mandates the use of such flexible instruments.

6.2.2 *Engagement Strategies*

TER regimes display a tremendous investment and variation in engagement strategies. Each of the studied cases goes well beyond the baseline of communicating regulatory content to the addressees. In fact, fostering addressee engagement emerges from the analysis as constituting the bulk of TER activity. As shown in the case of CNP certification and RGGI trading, the implementation of engagement strategies moreover tends to give rise to further layers of regulation as bonding and facilitation techniques become, themselves, subject to normalisation. Furthermore, notwithstanding the variety already on display in the five case studies, the engagement strategies they exemplify are not exhaustive. In the wider TER landscape, we also find engagement through negotiation. Regulation through negotiation and the agreement of voluntary covenants has been particularly prolific in the field of waste regulation, both at transnational and national levels.[19] In recent years, negotiation strategies have been keenly put to the test in pursuit of transnational

[15] Andrew J. Jordan, Rüdiger K. W. Wurzel & Anthony R. Zito, 'Still the Century of "New" Environmental Policy Instruments? Exploring Patterns of Innovation and Continuity' (2013) 22 (1) *Environmental Politics*, pp. 155–173, at p. 161.

[16] Light & Orts, 'Parallels', pp. 34–35.

[17] Jonathan Baert Wiener, 'Global Environmental Regulation: Instrument Choice in Legal Context' (1999) 108(4) *Yale Law Journal*, pp. 667–800, at 752.

[18] Jordan et al., 'Still the Century', p. 161.

[19] Eduardo Croci (ed.), *The Handbook of Environmental Voluntary Agreements* (2005, Springer).

conservation objectives, through the development of instruments such as conservation concessions and debt-for-nature swaps.[20]

The wide diversity of engagement strategies complicates the task of distilling a typical TER engagement profile. Moreover, it should be recalled that national environmental regulators, too, deploy an expanding range of mechanisms to foster engagement,[21] making it all the more difficult to distinguish a set of 'unique' TER engagement features. Yet some dominant traits do stand out. First, transnational environmental regulators often frame their endeavours in cooperative terms and markedly favour persuasive over mandatory language in their regulatory communications. Regulatory addressees are often 'encouraged' and 'advised' to act in accordance with regulatory prescriptions, even if the underlying intention is for the addressees to consider the provision as binding.[22] Additional dominant features of TER engagement strategies are the ubiquity of reporting requirements; labelling strategies that encourage bonding through valorisation; heavy reliance on facilitation and certification as a functional equivalent for licensing or permitting.

The most widespread TER bonding technique is the reporting requirement. Every one of the examined frameworks expects its addressees to report on their performance, and several have differentiated requirements for different groups of addressees.[23] Reporting requirements are certainly not exclusive to transnational regulation, but they do play a uniquely vital role in non-state regulatory regimes which have a limited capacity for inspection and detection of non-compliance. Reporting and failures to report offer a first, quick-and-dirty indicator of compliance. If a regulatory addressee fails to report on compliance, it is likely that substantive compliance with the regime's regulatory prescriptions, too, will be deficient. Admittedly, the reverse does not hold: regulatory addressees who report may still be non-compliant. However, reporting requirements are instrumental in enabling willing but non-compliant regulatory addressees to self-diagnose failures and work towards improvement. Moreover, even for those regulatory addressees who display a more cavalier attitude towards compliance, reporting requirements may be a game changer. Whereas failures to comply can be caused by a combination of complicating, arguably excusable factors, a failure to report the failure tends to be the result of a deliberate decision to breach. It is one thing to be considered negligent in one's

[20] Paul J. Ferraro, 'Global Habitat Protection: Limitations of Development Interventions and a Role for Conservation Performance Payments' (2001) 15(4) *Conservation Biology*, pp. 990–1000; Natasha Affolder, 'Transnational Conservation Contracts: A Primer' (2012) 106 *Proceedings of the Annual Meeting (American Society of International Law)*, pp. 508–511.

[21] See Elizabeth Fisher, Bettina Lange & Eloise Scotford, *Environmental Law: Text, Cases and Materials* (2013, Oxford University Press), pp. 491–494.

[22] This is particularly prominent in the Paris Agreement, which relies heavily on persuasive language but at the same time presents the overall target of staying within a 2° C rise as a binding target.

[23] The Paris Agreement (differentiation depending on common but differentiated responsibilities in the light of respective capacities), the FQD and the RGGI.

fulfilment of regulatory obligations, and quite another to appear fraudulent. Hence, even for less well-intentioned addressees, reporting requirements raise the stakes and may turn compliance into the lower risk, and therefore less costly, option.[24] Given TER's stronger reliance on self-diagnosis and self-disciplining, reporting requirements become the indispensable glue that binds the different stakeholders to the regulatory enterprise.

Labelling strategies, too, feature prominently as TER bonding techniques. TER labelling is often used to promote what Rieneke Slager refers to as bonding 'through valorization': the regulatory regime fosters allegiance through the creation of a brand that enables the regulated parties to capitalise on their investment in compliance.[25] The preconditions for labelling vary considerably between regimes, with the CNP requiring that regulatory addressees are vetted through an externally organised, intensive certification process and others, such as the Compact of Mayors, affording a much lighter-touch approach in the guise of self-certification. The FQD, too, deploys labelling with respect to the implementation of MMT maximum concentration limits. It should be noted, however, that the dynamics that drive MMT labelling are very different from those supporting bonding through valorisation. In the latter case, the promise of a label incentivises participation and compliance. It is therefore essentially facilitating in nature. In the FQD scenario, the regulation is legally binding and its labelling prescriptions are mandatory for all EU fuel suppliers. MMT labelling is not designed primarily to attract fuel suppliers to the regulatory framework, but instead to enable third parties to perform compliance checks and, thus to enhance the regime's capacity for learning and response. Whereas labelling to enable compliance verification is a bonding strategy relevant for state regulators and transnational regulators alike, bonding through valorisation is distinctive of transnational regulation.

A fourth point of note relates to TER's heavy reliance on facilitation strategies, and the extent to which TER regimes communicate the availability of facilitation. Facilitation infrastructure, which may result in the establishment of 'regimes within regimes' such as financial mechanisms in the Paris Agreement, the POPs Convention and the Montreal Protocol, is particularly prominent in regulatory initiatives that primarily engage with public authorities. In addition to financial mechanisms, the five case studies reveal the use of technology transfer mechanisms, transparency guarantees, staggered compliance timeframes and derogations and exemption options to facilitate regulatory compliance.

Finally, one engagement strategy which is notable by its absence is bonding through licensing or permitting; one of the staples of the national regulatory toolbox.

[24] On the relevance of disposition for compliance, see Robert Baldwin & Julia Black, 'Really Responsive Regulation' (2008) 71(1) *The Modern Law Review*, pp. 59–94.

[25] Rieneke Slager, Jean-Pascal Gond & Jeremy Moon, 'Standardization as Institutional Work: The Regulatory Power of a Responsible Investment Standard' (2012) 33(5/6) *Organization Studies*, pp. 763–790.

In the studied examples, permitting requirements only feature indirectly in the context of the RGGI, which demands that emitters participating in the inter-state trading programme are duly permitted by their respective participating state. Looking beyond the five case studies, we find a few instances of permitting requirements imposed via EU product and industrial regulation,[26] but beyond the EU zone transnational licensing and permitting schemes remain exceedingly rare. However, it should be remembered, first, that public authority regulatory addressees may implement their transnational regulatory commitments through the establishment of a licensing or permitting scheme at the national level. Secondly, while licensing and permitting are exceptional, certification as a bonding strategy is not, and it operates in a highly similar way. Both processes involve an application by the prospective licensee/certificate holder, and successful applications are typically conditional upon the submission of extensive documentation regarding the activity to be licensed/certified, as well as the payment of a fee. The application is examined by a licensing agency/certification authority, which will determine the appropriate licensing/certification conditions and decide on the application. Like licenses and permits, certificates are typically issued for a limited period of time and are subject to review. Non-compliance with the attached conditions in both cases may result in suspension or revocation of the permit/license/certificate. Undeniably, the reality that permitting and licensing bodies tend to be public authorities, whereas certification bodies usually operate in the private sphere, impacts upon both the relationship between applicant and issuing authority, and upon the enforcement tools at the latter's disposal.[27] However, such distinctions do not undermine the basic structural and operational similarities between permitting, licensing and certification. Hence, even if the former are rarely deployed in the transnational landscape, the basic dynamics of the process are alive and well by virtue of the widespread use of certification strategies in the TER sphere.

6.2.3 *Learning and Response in TER*

It is in the domain of learning and response strategies that the five case studies differ most starkly from the 'classical' model of regulation associated with command-and-control, which depends on inspection and response through penalties, threat of suspension and judicial enforcement. A first important point of note is that, while TER learning and response strategies deviate, and at times deviate significantly, from the 'base model', each of the examined regimes does have at least some mechanisms for learning and response in place. Secondly, the variation which characterises TER

[26] E.g., EU regulation requires authorisation for the use of dangerous chemicals, pesticides and GMOs. The Industrial Emissions Directive demands that regulated sectors obtain an environmental permit. See Suzanne Kingston, Veerle Heyvaert & Aleksandra Čavoški, *European Environmental Law* (2017, Cambridge University Press), pp. 321–325, 456–457 & 474–480.

[27] See Chapter 6.4.

normalisation and engagement strategies is equally present at the learning and response stages of regulation. For instance, the Compact of Mayors makes no mention of consequences of a participant city's failure to uphold the Compact's standards, whereas the threat of suspension is prominently emphasised in the European Covenant of Mayors. The RGGI explicitly disclaims enforcement authority,[28] and provides no mechanisms for participating US states to interpellate each other in the framework of the initiative. The Paris Agreement, in contrast, does affirm the availability of a dispute settlement mechanism between states, which could theoretically be deployed to address a member country's failure to abide by international regulatory prescriptions. However, in contrast to the FQD and a range of international regulations such as the Kyoto Protocol and the 1994 Protocol to the 1979 UN ECE Convention on Long-Range Transboundary Air Pollution on Further Reduction of Sulphur Emissions (1994 Sulphur Protocol),[29] it does not provide a non-compliance procedure by means of which a transnational body can hold a member country to account.[30] The CNP, finally, does not articulate any enforcement strategies, but its contractual organisation implies the existence of alternative opportunities to pursue individual compliance and deterrence.[31]

With regard to learning, the case studies bear out that transnational regulators only very exceptionally have the authority and required resources to learn through inspection. Even the FQD, which is arguably closest to the traditional model in terms of normalisation and engagement practices, is devoid of inspection powers to be assumed by a transnational regulatory authority (which most plausibly would be the European Commission). Some TER regimes introduce inspection indirectly by calling on national or local public authorities to deploy inspection in the implementation of transnational regulatory requirements. However, even this level of transnational intervention is exceptional. More frequently, the expectation is simply that implementing public authorities 'duly give effect to' TER provisions, leaving the choice of learning strategy to domestic discretion.[32] Overwhelmingly, TER regimes learn through reporting; they display a much stronger reliance on self-assessment and self-policing techniques than associated with more conventional, state-based learning. By the same token, many TER regimes build in a stronger

[28] www.rggi.org/rggi. The RGGI mission statement disclaims both enforcement and regulatory authority. For observations on the RGGI's regulatory character notwithstanding the disclaimer, see Chapter 4(1).

[29] Oslo (Norway), 14 June 1994, in force 5 Aug. 1998, available at www.unece.org/env/lrtap/fsulf_h1.html.

[30] Gunther Handl, 'Compliance Control Mechanisms and International Environmental Obligations' (1997) 5 *Tulane Journal of International and Comparative Law*, pp. 29–50; Anna Huggins, 'The Desirability of Depoliticization: Compliance in the International Climate Regime' (2015) 4(1) *Transnational Environmental Law*, pp. 101–124.

[31] But see discussion in Section 6.4.

[32] E.g., Art. 7(C)(3) FQD provides that 'Member States *shall take measures to ensure* that economic operators submit reliable information and make available to the Member State, on request, the data that were used to develop the information' (emphasis added).

expectation that regulatory addressees will address identified compliance failures themselves rather than await a regulatory response.

On the subject of response strategies, too, the TER landscape looks very different from the traditional model. Most of the studied cases do have provisions built in for systemic response, with several guaranteeing periodical reviews of the regulatory framework. As to individualised responses, the case studies *prima facie* display very limited regulatory reliance on deterrence strategies. The Paris Agreement is entirely geared towards compliance facilitation. The FQD is more deterrence-oriented, but judicial enforcement remains very much a last resort within the EU enforcement mechanism.[33] The CNP, the Compact of Mayors and the RGGI, in turn, do not articulate strategies towards individualised enforcement.

6.3 REVISITING ASSUMPTIONS ABOUT ENVIRONMENTAL REGULATION IN THE LIGHT OF REGULATORY COMPLEXITY

If not a truth universally acknowledged, it is hardly counter-intuitive to claim that regimes are more complex than their representation. Nevertheless, when it comes to TER strategies it remains important to emphasise the point because a failure to appreciate complexity can undermine attempts to understand and think critically about this new and rapidly evolving field of regulatory enterprise. Moreover, a firmer grasp on the variation and complexity of TER safeguards its students from making hasty associations and jumping to erroneous conclusions about TER's normative implications.

Thus, routine associations between 'transnational regulation', 'new governance' and 'flexibility' lure the attention towards TER's deployment of broad and principle-based standardisation, and towards the prominence of meta-standardisation, but they simultaneously obscure the equally relevant fact that a significant proportion of TER standards is moderately to highly prescriptive. Performance-based and technical standards may not dominate in transnational regulation, but neither are they absent. This goes not only for EU regulation, which is often regarded as a special case among TER regimes because of its uniquely advanced level of regulatory integration compared to other regional or international regimes,[34] but also for a large proportion of private TER.[35] Moreover, although the Paris Agreement in the case studies epitomises TER's propensity for flexible normalisation, other examples of public/

[33] Damian Chalmers, Gareth Davies & Giorgio Monti, *European Union Law*, 3rd edn. (2014, Cambridge University Press), pp. 340–342.

[34] Burkard Eberlein & Edgar Grande, 'Beyond Delegation: Transnational Regulatory Regimes and the EU Regulatory State' (2005) 12(1) *Journal of European Public Policy*, pp. 89–112, at 95.

[35] Cf. Jürgen Friedrich, *International Environmental 'Soft Law'* (2013, Springer Verlag), p. 131: '[o]ne must discard the assumption that nonbinding instruments are typically unspecific and vague. Nonbinding does not always mean soft and imprecise norms, but rather there is often a correlation between nonbinding norms and precise substance. Nonbinding instruments such as codes of conduct often contain surprisingly detailed measures'.

public, collective action TER do set precise and concrete standards with limited room for flexibility in implementation and application.[36] Hence, the flexibility of TER strategies should not be automatically assumed, but should instead be examined on a case-by-case basis.

The analysis also underlines the need for greater thoughtfulness in conceptualising the relationship between TER and incentive-based regulation. In the scholarly literature, TER regimes are readily portrayed as vehicles for incentive-based regulation, and TER's favouring of incentive-based approaches is typically explained by the assertion that these 'work' better at the transnational level than command-and-control strategies.[37] Observations made in this context frequently refer to transnational regulators' weaker claims to authority and credibility compared to their state-based counterparts, which lead them to promote approaches that promise greater efficiency in the achievement of environmental objectives, as these are less likely to encounter resistance from the private sector.[38] On this account, the promotion of incentive-based strategies is presented as a concession on the part of the transnational regulator in order to secure the cooperation of the private sector.

This account is not wrong, but neither is it complete. As it uncovers the various engagement strategies contained within transnational incentive-based instruments, targeted at different groups of regulatory addressees, an activity-based analysis of transnational regulatory processes invites us to question exactly *which* addressees are being wooed by the promise of flexibility. The cases of the RGGI and EU ETS are two of the very few regimes to introduce transnational emissions allowances. Even here, the RGGI takes pains to emphasise that the regulatory power formally resides with the state. More frequently, transnational regimes such as the Montreal or Kyoto Protocol encourage the use of incentive-based strategies at the national level, in implementation of transnational norms. The case is even more pronounced with regard to prices: barring some internal company-based initiatives,[39] there are no instances of transnational pollution or emissions prices or taxes.[40] The reason is that the creation of new entitlements, which has significant financial ramifications, as well as the levying of charges and taxes, can only be done legitimately, and in most cases lawfully, by the state. From this vantage point, TER's enthusiasm for incentive-based mechanisms can also – perhaps more convincingly – be viewed as an attempt

36 See, for instance, the Annexes to MARPOL, the Stockholm Convention and the Montreal Protocol to the Vienna Convention.

37 Jerneja Penca, 'Marketing the Market: The Ideology of Market Mechanisms for Biodiversity Conservation' (2013) 2(2) *Transnational Environmental Law*, pp. 235–257, at 240: 'Economic incentives are seen as a way of overcoming the treaty's weaknesses of very few strict obligations, absence of enforcement mechanisms, and insufficient buy-in/participation by the private sector'.

38 Robert Baldwin, 'Regulation Lite: The Rise of Emissions Trading' (2008) 2(2) *Regulation & Governance*, pp. 193–215.

39 Light & Orts, 'Parallels', pp. 34–35.

40 Wiener, 'Global Environmental Regulation', p. 684.

to get buy-in from the public regulatory addressees, rather than an attempt to get the private sector on side. The advocacy of a strategy that hinges on a high level of state involvement results in carving out a new, indispensable role for national authorities in the transnational sphere, and may therefore reconcile them to the emergence and consolidation of transnational regulatory authority. This is an aspect of TER strategising that has been underexplored so far. It might explain why, in spite of flexible mechanisms' limited success in delivering on their much vaunted superior economic efficiency,[41] there is no change in the narrative. Flexible instruments are thought to represent a shift from state to market power, but it is argued that they are also a means of keeping the state engaged and relatively empowered in TER networks.

A third set of assumptions in need of further reflection concerns the association of information-based strategies with 'light-touch' approaches.[42] A first observation regards labelling requirements. These are commonly considered non-interventionist compared to, say, binding performance-based standards because they do not constrain the addressee's behavioural choices. Under a labelling strategy, provided consumers are duly informed of the environmentally harmful properties of a dishwasher detergent or the carbon footprint of the dishwasher, both products may be lawfully marketed.[43] However, many of the labels encountered in the TER sphere are more accurately understood as brands or logos.[44] These tend to be accompanied by far more restrictive requirements than purely informative labels: regulatory addressees need to fulfil precise, at times demanding conditions prior to affixing the logo, otherwise their actions jeopardise brand credibility and risk misleading the consumer. While some logo-based approaches are reasonably relaxed, others tightly police compliance with the environmental quality standards that the brand conveys. Thus, whereas the Compact of Mayors relies on self-assessment and self-policing, companies that subscribe to the CNP must jump over a succession of hurdles before they can get certified and display the logo. Moreover, their compliance must pass through a third-party assessment and review process. Hence, the deployment of labelling strategies does not necessarily signal regulatory flexibility, let alone permissiveness. Secondly, even 'purely informative'

41 Frédéric Branger, Oskar Lecuyer & Philip Quirion, 'The European Union Emissions Trading Scheme: Should We Throw the Flagship out with the Bathwater?' (2015) 6(1) *WIREs Climate* Change, pp. 9–16; Brigitte Knopf et al., 'The European Emissions Trading System (EU ETS): Ex-Post Analysis, the Market Stability Reserve and Options for a Comprehensive Reform', 19 Sept. 2014, *FEEM Working Paper* No. 79.2014. Available at SSRN: https://ssrn.com/abstract=2499457 or http://dx.doi.org/10.2139/ssrn.

42 Christopher Taylor, Simon Pollard, Sophie Rocks & Andy Angus, 'Selecting Policy Instruments for Better Environmental Regulation: A Critique and Future Research Agenda' (2012) 22 (4) *Environmental Policy and Governance*, pp. 268–292, at 280.

43 See Andrew Jordan, Rüdiger K. W. Wurzel & Anthony R. Zito, *New Instruments of Environmental Governance?: National Experiences and Prospects* (2003, Frank Cass) p. 11.

44 Slager et al., 'Standardization as Institutional Work', p. 779, on valorising.

disclosure-based regimes may be more behaviour-constraining than they initially appear. For example, a requirement to report on environmental investment selection processes will generate a degree of pressure for such processes actually to be established within the enterprise affected, even if their presence is not formulated as a precondition for the enjoyment of other benefits.[45]

Fourthly, the outcomes of the activity-based analysis of TER strategies also invite us to revisit commonly held assumptions regarding the relation between command-and-control and private environmental regulation. The juxtaposition of command-and-control with alternative approaches to regulation is a key feature of the standard account of the evolution of environmental regulation. Since private regulation is typically grouped with the alternatives to command-and-control, it is therefore easily assumed that, as a regulatory strategy, it must be clearly different from command-and-control; it must have different approaches towards issues such as standardisation and compliance from those that characterise command-and-control. However, an activity-based analysis of the CNP shows that, but for the fact that it is private governed, the CNP shares more features with a typical command-and-control strategy than it does with TER strategies as displayed in, say, the Paris Agreement, the RGGI or the Compact of Mayors. The full content of CNP standards may not be publicly accessible, but this does not alter the fact that, from the perspective of the regulatory addressee, the CNP is a regime that deploys detailed and prescriptive normalisation.[46] The CNP's key engagement strategy is certification, which is a closer functional equivalent to the licensing and permitting regimes that epitomise 'classical' approaches to environmental regulation than the reporting and facilitating mechanisms that are so prominent in, for instance, the Paris Agreement, the Compact of Mayors and even the FQD. Finally, on the matter of individualised responses, the contractual basis of the relationship between regulator and regulatee, and the scope for suspension of CNP membership, imbue the regime with a considerable level of deterrent force.[47] Indeed, the threshold to breach a requirement set by peers, and implemented through a private network, may be higher than the threshold to disregard the commands of a public regulator. Finally, both state-based command-and-control regulation and the CNP can summon external force in the pursuit of compliance – police force and court action for state regulation; consumer power and adjudication or arbitration in contractual litigation for the CNP. When we compare the characteristics of the CNP's regulatory strategy to the features of command-and-control as retold through the activity-based analysis,[48] the overlap becomes clear. Again, the message is that it is important not to

[45] Cf. Light & Orts, 'Parallels', pp. 43–44.

[46] Ibid., p. 29.

[47] See Jacco Bomhoff & Anne Meuwese, 'The Meta-regulation of Transnational Private Regulation' (2011) 38(1) *Journal of Law and Society*, pp. 138–162, at 150.

[48] See Chapter 4. 4.

collapse expectations and treat all instances of governance beyond the state as similar and therefore likely to confront similar problems and require similar responses.

6.4 RETHINKING COMPLIANCE AND DETERRENCE IN THE TRANSNATIONAL SPHERE

There is a broad consensus in the literature and among practitioners that a key difference between transnational regulation and 'conventional' state-based regulation, as epitomised in the command-and-control model or its reconstruction through an activity-based lens,[49] resides in the extent to which regulators can compel their addressees to comply with regulatory prescriptions. National regulatory authorities can tap into the coercive apparatus of the state and marshal state policing powers and courts to the end of enforcing their commands. Transnational authorities must instead rely on the intermediacy of national authorities or devise alternative mechanisms to secure compliance.[50] It is because of this key difference that transnational regulatory regimes are often considered weaker or 'softer' than national regulation and, consequently, both less prestigious and less threatening to individual freedom.

A review of the learning and response stages in the case studies indeed confirms that deterrence measures such as financial penalties and court orders, which are strongly associated with the enforcement of state regulation, are exceedingly rare in the transnational sphere. Of the different TER regimes analysed, EU environmental regulation (as exemplified in the FQD) emerges as bearing the closest resemblance to the national enforcement model. In its relation with Member States as regulatory addressees, the FQD comes equipped with the means for judicial enforcement, backed up with the threat of financial penalties, via the Articles 258 to 260 TFEU infringement procedure. However, enforcement vis-à-vis private parties, such as fuel suppliers in the framework of the FQD, hinges on cooperation at the national level: EU institutions must rely on national governments establishing and putting into effect the necessary institutions to secure compliance and deter non-compliance. The European Commission can hold Member States legally accountable for a failure to effectively enforce EU regulatory requirements, and indeed it has done so in various instances in matters concerning EU environmental regulation,[51] but its opportunities to respond to private and individual breaches of EU regulation are extremely curtailed.

If the pathways towards direct enforcement are more limited for EU regulation than state regulation, they are even further restricted for other, non-EU forms of

49 Ibid.

50 Abram Chayes & Antonia Handler Chayes, 'Compliance without Enforcement: State Behavior under Regulatory Treaties' (1991) 7(3) *Negotiation Journal*, pp. 311–330, at 312.

51 Kingston et al., *European Environmental Law*, pp. 186–200.

TER. The activity-based analysis shows that non-EU TER is relatively lighter on learning and response strategies and typically presents without those design and operationalisation choices that are associated with deterrence. Self-assessment is far more prominent in TER regimes than inspection; transnational regulators rarely have the right or ability to impose penalties and vindicate them via judicial prosecution. The five case studies in the preceding chapter fully conform to this picture.

However, while corroborating the core message, the activity-based analysis also urges us to ask further questions. First, not all TER regimes are weak on deterrence to the same degree, or in the same way. We recall from the discussion in Section 6.2.3 that, notwithstanding the impending merger between the Compact of Mayors and the European Covenant of Mayors into the 'Global Compact', the former does not allude to any consequences for breach, whereas the latter explicitly emphasises the threat of suspension. The Paris Agreement incorporates the UNFCCC's dispute settlement mechanism between states, whereas the RGGI provides no avenue for participating US states to challenge each other in the framework of the initiative. The Paris Agreement does not include non-compliance procedures by means of which a transnational body can hold a member country to account; the FQD does. The CNP does not articulate any individual enforcement strategies.

The CNP example yields a second important lesson: the absence of an explicit reference to compliance and deterrence mechanisms should not be confused with their non-existence. Indeed, to take the CNP's reticence on individualised enforcement as a sign of weakness would be to overlook the dense contractual networks that connect the Protocol, certifiers, auditors and clients to the regulatory regime, and the concomitant opportunities for arbitral or judicial vindication of contractual breaches. Moreover, it would ignore the leverage created through processes of accreditation and certification: the threat of losing one's certificate or CNP accreditation, with the reputational costs this entails, may be a more decisive incentive for compliance than a fine levied by a national environmental authority. In sum, blanket assumptions regarding the enforcement strength of TER, even if the relatively more forceful nature of EU environmental regulation is accounted for, underplay the variation in enforcement choices, opportunities and effectiveness between different TER regimes.

Thirdly, strength in deterrence is often taken to equate effectiveness in regulation. More frequent inspections, and a credible threat of stiff sanctions for breach, are deemed to translate into higher levels of regulatory compliance. However, if strong deterrence has a positive influence on effectiveness,[52] it does not necessarily follow

[52] See, e.g., Wayne B. Gray & Jay P. Shimshack, 'The Effectiveness of Environmental Monitoring and Enforcement: A Review of the Empirical Evidence' (2011) 5(1) *Review of Environmental Economics and Policy*, pp. 3–24. They identify a positive correlation between investment in inspection and enforcement and regulatory compliance, yet at the same time underline the need for further research in relative effectiveness of enforcement versus alternative compliance strategies.

that weak deterrence results in ineffective regulation. Arguably, the overall 'compliance pull' of regulation is determined by factors including but not limited to deterrence. On the basis of a recent, large-scale empirical study, Christine Parker and Vibeke Lehman Nielsen identify no fewer than fourteen factors that affect compliance.[53] Six are related to deterrence,[54] but the majority of identified compliance factors refer to conditions that may be equally present in so-called weaker regulatory regimes.[55] Moreover, a review of Parker and Nielsen's list of fourteen reveals potential tensions between deterrence-related and non-deterrence factors. For example, the severity of a prospective sanction may deter non-compliance, but if experienced as draconian it could negatively influence the regulatory addressee's respect for the regulator, their acceptance of the regulation and, even, their respect for the law in general. For these reasons, and considering TER's observed high level of investment in engagement strategies, it would be mistaken to automatically equate the absence or scarcity of deterrence mechanisms characteristic of TER with lack of enforcement or, relatedly, regulatory ineffectiveness.

Fourthly, in order to fully understand the relative strength of TER compliance mechanisms, we need to take into account the particular identity of the players and the particular context in which TER unfolds. The point has been persuasively made by Robert Baldwin and Julia Black that a command that strikes the fear of god into a well-intentioned regulatory addressee with limited capacity may be received with relative insouciance by an ill-intentioned, highly capable party.[56] As to the importance of context, the deterrent force of, for instance, membership suspension from a voluntary regulatory scheme depends not only on the intentions and capacity of the member involved, but also on how such measure is likely to be perceived by parties that are in a position of influence vis-à-vis the suspended member, such as shareholders, insurers and consumers.

When the identity of the addressees and the context in which transnational regulatory enforcement unfolds are taken into consideration, the complexity of evaluating transnational regulatory compliance and the wide gaps in our knowledge come into stark relief. A first key point of note is that TER regulatory addressees are often public authorities, from national governments to city councils, or a

[53] Christine Parker & Vibeke Lehmann Nielsen, 'Compliance: 14 Questions' in Peter Drahos (ed.), *Regulatory Theory: Foundations and Applications* (2017, The Australian National University Press), pp. 217–232.

[54] Ibid. The six deterrence-related factors are: 1) risk that any violations of the rules will be reported to the authorities; 2) risk of inspection; 3) risk of detection; 4) selectivity of inspection and detection by the regulator; 5) risk of sanction and 6) severity of sanction.

[55] Ibid. The remaining compliance factors are: 1) the social and economic costs and benefits of the regulation; 2) degree of acceptance of the regulation; 3) respect for the law in general; 4) existence of non-official influence over the targeted group's compliance; 5) relevance of compliance to the target group's business model; 6) knowledge of the rules; 7) capacity to comply and 8) respect for the regulator.

[56] Baldwin & Black, 'Really Responsive Regulation'.

combination of public and private actors. It is eminently conceivable that public authorities respond in a different way to compliance and deterrence stimuli than private actors. Consequently, the coercive force or 'strength' of a particular response mechanism may vary depending on whether it engages with the public or private sector. For example, having a bad compliance track record published may be a far more shaming and discrediting experience for an environment agency which is supposed to act in the public interest, uphold standards of good governance and ensure environmental compliance, than it is for a private enterprise which is expected to put business considerations above environmental concerns. Conversely, private actors whose success or failure hinges on their customers staying loyal to the brand may be more vulnerable to suspension from a voluntary scheme than a public actor would be in a comparable situation. Constituents and members of the public typically have limited means at their disposal to convey their displeasure vis-à-vis the city council, the environment agency or the national government. There is an urgent need for further investigation and empirical research to create a better understanding of the relative responsiveness of different categories of addressees in the TER sphere to different enforcement techniques, so that a better grounded appreciation of the relative forcefulness of transnational compliance and deterrence regimes is enabled.

By the same token, an evaluation of the compliance and deterrence capacity of TER needs to fully engage with the networked structure of transnational regulation. As with the distinction between public and private body addressees of TER, preliminary indications on the impact of the network structure either weakening or amplifying the force of regulatory response mechanisms point in different directions. On the one hand, the regulatory complexity that characterises multilevel governance structures is frequently considered to have a diluting impact on the authoritative force of the regulatory framework. This is because of diffusion of accountability within the regulatory network,[57] and because the remoteness of enforcing authorities from the rule-making powers exacerbates the risk of errors in the interpretation and implementation of transnational regulatory communications.[58] Moreover, institutional disconnection between the stages of goal setting, normalisation, engagement, learning and response might strip the various decision makers involved of a sense of ownership and investment in the regulatory regime, which could erode their willingness to pursue compliance and enforce effectively. Yet on the other hand, the interdependence between different actors with regulatory responsibilities, whether in the context of multilevel governance or between a network of standard setters, certifiers, auditors and verifiers, equally multiplies lines of accountability.

[57] Julia Black, 'Constructing and Contesting Legitimacy and Accountability in Polycentric Regulatory Regimes' (2008) 2(2) *Regulation & Governance*, pp. 137–164.

[58] Andrew Jordan, 'The Implementation of EU Environmental Policy: A Policy Problem without a Political Solution?' (1999) 17 *Environment and Planning C: Government and Policy*, pp. 69–90.

Underperformance by one player in a transnational regulation chain may tarnish the reputation of the regime as a whole, which significantly raises the stakes for all involved.[59] Just as standard setting by reference may boost the credibility of external standardisation bodies, their standards becoming associated with sub-par implementation in practice may have a discrediting effect. Mutual interdependence might therefore increase the regime's commitment towards achieving effective compliance. Here too, further research is required to obtain a richer understanding of the connection between the networked structure of TER and its capacity to ensure compliance.

A final issue regarding which current knowledge gaps prevent a full evaluation of the strengths and limits of TER enforcement concerns the effectiveness of non-judicial pathways to third-party enforcement. Domestic courts are rarely defied. Hence, the ability to operate in the shadow of judicial enforcement imbues national regulatory communications with considerable force. The relationship between national courts and transnational regulators, on the other hand, is far less robust. In many cases, the path towards national judicial enforcement will be foreclosed, particularly when the non-compliant party is a public rather than a private actor. A domestic court could not entertain, say, a complaint instigated by a UN or UN-affiliated body against a signatory of the Paris Agreement for failure to meet the Agreement's regulatory requirements. Alternatively, in the context of multilevel governance, transnational regulators must rely on the willingness of local authorities to marshal the power of the courts vis-à-vis private addressees. The FQD includes several requirements that directly affect the private sector, yet any enforcement action before a national court must be initiated by national authorities, not the European Commission. Finally, some transnational regulators may have recourse to national civil courts by virtue of the contractual nature of the relationship between regulator and regulatee, yet the dearth of case law suggests that this pathway remains overwhelmingly unexplored.

The reputation for effectiveness of national judicial enforcement, combined with the limited availability of judicial pathways for TER enforcement, naturally helps to consolidate the assumption that TER enforcement is relatively weak. However, it is important to remember that, whereas we have solid information on the success of courts as third-party enforcers of regulatory requirements, less is known about the success rate of other third-party enforcers. Subscribers to the UN Global Compact for Multinational Enterprises (MNE), for example, cannot be sued for breach of the Compact's voluntary standards, but they do submit to internal review and mediation processes to address alleged instances of non-compliance.[60] Similarly, the absence

[59] Randy Starr, Jim Newfrock & Michael Delurey, 'Enterprise Resilience: Managing Risk in the Networked Economy' (2005) *Strategy and Business*, pp. 1–11, at 5, available at http://theicor.org/art/present/art/ARORRM00030.pdf.

[60] Friedrich, *International Environmental 'Soft Law'*, pp. 347–353.

of court judgements policing the contractual relations between private regulators and their regulatees may indicate deficient enforcement, but it could also be explained by a preference for the more discrete alternative of arbitration. Moreover, for those transnational regimes that govern the environmental performance of products and services suppliers, the court of public opinion may be as effective a third-party enforcer as a more conventional judicial body. Here, again, further research is needed to fully gauge the extent and force of non-judicial third-party enforcement in TER.

6.5 CONCLUDING REMARKS

To understand TER, it is essential to have a firm grip on the strategies through which transnational regulation is operationalised. The past three chapters have built up such understanding by, first, exploring the landscape of TER strategies by means of the familiar categorisations of 'command-and-control and alternatives'. This standard account was then enriched by analysing TER from an activity-based perspective, which organises regulation into recursive sets of activities in support of goal setting, normalisation, engagement, learning, and response. Applied to a sample of five transnational regulatory initiatives concerning climate change, the activity-based analysis yielded a range of important insights, some of which were more predictable and others less expected. Three important lessons to take from the analysis are that, first, at the transnational level, institutional interdependence is an essential feature of regulatory design. This analytical realisation has important implications for normative assessments because it means the strength or weakness of a transnational regulatory measure cannot be understood in isolation. Instead, it must be evaluated taking into account its functioning as part of a network of regulatory activity.

Secondly, the analysis confirmed the widely held assumption that TER regimes rely heavily on broadly framed, procedural and principle-based approaches to standardisation. At the same time, however, it put the spotlight on two normalisation strategies that are extremely prominent across TER case studies but are thus far relatively underexplored. Standardisation by reference, which further harnesses the network features of TER, and methodological standardisation, which can considerably shape and even limit the decision-making discretion typically associated with flexible approaches to normalisation, emerge as key features of TER strategies. To enhance our understanding of the dynamics of TER normalisation, standardisation by reference and methodological standardisation should become a focal point in further studies.

Finally, the activity-based analysis injects much-needed nuance into discussions of the enforceability of TER. Mapping out the wealth of engagement mechanisms, learning techniques and response options available to transnational regulators helps to highlight the multi-dimensional character of transnational enforceability. It underscores that the compulsive quotient of regulatory communications depends on more than the legal or alternative form in which they are expressed. It is equally affected by factors such as type of regulatory addressee involved, the visibility of (non) compliance, and the presence or absence of non-judicial third-party enforcers. The forcefulness of TER is rarely reducible to the sum of its expressly articulated individualised responses, and therefore easily underestimated. As a response to the question of TER enforcement, this message arguably serves as a double-edged sword. On the one hand, it affirms TER's potential to make a meaningful contribution to environmental protection by effectively influencing and steering the behaviour of its regulatory addressees towards relatively greener practices. On the other hand, it cautions against blithe assumptions that, as TER is rarely backed up by traditional administrative and judicial enforcement mechanisms, it is therefore mostly harmless and benign. With power comes responsibility, and thus, the need for TER regimes to be effectively governed. This opens up the question of TER's relation to law and to governance principles. The next two chapters explore both issues in greater detail.

7

Transnational Environmental Regulation and the Challenge to Law

So far, our explorations into the identity of TER have focused on the intentionality of TER and on the strategies through which TER is pursued. In the third and final segment of this study, we turn our attention to the relationship between TER and law. In Chapter 7, the argument is developed that, just as the transnationalisation of regulation prompts a reconceptualisation of the concept of regulation, it also compels us to reflect anew on the meaning and attributes of law. Chapter 8, then, delves into the normative content of TER through a discussion of proposed and emerging legal principles for TER governance.

An examination of the impact of TER on the concept of law necessarily requires the establishment of some core assumptions of what 'law' means outside the context of the particular transnational challenges which will be examined in this chapter. As briefly discussed in Chapter 2, the notion which constitutes the starting point of reference is that of law as a specific form of authoritative communication, which can be distinguished from other, non-legal forms of authoritative communication by means of a stable set of conventions.[1] It is roundly acknowledged that this is *an account* of law rather than the incontestable truth about law, and that alternative perspectives on the meaning of law have and continue to be developed. However, for the purpose of this investigation, the account has been chosen because it represents, in my opinion, the most influential and mainstream conception of law, which tacitly underscores a critical mass of legal writing.

The stable conventions (or, in a Hartian vein, the rules of recognition) by means of which societies distinguish legal from non-legal forms of authoritative communication are not immutable, but in contemporary constitutional regimes they are closely tied to the premise that, in order to be 'really law', authoritative communications must derive their authority either directly or indirectly from a constitutional basis. Law, in this particularised, late-modernity constitutionalised iteration, has a

[1] See Chapter 2.1.

number of pronounced qualities or 'attributes'. This chapter identifies and focuses on five dominant attributes which inform mainstream understandings of what law is and how it works in contemporary society: its territoriality; its emanation from the state; its organisation into a public and a private sphere; its constitutive, regulative and communicative functions; and its cohesive and regimented structure. It will be argued that the rise of transnational regulation problematises each of these conceptualisations and, ultimately, calls into question the continued reliability of the very conventions that serve to distinguish law from other forms of authoritative communication. This development, as a consequence, invites reflection on the appropriate response to law's conceptual crisis in the wake of TER. I refer to this process of problematisation, contestation and response as the 'transnationalisation of law'.

7.1 TER AND THE CHALLENGE TO LAW ILLUSTRATED

Transnational environmental regulatory initiatives cause legal complexity. Consider, for instance, the intricate legal and regulatory context in which the Covenant of Mayors for Climate and Energy operates. The Covenant, we recall, is a climate change initiative to which many of Europe's major cities voluntarily subscribe. It is administered by the Covenant of Mayors Office (COMO), which is established and funded by the European Commission. Participating towns and cities must develop a baseline emission inventory and are required to submit a Sustainable Energy Action Plan (SEAP), which maps out the different approaches and policies that they intend to implement to achieve the minimum 20% CO_2 emissions reduction target by 2020. Additionally, participating towns and cities are expected to submit regular implementation reports.[2] Failure to meet the membership criteria can negatively impact a city's access to the funding opportunities created within the framework of the Covenant, and may result in their membership being suspended.

Which legal regime governs the relation between the Commission, the COMO and the signatory towns and cities? The answer is supremely challenging. The official text of the Covenant gives no indication as to applicable law;[3] nor does the adhesion form that town and city councils are requested to sign as a confirmation of their intent to join.[4] Should such determination need to be made, several jurisdictions could credibly vie for the spot. At the very least, a claim could be made for the relations between Covenant parties to be governed by EU law, or Belgian law (the law of the jurisdiction in which the European Commission and the COMO are located), or the law of the country in which the town or city concerned is located.

[2] Veerle Heyvaert, 'What's in a Name? The Covenant of Mayors as Transnational Environmental Regulation' (2013) 22(1) *Review of European, Comparative & International Environmental Law*, pp. 78–90, at 81.

[3] Information available at www.eumayors.eu/IMG/pdf/covenantofmayors_text_en.pdf.

[4] See www.eumayors.eu/support/library_en.html.

Either choice creates different advantages and limitations. A choice for EU law would reflect the relevance of both EU institutions in the scheme and of EU legal commitments as the key reference points to determine the minimum aspirations that Covenant members agree to embrace in the fight against climate change. On the other hand, it would arguably defeat the deliberate establishment of the Covenant outside the institutional apparatus of the EU. It might be seen to favour EU-based participating cities over participants from outside the European Union, and it would subject the Covenant to a legal regime that has less experience in both judicial review and adjudicating contractual relationships than national legal systems. This may not be the best choice for the governance of such complex, multi-partite relationships.

Alternatively, the Brussels location of both the European Commission and the COMO point towards Belgian law. This choice shares with the previous one the advantage of consistency in that all relations under the Covenant would be reviewed against the same legal standards, without suffering from the relative paucity of experience that characterises EU law. On the other hand, the choice is highly formalistic and could produce inefficient, artificial and potentially unfair results. The prospect that, say, a disagreement between an Italian funding body and an Italian town or city would be shoehorned into the Belgian jurisdiction purely because the facilitating bodies are formally established there, is unattractive. This is all the more so since the connection between these facilitating bodies and the Belgian state is, itself, tenuous. Yet reverting to the law of the country in which the parties involved in the proceedings are located, would lead to both legal fragmentation and considerable complexity, as various authorities in different countries could stamp their own, disparate interpretations on the legal arrangements under the Covenant and the ensuing rights and responsibilities.

The choice of law challenges represented by the Covenant extend beyond the determination of the governing regime, and include the identification of the appropriate legal discipline. It is by no means clear whether any conflict between, for instance, the COMO and a signatory city regarding the former's decision to suspend membership rights is contractual, administrative or even tort-based in nature. If the Covenant is treated as a regulatory regime, the first option seems appropriate. However, the voluntary nature of membership, with no overt scope for administrative sanctions beyond exclusion from the club for non-adherence to club rules, makes the case for contract law. From a formalistic angle, the unilateral commitment structure of the Covenant might argue in favour of treating any disagreement between parties as being of a private but non-contractual nature.

These reflections convey a first impression of the destabilising impact of transnational regulatory activity on assumptions about legal governance. But the examples still underplay the potentially disruptive impact of TER on the very concept and content of law. Law, in the preceding example, refers to the pre-existing governance regime under which the Covenant resorts. The latter is portrayed, for all intents and purposes, as the passive subject that undergoes law and adjudication. Yet if we embrace the notion that the Covenant produces behaviour that is at least in part regulatory, then the question emerges whether it still makes sense to treat the authoritative communications emanating from this regulator as something other than law, whereas those of many other regulators *do* form part of the corpus of law.[5] The similarity in organisation, content and authority between the Covenant's communications and, say, the 20% emissions reduction target in EU law cast a shadow on the rationality of the conventions deployed to distinguish law from non-law and open the prospect of the Covenant as not only a subject but also a source of law. Hence, the Covenant does not merely operate in an intricate legal context; it arguably also creates an intricate legal context.[6] Transnational, decentred regulation thus co-produces transnational, decentred law. Moreover, this transnationalisation of law calls into question the usefulness of many of the attributes that we now conventionally associate with law and that are used to reinforce the distinction between law and non-law, such as its territoriality and its emanation from the state.[7]

7.2 MAPPING THE IMPACTS OF TRANSNATIONAL ENVIRONMENTAL REGULATION ON THE CONVENTIONAL ATTRIBUTES OF LAW

The following sections offer a framework for organising and discussing the transnationalisation of law. It is argued that, in order to understand the breadth and richness of reactions to the rise of TER, account must be taken of its impact on assumptions regarding the location, the sources, the organisation, the functions and the structure of law. The framework enables us to map the range of challenges to law encapsulated in the emergence of transnational regulation. This, in turn, fosters appreciation of the different and often divergent reactions to the transnationalisation of law, which are reviewed in the third part of this chapter.

7.2.1 *Location: Transnational Environmental Regulation and the 'End of Geography'*

Law is an intensely territorial concept. Laws emanate from the city, the state, the empire, and hold sway within – and only within – the geographical zone that falls

5 For example, the decisions of the Conference of the Parties adopted under the auspices of international treaties are considered part of international law. See Robin R. Churchill & Geir Ulfstein, 'Autonomous Institutional Arrangements in Multilateral Environmental Agreements: A Little-Noticed Phenomenon in International Law' (2000) 94(4) *American Journal of International Law*, pp. 623–659.

6 Cf. Roger Cotterrell, 'What Is Transnational Law' (2012) 37(2) *Law & Social Inquiry*, pp. 500–524, at 515; Karl-Heinz Ladeur, 'The Evolution of General Administrative Law and the Emergence of Postmodern Administrative Law' (March 21, 2011). Osgoode CLPE Research Paper No. 16/2011. Available at SSRN: http://ssrn.com/abstract=1792062 or http://dx.doi.org/10.2139/ssrn.1792062, p. 3, 8.

7 Cf. Cotterrell, 'What Is Transnational Law', pp. 512 & 515; Peer Zumbansen, 'Transnational Private Regulatory Governance: Ambiguities of Public Authority and Private Power' (2013) 76(2) *Law & Contemporary Problems*, pp. 117–138, at 130–131.

TABLE 7.1 *Impact of Transnationalisation on Key Attributes of Law*

	Conventional context	Transnational context
Location	Territorial	De-localised
Source	Based in or derived from the state	Plural
Organisation	Public and private law	Inchoate
Functions	Constitutive, regulatory, communicative	Cognitive, reflexive, coordinative
Structure	Cohesive and regimented	Polycentric

under the governing bodies' control, a zone bordered by physical and frequently contested frontiers. The intimacy of the bond between government, territory and law resonates in the notion of 'jurisdiction', which means both the official power to make legal decisions and judgements, and the territory over which legal authority extends. The exclusivity of the relationship is encapsulated in our understanding of legal sovereignty, which represents the entitlement to legal autonomy and self-determination and 'rests fundamentally on the notion of exclusive authority over discrete parcels of territory'.[8] Indeed, the very notion of independent statehood signifies a successful claim to a connection between a governance regime, a physical territory and its population. This connection conveys the entitlement to militarily defend the territory, to levy taxes within the territory, to issue laws for the territory and enter into international agreements on behalf of the territory.[9]

The rise of transnational regulation threatens the bond between law and geography in two ways. First, it is difficult to locate transnational actors in a particular jurisdiction; they do not have a 'seat' of authority in the way that state regulators do. Secondly, there is no clearly demarcated field of application of the normative content they produce. For private environmental standard setters, for example, the size of their field of application depends entirely on the successful uptake of the standards.

The challenges that TER poses to law and geography are particularly pressing with regard to transnational regulatory activity that takes place outside the auspices of a pre-established supra- or international legal framework. Unless they restrict their membership and field of action explicitly to a single state, private environmental regulators are genuinely and doubly de-localised. As illustrated in the Covenant of Mayors example, there is no obvious candidate jurisdiction in which to ground regulatory behaviour that occurs in a transnational network. Often, there will be no legal discipline that can claim undisputed governance over the relations that unfold within the network.[10] Secondly, the normative content that is generated through the

8 See Daniel Bethlehem, 'The End of Geography: The Changing Nature of the International System and the Challenge to International Law' (2014) 25(1) *European Journal of International Law*, pp. 9–24, at 13.

9 Ibid., pp. 13–14.

10 Cf. Joost Pauwelyn, Ramses A. Wessel & Jan Wouters, *Informal International Lawmaking* (2012, Oxford University Press), p. 2.

transnational network is, itself, de-localised. The Forest Stewardship Council (FSC) does not create American, Japanese or French sustainable forestry standards; it produces FSC sustainable forestry standards. If the FSC standards are treated as transnational law,[11] then this is indeed law that has sprung up in the absence of claims to territory and sovereignty. In the context of the OECD Guidelines for Multinational Enterprises,[12] de-localisation was a deliberate strategy: until 2000, the OECD Guidelines were addressed only to the multinational enterprises situated within OECD countries. However, this territorial reference has since been removed and enterprises from adhering countries are now exhorted to adhere to OECD standards 'wherever they operate'.[13]

Transnational regulation developed in implementation of regional or international legal frameworks, such as pollutant emission limit values adopted under the EU Industrial Emissions Directive[14] or decisions to include further species in the endangered lists annexed to the CITES Convention,[15] are comparatively less problematic. The geographical reach of such regional and international regulatory measures formally corresponds to the territory of the signatory states, which functions as an expanded field of jurisdiction. Nevertheless, in this context, too, challenges arise. They are perhaps less acute than those created by the rise of private transnational regulation, but they are certainly not negligible. In the EU, tensions arise because of a perennial need to mediate competing claims to territorial exclusivity. At the international level, in turn, the relevance of territoriality is significantly eroded by the growing complexity of international decision making and the dearth of international administrative law. The following paragraphs explain each point in turn.

In the EU context, the growth of a level of legal authority that geographically overlaps that of the Member States has put enormous pressure on domestic conceptions of the relation between law, territory and sovereignty.[16] Many of the landmark European constitutional cases of the past decade reflect, precisely, a preoccupation to reconceptualise or reclaim sovereignty over the national 'parcel of territory' in the

[11] Ibid.

[12] See http://mneguidelines.oecd.org/about/.

[13] As reported in Jürgen Friedrich, *International Environmental 'Soft Law'* (2013, Springer Verlag), p. 109.

[14] Directive 2010/75/EU on industrial emissions (integrated pollution prevention and control) [2010] OJ L334/17.

[15] Convention on International Trade in Endangered Species of 29 Wild Fauna and Flora (CITES), Washington, DC (US), 3 Mar. 1973, in force 1 July 1975, available at www.cites.org/eng/disc/text.php.

[16] Chris Thornhill, 'National Sovereignty and the Constitution of Transnational Law: A Sociological Approach to a Classical Antinomy' (2013) 3(4) *Transnational Legal Theory*, pp. 394–460, at 406; Armin von Bogdandy & Stephan Schill, 'Overcoming Absolute Primacy: Respect for National Identity under the Lisbon Treaty' (2011) 48(1) *Common Market Law Review*, pp. 1–38; Nico Krisch, 'Who Is Afraid of Radical Pluralism? Legal Order and Political Stability in the Postnational Space' (2011) 24(4) *Ratio Juris*, pp. 386–412 at 407.

face of competing claims from a centralised, de-localised legal authority.[17] In the EU context, the rise of transnational regulation has not resulted in the absence of geography but has generated competing claims to territorial sovereignty which, from a different vantage point but with equal urgency, call for a reconsideration of mainstream assumptions regarding the relation between law and geography.

Regulatory measures adopted under the auspices of international treaties put relatively less pressure on domestic claims to territorial sovereignty because their authority is typically contingent on ex-post state validation. Yet at the international level, too, the bond between law and geography is increasingly strained. A first contributing factor to de-localisation is the growing institutional complexity of international regulatory and administrative decision making. Consider, for example, the approval of CDM projects under Article 12 of the Kyoto Protocol. For such approval to come about, at least three different entities need to make affirmative decisions: the Designated National Authority (DNA), which approves the participant's project proposal and forwards the project for validation; the Designated Operational Entity (DOE), a private third-party certifier who validates the project, and the CDM Executive Board (CDM EB), which registers and thereby formally accepts a validated project as a CDM project activity.[18] Given the geographical spread of DNAs, DOEs and the CDM EB, it is difficult to anchor the set of decisions that culminates in CDM approval within a particular jurisdiction. A potential determination that, ultimately, the decision is taken in furtherance of the Kyoto Protocol and that, therefore, its jurisdiction corresponds to the combined territory of the signatory states, does not offer a genuine resolution. The public international law regime is arguably too limited on administrative principles and standards to effectively govern CDM decision making.[19] Resorting to the administrative law bodies of the signatory states instead is equally problematic, because these bodies differ from state to state. Hence, CDM decisions are floating entities: they are disconnected from the national level without having been fully relocated in the international sphere. The need for their governability pushes policy makers and commentators to look beyond the traditional realms of national and international treaty law for legal disciplines, or nascent disciplines, to deliver guidance.[20]

In sum, the intensity and precise nature of the challenge differs, but all main variants of TER cause a degree of de-localisation of law.

[17] 2 BVerfGE 2/08 *Treaty of Lisbon*, Judgment of 30 June 2009 (German Constitutional Court); BVerfGE 37, 271 2 BvL 52/71 (Solange I-Beschluß); K 32/09 *Treaty of Lisbon*, Judgment of 24 Sept. 2010) Polish Constitutional Court)' Pl. US 5/12: *Slovak Pensions*, Judgment of 31 Jan. 2012 (Czech Constitutional Court).

[18] Moon Jung Kang & Jihyoun Park, 'Analysis of the Partnership Network in the Clean Development Mechanism' (2013) 52 *Energy Policy*, pp. 543–553, at 543.

[19] See further Chapter 8.2.3.

[20] The potential legal disciplines explored in this context are discussed in Chapter 8.

7.2.2 *Source: Transnational Environmental Regulation and the Triple Challenge to the State*

Stronger even than the link with physical territory is the connection between law and the concept of the state. The nineteenth and twentieth centuries, in equal parts celebrated and denounced as the heyday of the nation-state, witnessed the consolidation of the trinity of state government, legislature and judiciary as a dominant, even exclusive source of law. In the third millennium, in contrast, the exclusivity – even the dominance – of the state as source of law is under threat.[21]

The proliferation after World War II of public international law in policy fields outside the traditional zones of international relations, including environmental protection, introduced a greater degree of diversity in recognised sources of law. However, this development did not yet genuinely call into question the centrality of the state because international legal authority is understood as derived from state authority.[22] *States* sign up to international agreements. *States* agree to recognise the competence of international courts and tribunals. *State* law and practice are the key benchmarks for the recognition of customary international law. Instead of constituting a threat, public international law validates the state as the inescapable, original source of law.

The arrival on the scene of the European Union as a source of law within the European region, on the other hand, heralded a more challenging proposition. The extent to which the exercise of legal authority at the EU level is reducible to the (member) state is a topic of endless examination and contestation. This is not the place to discuss the range of positions in this rich and ever evolving debate. It suffices to say that, to many participants in the debate, the representation of EU law as an affirmation of its Member States' prerogative to enter into international binding agreements, which therefore shores up the legal sovereignty of the state, strains the limits of credibility. Arguably, such representation overlooks the role of key players, such as the European Commission and the European Parliament, that are not accountable to the state.[23] It ignores the existence of majority voting among Member States.[24] It does not account for the enormous issue-interdependence and complexity of EU decision making, which easily reduces Member State day-to-day

[21] Thornhill, 'National Sovereignty and the Constitution of Transnational Law', p. 406.

[22] Brütsch & Lehmkuhl, *Law and Legalization*, pp. 22–23; Joseph H. H. Weiler, 'The Geology of International Law – Governance, Democracy and Legitimacy', (2003) 63 *Zeitschrift für ausländisches öffentliches Recht und Völkerrecht*, pp. 547–562, at 553–556.

[23] Antonis A. Ellinas & Ezra N. Suleiman, 'Supranationalism in a Transnational Bureaucracy: The Case of the European Commission' (2011) 49(5) *Journal of Common Market Studies*, pp. 923–947; Erik Oddvar Eriksen & John Erik Fossum (eds.), *Democracy in the European Union. Integration through Deliberation* (Routledge, 2002), p. 4.

[24] Cf. Stephen C. Sieberson, 'Inching towards EU Supranationalism? Qualified Majority Voting and Unanimity under the Treaty of Lisbon' (2010) 50(4) *Virginia Journal of International Law*, pp. 919–996, at 926–932.

self-determination to a purely theoretical possibility.[25] To a more significant extent than public international law, EU law worries at the fabric of state-centred conceptualisations of law and legality. Its existence calls into question prevalent iterations of the rule of recognition which inexorably lead back to the constitutional authority of the state.

The proliferation of transnational regulation intensifies this challenge in several ways. First, the provenance of the rules that are deemed to govern much of transnational regulatory activity is unclear. This is definitely the case for private transnational regulation, which typically has no obviously identifiable 'home jurisdiction'. But it is also the case for transnational regulation under the auspices of international legal instruments, because neither these instruments nor public international law are rich on legal provisions that are, essentially, administrative in nature. It is therefore not surprising that discussions on the legality and legitimacy of TER, for example, often refer to abstract notions of, e.g., accountability or transparency without clarifying which legal regime's rendition of accountability or transparency is targeted.[26] They seemingly operate on the assumed existence of an inchoate, common conception of the meaning of administrative standards, but it is rarely made explicit where this common conception comes from and what it consists of.[27] Karl-Heinz Ladeur recognises this and advocates the development of an experimental, inductive approach to the production of a new administrative legality: 'Particular emphasis should be placed on the question of the "sources" of the emerging regulatory order. Arguably, the new relational "rationality of networks" can no longer be regarded as being "deposited" in a canonical (legal) text; instead, legal meaning must be generated from several overlapping texts and contexts of practice in an experimental approach that comprises both the domestic and the transnational realms'.[28]

The reference to 'contexts of practice', which are treated as (co-)constitutive of legal normativity, is a reminder that TER does not only frustrate conventional understandings of the attributes of law in its guise as a problematic subject of law, but also as a potential source of law. It thus raises the prospect of a source of law which is emphatically not traceable to the state. Hence, the legal content produced by transnational environmental regulators does not merely call into the state's dominance as a source of law (as EU law does), it raises the possibility of law in

[25] Raya Kardasheva, 'Package Deals in EU Legislative Politics' (2013) 54(4) *American Journal of Political Science*, pp. 858–874.

[26] See, for example, Robert L. Glicksman & Thoko Kaime, 'A Comparative Analysis of Accountability Mechanisms for Ecosystem Services Markets in the United States and the European Union' (2013) 2(2) *Transnational Environmental Law*, pp. 259–283.

[27] See Benedict Kingsbury, Nico Krisch & Richard B. Stewart, 'The Emergence of Global Administrative Law' (2005) 68(3/4) *Law and Contemporary Problems*, pp. 15–61, at 29–31 (on the difficulty of identifying the source[s] of global administrative law).

[28] Ladeur, 'The Evolution of General Administrative Law', p. 249.

the very absence of the state. Roger Cotterrell speaks of a paradigm shift: 'One might think of transnational networks of community as the ultimate source of their own legal regulation but, equally, as being subject to legal regulation created in other such networks that impinge on them … So it is possible to envisage a kind of paradigm shift in legal inquiry provoked in part by the development of transnational law: a shift away from a limited nation-state focus and towards a new emphasis on the law-creating potential of complex, interpenetrating networks of social relationships of community'.[29]

Both as author and subject, TER calls into question the assumption that the construction of law is the privilege of a single actor (the state) or, at most, a select few.[30] If we take TER seriously as a source of law, the question arises whether legal authorship is genuinely knowable and attributable. In the multi-directional and reflexive environment of transnational regulatory networks, the distinction between regulator and regulatee fades.[31] In a Habermasian sense, it could be argued that TER blurs the distinction between strategic action and communicative action.[32] With it, opportunities to designate with conviction those nodes within the network that constitute the source of law, recede. TER thus erodes the conceptual walls protecting formal representations of law and regulation – representations that thrive on binary distinctions between regulator and regulatee, law maker and legal subject, legality and illegality – and uncompromisingly confronts us with the much messier, reflexive reality in which law is being made and experienced through the countless interactions of ever permutating groups and networks.

7.2.3 *Organisation: Transnational Environmental Regulation and the Dissolution of Disciplinary Divides*

Possibly the most tangible pressure that regulatory transnationalisation exerts on the legal system is exercised through the problematisation of public/private disciplinary divides.[33] This is largely a consequence of private and hybrid actors stepping into roles that are traditionally associated with public authority. The tension is most eloquently illustrated in the context of private/private TER. Since regulators as well as regulatory addressees are private entities, and since the latter's membership is typically a matter of choice rather than a legal requirement, private/private TER

[29] Cotterrell, 'What Is Transnational Law', p. 515.

[30] Thornhill, 'National Sovereignty and the Constitution of Transnational Law', p. 406.

[31] Christian Brütsch & Dirk Lehmkuhl (eds.), *Law and Legalization in Transnational Relations* (2007, Routledge), p. 23.

[32] Jürgen Habermas, *Theorie des kommunikativen Handlens* (1981, Surhkamp).

[33] Cf. Sabino Cassese, 'Administrative Law without the State? The Challenge of Global Regulation' (2005) 37 *NYU Journal of International Law & Politics*, pp. 663–694, at 669 and 679; Lorenzo Casini, 'Down the Rabbit-Hole: The Projection of the Public/Private Distinction beyond the State' (2014) 12(2) *International Journal of Constitutional Law*, pp. 402–428.

prima facie presents as a private arrangement that should be governed by private law. Yet, other aspects of private/private TER call into question the appropriateness of this determination. Most prominently, the overt public interest mission defies expectations regarding the behaviour of private groups, as does its often close entanglement with public authorities, which may assume the roles of supporters, interlocutors, target audience or even members of the private regulatory network. Moreover, the compliance pull that radiates from these initiatives often belies their modest formal status.[34] In fact, their real but informal authority, and the accompanying opportunities to ensure the initiative's effectiveness without resorting to the apparatuses of administrative and criminal law, are one of the key benchmarks to distinguish regulatory initiatives from other, non-regulatory governance structures.[35]

The regulatory character of transnational environmental initiatives provokes by now familiar dilemmas of legal governance: should the legality of the interactions within the group or network be judged by public or private law standards? The question is deeply relevant for the day-to-day organisation and conduct of TER since private, contractual behaviour is judged against considerably different yardsticks from those used for public, administrative behaviour.[36] Transparency and openness, for example, are keystone virtues in public law. In a private, contractual setting, the qualities of exclusivity and confidentiality often take precedence. A recent article by Armin Von Bogdandy, Matthias Goldmann and Ingo Venzke on the growing expectations for the legitimacy and effectiveness of international institutions, and their impact on the development of public international law, illustrates the difficulty.[37] While acknowledging the pressures caused by transnational governance and regulation, the authors nonetheless argue for the continued relevance and feasibility of a public/private divide. Their approach towards settling the thorny question of determining whether a transnational regulatory regime should be governed by private or public law takes intentionality as its key determinant: 'If the activity is part of the sphere where self-interest is a sufficient justification, the act is private; if it belongs to the sphere where common interests are predominant, it is public'.[38] The solution appears both pragmatic and elegant, however we recall from the analysis in Chapter 3 that the border between public and private motivations, too, is considerably less sturdy than assumed. What is a risk management regime for one actor may constitute substitute TER for another. There are no quick fixes to the public/private dilemma.

34 See Chapter 6.4.
35 See Chapter 2.3.
36 Cf. Zumbansen, 'Transnational Private Regulatory Governance', p. 120.
37 Armin von Bogdandy, Matthias Goldmann & Ingo Venzke, 'From Public International to International Public Law: Translating World Public Opinion into International Public Authority' (2017) 28(1) *European Journal of International Law*, pp. 115–145.
38 Ibid., p. 136.

Moreover, as in matters concerning location and source, the ambiguity of TER problematises both the determination of the legal system to which regulatory behaviour ought to subjected, and the disciplinary affiliation of the legal content it produces. The potential ramifications of classifying, say, a conservation contract as a public act or a private contract are hugely significant, particularly when it comes to determining the rights and responsibilities of third parties. In a public law sphere, interested outsiders would have greater opportunities for involvement in the decision-making process and for judicial review. In the private sphere, third-party rights derived from contract are virtually non-existent. On the other hand, any external negative impact from the conservation contract may be more easily vindicated if the contract is considered a private arrangement than if it is treated as an administrative decision in the pursuit of the public interest.

The position of much of transnational environmental activity at the crossroads of public and private law presents a taxing intellectual puzzle. Yet the challenges run deeper: it calls into question the very usefulness of organising the discipline of law into demarcated public and private spheres. Pioneering case studies, such as Natasha Affolder's work on transnational conservation contracts and Benjamin Richardson's exploration of tensions between fiduciary and environmental law prescriptions in the field of socially responsible investing (SRI), suggest that it is not a question of ascertaining the 'right' sphere in which to house TER; neither private nor public law can autonomously deliver the regulating and legitimising qualities that are necessary for such conservation contracts or responsible investment practices to flourish.[39]

In the transnational regulatory sphere, the walls that separate public and private law may therefore lose both their resilience and their usefulness. Their crumbling can be read as another tell-tale symptom of the weakening bond between state, territory and law.[40] The affirmation of private law is, after all, an exercise of public authority. Such affirmation may be highly explicit, as in the strategic enactment of civil law codes in the Napoleonic era.[41] It might also be residually established through the legal construction of public institutions with clearly and exhaustively designated competencies, privileges and responsibilities. This fences off newly established bastions of public authority and lifts them out of the mass of private entanglements fomented from human interaction. TER questions both the sturdiness and the relevance of the fence.

39 Natasha Affolder, 'Transnational Conservation Contracts' (2012) *Leiden Journal of International Law*, pp. 443–460; Benjamin J. Richardson, 'Socially Responsible Investing for Sustainability: Overcoming Its Incomplete and Conflicting Rationales' (2013) 2(2) *Transnational Environmental Law*, pp. 311–338.

40 Thornhill, 'National Sovereignty and the Constitution of Transnational Law', p. 406.

41 Jean-Louis Halpérin, 'L'Histoire de la Fabrication du Code le Code: Napoléon' (2003) 4(107) *Pouvoirs*, pp. 11–21.

7.2.4 *Function: Transnational Environmental Regulation and the Enhanced Reflexivity of Law*

Transnationalisation has re-energised debates regarding the role of law in global society. Preliminarily, it should be acknowledged that to talk of 'the role of law' and the impact of TER on the role of law suggests that, outside the context of transnational regulation, the role of law is a singular, universally understood and agreed upon concept. Centuries of heated jurisprudential exchange attest that this is certainly not the case. Viewpoints abound about what role – or, what combination of roles – law fulfils for society, about the relation and ranking between different roles and the desirability to enhance or suppress particular functionalities. The point is, rather, that the emergence of transnational regulation, and TER in particular, suits some accounts of what law does for society, but problematises others. TER thus productively destabilises the debate and creates a new agenda both for those who see their account of the role of law affirmed by the rise of TER, and those who see law's functions as frustrated by transnational regulatory activity.

This examination of the impact of TER on the functions of law starts from a familiar place, namely, the mainstream account of the role of law as constitutive of regulatory and administrative authority.[42] Law sets the terms for the institutionalisation of power and thereby enables the very establishment of regulatory and administrative institutions. The constitutive force of law is embodied by the 1995 UK Environment Act, which opens with the lofty words 'There shall be a body corporate to be known as the Environment Agency'; by Article 4 of the 2014 Environmental Protection Law of the People's Republic of China, which recognises environmental protection as a basic national policy and mandates the state to adopt measures in its furtherance;[43] by the provisions mapping out the composition and competencies of the European Commission, the Council, and the European Parliament in the TEU, and by any international convention article entitled 'Conference of the Parties'. The latter two examples simultaneously affirm that the constitutive role of law does not disappear beyond the level of the state. However, it is severely impacted.[44] For every transnational environmental regulator that operates under the auspices of exogenous, binding terms of reference, there is a counterexample that does not. Private and hybrid regulators such as the MSC and the ISO, as well as transnational networks such as the Covenant of Mayors, all organise without the constitutive *pneuma* of law.

[42] Ming-Sung Kuo, 'From Administrative Law to Administrative Legitimation? Transnational Administrative Law and the Process of European Integration' (2012) 61(4) *International & Comparative Law Quarterly*, pp. 855–879, at 863.

[43] Translation available at www.chinadialogue.net/Environmental-Protection-Law-2014-eversion.pdf.

[44] Thornhill, 'National Sovereignty and the Constitution of Transnational Law', pp. 403–404.

TER equally puts severe pressure on the regulating functions of law. In its regulating guise, law is a supplier of procedural and substantive norms that constitute a framework capable of structuring, supervising and disciplining the conduct of regulation.[45] This function is typically associated with administrative law. It is readily apparent that the triple impacts of de-localisation, institutional decentring and the blurring of disciplinary boundaries limit opportunities for administrative law to fulfil the functions of structuring, supervising and disciplining regulatory behaviour. With the possible exception of EU administrative law, supranational administrative legal regimes are normatively thin and disconnected from the institutional enforcement apparatus that is vital to enhancing the effectiveness of the structuring and disciplining influence of administrative law. As the roster of transnational regulators expands, the perceived deficit of administrative law to govern their conduct becomes ever more acute.[46]

The erosion of the constitutive and regulatory functions of law vis-à-vis transnational regulation can also impede law's communicative function.[47] Law is a vital channel through which governments and courts publicise their vision of what constitutes good regulation and administration. A dearth in constitutive and administrative law reduces opportunities for interpellation, debate and, consequently, government accountability.

From this vantage point, TER has a profound and potentially crippling impact on law's functionality. However, not everyone subscribes to the idea of law as conceptually and operationally separate from that which it professedly governs. According to Ladeur, the constitutive role of law as an external organising principle that beams down on regulatory and administrative behaviour has always been an illusion: 'The fundamental forms and components of general administrative law have not been developed by the legislator nor by the judiciary (which has made some of its implicit rules explicit) but by an experimental search process of the administration itself'.[48]

This account represents a more self-generating and organic understanding of law: one in which the role of law is not to create normative content but to reflect rules and standards as they emerge and consolidate within the day-to-day reality of regulatory and administrative decision making. Law is not superimposed on the regulatory and administrative life world; it is produced and reabsorbed within

45 Cf. Christopher Anderson, 'Contrasting Models of EU Administration in Judicial Review of Risk Regulation' (2014) 51(2) *Common Market Law Review*, pp. 425–454; Alberto Alemanno, 'The Shaping of European Risk Regulation by Community Courts', Jean Monnet Working Paper No. 18 (2008), pp. 7–10 available at https://papers.ssrn.com/sol3/papers.cfm?abstract_id=1325770.

46 Kuo, 'From Administrative Law to Administrative Legitimation?' p. 863.

47 Veerle Heyvaert, 'Levelling Down, Levelling Up, and Governing Across: Three Responses to Hybridization in International Law' (2009) 20(3) *European Journal of International Law*, pp. 647–674, at 662.

48 Ladeur, 'The Evolution of General Administrative Law', p. 5.

the very processes and practices that it codifies. It is, in Lon Fuller's words, a 'language of interaction'.[49]

If law is a co-product rather than a determinant of decision making, then our expectations of its autonomous constitutive and disciplining power have been overstated. At most, law can contribute to the 'stabilization of normative expectations'[50] and foster 'the selection and upholding of such expectations even in the face of disappointment'.[51] Law is informative rather than formative; law facilitates stable self-ordering rather than impose order.

The key functions of law, in the autopoietic/constructivist perspective associated with the writing of Niklas Luhmann, Günther Teubner, Karl-Heinz Ladeur, Gralf-Peter Calliess and Moritz Renner, are facilitative and cognitive. The rise of TER changes the way in which law is co-produced, but it does not fundamentally threaten its facilitative and cognitive functionality. Evidently, the existing corpus of international, administrative, environmental and contract law does enough to manage uncertainty to an extent that it does not impede the blossoming of manifold TER initiatives. Expectations between the participants in governance networks are stable enough for these networks to persist and even thrive.[52] Simultaneously, a developing body of decision-making protocols and standard-setting practice is being documented. Protocols and standards fulfil a vital informative function about what the normative expectations within the transnational regime are.[53] The information thus created is diverse and differentiated, but it does contribute to an evolving, flexible understanding of the normativity of TER, which then in turn helps to stabilise continuing transnational regulatory and administrative behaviour.

In sum, accounts that position law as a hierarchically superior force external to administration yet capable of shaping its design and operation, are threatened by the rise of transnational regulatory regimes[54]. The latter seem to exemplify much more aptly law's reflexive potential. To some, the shift in representation from 'law as authority' to 'law as reflection' constitutes a diminishment of the status of law and its role in society. To others, it instead signals a closing of the gap between the myth and the reality of law.

[49] Lon L. Fuller, 'Law and Human Interaction' (1977) 47(3/4) *Sociological Inquiry*, pp. 59–89, at 61.

[50] Gralf-Peter Calliess & Moritz Renner, 'Between Law and Social Norms: The Evolution of Global Governance' (2009) 22(2) *Ratio Juris*, pp. 260–280, at 267.

[51] Ibid.

[52] Fuller, 'Law and Human Interaction', pp. 61–64.

[53] On the cognitive function of law, see also Franz von Benda-Beckmann & Keebet von Benda-Beckmann, 'The Dynamics of Change and Continuity in Plural Legal Orders' (2006) 53(4) *Journal of Legal Pluralism & Unofficial Law*, pp. 1–44, at 12.

[54] Cf. Colin Scott, 'Analysing Regulatory Space: Fragmented Resources and Institutional Design' (2001) *Public Law*, pp. 329–353, at 333.

7.2.5 *Structure: Transnational Environmental Regulation and Regime Polycentricity*

As it challenges the monopoly of the state as the source of law, so does TER call into question the accuracy of representing the legal system as a hierarchically organised, regimented and fully articulated structure.[55] Concepts such as the 'architecture' of law evoke an image of law as a cohesive, comprehensive system built on solid, singular foundations – national constitutions for domestic law; the EU Treaties for the EU legal regime; the Vienna Convention on the Law of Treaties for international law.[56]

The difficulties in determining which sets of laws and rules should govern TER, illustrated in the examples of the Covenant of Mayors and CDM decision making, cast a shadow on the assumption of architectural cohesion of the legal edifice. Doubts only mount if we moreover engage seriously with the notion that, in the wake of transnational regulation, a reconsideration of the distinction between law and non-law may be in order. Indeed, any claim to legal status of the normative content produced through transnational regulatory decision making, is even harder to reconcile with a systemic, pyramidal vision of law. Instead, law unfolds as a network; one with stronger, weaker and even missing links – maybe a patchwork more than a network.[57] The law that feeds into and emanates from transnational regulatory decision making does not self-organise into a monolithic structure; it is fragmented and polycentric. The normative practices developed and replicated within, for example, ISO standard setting certainly reflect aspects of domestic and regional administrative law regimes that are imported into the proceedings via the expectations and routines of governmental as well as non-governmental ISO members, but they cannot be properly 'housed' within a pre-established organigram of international, regional or national administrative law. Law's structure is perennially inchoate.

55 Brütsch & Lehmkuhl, *Law and Legalization*, pp. 22–23.

56 Neil Gunningham's work illustrates both the assumption of stability and the extent to which this assumption is under threat in Gunningham, 'Environment Law, Regulation and Governance: Shifting Architectures' (2009) 21(2) *Journal of Environmental Law*, pp. 179–212.

57 Benvenisti observes a similar sensibility reflected in recent American writing on international law: 'a view shared by scholars who deny that there is anything "out there" other than solitary treaties floating around in no particular hierarchy in the abyss of international anarchy'. It should, however, be noted that representation is typically used not to challenge the systemic vision of law at a fundamental level, but to buttress claims for a return to the values of state sovereignty and subordination of transnational to national law. See Eyal Benvenisti, 'The Future of International Law Scholarship in Germany: The Tension between Interpretation and Change' (2007) 67 *ZaöRV*, pp. 585–598, at 587.

7.3 RESPONDING TO TRANSNATIONALISATION: RECLAIMING, RECONSTRUCTING OR RECONCEPTUALISING LAW

Both as subject and potential source of law, transnational regulation calls into question established assumptions about the key attributes of law. Law is perceived as increasingly de-localised, pluralistic, inchoate, reflexive and polycentric. The preceding discussion also affirms that not every variant of TER exerts an equal amount of pressure. The decisions of transnational environmental standard setters such as the ISO, which defy easy classification under any legal regime or discipline, present a more acute challenge than those of the European Commission, which are generated through a highly developed, supranational legal regime that replicates many features and functions of domestic law. Yet whether nagging or acute, it would be desperately short-sighted to ignore the practical and conceptual problems that accompany the rise of TER.

The following pages map out a variety of possible responses to the transnationalisation of law. For the sake of clarity, the material is organised into three distinctive categories, namely, responses that aim to reclaim law as conventionally conceived; those that seek to reconstruct law and thereby restore its conventional attributes and functionalities and a third group of responses that advocate a reconceptualisation of law that is more in tune with the changes prompted by transnationalisation.[58] It goes without saying that the full wealth of reactions to the transnationalisation of law, as expressed in regulation, case law and scholarship, does not always allow itself to be neatly stored into one of three mutually exclusive categories. Nor are commentators necessarily aware of whether their suggestions have an essentially defensive, conservative or creative bent. However, a more systematic understanding of the range of possible reactions to transnationalisation, whether expressed in case law, in scholarship or through legislative reform initiatives, strengthens our ability to process, contexualise and critically engage with individual responses.

7.3.1 *Conservative and Defensive: Reclaiming Law*

The transnationalisation of law unlocks a Pandora's box of conceptual dilemmas, uncertainties and transitional problems. One way to solve the deluge of new

[58] For comparison, see Nico Krisch's discussion of 'containment', 'transfer' and 'break' as three reactions to the democracy challenges represented by the emergence of postnational law. See Nico Krisch, *Beyond Constitutionalism: The Pluralist Structure of Postnational Law* (2010, Oxford University Press), pp. 14–22. Krisch's brief analysis focuses chiefly on the different interpretations of the relation between democracy, legitimacy and constitutionalism that underscore the diverse responses. The following analysis, in contrast, focuses its attention on the consequences of embracing one or other viewpoint. See also Berman's discussion of sovereigntist, universalist and pluralist constructions of the global legal order. Paul Schiff Berman, *Global Legal Pluralism: A Jurisprudence of Law Beyond Borders* (2014, Cambridge University Press), p. 14.

challenges is to re-seal the box and reassert the traditional boundaries of law. To this end, the transnationalisation of law is resolutely kept outside the zone of 'law proper'. Defensive responses to transnationalisation seek to keep intact the formal distinction between state-sanctioned public regulation and private regulation, however similar their impact. The barrier between officially promulgated, binding laws that are made effective through national enforcement mechanisms and backed up by punitive sanctions on the one hand, and conventional norms that derive their authority primarily from expertise, persuasion and widespread voluntary compliance on the other, is strictly maintained.

Consequently, defensive responses relegate the lion's share of TER to the private legal sphere. The standards adopted by, for instance, the FSC are treated as private conventions; the relation between the FSC and its members is a contractual one. Choice of law questions that may arise in a dispute between parties in the FSC network are resolved through conflict of law rules (also known as '*private* international law') as applied by the dispute settlement body seized of the conflict. Third-party ramifications of the contractual standards agreed to by FSC members are legally relevant only to the extent that such standard setting might constitute anti-competitive behaviour.

More nuanced defensive responses to transnationalisation combine the desire to safeguard the formal divisions between law and non-law with an awareness of the de facto similarities between legal and non-legal norms.[59] This resonates in the popularity of concepts such as 'soft law', 'quasi-regulation' and 'governance', which simultaneously underscore the similarity and the otherness of normative dynamics in the transnational field. OECD codes of conduct are like law yet not law; they are 'soft law'.[60] Transnational cooperation in standard setting for sustainable farming is like regulation but not regulation; it is 'quasi-regulatory'[61] or constitutive of 'governance' rather than a regulatory regime.[62] The introduction of a *sui generis* set of para-legal terminology offers the benefit of locating the transnationalisation of law close enough to the legal sphere to legitimise its colonisation by lawyers, but simultaneously affirms the specialness and authority of the newly buttressed 'core' of law and regulation.[63] State-issued law is no longer merely law; it is 'hard law'.

The establishment of a para-legal zone conceptually shelters the core of 'real' law from the challenges triggered by transnationalisation, and stimulates inquiries into the nature and status of this newly established soft-, para- or quasi-legal periphery.

59 Ladeur, 'The Evolution of General Administrative Law', p. 9.

60 Martin Marcussen, 'OECD Governance through Soft Law' in Ulrika Mörth (ed.), *Soft Law in Governance and Regulation: An Interdisciplinary Analysis* (2004, Edward Elgar), pp. 103–128.

61 Christopher Ray, 'Transnational Co-operation between Rural Areas: Elements of a Political Economy of EU Rural Development' (2001) 43(3) *Sociologia Ruralis*, pp. 279–295.

62 Cf. Louis Kotzé, *Global Environmental Governance: Law and Regulation for the 21st Century* (2012, Edward Elgar), p. 83.

63 Friedrich, *International Environmental 'Soft Law'*, p. 7.

Soft law is the subject of a rich vein of scholarship that explores the main reasons why actors resort to non-binding modes of norm setting; the variety of formats in which soft law is encapsulated and the ways in which soft law has been used alongside or distinguished from hard law by traditional sources of legal authority.[64] Many writings emphasise soft law's precursor status: it often functions to lower the threshold for agreement and as a stepping stone towards a final, binding legal product.[65] This is an affirmative account, but it does portray non-traditional legal activity as instrumental and in support of a more enduring, prestigious end goal. The final destiny for successful soft law is elevation to the ranks of real, hard law.

Advantages and Disadvantages of Reclaiming Law

Defensive responses to the transnationalisation of law have an obvious appeal. They avoid the disruption that accompanies attempts at reconceptualisation, preserve the relevance of generations of legal knowledge and praxis, and imbue decision making with continuity and, hence, predictability. On the other hand, unwillingness to confront the impacts of transnationalisation widens the gap between 'the law on the books' and 'what really happens', which may dent law's credibility as an effective disciplining force of political power. Moreover, the decision not to engage with the regulatory character of transnational arrangements arguably represents a missed opportunity to lend structure and support to innovative attempts at public interest regulation. Considering the gaping chasm between the scope and pace of, for instance, 'traditional' climate change regulation and the extent of intervention required to achieve sustainable climate targets, such opportunities may be too costly to miss.

Ultimately, the main shortcoming of boundary drawing exercises is that they tend to ignore or displace rather than truly resolve the tensions caused by transnationalisation. The conceptual clarification that comes from firmly locating, say, the environmental instruments adopted under the 2007 ASEAN Charter[66] outside the sphere of real law, does little to alleviate concerns about the transparency and responsiveness with which such measures were adopted. Housing the same

[64] Fabien Terpan, 'Soft Law in the European Union – The Changing Nature of EU Law' (2015) 21(1) *European Law Journal*, pp. 68–96; Jean d'Aspremont & Tanja Aalberts (eds.), 'Symposium on Soft Law' (2012) 25(2) *Leiden Journal of International Law*, pp. 309–378; Heyvaert, 'Levelling Down, Levelling Up', note 3 (overview of key publications on soft law between 1990 and 2009).

[65] Gregory Shaffer, 'Theorizing Transnational Legal Ordering' (2016) 12 *Annual Review of Law and Social Science*, pp. 231–253, at 246; Kenneth W. Abbott & Duncan Snidal, 'Hard and Soft Law in International Governance' (2000) 54(3) *International Organization*, pp. 421–456; Gregory Shaffer & Mark A. Pollack, 'Hard vs. Soft Law: Alternatives, Complements, and Antagonists in International Governance' (2010) 94 *Minnesota Law Review*, pp. 706–799.

[66] Koh Kheng-Lian, 'Transboundary and Global Environmental Issues: The Role of ASEAN' (2012) 1(1) *Transnational Environmental Law*, pp. 67–82.

instruments into the 'soft law' category does create some space for these issues to be debated, but offers little instruction on how such debates should be settled.

Arguably, the introduction of notions such as soft law, quasi-regulation and governance do not so much fix the boundaries between law and non-law as represent an institutional choice about the appropriate forum for determination. The question of exactly what consequences to attach to the label of 'soft law' usually remains suspended until it falls in the lap of judicial and arbitration bodies.[67] The CJEU ruling in *Fra.bo* exemplifies this.[68] Here, the CJEU was asked whether the refusal by a German certification body, the Deutsche Vereinigung des Gas- und Wasserfaches eV (DVGW), to recognise the validity of a certificate issued by an Italian certification entity which was not on DVGW's approved list, could be construed as an impediment to the free movement of goods (Article 34 TFEU, then 28 of the Treaty establishing the European Community). The catch was that DVGW is a private organisation. Under German law, DVGW certification is not essential to prove that construction products (in this case, copper fittings) meet mandatory safety standards, but the DVGW certificate bestows a presumption of conformity. Alternative avenues to prove compliance are underspecified and costly.[69] In its submission, the DVGW asserted that only the German state was bound by Article 28 EC. Consequently, there was 'nothing preventing the DVGW from drawing up technical standards which go beyond those in place in member states other than the Federal Republic of Germany and to apply them to its certification activities. It is also free, on quality-related grounds, to take account only of laboratories accredited by it'.[70] The CJEU did not dispute DVGW's status as a private body, but considered that because, first, German legislation provided that goods certified by DVGW would be compliant with national law, secondly, the DVGW was the only body that certified copper fittings in Germany and, thirdly, a lack of certification by DVGW would result in serious difficulties in placing the product on the market, the DVGW 'in reality (held) the power to regulate'.[71]

Fra.bo relies on a preponderance of the evidence approach to resolve the boundary dispute and situate DVGW's certification activities on the public side of the public/private divide. The case-by-case, problem-solving approach to questions regarding the legal status of non-traditional regulators, which is inherent in judicial determination, imbues the process with a considerable degree of flexibility and scope for fairness in decision making. At the same time however, it is not the most

67 See Emilia Korkea Aho, 'Laws in Progress? Reconceptualizing Accountability Strategies in the Era of Framework Norms' (2013) 2(2) *Transnational Environmental Law*, pp. 363–385, at 378–384.

68 Case C-171/11, *Fra.bo SpA* v *Deutsche Vereinigung des Gas- und Wasserfaches eV (DVGW) – Technisch-Wissenschaftlicher Verein*, judgment of 12 July 2012, ECLI:EU:C:2012:453.

69 Ibid., at 29.

70 Ibid., at 14.

71 Ibid., at 31.

conducive to establishing general criteria regarding the legal status of de facto authoritative bodies. It takes more than one ruling to confidently crystallise generalisable rules. In this manner, too, the institutional choice to settle 'boundary disputes' through (individual) judicial determination instead of through (general) rule making presents itself as a defensive rather than offensive response to the transnationalisation of law.

7.3.2 *Conservative and Adaptive: Reconstructing Law*

A second cohort of responses to the transnationalisation of law shares with the first that it is essentially conservative: it seeks to alleviate the pressures on conventional understandings of the location, sources, functions, disciplines and structure of law. But in contrast to the first, commentators who espouse conservative and adaptive perspectives display a greater willingness to confront the undesirable consequences of maintaining a strict law/non-law, public/private divide. Such undesirable consequences may manifest in, for example, the inability of contract law to address the lack of transparency with which private transnational regulators behave. Or in the inability to appeal against decisions adopted by transnational environmental regulators, such as the CDM Executive Board.[72] Following a conservative and adaptive approach, law should be tweaked, adapted and, where necessary, newly produced to bridge the discrepancy between the private form and the public substance of transnational regulation. New law should fix the gaps in the fabric of legal protection torn by the emergence of transnational regulators. Conservative and adaptive responses to the transnationalisation of law aim to reconstruct the conventional role and functions of law through the creation of new generations of public transnational law.

Views differ on whether adapting law to the transnational context is a matter of implementing a few discrete fixes, or instead calls for a large-scale overhaul. It has been argued that, in their enthusiasm for the new and challenging, scholars easily overestimate the proportion and weight of transnational regulation. In reality, it is countered, the irritation caused by the transnationalisation of law remains modest, and most of it can be managed with old-fashioned legal tools.[73] Conflict of laws doctrines may not provide perfect answers to problems of dislocation, but they still perform the core task of identifying possible forums and plausible legal regimes

[72] Charlotte Streck & Jolene Lin, 'Making Markets Work: A Review of CDM Performance and the Need for Reform' (2008) 19(2) *European Journal of International Law*, pp. 409–442, at 426–428.

[73] Ralf Michaels, for example, has proposed a more inclusive approach to conflicts of law as a way to resolve competing claims between state and non-state law: Ralf Michaels, 'The Re-Statement of Non-State Law: The State, Choice of Law, and the Challenge from Global Legal Pluralism' (2005) 51(3) *The Wayne Law Review*, pp. 1209–1258, at 1250–1258. See also Zumbansen, 'Transnational Private Regulatory Governance', p. 127. Note that Zumbansen discusses this view in the literature but does not personally espouse it.

under which transnational legal conflicts can be housed. Similarly, in response to the challenges associated with the blurring public/private divide, it is possible to expand the scope of state regulation of the private sector to introduce requirements that specifically address the increasingly regulatory character of private governance. Such requirements may be adopted under the mantle of shareholder protection, consumer protection or environmental protection. Their main target is to imprint an ethos of good governance on the private sector that is comparable to the expectations of administrative law vis-à-vis public regulators. The official justification of transparency, consultation and review requirements may be the protection of shareholder or consumer interests, but their introduction simultaneously supports the development of a broader concept of responsibility and accountability of (private) transnational regulators.

Thus, the tensions that result from maintaining a formal distinction between public and private regulators are alleviated through the introduction of functional equivalents of public law expectations in the private sphere.[74] As an example, Kähler refers to the US Sarbanes–Oxley Act (2002), which requires private companies to establish a contract-management system. Such systems can reduce the risk of contract failure, but whether it was cost effective to implement them was formerly down to the individual enterprise to decide. The introduction of the contract-management requirement as a legal obligation could be viewed as a response to the growing expectation that private as well as public organisations conform to 'best practice' or 'good governance' as a matter of law, in the interest of both their contractual partners and the public at large.[75]

Others consider that the disruptive consequences of the transnationalisation of law cannot be countered by mere tweaking, but require more thorough and systematic legal reform efforts.[76] Natasha Affolder's aforementioned study of transnational conservation contracts leads her to examine the notions of fairness in private (contractual) law and in public (international environmental) law. Her conclusion is that the two notions are not fully reconcilable; in fact they pull in opposite directions. Fairness in contract law refers to the fairness between the contracting parties, and is typically protected by ensuring the privity of the contractual relations and prioritising contractual interests over external concerns. Fairness in international environmental law, in contrast, is closely bound with notions of transparency and access to the negotiation process. In these circumstances, it is difficult to simply tweak notions of fairness in contract law to reflect the regulatory aspects of transnational conservation contracts without such adaptation effectively constituting a distortion. Correspondingly, Affolder calls for a more advanced

[74] See Henry J. Steiner & Detlev F. Vagts, *Transnational Legal Problems*, 2nd edn. (1976, Foundation Press), p. xvii.

[75] Lorenz Kähler, 'Contract-Management Duties as a New Regulatory Device' (2013) 76(2) *Law & Contemporary Problems*, pp. 89–103, at 90 & 94.

[76] Bethlehem, 'The End of Geography', p. 19.

response in the development of a transnational legal concept of fairness that 'extends rather than simply recycles fairness thinking in domestic and international law'.[77] In a similar vein, Benjamin Richardson uncovers fundamental tensions between Socially Responsible Investment as a transnational governance regime and fiduciary finance law: 'The seemingly exclusive focus of fiduciary law on the interests of investors, especially their financial interests, potentially clashes with any vision of SRI prioritizing environmental and social responsibility'.[78] The reconciliation, he argues, involves adopting both a more productive rationale for SRI *and* a reconceptualisation of fiduciary law.[79]

In their most expansive expression, conservative and adaptive responses to the transnationalisation of law advocate the establishment of new, encompassing legal frameworks to govern TER. EU administrative law, an initially underdeveloped tenet of EU legal integration that has gradually matured in response to the growing presence and immediacy of EU regulation,[80] is often advanced as a model for the development of additional regional, or potentially global, regimes of public law.[81] Alternative conceptions for models of public transnational law include the development of 'an international law of corporate social responsibility'. The idea starts from the premise that contemporary international law, although formally established through and for states, usually has major economic actors as its real addressees. Their differentiated status is increasingly recognised in international law, for example, in the context of investor-state dispute settlement mechanisms. An international law of corporate social responsibility could constitute the 'differentiated responsibility pillar' to match the differentiated position and access that major economic actors increasingly enjoy in the international legal sphere.

Along similar lines, Daniel Bethlehem suggests a *lex congregatio* or law of society. In a preliminary attempt to operationalise this model, he proposes the following features:

> [F]irst, an instrument of traditional inter-state law that would act as a platform on which would stand a second tier set of protocols and principles addressing the application and mutual recognition of rules and standards relevant to particular conduct; thirdly, a further tier of industry-driven and derived minimum standards of conduct; and all this finally held together by a basic principle that actors are bound

77 Affolder, 'Transnational Conservation Contracts', pp. 456–460.
78 Richardson, 'Socially Responsible Investing', p. 327.
79 Ibid., pp. 332–337.
80 Hanns Peter Nehl, *Principles of Administrative Procedure in EC Law* (1999, Hart Publishing), pp. 214.
81 Kuo, 'From Administrative Law to Administrative Legitimation?' pp. 857–8; 862; Ellen Vos, 'Making Informal International Law Accountable: Lessons from the EU' in Joost Pauwelyn, Ramses A. Wessel & Jan Wouters (eds.), *Informal International Lawmaking* (2012, Oxford University Press), pp. 369–381.

by what they accept – whether by their conduct, by the click of a mouse button on an 'I agree' icon on a software program, or in some other manner.[82]

Reconstructing Law: Strengths and Weaknesses

The strongest appeal of conservative and adaptive responses is that they acknowledge the disruptive impact of transnationalisation head-on, and seek to mend the fissures between the idea of law and law in practice through enduring, sustainable solutions. These solutions, which usually consist of the introduction of new layers of public law to govern transnational action and clarify the status of transnational regulatory decisions, enable law to regain a sense of locality, exclusivity in authorship, disciplinary clarity, constitutional and regulatory functionality, and comprehensiveness. They recast the net in order better to cover the richness and variety of transnational regulatory activity, which helps to restore the concept of law in its traditional splendour.

Less felicitously, the reconstruction of law engenders an extensive degree of juridification in an already heavily legalised world. Moreover, it raises the difficult question of whom should be in charge of developing and, indeed, enacting this new layer of law. The conventional starting assumption would be that such a new, transnational level of public law should emanate from all states acting in concert and adopting a novel instrument of public international law. However, there is no global political appetite to speak of for such a large-scale undertaking – a situation which is unlikely to change in the foreseeable future. In the absence of traditional legislative action, a raft of voluntary, expert- and civil society-driven initiatives have cropped up to fill in the void. They range from legal commentators proposing principles and prescriptions of generally unspecified origin as appropriate norms to govern one or other transnational regulatory initiative,[83] to the more high profile launch of informal codes and principles endorsed by bodies of experts, often acting in association with NGOs and, even, private enterprises.[84] However, the authority of such initiatives is questionable, as is their own legal status. In fact, unless they are explicitly pitched as proposals for the exclusive consideration by recognised legislative bodies, their production creates a paradox. The introduction of public law

[82] Bethlehem, 'The End of Geography', p. 24.

[83] See, for example, Glicksman and Kaime's proposals for the introduction of accountability requirements to remedy the vulnerability of ecosystem markets to underperformance, abuse and fraud. Glicksman & Kaime, 'A Comparative Analysis of Accountability Mechanisms', p. 271.

[84] See, for example, the International Corporate Governance Network (ICGN) Global Governance Principles, available at http://icgn.flpbks.com/icgn_global_governance_principles/#p=1; Expert Group on Climate Obligations of Enterprises, *Principles on Climate Obligations of Enterprises* (2018, Eleven International Publishing); the Oslo Principles on Global Climate Obligations, available at https://globaljustice.yale.edu/sites/default/files/files/OsloPrinciples.pdf.

norms designed to govern the behaviour of transnational regulators may help to reassert the boundaries between public and private law, restore law's constitutive and regulative functions, as well as its image as a cohesive and comprehensive structure. However, the requisite treatment of such proposals or informal codes as legally meaningful simultaneously undermines the conventions of law as territorial and state-based and, ultimately, destabilises the conventions by which societies distinguish law from non-law.

Expertise-driven proposals for the reconstruction of law at the transnational level must also confront the uneasy reality that they are, in essence, undemocratically formulated responses to problems that are, themselves, in no small measure a consequence of the dissolution between regulation and democratic oversight in the transnational sphere.[85] The EU legal regime, we recall, faces unrelenting 'democratic deficit' allegations, in spite of having incorporated over the years a veritable arsenal of checks and balances, institutional innovations and decision-making mechanisms in a continuing quest to boost the democratic credibility of its legislative and regulatory output. The EU experience serves as a cautionary reminder that the mission of reconstructing law at the transnational level to govern transnational regulatory activity would inevitably be fraught with political controversy and ongoing challenges to the authority of the transnational legal regime.

7.3.3 *Creative and Adaptive: Reconceptualising Law*

Whether a fringe event or a development that affects vast swathes of the legal system, the transnationalisation of law presents a problem that needs to be managed. That is the view shared by those who seek to reclaim or reconstruct law. The implicit assumption from which both lines of thought depart, is that the traditional understanding of law as territorial, emanating from the state, organised in public and private domains, functionally constitutive, regulating and structurally comprehensive, is a notion worth protecting and preserving. However, what if we relinquish the idea that law is and must always remain defined by these traditional attributes, and instead embrace the possibility of the metamorphosis of law into a ubiquitous, pluralistic, fragmented and reflexive phenomenon? Or, what if we start from an alternative assumption, namely, that the traditional attributes of law have always been mythical? Arguably, law has never really lived up to its territorial, state-based and comprehensive billing.[86] If that is the case, then the rise of transnational regulation has not transformed the nature of law but instead tipped the veil on the artificiality of the dominant paradigm.[87]

[85] Cf. Alexander Somek, 'Constituent Power in National and Transnational Contexts' (2012) 3(1) *Transnational Legal Theory*, pp. 31–60.

[86] Ladeur, 'The Evolution of General Administrative Law', p. 5.

[87] Brütsch & Lehmkuhl, *Law and Legalization*, p. 23.

The latter perspectives are likely to elicit adaptive and creative responses that seek not to restore but instead to reconceptualise law.[88] The transnationalisation of law is not so much a disruption to be managed as it is an opportunity to further our knowledge about law's nature and dynamics; to adapt the cognitive frameworks through which legal processes are perceived and constructed, and to develop a paradigm that is better attuned to the new (or newly revealed) reality of law. In this context, transnational law is no longer a shorthand for law that does not fit the within mainstream paradigm, but becomes the signpost of an alternative account of law that 'methodologically responds to the fragmented, embedded evolutionary dynamics of norm creation in the context of world society'.[89]

The reconceptualisation of law necessitates the development of new tools to organise and structure our thinking about law; tools that are not reliant on conventional tropes (e.g., sovereignty, jurisdiction), dividing lines (e.g., the public/private divide) and decisionistic mechanisms (primacy). The creative effort of rethinking law in a mode that is less beholden to its conventional attributes echoes the intellectual challenges experienced in the quest for a de-institutionalised, de-centred concept of regulation. As in that case, it is difficult to break free from the shackles of conventional thinking; we all too easily equip new models with thinly disguised reworkings of old formulae. In a second parallel with the reconceptualisation of regulation, the development of a paradigm of transnational law is very much work in progress. The following paragraphs introduce some of the key exponents of the process so far.

The Organisation of Transnational Law

A first prominent feature in transnationalisation scholarship is the demarcation of nascent legal spheres that are neither territorially defined nor clearly reducible to the public or private sphere. Attempts to chart domains of law that are united by characteristics other than their shared geography or location in the public or private field, respond to our abiding need for boundaries to structure legal thought and action. The existence of disciplinary boundaries facilitates the performance of a number of essential operations including, to name but a few, the framing and scoping of legal conflicts; the selection of relevant bodies of legislation, case law and literature for the purpose of research and argumentation; and the identification of fields of professional expertise. The waning relevance of territorial boundaries and public/private divides is therefore as disorienting as it is liberating, and fuels a demand for new categorisations and criteria to organise the vast expanse of law into manageable segments.

The quest for functional equivalents to territorial and traditional disciplinary divides may well explain why the *lex mercatoria*, for instance, is experiencing

88 Zumbansen, 'Transnational Private Regulatory Governance', p. 133.
89 Ibid.

something of a revival in today's legal scholarship. In contemporary writing, it is frequently held up as a model for transnational law that has an autonomous identity and an internal logic without being territorially confined or anchored to a predetermined source of legal authority.[90] It serves as both a structural and, evidently, linguistic inspiration for the denomination of new transnational fields such as the *lex digitalis*, which refers to the burgeoning body of principles, conventions and rules that structure the online environment, and the *lex sportiva*, which fulfils a parallel function for sports.[91]

The identification of de-localised fields of law may be accompanied by proposals to align emerging legal frameworks along traditional formats, which imbue the discussion with a reconstructive élan. Yet others eschew the stable conventions to locate law and are instead geared towards the analytical exercise of uncovering transnational normativity as they find it. Compare, for example, Bethlehem's aforementioned proposal for a *lex congregatio* with von Benda-Beckmann's discussion of 'project law'. The former derives its legal status from 'an instrument of traditional inter-state law that would act as a platform'.[92] 'Project law', in contrast, refers to an organically evolving body of principles, rules and procedures made and replicated by transnationally operating funding agencies and development projects. It is a flexible category that may expand to include stipulations determined by law and political conditions of the donor country, but its identity as project law and its internal organisation are not dependent on the involvement of state law.[93]

The turn towards de-localised fields of law that are neither public nor private, has important institutional ramifications. The dissolution of clear public/private distinctions between actors connected to a transnational project or linked via commercial practices, digital networks or sporting events, creates scope for access on equal terms to institutional resources such as review processes and dispute settlement mechanisms. The multiplication of legal authorship may thus constitute the basis for an expansion of external accountability. Thus far, the cracks in the institutional wall between the public and private spheres have mostly favoured large transnational firms, granting them privileged standing in claims vis-à-vis state bodies, most controversially so in litigation on the basis of investment treaty provisions.[94] However, a fuller reconceptualisation of law in the transnational context might open the door towards a finer calibration of actors' rights and responsibilities that is no longer

[90] E.g., Gunther Teubner, 'The Project of Constitutional Sociology: Irritating Nation State Constitutionalism' (2013) 4(1) *Transnational Legal Theory*, pp. 44–58, at 49; Klaus Peter Berger, *The Creeping Codification of the New Lex Marcatoria*, 2nd edn. (2010, Center for Transnational Law); Alec Stone Sweet, 'The New *Lex Mercatoria* and Transnational Governance' (2006) 13(5) *Journal of European Public Policy*, pp. 627–646.

[91] Ladeur, 'The Evolution of General Administrative Law', p. 10.

[92] Note 82 in this chapter.

[93] von Benda-Beckmann & von Benda-Beckmann, 'The Dynamics of Change', p. 19.

[94] Cf. Jan Kleinheisterkamp, 'Financial Responsibility in European International Investment Policy' (2014) 63(2) *International & Comparative Law Quarterly*, pp. 449–476.

determined by their public or private status, and that instead takes its cue from their relative position in the commercial/digital/project/sporting network.

The Plurality of Transnational Law

A pressing agenda point for advocates of reconceptualisation, is to devise productive solutions to the loss of hierarchy as an ordering mechanism and a problem-solving technique. The sources of transnational law are understood as plural, heterarchical, and theoretically infinite: there is no pre-ordained limit on the range of actors that engage in transnational norm-generating behaviour.[95] Moreover, no single institution – whether state, intergovernmental organisation or association of large commercial enterprises – can credibly lay claim to the exclusive competence to recognise and validate the creation of transnational law. Transnational law can thrive in the absence of a discernible *Grundnorm* and beyond the control of a designated authority equipped to sanction and rank its normative communications. The rise of transnational law thus creates a double bind: it generates new layers of normativity, which increases the likelihood that situations will be governed by multiple, potentially conflicting bodies of law. Yet it simultaneously strips law of its most effective decision-making technique, namely, resolving conflict through determinations of primacy, made by institutions that have been constitutionally empowered to that effect.

The most obvious way of dealing with the plurality of law is, simply, to bear it. That is, to resist the urge to stratify spheres of legality and to tolerate accompanying incommensurability in legal decision making as the inevitable side-effect of high levels of diversified legal productivity. One of the most developed exponents of this approach can be found in Nico Krisch's postnational, radical pluralism. Radical pluralism embodies an appealingly optimistic disposition: it expresses faith in the resilience of legal structures; they can bear a quantity of dissonance without descending into chaos.[96] Moreover, Krisch argues that it is important not to overstate the degree of conflict that legal pluralism will elicit: for all its diversity, there are strong similarities and overlaps in our normative heritage that influence legal decision making within and outside conventional legal regimes. Finally, an absence of hierarchy does not necessarily equate an unwillingness to take inspiration from others. Plurality leaves scope for informal coordination, which could potentially reap more stable results than hierarchically imposed assimilation.

The Functions and Structure of Transnational Law

Creative and adaptive responses to transnationalisation are less preoccupied with restoring law's waning constitutive and disciplining force vis-à-vis TER, and more with harnessing the reflexive and communicative strengths of law. In this vein, one

95 Thornhill, 'National Sovereignty and the Constitution of Transnational Law', pp. 398–399.
96 Krisch, 'Who is Afraid of Radical Pluralism', pp. 397–400.

of transnational law's chief functions is to enable the 'peaceful co-existence' of heterarchical normative regimes. Importantly, transnational law does so not by exogenously imposing a superstructure of constitutional and administrative prescriptions to which transnational regimes must be subjected, but through the introduction of interstitial norms[97] that serve to coordinate, orchestrate and moderate.[98] The emphasis on the liaising, facilitating functions of law has a profound structural impact. Under a creative, adaptive conceptualisation of transnational law, the norms that govern transnational regulatory behaviour are not created outside the regulatory context but are better understood as composite co-products of the very practice of transnational regulation.[99] They are not situated above but in-between an indeterminate and changing number of regulatory regimes, their content and status constantly evolving through processes of regulatory application and feedback.

Reconceptualising Law: Strengths and Weaknesses

Creative and adaptive responses to transnationalisation exercise a powerful draw on the legal imagination. Although less familiar, the idea of organically co-produced norms that emerge from the very behaviour that they seek to govern, arguably rings truer to experience than the sterile representation of law and action as essentially separate spheres.[100] In this vein, Peer Zumbansen comments on the concreteness, the earthiness of legal pluralism: 'Legal pluralists, by drawing on anthropological and sociological accounts to more adequately capture the dynamics of norm-creation and regulatory practice, scrutinize the distinction between a legal and a social norm to better understand the concrete process through which a norm comes into existence and is adhered to or rejected'.[101]

The lure of reconceptualising law seems to grow even stronger when contrasted with the repressive inclination of attempts to reclaim law. The former's willingness to acknowledge 'norms that do not fit' throws into sharp relief the tendency of defensive responses to ignore or define them out of existence. Such responses may bring short-term relief, but they are hardly sustainable attempts at problem solving.

The reconceptualisation of law along more heterarchical, pluralistic and reflective lines could also be preferable to conservative and adaptive (reconstructive) approaches. Pragmatically speaking, reconceptualisation may be more attainable than the large-scale legislative efforts that would be required to replicate the

97 Cf. Virginie Barral, 'Sustainable Development in International Law: Nature and Operation of an Evolutive Legal Norm' (2012) 23(2) *European Journal of International Law*, pp. 377–400, at 388–390.

98 Olaf Dilling, 'Legitimacy Collisions in 3D: Some Queries with the Third Dimension of Joerges' Conflicts Law' in Christian Joerges & Tommi Ralli (eds.), *After Globalisation: New Patterns of Conflict and Their Sociological and Legal Reconstructions* (2011, RECON Report Series), p. 8.

99 Ladeur, 'The Evolution of General Administrative Law', p. 5.

100 Berman, *Global Legal Pluralism*, p. 11.

101 Zumbansen, 'Transnational Private Regulatory Governance', p. 133.

conventional structure, organisation and functions of law at the transnational level. If developments in international environmental law over the past twenty years are an indication, there is currently a limited appetite for the kind of grand legislative orchestration that would be needed to develop a coherent, overarching transnational legal framework. The universalistic spirit of the 1992 UNFCCC and CBD, it transpires, did not set the mould for the future of environmental agreements, but instead contrasts with the more recent practice of international environmental lawmaking which, when it is not amending protocols and annexes to older treaties, tends to be either regional and/or narrowly sectoral in nature.[102] The only current exception to the narrowing remit of international agreements is the Aarhus Convention on Access to Environmental Information, Public Participation in Decision Making and Access to Justice, which is now nearly twenty years old and is, in fact, regional rather than global in scope.

Reconceptualisation and reconstruction also represent starkly different political choices, neither of them unproblematic. To many, the advanced juridification that accompanies reconstructive approaches, and the extent to which they would concentrate decision-making power in the hands of a global legal elite, are deeply unsettling.[103] The pluralism of creative and adaptive responses to transnationalisation could offer an antidote to the development of a winner-decides-all society. The absence of a supreme body of law, interpreted by a privileged set of transnational institutions, is a welcome reminder of the virtues of opposition and contestability. Moreover, as Krisch observes with regard to contestation, in instances where legal regimes collide, there is no reason to assume that law is better equipped than politics to resolve the ensuing tensions.[104]

Yet, for all their promise, creative and adaptive approaches are also seriously problematic. A pluralistic model of law, too, poses significant political risks. Pluralism may result in a greater diffusion of power than attempts to reconstruct law at the transnational level, but it is equally vulnerable to the democratic deficit critique.[105] The *lex mercatoria*, for example, is hardly the law of the people; it is made by and arguably in support of a global commercial elite with expert transactional knowledge, yet its reach extends far beyond its authors.[106]

Secondly, an open acknowledgement of legal pluralism may erode the legitimising function of law. Since the connection between TER and democratic

[102] For a counter-indicative but still very preliminary development, see the proposal to adopt a Global Pact for the Environment. Information available at: http://pactenvironment.org/. For a comprehensive overview of international environmental lawmaking activity through time, see the International Environmental Agreements Database Project at http://iea.uoregon.edu/page.php?query=summary&type=MEA.

[103] Berman, *Global Legal Pluralism*, p. 10.

[104] Krisch, *Beyond Constitutionalism*, p. 283.

[105] I am grateful to Gregory Shaffer for this observation.

[106] Cf. Thomas Schultz, *Transnational Legality: Stateless Law and International Arbitration* (2014, Oxford University Press), pp. 12–14.

representation is both weak and remote, the legitimacy of transnational regulators is strongly beholden to alternative claims to authority. These are typically partially based on qualities such as expertise and output efficiency, but they are also significantly furthered by the perception that the transnational actor under scrutiny is legally accountable and operates under the rule of law. Legal pluralism limits both the availability and robustness of accountability mechanisms and erodes the universal significance of the concept of the rule of law, thus diluting the alternative bases upon which transnational actors can justify the power they wield. Unless backed up by additional guarantees, diffusion is a very thin basis on which to legitimate the exercise of otherwise unchecked legislative power.

Thirdly, Krisch's analysis, although impressively expansive, does not take into account what might be labelled as the 'more advanced' forms of transnational law, namely, the norms generated by private, hybrid or networked regulators outside the auspices of an international legal regime established with the fiat of participating states. Mireille Delmas-Marty's work on Ordering Pluralism, too, stays within the confines of highly institutionalised legal orders such as the UN treaty regime, the WTO, the European Convention on Human Rights (ECHR) and the EU.[107] Whether the legal system possesses sufficient resilience to also productively respond to a legal normativity generated through private, hybrid and informal regulatory networks, remains untested.

A final weakness is that, although creative responses may be grounded in a more contextualised and resonant understanding of processes of norm creation than conservative ones, their very analytical richness can simultaneously stunt their normative potential. Like spontaneity, plurality is difficult to engineer. It is in the formulation of reform proposals that advocates of pluralism are most prone to fall back on conventional tropes. The previously mentioned 'interstitial norms',[108] which should serve to coordinate between heterarchical normative spheres, exemplify the slippery slope between coordination and juridification and, thus, between reconceptualisation and reconstruction. In Delmas-Marty's work, for example, the assertion is made that legal pluralism should in the first place be organised through practices of cross-referencing.[109] It is an elegant solution to the decisionistic void at the heart of legal pluralism, and there is widespread evidence of this practice in transnational regulatory and judicial decision making.[110] However, the suggestion does inevitably beg the question whether the requirement to cross-reference then becomes, itself, the hierarchically superior norm with which the plurality of legal

[107] Mireille Delmas-Marty, *Ordering Pluralism: A Conceptual Framework for Understanding the Transnational Legal World*, trans. Naomi Norberg (2009, Hart Publishing).
[108] Barral, 'Sustainable Development in International Law', pp. 388–390.
[109] Delmas-Marty, *Ordering Pluralism*, pp. 19–37.
[110] Ibid.

regimes must conform and, thus, carries within itself the seeds to undermine the pluralistic vision.[111]

7.4 CONCLUDING REMARKS

It makes intuitive sense that the emergence of new spheres of transnational and often informal authority would challenge conventional understandings of law. The contribution of this chapter was to pinpoint with greater precision where the impacts are being felt. To this end, the analysis identified five key pressure points, namely, conceptualisations of the location, source, organisation, functions and structure of law. For each of these attributes, the expansion of transnational governance regimes, such as those aimed at TER, provokes a problematisation of long held assumptions about what law is and how it works.

Beyond mapping the breadth of transformations that, together, constitute the transnationalisation of law, the discussion conveys a number of significant messages regarding the relation between TER and law. Not every variant of transnational regulation is equally challenging to mainstream conceptualisations of law. Unsurprisingly, regulatory initiatives that flourish under the auspices of well-established frameworks of international or regional law, with EU regulation as a prime example, pose less acute conceptual challenges than transnational private and hybrid regulatory networks, which may display an evolving composition and exert fluctuating levels of authority. However, the discussion equally confirmed that, if the presence of a mature regime such as EU environmental regulation is superficially reconcilable with traditional conceptualisations of law, dissonances remain. The EU legal regime may offer rough functional equivalents to the assumptions of territoriality, exclusivity, exhaustiveness and cohesion that support traditional understandings of legality, but closer inspection quickly reveals their frailty. Even the densely institutionalised, highly organised landscape of EU law cannot fully camouflage the gaps and fissures caused by the evolution of transnational regulatory authority.

A key message that resonates from the overview of possible reactions to the transnationalisation of law, is that seemingly 'commonsensical' proposals for the classification of new forms of environmental regulation, or for the extension or introduction of new rules and principles to govern them, represent important choices that are not only conceptual but also deeply political in nature. The term 'soft law' has become so ubiquitous that its use is hardly questioned. Yet it is important to remember that its deployment implies a clear choice to maintain a hierarchy between traditional and alternative sources of authority. In a similar vein,

[111] Similarly, in what van Asselt calls a 'constitutional twist', Krisch cannot resist the siren call of 'interface norms' that reintroduce a degree of layering or informal hierarchy into the system of law. See Harro van Asselt, 'Pluralism, Informality and Transnational Environmental Law' (2014) 3(1) *Transnational Environmental Law*, pp. 173–189, at 179.

the frequently voiced opinion that TER is likely to suffer from legitimacy deficiencies which should be overcome through the imposition of good governance standards, is not 'simply' a sound suggestion to respond to perceived shortcomings, but also implies a decision to either formally or informally centralise legislative authority; a decision with serious democratic and distributive consequences. Conversely, the approach to reconceptualise law as pluralistic, polycentric and reflexive may result in an alternative distribution of authority, but it is equally political, contentious and, especially, democratically fraught. The aim of the exploration in this chapter was not to elevate one of the three identified responses as superior, but to drive home the point that none of these choices are innocent. This is an important lesson to remember as we move, in the next chapter, to consider the procedural and substantive legal principles that are proposed and increasingly deployed as governance principles for TER.

8

Legal Principles for Transnational Environmental Regulation

The spread and diversity of TER frameworks poses a conceptual challenge to law because it problematises widely held assumptions about law as territorial, emanating from the state, composed of a public and private sphere, functionally constitutive and regulative, cohesive and regimented. It also creates a host of new questions about law's normative content and how to discover it. Beyond the specifics of rules and requirements that, for instance, determine by how many percentage points CO_2 emissions need to be reduced by which point in time, or which documentation needs to be submitted to have a paper processing plant certified, does TER recognise and respect an overarching set of shared principles that guide decision making under its auspices? If so, how can these principles be identified? These are the driving questions which motivate this final instalment of the exploration of TER. It will be argued that, while the well-documented range of TER does not allow for a single, clearly delineated set of principles to be cast as definitive, a number of clear trends in the identification and interpretation of principles for environmental regulation beyond the state nonetheless emerge. These include a growing prominence of procedural rights as environmental principles, which development has been keenly observed within academic circles and beyond, and also an up to now less frequently noted, but equally remarkable, trend towards managerial interpretations of both procedural and substantive environmental principles.

This chapter begins by taking stock of the different challenges that accompany attempts to identify the principles of TER. It then reviews the main bodies of law that could serve as plausible sources for principles to guide transnational environmental decision making, including international environmental law and global administrative law. The analysis subsequently uncovers the key principles for environmental decision making as discussed and deployed in a variety of TER documents, and follows up with a critical discussion of the evolution of legal principles for regulation in the wake of transnationalisation.

8.1 THE CHALLENGES OF IDENTIFYING PRINCIPLES FOR TER

Regulatory authorities are simultaneously governed and governing bodies. Consequently, the notion of TER principles can convey different meanings. First, TER principles could be understood as the norms and standards that external legal authorities, such as constitutional provisions, legal statutes, treaties and judicial or arbitral decisions, confirm as valid and applicable to TER decision making for this decision making to be lawful.[1] Secondly, they might refer to those principles that transnational regulatory authorities proclaim themselves to be governed by or, thirdly, to the principles that TER provisions impose upon their regulatory addressees. The three versions are conceptually distinctive but also inextricably linked. Legislative, judicial and regulatory conceptualisations mutually and continuously inform each other, to the extent that they are often considered 'co-produced'.[2] There is an equally close connection between the principles that govern, or self-govern, regulatory behaviour and those imposed by regulators upon their addressees. Indeed, a regulatory agency that acts transparently in decision making will be more likely to expect transparent behaviour from its addressees, and vice versa.[3] The correspondence between the principles *for* TER and the principles *of* TER is all the stronger when we consider the high quotient of meta-regulation that characterises transnational regulatory activity. The addressees of TER often are, themselves, regulators, or act in a delegated regulatory capacity.

The multiple and interactive generation of TER principles entails that their analysis can commence from a variety of starting positions. The exploration of TER principles could be conducted in a deductive manner, by examining the external standards for assessment of TER behaviour, as rendered in legislative instruments, judgements and decisions, and by reviewing scholarly commentaries on law and jurisprudence. Alternatively, it is possible to approach the question from an inductive angle, and search for the principles for decision making as they are

1 For example, proportionality as a legal principle for regulatory decision making is confirmed in, among others, the German Constitution, the ECHR and the TEU, and is fleshed out in a wealth of European Court of Human Rights (ECtHR), CJEU and German domestic case law. See, e.g., Dieter Grimm, 'Proportionality in Canadian and German Constitutional Jurisprudence' (2007) 57(2) *University of Toronto Law Journal*, pp. 383–397; Andrew Legg, *The Margin of Appreciation in International Human Rights Law: Deference and Proportionality* (2012, Oxford University Press); Tor-Inge Harbo, 'The Function of Proportionality in EU Law' (2010) 16(2) *European Law Journal*, pp. 158–185.

2 Elinor Ostrom, Marco A. Janssen & John M. Anderies, 'Going beyond Panaceas' (2007) Vol 104(39) *Proceedings of the National Academy of Sciences of the United States of America*, pp. 15176–15178; Sheila Jasanoff, 'The Idiom of Co-Production' in Sheila Jasanoff (ed.), *States of Knowledge: The Co-Production of Science and Social Order* (2004, Routledge), pp. 2–3; John Alford, 'The Multiple Facets of Co-Production: Building on the Work of Elinor Ostrom' (2014) 16(3) *Public Management Review*, pp. 299–316, at 302–304.

3 See OECD Guiding Principles for Regulatory Quality and Performance 2005, available at www.oecd.org/fr/reformereg/34976533.pdf.

promulgated by and within the transnational regulatory regime itself, either with respect to the exercise of regulatory authority, or in relation to the behaviour expected from the regulatory addressees. Traditional legal scholarship on the principles that govern regulation overwhelmingly favours the former pathway: principles are primarily identified through the study of sources of law that are formally external to the regulatory authority, such as constitutions, laws and, most importantly, court judgements in judicial review decisions.[4] It is precisely their affirmation in legal texts and binding rulings that is deemed to confirm their status as legal principles.

The proliferation of transnational regimes heralded a sharp rise of interest among legal scholars to expand their investigations from the state-based to the transnational plane and acquire a deeper understanding of the principles and expectations governing regulation beyond the state. This expansion, however, faces a number of complications, many of which were flagged up in the preceding chapter. We recall that transnational regulatory frameworks, and TER particularly, are rarely nested within a single jurisdiction. This characteristic obviously complicates the determination of the appropriate legal regime, and the corresponding body of case law, from which TER principles can be derived. An exception here is the case of EU environmental regulation, which is developed under the auspices of a broad, constitution-like legal framework in the form of the EU Treaties, is well-stocked with regulatory principles, and is further enriched by the relatively extensive judgements of the CJEU.[5] Similarly, environmental regulatory instruments that are embedded within, attached to, or developed in implementation of international conventions can call on public international law as their key source of law.[6] However, in contrast to the EU scenario, international law and jurisprudence are comparatively thin on both the promulgation and interpretation of principles for

4 See, for example, legal scholarship on the precautionary principle in EU regulatory decision making, or on notice-and-comment rulemaking in US regulation, which in both cases is overwhelmingly focused on case law analysis. E.g., Veerle Heyvaert, 'Facing the Consequences of the Precautionary Principle in European Community Law' (2006) 31(2) *European Law Review*, pp. 185–206; Elen Stokes, 'The EC Courts' Contribution to Refining the Parameters of Precaution' (2008) 11(4) *Journal of Risk* Research, pp. 491–507; Theofanis Christoforou, 'The Precautionary Principle and Democratizing Expertise: A European Legal Perspective' (2003) 33(1) *Science and Public* Policy, pp. 205–211; Mark Seidenfeld, 'Demystifying Deossification: Rethinking Recent Proposals to Modify Judicial Review of Notice and Comment Rulemaking' (1997) 75(3) *Texas Law Review*, pp. 483–524; Michael Abramowicz & Thomas B. Colby, 'Notice and Comment Judicial Decision Making' (2009) 76(3) *University of Chicago Law Review*, pp. 965–1036; Kristin E. Hickman & Mark Thomson, 'Open Minds and Harmless Errors: Judicial Review of Postpromulgation Notice and Comment' (2016) 101(2) *Cornell Law Review*, pp. 261–324; Catherine J. Lanctot, 'The Good Cause Exceptions: Danger to Notice and Comment Requirements under the Administrative Procedure Act' (1980) 68(3) *Georgetown Law Journal*, pp. 765–782.

5 Paul Craig, *EU Administrative Law*, 2nd edn. (2013, Oxford University Press); Hanns Peter Nehl, *Principles of Administrative Procedure in EC Law* (1999, Hart Publishing).

6 See Case Concerning Pulp Mills on the River Uruguay, *Argentina* v *Uruguay*, Judgment on the merits, ICGJ 425 (ICJ 2010), 20 April 2010, International Court of Justice.

transnational regulation. When we move our gaze towards private and hybrid forms of TER, the challenge only becomes more pronounced as potential jurisdictions multiply yet case law all but disappears.

Building on the previous chapter, it is possible to consider different strategies to overcome the absence of a readily available jurisdiction from which to derive universally applicable principles for the governance of transnational environmental regulatory activity. In accordance with a defensive line of reasoning, all but those TER regimes that clearly resort under a formally binding international or regional legal regime, such as endangered species listing under the CITES Convention or EU regulation on the deliberate release of GMOs, would be classed as non-regulatory and, therefore, governed by private law. Hence, for a significant segment of TER, the question of public governance principles, which discipline the exercise of regulatory authority, would not arise in the first place. A reconstructive approach to the phenomenon of transnationalisation, in turn, would focus on the development of new public law principles to govern transnational environmental activity. Ming-Sung Kuo's proposal to use the growing body of EU constitutional and administrative law as a basis for the development of transnational regulatory law more generally, exemplifies this strategy.[7] Others have looked to international environmental law as a source of inspiration,[8] or have undertaken comparative studies of constitutional provisions in a search for workable principles to govern transnational decision making.[9] Alternatively, a prominent stream in global administrative law (GAL) scholarship advocates the adaptation of widespread principles of international and domestic administrative law to a new, transnational context.[10] In a similar vein, commentators have argued for the development of a body of international public law to be applied in the more specific context of international organisations making determinations that affect global public goods.[11] The sources vary but, in each of these cases, legal principles are drawn from existing, well-established bodies of law and transferred to a different, transnational context. Finally, a reconceptualising response to transnationalisation would primarily seek to derive the principles of TER from the hustle and bustle of transnational regulatory

7 Ming-Sung Kuo, 'From Administrative Law to Administrative Legitimation? Transnational Administrative Law and the Process of European Integration' (2012) 61(4) *International & Comparative Law Quarterly*, pp. 855–879.

8 See David M. Ong, 'From "International" to "Transnational" Environmental Law? A Legal Assessment of the Contribution of the "Equator Principles" to International Environmental Law' (2010) 79 *Nordic Journal of International* Law, pp. 35–74.

9 James R. May & Erin Daly, *Global Environmental Constitutionalism* (2014, Cambridge University Press); Louis Kotzé, 'Arguing Global Environmental Constitutionalism' (2012) 1(1) *Transnational Environmental Law*, pp. 199–233.

10 Benedict Kingsbury, 'The Concept of "Law" in Global Administrative Law' (2009) 20(1) *European Journal of International Law*, pp. 23–57, at 29 ('sources of law').

11 Armin von Bogdandy, Matthias Goldmann & Ingo Venzke, 'From Public International to International Public Law: Translating World Public Opinion into International Public Authority' (2017) 28(1) *European Journal of International Law*, pp. 115–145.

activity itself, rather than from an external legal source. This in an approach more commonly found in writings on legal pluralism, which features alongside more reconstructive approaches in the GAL literature,[12] and in socio-legal studies. The adoption of an internalised, inductive perspective on the identification of TER principles does not imply that any available external legal source – for example, a judicial determination regarding the legality of a particular transnational regulatory decision – would be pushed aside as irrelevant to the analysis. However, it would be treated as representative, or reflexive, rather than constitutive of transnational regulatory authority.

Since the aim of this chapter is primarily analytical, in that it seeks to discover the key principles that structure TER governance, an inductive approach, which dives into the substance of TER itself and distils principles from its own assertions and strategies, at first sight seems most suited to the enquiry. Textbooks, treaties and even International Court of Justice rulings may proclaim, say, sustainable development to be a binding legal principle, but that does not mean that transnational regulatory decision making invariably (or even generally) lives up to the expectation of sustainability, or interprets the sustainable development principle as envisaged by international lawmakers or judicial bodies. Particularly those transnational regimes that do not fall under a clearly designated jurisdiction of international or regional law are unhindered to develop an autonomous understanding of the prerequisites of environmental governance, which may deviate significantly from the assumptions that animate public law. Yet on the other hand, it would be unwise to rely exclusively on inductive strategies to form an understanding of the principles that guide TER decision making. For one, this overlooks the co-productive nature of regulatory normativity. When transnational regulators, such as the MSC or the FLEGT initiative, espouse the virtues of sustainability, transparency or informed consent, they do not reinvent the wheel but are inevitably informed and influenced by conceptualisations and interpretations developed in other fora, including the sphere of international environmental law.[13] Secondly, analytical examinations are not necessarily devoid of critical reflection, nor should they be. To the extent that external and internal conceptualisations of the principles for TER deviate, an awareness of such differences aides the formation of a critical perspective on TER normativity.[14] For these reasons, the choice in this chapter is to pursue a twofold approach to the identification of TER principles. To this end, we will review, first, key sources of law that have been proffered as significant for the governance of transnational regulatory authority, and then have a closer look at the principles and their interpretation as discussed in various TER documents.

[12] Kingsbury, 'The Concept of "Law"', p. 24.

[13] Markos Karavias, 'Interactions between International Law and Private Fisheries Certification', (2018) 7(1) *Transnational Environmental Law*, pp. 165–184, at 182.

[14] Cf. von Bogdandy et al., 'From Public International to International Public Law', p. 121.

8.2 TER PRINCIPLES: A DEDUCTIVE APPROACH

On 1 March 2015, an assembly of legal experts drawn from the ranks of the judiciary, universities and organisations across the world issued the 'Oslo Principles on Global Obligations to Reduce Climate Change', a set of non-binding recommendations for responsible climate change management.[15] Particularly noteworthy about the Oslo Principles, in addition to their global scope, is that they are one of a few – yet rapidly expanding – group of public policy documents that are addressed to public as well as private actors. They target both states and enterprises, and although some segments of the text differentiate, the Oslo Principles exemplify a transnational approach to environmental governance that aims to overcome the public/private divide so deeply anchored in public policy, and distinguish instead on the basis of relative responsibility and capacity. The opening statements assert: 'all States and enterprises have an immediate moral and legal duty to prevent the deleterious effects of climate change. While all people, individually and through all the varieties of associations that they form, share the moral duty to avert climate change, the primary legal responsibility rests with States and enterprises'. In representing the shared responsibilities of states and enterprises as legal, the Oslo Principles overtly embrace both the reality and desirability of transnational law.

The expertise of the main contributors to the Oslo Principles project represents those legal disciplines that are deemed most pertinent to inspire the development of a body of transnational law to govern actors with enhanced responsibilities for climate change. Key among them are specialists in environmental and, particularly, international environmental law, as well as experts in public international law and human rights. According to the Oslo Principles drafters, neither discipline is individually capable of delivering the tools for effective climate change control: 'No single source of law alone requires States and enterprises to fulfil these Principles. Rather, a network of intersecting sources provides States and enterprises with obligations to respond urgently and effectively to climate change in a manner that respects, protects, and fulfils the basic dignity and human rights of the world's people and the safety and integrity of the biosphere. These sources are local, national, regional, and international and derive from diverse substantive canons, including, inter alia, international human rights law, environmental law and tort law'. This 'network vision' for the legal obligations that shape states' and enterprises' activities further resonates in the Oslo drafters' core understanding of the qualities that all laws, principles, policies and practices which affect the environment and, particularly, the climate, must embrace. They emphasise that all laws, policies and practices must be evidence-based, must heed the precautionary principle, and must respect the obligations to act cooperatively and protect and advance fundamental

[15] Oslo Principles on Global Climate Obligations, available at https://globaljustice.yale.edu/sites/default/files/files/OsloPrinciples.pdf.

human rights.[16] Hence, within a single paragraph, the Oslo Principles draw on administrative law ('evidence-based decision making'), environmental law ('precautionary principle'), international institutional law ('act cooperatively') and human rights to construct an image of the legally responsible state or enterprise in a context of climate change.

The following sections pay closer attention to the different legal disciplines that have been most influential in informing an emergent understanding of transnational environmental law and, particularly, the legal principles that govern TER. These are: international environmental law; human rights and public institutional law.

8.2.1 *International Environmental Law*

In recent decades, international law has reached beyond its traditional constituency of nation states and delivered principles that are increasingly seen as appropriate to structure the behaviour of non-state actors. For instance, in a thoughtful analysis of private fisheries certification under the MSC, Markos Karavias illustrates the 'referencing technique' in the Core Principles of the MSC Fisheries Standard and Guidelines, which precondition certification upon compliance with the requirements of 'local, national and international laws' and deploy the principle of 'maximum sustainable yield', a foundational principle governing state behaviour under international law, as a benchmark for private fisheries management.[17] Generally, we recall from discussions of the intentionality of TER in Chapter 3 that, for both substitute TER and risk management TER, coalition building by incorporating compliance with national and international law can be a strategy to reduce the regime's vulnerability to scrutiny and contestation.[18]

Predictably, in the context of environmental regulation, the principles of international environmental law are seen to have a particular relevance to secure the legality and legitimacy of transnational regulatory initiatives. It is well-known that there is no single, authoritative source of legally binding international environmental principles; their status solidifies and erodes gradually, through generations of treaty law, international court rulings, explicit or tacit state endorsement or, conversely, through law and policy reform, amendment or disuse.[19] Yet notwithstanding a degree of fluidity, in the past century legal scholarship and practice have developed a reasonably robust understanding of a core set of substantive, procedural and distributive principles to instruct the environmental behaviour of states in

[16] Ibid.

[17] Karavias, 'Interactions between International Law and Private Fisheries Certification', p. 175.

[18] See also Jürgen Friedrich, *International Environmental 'Soft Law'* (2013, Springer Verlag), p. 240.

[19] Cf. Pierre-Marie Dupuy, 'Formation of Customary International Law and General Principles' in Daniel Bodansky, Jutta Brunnée & Ellen Hey (eds.), *The Oxford Handbook of International Environmental Law* (2008, Oxford University Press), pp. 450–465.

international law. The 1992 Rio Declaration on Environment and Development constitutes a non-binding but authoritative source of such principles, listing, among others, states' sovereign right to exploit their natural resources and their corresponding responsibility to prevent transboundary environmental damage (Principle 2); the precautionary principle (Principle 15);[20] the principle of sustainable development (Principles 1, 3, 4, 8, 12, 24 and 25);[21] the polluter pays principle (Principle 16); the expectations that environmental impact assessments will be carried out to inform decision making (Principle 17) and that states will cooperate in the pursuit of environmental protection strategies and the prevention of environmental damage (Principles 5, 7, 9, 12–14, 18 and 27); the principles of public access to environmental information, participation in decision making, and access to justice (Principle 10); an expectation that the position of women, youth, indigenous groups and other vulnerable communities will be given particular consideration (Principles 20–23) and the principle that states have common but differentiated responsibilities for environmental protection (Principles 6, 7 and 11).

Iterations of these principles resonate in the preambles and the articles of various international environmental agreements, as well as in a compact but high-profile set of International Court of Justice rulings in international environmental disputes.[22] Moreover, international conventions and other large-scale proclamations have yielded additional principles not covered by Rio, most prominently the 'common heritage of (hu)mankind' principle, which 'represents the notion that certain global commons or elements regarded as beneficial to humanity as a whole should not be unilaterally exploited by individual states or their nationals, nor by corporations or other entities, but rather should be exploited under some sort of international arrangement or regime for the benefit of mankind as a whole'[23] and the related notion of 'common concern of humankind'. The latter equally reflects the view that some aspects of the environment need cooperative, cross-border action to enjoy effective protection, but shifts the focus

[20] The absence of full scientific evidence should not be used as a reason to postpone intervention for environmental protection, particularly if there is a threat of irreversible harm. See Heyvaert, 'Facing the Consequences'.

[21] Sustainable development is development that meets the needs of the present without compromising future generations' ability to meet their needs. World Commission on Environment and Development, *Our Common Future* (1987, Oxford University Press); see John Dernbach & Federico Cheever, 'Sustainable Development and Its Discontents' (2015) 4(2) *Transnational Environmental Law*, pp. 247–287, at 252–267.

[22] See, e.g., Nuclear Tests Case (*New Zealand* v *France*) [1995] ICJ Rep 288; Gabčikovo-Magymaros Project (*Hungary* v *Slovakia*) [1997] ICJ Rep 7, 90 91998} 37 ILM 162; Pulp Mills (*Argentina* v *Uruguay*) [2010] ICJ Rep 14.

[23] Edwin Egede, 'Common Heritage of Mankind', *Oxford Index on International Law*, see http://oxfordindex.oup.com/view/10.1093/obo/9780199796953–0109.

away from the politically charged language of exploitation and unilateralism which characterises the 'common heritage' notion.[24]

Principles of international environmental law traditionally govern inter-state behaviour, however, their instructive value as potential benchmarks against which to assess the regulatory behaviour of intergovernmental bodies as well non-state actors is frequently emphasised. Karavias underlines the importance of international law for the organisation of fisheries certification.[25] In an earlier study, David Ong examined the non-governmental Equator Principles (EP) through a lens of international environmental law, and found that several of the EP's core prescriptions correspond closely to familiar dictates of international environmental law, including the expectation of an impact assessment, transparency and a public participation in decision making.[26] Moreover, the EP lay down different standards and lending requirements depending on whether the financing projects are located in non-OECD, low-income OECD or high-income OECD countries, which Ong identifies as a functional equivalent for the principle of common but differentiated responsibilities in a transnational context.[27] In the same vein, the OECD Guidelines for Multinational Enterprises, a multi-stakeholder initiative to set standards for responsible entrepreneurial behaviour, draws heavily on the Rio Declaration, as well as on the Aarhus Convention on Access to Information, Public Participation in Decision-Making, and Access to Justice, to flesh out its Environmental Section.[28] Conversely, discussions within the international legal sphere increasingly reflect an awareness that the effective fulfilment of the principles and objectives of international environmental law cannot be achieved without the engagement of transnational regimes. In this spirit, Goal 17 of the UN Sustainable Development Goals proclaims: 'A successful sustainable development agenda requires partnerships between governments, the private sector and civil society. These inclusive partnerships built upon principles and values, a shared vision, and shared goals that place people and the planet at the centre, are needed at the global, regional, national and local level'.[29]

8.2.2 *Human Rights*

In the quest for principles against which to evaluate the legality and legitimacy of TER, human rights are an important point of reference. Overwhelmingly, human

[24] Friedrich Soltau, 'Common Concern of Humankind' in Cinnamon P. Carlarne, Kevin R. Gray & Richard Tarasofsky (eds.), The Oxford Handbook of International Climate Change Law (2016, Oxford University Press), pp. 203–211, at 206.

[25] Karavias, 'Interactions between International Law and Private Fisheries Certification'.

[26] Ong, 'From "International" to "Transnational" Environmental Law?', pp. 62 and 64–65.

[27] Ibid., p. 63.

[28] OECD Guidelines for MNEs, 2011 version, section VI, Commentary on the Environment section pt. 60.

[29] Information available at https://sustainabledevelopment.un.org/.

rights are now considered to encompass the right to a healthy environment, which is explicitly confirmed in most national constitutions,[30] or is alternatively inferred from pre-existing rights, such as the rights to life and privacy as expressed in Articles 2 and 8 ECHR.[31] Moreover, the connection between human rights and environmental regulation has been significantly strengthened with the rise in prominence of the so-called third generation or procedural human rights, which in the environmental sphere comprise the Aarhus rights of access to environmental information, participation in environmental decision making and access to justice.[32]

The relevance of third generation, procedural human rights as principles for TER is easy to discern. Although the Aarhus Convention only directly governs the behaviour of public authorities, the obligations it entails for regulators to act transparently and inclusively, and to provide an opportunity for the contestation of regulatory decisions, can be transported reasonably straightforwardly to the realm of non-state actors and hybrid constellations as well. This does not mean that the imposition of procedural environmental principles within a transnational regulatory context will always be unproblematic. For example, since the geographical reach of TER may fluctuate and is potentially unconstrained by national or regional borders, it may be considerably more difficult for transnational regulators to identify 'the public' which should be informed and consulted in decision making, than it is for state-based authorities. By the same token, the organisation of independent review mechanisms for transnational regulatory decisions may be onerous, complicated and fraught with credibility challenges outside the remit of well-established administrative and judicial review trajectories. Nevertheless, the directive significance of human rights-based procedural principles for TER is apparent.

In contrast, the contribution of a substantive right to the environment as a disciplining influence for transnational regulatory behaviour is harder to gauge. Indeed, since TER by definition pursues an environmental objective, it might be argued that all variants of TER harness a human right to the environment and none could possibly violate it. However, environmental rights have acquired a richer

30 For a full overview of national constitutions with environmental provisions, see Roderic O'Gorman, 'Environmental Constitutionalism: A Comparative Study' (2017) 6(3) *Transnational Environmental Law*, pp. 435–463.

31 See *López Ostra* v *Spain* [1994] App no 16798/90, ECHR 46, (1995) 20 EHRR 277; *Fadeyeva* v *Russian Federation*, App No 55723/00, ECHR 2005-IV, [2005] ECHR 376; *Öneryıldız* v *Turkey*, App no 48939/99, ECHR 2004-XII, (2005) 41 EHRR 20; Richard Desgagné, 'Integrating Environmental Values into the European Convention on Human Rights' (1995) 89(2) *American Journal of International Law*, pp. 263–294; Francesco Francioni, 'International Human Rights in an Environmental Horizon' (2010) 21(1) *European Journal of International Law*, pp. 41–55, at 48–54; Jonathan Verschuuren, 'Contribution of the Case Law of the European Court of Human Rights to Sustainable Development in Europe' in Werner Scholtz & Jonathan Verschuuren (eds.), *Regional Integration and Sustainable Development in a Globalised World* (2015, Edward Elgar), pp, 363–385.

32 Don Anton & Dinah Shelton, *Environmental Protection and Human Rights* (2011, Cambridge University Press), pp. 356–434.

texture in the past decades, with several countries developing a more detailed understanding of the actions that need to be undertaken for such rights to be effectively guaranteed. May and Daly's seminal study of global constitutionalism reports that, among others, Albania, Belgium, Bolivia, Ecuador, Kenya and South Africa connect the human right to the environment to the expectation that sustainable development will be respected in decision making.[33] The South African Constitution is particularly noteworthy in its specificity. After affirming everyone's right to an environment that is not harmful to their health or wellbeing, it provides that this includes the right 'to have the environment protected, for the benefit of present and future generations, through reasonable legislative and other measures that (i) prevent pollution and ecological degradation; (ii) promote conservation and (iii) secure ecologically sustainable development and use of natural resources while promoting justifiable economic and social development'.[34] Hence, it is possible to connect substantive rights with both more goal-oriented and operational prescriptions that can be applied within a regulatory setting.

A further remarkable aspect of the South African Constitution lies in its reference to 'reasonable legislative *and other measures*' in pursuit of environmental rights objectives. The broad phrasing could be read as an implicit nod to the environmental contribution from initiatives that fall outside the traditional remit of public policy conducted by government authorities. Here, we may see an opening towards a more active engagement with non-state actors as guarantors of constitutionally protected environmental rights.[35] The argument that private actors can be the bearers of human rights responsibilities also undergirds the pending petition against carbon majors, lodged with the Philippines Commission on Human Rights by environmental NGOs,[36] which asserts that the climate-related consequences of

[33] May & Daly, *Global Environmental Constitutionalism*, pp. 64–70 and 262. A draft version of the 2015 Paris Agreement, too, connected human rights and sustainable development, and suggested that sustainable development is, in itself a human right. See draft Art. 2 calling on states for the 'respect, protection, promotion and fulfilment of human rights for all, including indigenous peoples, including the right to health and sustainable development'. This wording did not make it into the final version, which only refers to human rights in the preamble. See draft agreement and draft decision on workstreams 1 and 2 of the Ad Hoc Working Group on the Durban Platform for Enhanced Action, Work of the ADP contact group, edited version of 6 Nov. 2015, re-issued 10 Nov. 2015.

[34] May & Daly, *Global Environmental Constitution*, p. 69. See also South Sudan, as discussed in May & Daly, *Global Environmental Constitutionalism*, p. 70.

[35] The argument that private entities may bear human rights responsibilities has a well-established pedigree in legal scholarship. See, for example, Stephen R. Ratner, 'Corporations and Human Rights: A Theory of Legal Responsibility' (2001) 111(3) *Yale Law Journal*, pp. 443–545; Denis G. Arnold, 'Corporations and Human Rights Obligations' (2016) 1(2) *Business and Human Rights Journal*, pp. 255–275; John Gerard Ruggie, *Just Business: Multinational Corporations and Human Rights* (2013, W. W. Norton & Company).

[36] 'Petition to the Commission on Human Rights of the Philippines Requesting for Investigation of the Responsibility of the Carbon Majors for Human Rights Violations or Threats of Violations Resulting from the Impacts of Climate Change', submitted by Greenpeace

corporate behaviour impair the lives and livelihoods and, hence, the human rights of present and future generations.[37] The Commission's acceptance of the petition, announced on the first day of the Paris Agreement concluding negotiations in December 2015, signals at least a willingness to engage with human rights-based argumentation beyond the traditional remit of state-individual relations.

8.2.3 *Public Institutional Law: Constitutional Law, Administrative Law and International Public Law*

A final cohort of legal sources for TER principles is composed of the public law disciplines which have as a focus or at least include a focus on governing the exercise of public authority. Key among these are constitutional law, international institutional law, and administrative law. Each discipline yields its own set of directives for the exercise of regulatory authority, although there are significant overlaps in the gist and even the substance of a number of their foundational principles. For instance, expectations that authority will be exercised transparently, and that binding acts and decisions will be reviewable, resonate in constitutional documents as well as in administrative law and international institutional law. The main reason why commentators favour one or other legal discipline as the anchoring point for the development of principles for transnational regulation arguably has less to do with the specific content of the respective legal principles, and more with their understanding of the scope of transnational regulation as either narrow or inclusive. Equally, the choice will be influenced by their view on the requisite qualities which a legal regime must possess in order to be capable of legitimising the exercise of regulatory authority, and by their favouring of a defensive, reconstructive or reconceptualising response to the transnationalisation of law. Indeed, the past decades have witnessed a vigorous debate between advocates of constitutionalism, international institutional law and administrative law as the appropriate foundation for transnational regulatory authority. The next few paragraphs cannot fully capture the richness and diversity of viewpoints represented in this debate, but do aim to convey the key points that are relevant in the context of this exploration of TER principles.

The first, constitutionalist perspective reflects the position that, to be legal and legitimate, regulation should be subject to an overarching, normatively superior level of control, which is typically secured through its submission to constitutionally

Southeast Asia and the Philippine Rural Reconstruction Movement on behalf of numerous other organisations and individuals. See https://secured-static.greenpeace.org/seasia/ph/PageFiles/735291/Human_Rights_and_Climate_Change_Consolidated_Reply_2_10_17.pdf.

[37] Sam Adelman, 'Human Rights in the Paris Agreement: Too Little, too Late?' (2018) 7(1) *Transnational Environmental Law*, pp. 17–36, at 36.

guaranteed principles and requirements.[38] It implies a belief in the need for a vertical, hierarchical relationship between the kind of authority that is exercised through regulatory decision making, and the superior authority that flows from foundational, primary legislation. The latter's superiority is typically justified with reference to the stronger democratic credentials of constitutional principles; they serve as the most reliable indicator of the ways in which and the extent to which a 'pouvoir constituant' is willing to rein in the freedom of its members for the greater good, and at the same time flag up the boundaries between permissible and impermissible intrusions upon individual self-determination.[39] As the exercise of regulatory authority necessarily implies that individual freedom is curtailed – directly in the form of the positive requirements, prohibitions or compelling incentives addressed to regulatory addressees; indirectly in terms of the inescapable consequences of regulated behaviour for third parties – this invasion must stay within constitutional boundaries in order to qualify as the type of restriction of which the public has expressed its approval in general terms in a constitutional act.

Although constitutions are traditionally understood to address the relationship between the citizen and the state, constitutionalist perspectives can accommodate a broader conception of public authority and, hence, expand the range of relationships that are considered to be caught within the constitutional dialogue.[40] Since the key motivation for subjecting regulatory structures to constitutional authority relates to their *impact* rather than their institutional design, constitutionalism need not necessarily stumble over the distinctions between public, private and hybrid regulatory authority. The determinative point is whether and how individual freedom is curtailed; not who does the curtailing. Reconciling the transboundary dimension of TER with a constitutional perspective represents a greater challenge since, with the arguable exception of the EU Treaties in the case of EU environmental regulation,[41] there is no readily discernible global or transnational constitution to which transnational regulatory frameworks and, specifically, TER can be subjected.[42] Here the notions of 'global constitutionalism' and 'global environmental constitutionalism', which have gained considerable traction in the last decade, might offer a resolution.[43] Rather than referring to a particular constitutional

38 Chris Thornhill, 'National Sovereignty and the Constitution of Transnational Law: A Sociological Approach to a Classical Antinomy' (2013) 3(4) *Transnational Legal Theory*, pp. 394–460, at 400.

39 Kotzé, 'Arguing Global Environmental Constitutionalism', p. 204.

40 Anne Peters, The Constitutionalist Reconstruction of International Law: Pros and Cons (NCCR International Trade Working Paper No. 11(07–2006)), p. 6.

41 'Arguable' because the democratic legitimacy of the EU Treaties is less robust than that of national constitutions in democratic states. See Claudia Schrag Sternberg, *The Struggle for EU Legitimacy* (2013, Palgrave Macmillan).

42 Daniel Bodansky, 'Is There an International Environmental Constitution' (2009) 16(2) *Indiana Journal of Global Legal Studies*, pp. 565–584.

43 May & Daly, *Global Environmental Constitutionalism*; Kotzé, 'Arguing Global Environmental Constitutionalism', pp. 199–233.

exercise, they reflect the proposition of a fluid but gradually maturing and converging body of constitutional principles that is drawn from yet transcends the national level.[44] The quest for global (environmental) constitutionalism has fuelled a keen interest in comparative constitutionalism[45] to unearth connective seams of globally overlapping perspectives on the organisation and legitimation of power, as well as on the appropriate values and strategies to support both the conceptualisation and the pursuit of the common good.[46]

As a source for TER principles, global constitutionalism taps into a wealth of national experience and delivers principles from the governance as well as the rights-based end of the legal spectrum. Constitutional principles cover institutional discipline as well as fundamental rights; general administrative matters as well as specifically environmental issues; proportionality as well as sustainability.[47] From this vantage point, constitutional traditions are a promisingly rich source for the development of transnational legal principles. On the other hand, it has been argued that, partly because of its 'global common denominator' premise, the substance of both global constitutionalism and global environmental constitutionalism is too broad and generic to be an effective foundation for transnational regulatory principles. Constitutional law, it is argued, does not supply the detail and specificity required to engage successfully with day-to-day regulatory and administrative decision making, whether in a national or a transnational context.[48]

The constitutionalist perspective could be represented as one that is essentially located at the national level with the potential to travel outwards. For constitutionalists, transnational regulatory authority is a variation on the theme of national regulatory authority and, to the extent that it mimics the coercive, freedom-constraining impact of state regulation, it may need to be subjected to the same or similar constitutional principles, requirements and restrictions as the latter. The international institutionalist perspective, by comparison, takes as its point of departure the actions of international governmental organisations, and draws other, transnational structures into its orbit on the basis of their proximity to or similarity with international organisations. The function of international institutional law as a discipline is to lay down common principles for the exercise of international legal authority. These principles focus heavily on the need for state consent, which is the driving legitimising force of international law and is expressed primarily through decision-making rules requiring member country unanimity, consensualism or

44 Kotzé, 'Arguing Global Environmental Constitutionalism', p 211.

45 von Bogdandy et al., 'From Public International Law to International Public Law', p. 128.

46 Cf. Miguel Poiares Maduro, 'The Importance of Being Called a Constitution: Constitutional Authority and the Authority of Constitutionalism' (2005) 3(2/3) *International Journal of Constitutional Law*, pp. 332–356, at p. 333.

47 Kotzé, 'Arguing Global Environmental Constitutionalism', p. 208.

48 Cf. Christoph Möllers, 'Ten Years of Global Administrative Law' (2015) 13(2) *International Journal of Constitutional Law*, pp. 469–472, at 471.

(qualified) majority voting. Additional key principles of international institutional law include the legality principle, which requires the exercise of international authority to be founded on an international legal mandate and in accordance with the procedural requirements set out in international law, and the prohibition for international organisations to act beyond their competence or *ultra vires*.[49]

The international institutionalist approach to transnational regulatory authority clearly does not struggle with the 'beyond the state'-quality of TER as its own premise is very much transboundary. However, international institutional law engages less easily with the non-state dimension of transnational regulation. There is a strong formalist expectation in international institutional law that the establishment of international organisations is secured and circumscribed through international agreements, treaties or conventions. Entities that flourish outside the strict boundaries of binding international instruments are inherently disruptive and problematic. In view of the proliferation of international organisations which lack such clearly enunciated international legal mandate, as well as the experience that international organisations may over time acquire powers that were not foreseen in their founding documents, commentators have tried to 'work around' the conceptual constraints of international institutional law and relax its boundaries. For instance, Jan Klabbers acknowledges that not all international organisations that are subject of international institutional law are the product of a binding treaty or convention. Some have been created through instruments adopted by pre-existing international organisations, such as the United Nations Children's Fund (UNICEF), which was established via United Nations General Assembly (UNGA) resolution. Others, such as the Nordic and the Arctic Council, are the product of informal inter-state cooperation.[50]

Other commentators emphasise the need for international organisations to have an official legal basis in order to constitute a legitimate subject of international law, but qualify that this may be a soft as well as a hard legal basis. Thus, Armin von Bogdandy, Matthias Goldmann and Ingo Venzke assert: 'The established sources of treaties, custom and general principles provide guidance in most cases. Some acts, however, are based on soft legal instruments – for example, the Basel Accords by the Basel Committee on Banking Supervision. Soft law created by states or international institutions should be included in the canon of possible legal bases because, in the context of global governance, it often plays a functionally equivalent role to hard law. The choice between soft law and hard law as a legal basis should not allow governments and international institutions to escape normative requirements, and,

49 Jan Klabbers, *An Introduction to International Institutional Law*, 2nd edn. (2009, Cambridge University Press), pp. 226–252.

50 Ibid., p. 11. On the Arctic Council, see Betsy Baker & Brooks Yeager, 'Coordinated Ocean Stewardship in the Arctic: Needs, Challenges and Possible Models for an Arctic Ocean Coordinating Agreement' (2015) 4(2) *Transnational Environmental Law*, pp. 359–394, at 368–372.

indeed, the respective legal regimes are often similar'.[51] Such proposed relaxations may enhance the relevance of international institutional law as a source of TER principles because they widen the range of regulators with which international institutional law engages, but either approach still hinges heavily on the presence of states as initiators of transboundary projects. The presence may be second-order or informal rather than confirmed via an internationally binding instrument, but it remains essential. Hence, it is highly questionable whether, from and international institutional law perspective, the discipline could serve as a legitimate source of legal principles to govern the activities of entities such as the Carbon Neutral Protocol or the FSC.

A further caveat regarding international institutional law as a source for TER principles relates to its relative substantive thinness when contrasted with constitutional or administrative law. Beyond the requirement of state consent and its derived values (voting provisions, mandate, *ultra vires* prohibition), the governance principles of international institutional law are rather opaque. Klabbers observes that requirements of legality and the doctrine of *ultra vires* imply the possibility for the validity of acts of international institutions to be judicially reviewed,[52] which suggests a general expectation of contestability of legislative acts. It is, however, unclear whether this amounts to a principle of international institutional law and, if so, whether it should be deemed transferable to regulatory decision making. Von Bogdandy, Goldmann and Venzke's proposal for the development of a body of international public law, to govern institutions founded upon international hard or soft law, reflects an awareness of the need for more and further developed governing principles, but it has not (yet) moved beyond the level of general advocacy.[53]

The third and most influential public law approach towards the identification of legal principles for transnational regulation proposes administrative law as a lens through which to view and evaluate transnational regulatory behaviour. In the past decade, the proposition popularised in the work of Benedict Kingsbury, Nico Krisch and Richard Stewart of a nascent body of 'global administrative law' (GAL), which governs a rapidly expanding array of transnational entities with regulatory and administrative functions and which needs to be further developed and defined, has captured the imagination of law and policy communities.[54] It offered a timely

[51] von Bogdandy et al., 'From Public International Law to International Public Law', p. 133. The authors distinguish their approach to the legal governance of international institutions, which engages with a broader range of entities than international institutional law *sensu stricto*, by labelling theirs an 'international public law' approach.

[52] Klabbers, *An Introduction to International Institutional Law*, pp. 235–247.

[53] von Bogdandy et al., 'From Public International Law to International Public Law', pp. 124–125.

[54] Benedict Kingsbury, Nico Krisch & Richard B. Stewart, 'The Emergence of Global Administrative Law' (2005) 68(3/4) *Law and Contemporary Problems*, pp. 15–61.

response to an ever more pressing concern about the proliferation of powerful transnational organisations and networks, ranging from the Internet Corporation for Assigned Names and Numbers (ICANN) and the Basel Committee on Banking Supervision to the International Council of Chemical Association's Responsible Care® programme, which adopt policies and make decisions that have a deep and lasting social impact but which operate beyond the purview of effective state control. Now, a little over ten years on from Kingsbury, Krisch and Stewart's landmark article, GAL has become an established player in the debate about transnational law and governance.

Beyond its timeliness, GAL's appeal is arguably explained by its direct and deliberate engagement with, precisely, those messy and complex regulatory regimes that are misfits in either a national or an international legal context.[55] Whereas constitutional provisions can be creatively applied outside their traditional interactional space between the individual and the state, and international institutional law can be stretched to cover those institutions established through soft as well as hard international law instruments, GAL needs no such tweaks; transnational structures are its focus rather than its sideshow. Moreover, GAL attempts to straddle the national and transnational divide by acknowledging national administrative legal traditions as its primary source yet simultaneously emphasising that administrative law takes on *sui generis* forms and meanings when exercised in a beyond-the-state context. GAL is not a cross-section of the administrative laws of all countries; it is a nascent body of transnational norms and operating principles which are informed by but have evolved from state-based iterations.[56] GAL scholarship also accommodates different perspectives on the extent to which such transnational norms and principles *ought to* come together as a cohesive body of law to govern all transnational regulatory activity, with some espousing reconstructive and others more reconceptualist and pluralistic agendas.[57] Finally, as a source of governance principles for regulation, administrative legal traditions are an

[55] Cf. Eyal Benvenisti, *The Law of Global Governance* (2014, Hague Academy of International Law), p. 80.

[56] Cf. Peer Zumbansen, 'Neither "Public" Nor "Private", "National" nor "International": Transnational Corporate Governance from a Legalist Pluralist Perspective' (2011) 38(1) *Journal of Law and Society*, pp. 50–75, at 59.

[57] See Eduardo Chiti, 'Where Does GAL Find Its Legal Grounding?' (2015) 13(2) *International Journal of Constitutional Law*, pp. 486–491; Richard B. Stewart, 'Remedying Disregard in Global Regulatory Governance: Accountability, Participation, and Responsiveness' (2014) 108 (2) *American Journal of International Law*, pp. 211–270, at 213; von Bogdandy et al., 'From Public International to International Public Law', p. 130. For a reconstructive take on GAL, see Kuo, 'From Administrative Law to Administrative Legitimation'; for a pluralistic take, see Nico Krisch, 'Who Is Afraid of Radical Pluralism? Legal Order and Political Stability in the Postnational Space' (2011) 24(4) *Ratio Juris*, pp. 386–412.

arguably richer well to tap than either constitutional or international institutional law.[58] GAL scholars can draw on a broad range of nationally established good governance requirements, including transparency, proportionality, 'sound science' or 'evidence-based' decision making, participation and reasonableness, and correspondingly rich bodies of case law, to examine and contribute to the juridification of the transnational legal sphere.[59]

Yet for all its attractions, GAL also has its limitations. The question has been raised whether administrative law can be an adequate and sufficient basis to legitimise the type of authority that is channelled through transnational regulatory structures and networks.[60] It could be argued that GAL's accommodating qualities, which enable it to engage with the broad and sprawling diversity of transnational regulatory activity, are also its Achilles' heel. It encompasses and relabels as 'administrative' a range of actions which, if functional equivalents were sought in the national sphere, would be considered of a legislative, executive or even judicial character,[61] and in the process devalues and misrepresents them. The legitimacy of GAL as a basis for transnational regulatory principles generally, and TER principles in particular, is even more tenuous when we consider what 'global' really means in this context. GAL principles may have a theoretical connection with administrative law traditions across the world but, in practice, the influence of North American and, to a lesser degree, West European and Australian jurisprudence is overwhelming.[62] Indeed, legal elites from these regions play key roles both in transnational governance circles and in the legal academic circles which are commenting upon and co-producing both concept and content of GAL.

Finally, after twelve years of vibrant GAL scholarship, it is difficult to escape the impression that, for all the talk of global administrative law, little progress has been made in pinning down its content (or its various bodies of content under a pluralist perspective) beyond familiar, broad and general 'good governance' exhortations. Publicness and accountability are the most frequently proposed qualities that transnational decision makers should embrace,[63] and transparency and participation the most frequently emphasised vehicles through which these qualities can be pursued, but a great deal of work remains to be done on what notions such as

[58] Cf. Möllers, 'Ten Years of Global Administrative Law', p. 471.

[59] Lorenzo Casini, 'Beyond Drip-Painting? Ten Years of GAL and the Emergence of a Global Administration' (2015) 13(2) *International Journal of Constitutional Law*, pp. 473–477, at 473–474.

[60] von Bogdandy et al., 'From Public International Law to International Public Law', pp. 130–131.

[61] Ibid. Cf. Stewart, 'Remedying Disregard', p. 217.

[62] Richard B. Stewart, 'The Normative Dimensions and Performance of Global Administrative Law' (2015) 13(2) *International Journal of Constitutional Law*, pp. 499–506, at 499.

[63] Kingsbury, 'The Concept of "Law"'; Stewart, 'Remedying Disregard'.

transparency and participation actually mean and should mean in a variety of transnational contexts. Even less is known about how other stalwarts of national administrative law, such as proportionality, reasonableness, evidence-based decision making and review, should be interpreted and applied as principles of GAL, as distinctive from their application within a domestic setting. Until such greater depth of knowledge is reached, the impact of GAL as both an organising and disciplining force on transnational regulatory authority and, in this case, TER, is limited.[64]

8.3 TER PRINCIPLES: AN INDUCTIVE APPROACH

Moving from the deductive to the inductive stage, we now turn the spotlight on the very TER regimes that are at the heart of the investigation and examine which principles are actually espoused by TER itself, rather than imprinted upon it by the respective disciplines of international environmental law, human rights law, or public institutional law in one of its various guises. As was the case for the examination of regulatory strategies, an exhaustive analysis of every known example of TER would far exceed both the capacity of the author and the forbearance of the reader. Nonetheless, the study is grounded in a broad range of examples which allows reasonable generalisation. The overview will proceed in two steps: first, shared general features of TER principles will be identified, followed by an itemised discussion of the most frequently affirmed and advocated principles in TER documents.

8.3.1 *General Characteristics*

Scanning the TER landscape, a first category of regulatory frameworks and regimes that is irrefutably distinctive in terms of its relation to legal principles, is the extensive body of European Union environmental regulation. To a considerable extent, the agonies that shape transnational debates about whether, say, private, constitutional or administrative law is the appropriate reference point to test the legitimacy of transnational authority, have dissipated with respect to EU regulation. This is because, under the auspices of the EU Treaties, a body of transnational institutional

[64] Cf. similar critique by von Bogdandy, Goldmann and Venzke with reference to organisations operating under international law or international soft law: 'The development of an operative legal vocabulary for international public authority is a pressing task. Most importantly, the frequent absence of elaborated legal standards leads to the unfortunate situation that international institutions exercise public authority that many might perceive to be illegitimate but cannot claim to be illegal for lack of such standards'. von Bogdandy et al., 'From Public International Law to International Public Law', pp. 124–125.

and administrative law has flourished.[65] EU environmental regulation is well-structured and guided by both governance principles and procedural rights, including both a general layer and a set of directives that particularly pertains to environmental decision making. The core set of general standards that EU decision making must adhere to includes the principles of subsidiarity, proportionality, transparency, participation and the duty to give reasons.[66] Moreover, Articles 191(2) and (3) TFEU articulate principles that particularly – although not exclusively[67] – relate to EU environmental policy:

> 2. Union policy on the environment shall aim at a high level of protection taking into account the diversity of situations in the various regions of the Union. It shall be based on the precautionary principle and on the principles that preventive action should be taken, that environmental damage should as a priority be rectified at source and that the polluter should pay.
>
> In this context, harmonisation measures answering environmental protection requirements shall include, where appropriate, a safeguard clause allowing Member States to take provisional measures, for non-economic environmental reasons, subject to a procedure of inspection by the Union.
>
> 3. In preparing its policy on the environment, the Union shall take account of:
> – available scientific and technical data,
> – environmental conditions in the various regions of the Union,
> – the potential benefits and costs of action or lack of action,
> – the economic and social development of the Union as a whole and the balanced development of its regions.

Through years of implementation, as well as a considerable body of EU case law, both the general principles and particular environmental provisions have shaped the EU approach to environmental regulatory decision making, although some principles feature more prominently than others. The general transparency and participation requirements in Articles 11 and 15 TFEU are particularly influential, all the more so because their importance is amplified by the EU's adherence to and active support of the Aarhus Convention on Access to Information, Public Participation in Decision-Making and Access to Justice in Environmental Matters. Access to justice is the weaker link in this triad. It does not have a general corollary in Article 15 TFEU, and opportunities for third parties judicially to contest EU environmental regulation are notoriously strapped by the EU's stringent standing requirements for

[65] Craig, *EU Administrative Law*; Nehl, *Principles of Administrative Procedure in EC Law*.

[66] Art. 5 TEU (subsidiarity and proportionality); Art. 15(3) TFEU (transparency); Art. 11 TEU (participation); Art. 296 TFEU (duty to give reasons).

[67] The precautionary principle, for example, has been recognised as a general principle of EU law, see Joined Cases T 74/00 et al., *Artegodan GmbH* v *Commission* [2002] ECR II-4945, at para. 184.

so-called non-privileged applicants.[68] Instead, the main avenue for third parties to challenge EU regulatory provisions is via a request for the internal review of an administrative act, which is only granted to a list of recognised NGOs and which does not cover broad regulatory measures.[69] As to the principles in Article 191 TFEU, the high level of environmental protection (HLP) principle, the prevention, proximity and polluter pays principle are routinely alluded to in the preambles of EU environmental directives and regulations, but their justiciability has rarely been tested[70] and they exert limited discernible disciplining force on the processes and practice of EU environmental regulation. In contrast, the precautionary principle and the requirements under Article 191(3) TFEU have been both more intensively discussed and tested in case law. As a consequence, their contribution to the EU's environmental regulatory ethos is both more pronounced and defined.[71]

Compared to EU environmental regulation, other sources of public TER are generally much more tight-lipped about the governance principles that animate their environmental decision making. To the extent that international legal instruments with a clear regulatory content such as the Basel Convention on Hazardous Waste,[72] the Minamata Convention on Mercury, the Stockholm Convention on Persistent Organics Pollutants, the Kyoto Protocol and Paris Agreement in implementation of the UNFCCC express governance principles, they typically do not serve to guide the behaviour of the intergovernmental decision makers themselves or that of bespoke bodies set up in service of the international regime. Any rules of procedure and decision-making conventions expressed in this context tend to concern internal organisation on matters such as frequency of meetings, internal circulation of documents and, most crucially, voting rules. For example,

68 Damian Chalmers, Gareth Davies & Giorgio Monti, *European Union Law*, 3rd edn. (2014, Cambridge University Press), pp. 444–455.

69 See Regulation (EC) No 1367/2006 of the European Parliament and of the Council on application of the provisions of the Aarhus Convention on Access to Information, Public Participation in Decision-Making and Access to Justice in Environmental Matters to Community institutions and bodies [2006] OJ L264/13 and Commission Decision of 13 Dec. 2007 laying down detailed rules for the application of Regulation (EC) No 1367/2006 as regards requests for the internal review of administrative acts [2008] OJ L13/24.

70 There is a compact body of case law regarding the HLP principle (see Delphine Misonne, 'The Importance of Setting a Target: The EU Ambition of a High Level of Protection' (2015) 4(1) *Transnational Environmental Law*, pp. 11–36, at 17–22) and the prevention and proximity principle (see Suzanne Kingston, Veerle Heyvaert & Aleksandra Čavoški, *European Environmental Law* (2017, Cambridge University Press), pp. 99–102). On the latter, however, case law chiefly concerns the compatibility of *national* environmental policies with EU law, not EU environmental regulation itself. See Case C-2/90, *Commission* v *Belgium* (*Walloon Waste*) ECLI:EU:C:1992:310; Case C-209/98, *Sydhavnens*, ECLI:EU:C:2000:279.

71 See Kingston et al., *European Environmental Law*, pp. 26–35 and 94–99; Ellen Vos (ed.), *European Risk Governance: Its Science, Its Inclusiveness and Its Effectiveness*, Connex Report Series No 6 (2008).

72 Basel (Switzerland), 22 Mar. 1989, in force 5 May 1992, available at www.basel.int/TheConvention/Overview/TextoftheConvention/tabid/1275/Default.aspx.

environmental governance principles and procedural guarantees for third parties are scarce among the extensive rules and principles governing the International Seabed Authority (ISA),[73] even though it exercises a number of clear environmental regulatory functions with a transnational impact.[74]

Instead, the governance principles in public and also hybrid TER with a significant 'public authority quotient' are typically addressed to the regulatees, which may be implementing countries, cities, regional actors, private corporations or, even, individuals. Thus, the Basel Convention, Stockholm Convention and Paris Agreement all warmly embrace transparency as a governance principle, but the regulatory authorities which are expected to behave transparently are, in the first place, the national competent authorities when devising and implementing national regulation in compliance with the respective Conventions. Hence, governance principles and procedural rights in this cohort of TER are mostly 'second-order' or meta-regulatory principles which instruct the addressees in their implementation of transnationally agreed objectives.

The most common explanation for the dearth of governance principles in international legal instruments is that state consent obviates the need for an alternative basis of legitimation;[75] the concern of a runaway bureaucracy does not materialise when all binding decisions are directly approved by national governments, either through signature and ratification or via voting in the Conference of the Parties. This would also help to explain the distinctive situation of EU environmental regulation: as the legitimising force of state consent is weakened through increased delegation to supranational bodies such as the European Commission and through a shift to majoritarian decision making, the importance of governance principles and procedural rights ascends. However, there may be additional factors at play to explain the presence or absence of governance principles and procedural

[73] Rules and principles are laid down in the United Nations Convention on the Law of the Sea (UNCLOS) (Montego Bay, Jamaica), 10 Dec. 1982, in force 16 Nov. 1994, available at www.un.org/depts/los/convention_agreements/texts/unclos/unclos_e.pdf); the 1994 agreement relating to the implementation of Part XI of the United Nations Convention on the Law of the Sea of 10 Dec. 1982 and the respective Operational Rules of Procedures of the ISA Council, Assembly, Finance Committee, and Legal and Technical Commission (available at www.isa.org.jm/authority). Rudimentary governance principles cover a possibility for consultation of pre-approved NGOs and expectations that ISA decisions are supported by an environmental impact assessment and that general policies are open to review.

[74] See Michael Lodge, David Johnson, Gwenaëlle Le Gurun, Markus Wengler, Phil Weaver & Vikki Gunn, 'Seabed Mining: International Seabed Authority Environmental Management Plan for the Clarion–Clipperton Zone: A Partnership Approach' (2014) 49 *Marine Policy*, pp. 66–72, at 67–68.

[75] *Case of the SS Lotus* [1927] Publ. PCIJ, Series A, No. 10, p. 18. See Klabbers, *An Introduction to International Institutional Law*, p. 64; Nico Krisch, 'The Decay of Consent: International Law in an Age of Global Public Goods' (2014) 108(1) *American Journal of International Law*, pp. 1–40, at 3, Joost Pauwelyn, Ramses A. Wessel & Jan Wouters, 'When Structures Become Shackles: Stagnation and Dynamics in International Lawmaking' (2014) 25(3) *European Journal of International Law*, pp. 733–763, at 748.

rights. Intentionality may also play a role. Among public TER, trade facilitation TER tends to place a stronger emphasis on governance principles and procedural rights than collective action TER. This is exemplified in the context of ASEAN. ASEAN relies overwhelmingly on consensual, intergovernmental decision making and, consequently, can be presumed to benefit from the legitimising force of state consent. Nevertheless, its 2025 Economic Community Blueprint heavily emphasises the importance of good governance standards, in particular stakeholder engagement, and mandates respect of governance principles and procedural rights most emphatically for the adoption of trade harmonisation measures.[76] Similarly, the GHS, while not exactly voluble on the subject, does preliminarily set out its agreed principles for harmonisation, which include a requirement that levels of environmental protection should not be reduced as a consequence of harmonisation; requirements of stakeholder engagement and an expectation of transparency in that agreed classifications and labels must be comprehensible for workers, consumers and the general public.[77]

By the same token, enhancement TER typically articulates fewer 'first-order' governance principles and procedural rights than substitute or risk management TER. This is remarkable because accession to either category of TER is formally voluntary: private actors are free but not forced to sign up to the Roundtable on Sustainable Palm Oil (RSPO), or Responsible Care®, or the FSC, just like cities choose to join C40, the Compact of Mayors or the Global Sustainable Tourism Council, and states or regional actors opt to accede to the RGGI or WCI. Hence, regulatory purpose may be a better predictor of the likelihood of a TER regime observing procedural rights and having a set of clearly articulated governance principles, than its binding or voluntary status. Indeed, a considerable number of the private environmental regulators, which typically serve a substitute or risk management purpose, are members of the International Social and Environmental Accreditation and Labelling (ISEAL) Alliance and subscribe to the ISEAL Code of Good Practice for Setting Social and Environmental Standards.[78] The Code defines effective standard-setting processes which are intended to convey credibility upon adherent organisations. ISEAL does not publish its Code in full detail – it is a proprietary asset accessible only to paying ISEAL members – but its general ethos is built around ten governance principles. These include sustainability; transparency and meaningful engagement with stakeholders; expectations that standards will be accessible to addressees, fit for purpose, rigorous and efficient and adopted with an eye to improvement in performance over time.

76 Information available at www.asean.org/storage/images/2015/November/aec-page/AEC-Blueprint-2025-FINAL.pdf.

77 GHS s. 1.1.1.6, available at www.unece.org/trans/danger/publi/ghs/ghs_welcome_e.html.

78 Information available at www.isealalliance.org/get-involved/resources/iseal-codes-good-practice.

8.3.2 *Key TER Principles*

Notwithstanding the extensive variety between individual TER instruments, a broad and admittedly impressionistic survey of the actual principles proclaimed or endorsed by different types of transnational environmental regimes does reveal some patterns and trends. First, procedural governance principles are more widespread than substantive ones. Virtually every example of a TER regime which offers some degree of information about its own governing principles espouses transparency and stakeholder engagement. In comparison, commitments to observe the prevention principle or the proximity principle are much harder to find. Even the most intergovernmental variants of TER, such as the regulatory provisions contained in MEAs, tend to emphasise procedural over substantive principles. Secondly, among procedural principles, access to information and participation are better covered than access to justice; TER regimes tend to be distinctly more accessible to notions of ex-ante involvement[79] than ex-post contestation. Thirdly, TER principles evolve over time: while principles such as 'polluter pays' nowadays rarely feature in an environmental regulatory context, other notions are on the rise, such as an expectation of progression. The following paragraphs offer more detail on individual TER principles.

Transparency

Commitments to transparency feature in all categories of TER. They occur in, to give a handful of examples, every instance of EU environmental regulation; the Minamata Convention on Mercury;[80] the ASEAN Regulatory Practice Guide for the adoption of harmonisation measures;[81] The UN Programme on Reductions in Emissions from Deforestation and Forest Degradation (UN REDD Programme);[82] public statements released by the Compact of Mayors;[83] and the ISEAL principles for standard setting which, in turn, are observed by a wide range of TER initiatives.[84] Many other TER regimes may not explicitly commit to transparency, but overtly

79 Stewart, 'Remedying Disregard', p. 239.

80 Minamata Convention, Art. 5(4): 'The Secretariat shall, on the basis of information provided by Parties, collect and maintain information on processes that use mercury or mercury compounds and their alternatives, and shall make such information publicly available'.

81 See http://regulatoryreform.com/wp-content/uploads/2015/08/ASEAN-Good-Regulatory-Practice-GRP-Guide-2009.pdf, Section 2.1: 'Taking into consideration current practices by national and regional bodies and obligations on good regulatory practice, there is a convergence of views on common principles for good regulatory practice, whereby good regulation should … g) be transparent to both regulators and those affected by regulation.'

82 Information available at www.un-redd.org/how-we-work.

83 Information available at www.globalcovenantofmayors.org/wp-content/uploads/2015/07/Compact-of-Mayors-Full-Guide_July2015.pdf.

84 Cf. Joanne Maimaris, 'ISEAL membership linked to improved transparency, accessibility and rigour of a standards systems' (14 July 2017), available at www.isealalliance.org/sustainability-news/iseal-membership-linked-improved-transparency-accessibility-and-rigour.

take pains to be open and informative about their decision-making process and its outcomes. Such is the case for, among others, the ISO,[85] the RGGI, and the EP. The latter also illustrates the evolving importance attached to governance principles in a transnational regulatory context: with every new iteration of the EP, its governing bodies go to greater lengths to structure and document internal decision-making processes.[86] In April 2017, the EP Association published its governance rules, which include information on, inter alia, decision-making thresholds and requirements for the EP Steering Committee, a body which has 'the power and authority to plan, lead, and commission work or activities related to the administration, management, and development of the Equator Principles'.[87]

Transparency equally features prominently among 'second-order' or meta-regulatory principles endorsed by TER. The Paris Agreement,[88] the Basel Convention on Hazardous Waste[89] and the UNEP Cairo Guidelines and Principles for the Environmentally Sound Management of Hazardous Wastes,[90] the Minamata Convention,[91] the Stockholm Convention on Persistent Organic Pollutants,[92] ASEAN, the OECD Guidelines for Multinational Enterprises and, again, every piece of EU regulation, all exhort and in some instances oblige their addressees to behave transparently.

Approaches to transparency differ, yet TER initiatives tend to conceptualise transparency as a primarily active rather than a passive responsibility. Transparency is achieved by the regulator deliberately creating and disseminating information about the decision-making process, about implementation and enforcement actions, or about complaints and their resolution. Apart from EU environmental regulation, which is subject to the provisions of the Aarhus Convention, transnational environmental regulators rarely connect transparency explicitly to 'access to environmental information' or the 'right to know';[93] they increasingly recognise a responsibility to

85 See Evisa Kica, 'The Drive towards Nanotechnology Standardization: Shifting Roles in Governance and Key Challenges', (2012) 3(2) *European Journal of Risk Regulation*, pp. 227–234, at 230: 'According to Hatto (a former chairman of the ISO committee on nanotechnology ...), standards can demonstrate legitimacy in the sense that "they are proposed, commented on and approved by stakeholders from the international community to provide an agreed benchmark ... and the standardization process is robust, transparent, consensual and voluntary"'.

86 Ong, 'From "International" to "Transnational" Environmental Law?', p. 72.

87 See http://equator-principles.com/wp-content/uploads/2018/01/governance-rules-april-2017-v2.pdf.

88 Arts. 4(8) and 4(12) PA.

89 Art. 13 Basel Convention.

90 Guideline 20. Information available at.

91 Art. 18 Minamata Convention.

92 Art. 10(2) Stockholm Convention.

93 For an exception see Art. 10(2) Stockholm Convention: 'Each Party shall, within its capabilities, ensure that the public has access to the public information referred to in paragraph 1 and that the information is kept up-to-date'.

inform but consider this generally as a tenet of their commitment to 'good governance'[94] or 'regulatory excellence'[95] rather than as the consequence of an obligation to respect fundamental rights.

Secondly, many TER regimes, particularly those with a high level of private actor engagement in regulatory decision making, face considerable challenges in balancing transparency against confidentiality.[96] The protection of sensitive commercial information is an issue which confronts environmental regulators regardless of whether they are state-based, transnational, public, private or hybrid. However, balancing exercises to reconcile transparency and confidentiality have a different starting point for public and private actors, since generally only the former operate under a legal duty to grant access to information. Moreover, in some scenarios the commercial actor whose interests are jeopardised through disclosure of regulatory information is the transnational regulator herself. For example, the standards adopted in the context of substitute, risk management or enhancement TER may constitute a business asset only to be released to (paying) subscribers to the regulatory scheme. Indeed, their public unavailability may be the key reason why companies accede to the scheme in the first place. This is a complication that generally does not affect 'traditional' state-based environmental regulators, and it requires devising alternative strategies to introduce a credible level of transparency without undermining the raison d'être of the initiative. Hence, both the different balance between transparency and confidentiality expectations in many TER regimes, and the potentially proprietary nature of TER standards and rules, affect the implementation of transparency within a transnational context in a distinctive manner.

Participation

Stakeholder participation as a TER principle has a similar profile to transparency. It is one of the most frequently featured governance principles and can be found across the rungs of public, private and hybrid TER.[97] Participation appears both as a first- and second-order principle, to be observed by transnational regulators as well as their addressees in implementation of overarching environmental regulatory requirements. In some cases, participation must be inferred from the regime's operation in practice, but overwhelmingly TER instruments explicitly affirm their endorsement of participatory decision making. For example, the ISO, which does not explicitly mention transparency among its key decision-making principles, does

94 Kingston et al., *European Environmental Law*, pp. 41–43.

95 See Cary Coglianese (ed.), *Achieving Regulatory Excellence* (2017, Brookings Institution Press).

96 See, for example, provisions on transparency and confidentiality with respect to the financial institutions subscribing to the Equator Principles, http://equator-principles.com/wp-content/uploads/2018/01/governance-rules-april-2017-v2.pdf.

97 Cf. John Braithwaite & Peter Drahos, *Global Business Regulation* (2000, Cambridge University Press), p. 36.

emphasise that its standards are developed through a multi-stakeholder process.[98] Furthermore, as with transparency, participation expectations tend to become more deeply embedded in transnational regulation over time. Jürgen Friedrich contrasts older OECD decision-making procedures, which he describes as 'opaque' and lacking 'any participatory element in decision-making' with the 2000 and 2011 revisions of the OECD Guidelines for MNEs, which were accompanied 'by a full-fledged public consultation process' and 'drew heavily on the various stakeholders represented through BIAC, TUAC and OECD Watch as well as the expertise of the OECD Secretariat'.[99]

A final important point is that TER tends to frame participation, like transparency, as an active rather than a passive requirement. The wording of participation, or 'stakeholder consultation', provisions generally reflects the regulator's positive commitment to inclusiveness rather than her observance of an individual right to participation. This approach enables TER regimes to claim inclusiveness while remaining strategic and, conceivably, selective about who they involve in the decision-making process.[100] EU environmental regulation is, again, exceptional in this regard as it is subject to the public participation provisions of the Aarhus Convention although, even in the EU context, the right to participation strictly applies to 'plans and programmes relating to the environment' rather than to the very act of regulatory decision making itself.[101]

Contestability

The principle of contestability, or the availability of an opportunity to contest a regulatory decision, is a rather more challenging proposition than transparency or participation. EU environmental regulation and administrative decisions, for example, have a solid reputation as to their accessibility and inclusiveness, but are famously hard to interpellate, particularly if the challenge comes from third parties who are indirectly affected by an EU rule or decision, instead of parties directly addressed in the regulatory or administrative act.[102] Observance of the Aarhus principles has brought some degree of relief as it has introduced a requirement for the availability of internal review of so-called administrative acts of individual scope, but this requirement by no means covers the full range of EU environmental

98 Information available at www.iso.org/developing-standards.html.

99 Friedrich, *International Environmental 'Soft Law'*, pp. 118–119.

100 Ibid, p. 119: 'One can assume that the secretariat influenced the process through a selection process of which comments were taken into account and which were not' and p. 120.

101 See Regulation (EC) No 1367/2006 on the application of the provisions of the Aarhus Convention on Access to Information, Public Participation in Decision-Making and Access to Justice in Environmental Matters to Community institutions and bodies [2006] OJ L264/13, Arts. 2(1)e and 9.

102 Chalmers et al., *European Union Law*, pp. 444–455.

regulation and the mechanism is moreover reserved for environmental NGOs rather than open to the public generally.[103]

By the same token, avenues for recourse against regulatory decisions taken under the auspices of MEAs are typically very limited, particularly if such decisions are taken by or on behalf of national governments in accordance with unanimity or consensual voting rules. Some instruments do introduce a modest level of contestability, such as the Stockholm Convention on POPs, which enables member countries to resubmit proposals for the inclusion of additional substances on the list of restricted chemicals after they have been set aside by the POPs Committee, and furthermore allows members to challenge POPs Committee decisions. Any challenged decisions are forwarded for the consideration of the COP.[104] This provision exposes POPs Committee decision making to some level of contestation, but only to a limited extent: the review mechanism is set up as an internal process exclusively for the benefit of parties involved in TER decision making, and does not introduce opportunities for external interpellation and accountability.

The characteristic of limited contestability extends beyond TER adopted in implementation of international agreements. As a rule of thumb, transnational regimes with a high degree of public authority involvement in the design and application of environmental regulatory provisions are thin on review and redress mechanisms. This is the case whether the regulatory framework is binding or voluntary, and regardless of the primary purpose which the regime serves – collective action or trade facilitation; substitution or enhancement.[105] By comparison, TER initiatives with a high quotient of private regulatory involvement tend to score better on contestability. For example, the FSC and the RSPO are open to receiving complaints about the organisation itself as well as about the behaviour of certified parties, and both have established dispute resolution systems. The FSC dispute resolution center enables stakeholders, rather than only FSC members, to express their 'concerns about the operation of the FSC system', which covers the FSC certification strategy; the FSC Network; the FSC accreditation programme and the performance of FSC accredited certification bodies.[106] The RSPO Complaints System, too, admits complaints against individual members and against the regime itself, and is accessible to members as well as '[n]on-members including affected communities (and their nominated representative), workers (and their nominated representative), other interested parties etc'.[107] The Roundtable moreover has an

[103] Arts. 10 & 11 Reg. 1367/2006. Cf. Benedikt Pirker, 'Access to Justice in Environmental Matters and the Aarhus Convention's Effects in the EU Legal Order: No Room for Nuanced Self-Executing Effect?' (2016) 25(1) *RECIEL*, pp. 81–91, at 86–87.

[104] Art. 8 Stockholm Convention.

[105] Risk management is not listed because this TER of this nature is overwhelmingly private/private; see Chapter 3.3.4.

[106] See https://ic.fsc.org/en/what-is-fsc/what-we-do/dispute-resolution.

[107] Information available at https://rspo.org/members/complaints.

RSPO Dispute Settlement Facility to support those aggrieved parties who face particular barriers to access to information, advice and expertise, which would prevent them from engaging in the complaints process 'on fair, informed and respectful terms'.[108] The professed overall aim of the RSPO Dispute System is to ensure that 'any alleged breaches of specified RSPO Statutes, By-laws, motions approved by the General Assembly, or any other approved articles, including the Principles & Criteria for Sustainable Palm Oil Production, Certification System and RSPO Code of Conduct are fairly, impartially and transparently resolved'. While stated intentions reveal very little about the System's actual success at securing contestability, they do unequivocally confirm its openness to a broad range of legality and legitimacy challenges.

In practice, however, the difference in contestability between TER with a high level of public versus private involvement may not be as pronounced as the preceding paragraphs suggest. First, the divide is not static: public TER seems to be evolving towards greater degrees of openness to complaints. The decisions of the Clean Development Mechanism Executive Board (CDM EB), taken in pursuit of the flexible mechanisms laid down in the Kyoto Protocol, are closed off to third party review or appeal.[109] In contrast, the more recent UN REDD Programme places a stronger emphasis on the availability of grievance mechanisms for all parties affected by decisions taken by REDD Delivery Partners, whether they are country participants or transnational actors.[110] Secondly, it is important to recall that a considerable proportion of the regulatory content produced by transnational regulators is subject to further elaboration and implementation at the local level. Affected parties may therefore have the opportunity indirectly to query transnational regulatory decisions by challenging their national or otherwise decentralised implementation. They may be facilitated in this task by the provision of second-order TER principles, which require the regulatory addressees to make available grievance mechanisms and complaints procedures in their dealings with individual applicants or other impacted parties. This is the case for, for instance, the OECD Guidelines for MNEs and the UN Global Compact.[111] Both establish certain expectations that aggrieved parties, affected by the policies and decisions of enterprises who subscribe to the Guidelines of Compact, will be granted access to some form of review process, either in the context of mediation, reconciliation or a complaints

[108] Ibid.

[109] Charlotte Streck & Jolene Lin, 'Making Markets Work: A Review of CDM Performance and the Need for Reform' (2008) 19(2) *European Journal of International Law*, pp. 409–442, at 426–428.

[110] See www.forestcarbonpartnership.org/sites/forestcarbonpartnership.org/files/Documents/PDF/Aug2012/FCPF%20Readiness%20Fund%20Common%20Approach%208–209-12.pdf and www.forestcarbonpartnership.org/sites/forestcarbonpartnership.org/files/Documents/PDF/May2011/FCPF%20UN-REDD%20Stakeholder%20Guidelines%2005–18–11.pdf.

[111] Friedrich, *International Environmental 'Soft Law'*, pp. 120–123 and 347–353.

procedure. Such 'second-order contestability' may fall significantly short of the administrative and judicial review guarantees that tend to discipline state-based regulatory authorities,[112] but it goes some way towards enhancing the accessibility of the transnational regime.

Sound Science and Precaution

In addition to transparency and participation, 'sound science' requirements, or the expectation that regulatory decision making will be based on the best available scientific evidence and expertise, are among the most widely endorsed TER principles. They constitute a firm pillar of EU environmental regulation[113] and feature prominently in other public, private and hybrid TER.[114] They occur both as first-order and second-order principles.[115]

It is arguably unsurprising to find broad adherence to sound science and best available science across TER instruments. References to science and expertise tend to boost the credibility of decision-making regimes, and are all the more vital in constellations where the regulator has few representative, directly democratic or alternative credentials to justify its exercise of regulatory authority. What is conceivably more unexpected is the frequency with which the precautionary principle is mentioned and endorsed in TER documents. The precautionary principle permits regulatory decision making under conditions of scientific uncertainty and advocates that, particularly when irreversible harm might ensue, interventions may happen proactively and in the absence of conclusive scientific evidence.[116] It is far more permissive of the exercise of regulatory discretion than a requirement that all regulation must be based on sound scientific evidence and, consequently, considerably more controversial and divisive. The United States' opposition to precaution as

[112] Ibid.

[113] Art. 191(3) TFEU; see Kingston et al., *European Environmental Law*, pp. 31–36.

[114] Present in, inter alia, the Vienna Convention; the Montreal Protocol; the preamble to the Gothenburg 1999 Protocol to Abate Acidification, Eutrophication and Ground-level Ozone to the Convention on Long-range Transboundary Air Pollution (Gothenburg [Sweden]; 30 Nov. 1999, in force 15 May 2005, available at www.unece.org/env/lrtap/multi_h1.html); the International Seabed Association's Mining Code. See Rosemary Rayfuse, 'Precaution and the Protection of Marine Biodiversity in Areas beyond National Jurisdiction' (2012) 27(4) *The International Journal of Marine and Coastal Law*, pp. 773–781, at 779; the Covenant of Mayors for Climate and Energy; the ISEAL Code for Standard Setting; the RGGI; the ASEAN Good Regulatory Practice Guide (2009) at http://regulatoryreform.com/wp-content/uploads/2015/08/ASEAN-Good-Regulatory-Practice-GRP-Guide-2009.pdf and the ISO key principles for standard development.

[115] Second-order sound science principles can be found in, inter alia, the OECD Guidelines for MNEs and the Oslo Principles.

[116] Kingston et al., *European Environmental Law*, pp. 94–99; Philippe Sands & Jacqueline Peel, *Principles of International Environmental Law* (2012, Cambridge University Press), pp. 217–228.

a guiding principle for environmental decision making, for example, has been widely documented.[117]

Taking these factors into account, the precautionary principle has been remarkably successful as a TER principle. It is an EU legal principle for both environmental governance and public policy more generally, and is endorsed in the preambles and articles of a broad array of international environmental agreements, from the Montreal Protocol to the Convention on Biological Diversity. Moreover, the most noteworthy aspect of the principle's success is that it features in a number of voluntary TER initiatives, both governed by the public and the private sector. It is not part of the ISEAL Principles for Standard-setting, to which a substantial number of private TER regimes subscribe, but some ISEAL subscribers such as the FSC do endorse the precautionary principle or a precautionary approach in certain aspects of their decision making, alongside the ISEAL principles.[118] Both the UN Global Compact and the OECD Guidelines for MNEs exhort their addressees to 'support a precautionary approach to environmental challenges' and 'not use the lack of full scientific certainty as a reason for postponing cost-effective measures',[119] particularly when 'there are threats of serious damage to the environment, taking also into account human health and safety'.[120]

One domain of TER in which the precautionary principle has become particularly well-embedded is marine governance. Although absent from the environmental provisions of the UN Convention on the Law of the Sea (UNCLOS),[121] which was adopted ten years before the 1992 Rio Declaration propelled the precautionary principle to global visibility, precaution is a key tenet of the 1995 UN Fish Stocks Agreement (FSA), which insists on a precautionary approach 'in the management of straddling and highly migratory fish stocks'.[122] Moreover, in contrast to, for example, the UNFCCC which contents itself with a general and unspecified reference to precaution, the FSA sets out a methodology for the development and application of precautionary management strategies, which cover harvested marine species as well as associated and dependent species.[123] Precautionary prescriptions have since been adopted by a wide range of regional fisheries management organisations (RFMOs)

[117] See Cass R. Sunstein, *Laws of Fear: Beyond the Precautionary Principle* (2005, Cambridge University Press); Frank B. Cross, 'Paradoxical Perils of the Precautionary Principle' (1995) 53 (3) *Washington and Lee Law Review*, pp. 851–928.

[118] Principle 9 (on maintenance of high conservation value forests) of the FSC Principles and Criteria for Forest Stewardship, see https://ic.fsc.org/en/what-is-fsc-certification/principles-criteria.

[119] Global Compact, Principle 7.

[120] OECD Guidelines MNEs Section VI, pt. 4.

[121] Montego Bay (Jamaica), 10 Dec. 1982, in force 16 Nov. 1994, available at www.un.org/depts/los/convention_agreements/texts/unclos/unclos_e.pdf.

[122] Rayfuse, 'Precaution and the Protection of Marine Biodiversity', p. 775. UN Fish Stock Agreement 1995, New York (NY, US), 4 Aug. 1995, in force 11 Dec. 2001, available at http://www.un.org/depts/los/convention_agreements/convention_overview_fish_stocks.htm.

[123] Rayfuse, 'Precaution and the Protection of Marine Biodiversity'.

and assume a prominent place in the Code of Conduct for Responsible Fisheries (CCRF), a voluntary instrument adopted by the FAO and addressed to national governments, regional organisations, NGOs and fishing enterprises alike.[124] Precautionary strategies have also been absorbed into various fisheries certification initiatives, such as the MSC-run scheme, which deploys what it refers to as 'highly' precautionary risk-based indicators for the assessment and consequent accreditation of fisheries regarding which limited data is available.[125] The highly networked structure of transnational fisheries governance, in which public, private and hybrid forms of TER intersect, overlap and refer to each other,[126] is arguably conducive to both the effective embedding of TER principles and their further development into benchmarks and indicators against which regulatory and administrative decision making can be measured.

Sustainability and Progression

The vast majority of transnational environmental regimes identify sustainable development or sustainability as a guiding principle for both regulation and actions taken in implementation of regulatory incentives or requirements.[127] As with previously identified TER principles, sustainable development cuts across different categories of TER and is endorsed as a first- as well as a second-order principle for regulatory decision making.

Sustainable development is a complex concept with a rich history and a formidable body of scholarly literature to match. An examination of this history, and the many legal and policy debates surrounding the interpretation and application of the principle, is beyond the scope of this discussion.[128] Yet it is useful to reflect briefly on the most likely reasons why references to sustainable development and sustainability are close to ubiquitous in TER legal texts, preambles, mission statements and other

[124] Friedrich, *International Environmental 'Soft Law'*, pp. 68–70 & 182: 'the CCRF is referred to explicitly in some regional fisheries treaties. Thus, the Agreement on the International Dolphin Conservation Program initiated by the Inter-American Tropical Tuna Commission provides in its general principles that "the Parties shall ... take measures to ensure the conservation of ecosystems as well as conservation and management measures ... and apply the precautionary approach, consistent with the relevant provisions of the FAO CCRF and the UN Agreement on Straddling Fish Stocks and Highly Migratory Fish Stocks"'.

[125] Information available at www.msc.org/about-us/standards/fisheries-standard/msc-risk-based-framework.

[126] Karavias, 'Interactions between International Law and Private Fisheries Certification'.

[127] The principle of sustainable development is affirmed in, to name but a few, Art. 3(3) TEU; the CBD, the UNFCCC, the Basel Convention on Hazardous Waste, the Vienna Convention, the CNP, the FSC and MSC, the Global Compact, Responsible Care® and the WCI.

[128] For some key recent contributions, see Dernbach & Cheever, 'Sustainable Development and Its Discontents'; Norichika Kanie & Frank Biermann (eds.), *Governing through Goals: Sustainable Development Goals as Governance Innovation* (2017, The MIT Press); Klaus Bosselmann, *The Principle of Sustainability: Transforming Law and Governance*, 2nd edn. (2016, Routledge); Timothy Cadman et al. (eds.), *The Political Economy of Sustainable Development: Policy Instruments and Market Mechanisms* (2015, Edward Elgar).

governance-related TER documents. A key factor is sustainable development's unchallenged status as the most iconic concept in the history of environmentalism. Over the years, it has developed an enduring, although not uncontested, appeal as an informed yet flexible conceptual framework through which to normalise humankind's relationship to the environment. Erected on the core premise that society should strive to meet its own development needs without compromising the ability of future generations to meet theirs, it offers sufficient direction to support the development of tangible yardsticks against which to gauge the sustainability and, hence, acceptability of regulatory structures, interpretations and decisions.[129] At the same time, owing to the balancing dynamic inherent in the sustainability paradigm and its openness towards different economic, political and ideological readings of the very needs of present and future generations, it is experienced as less constraining on decision making than alternative environmental principles such as prevention, proximity and polluter pays.

Transnational environmental regulators operationalise sustainable development in different ways. Some effectively do not; they simply refer to sustainable development and present the regulation as an *expression of* sustainable development rather than as an exercise of authority that needs to be guided and, conceivably, policed by the principle.[130] In other cases, sustainable development is reconstituted as an umbrella objective, the attainment of which hinges on the observance of a collection of environmental and governance principles such as precaution, polluter pays, environmental impact assessment and cooperation.[131] An alternative iteration of this approach sees sustainable development primarily operationalised as a check against fragmentation in environmental regulatory decision making. This approach has been particularly noticeable in the context of carbon offsetting regimes, which were vulnerable to supporting, for instance, the generation of carbon credits that came at the expense of biodiversity losses, or air, water or soil pollution. Contemporary regulatory requirements for, among others, decision making under the CDM and the UN REDD Programme include sustainable development standards which aim to avert environmentally deleterious carbon mitigation.[132] Thirdly, sustainable development in a TER context may be interpreted to require the adoption of particular

[129] See, for example, the seventeen UN Sustainable Development Goals, which add a considerable degree of implementation detail to the concept, at www.un.org/sustainabledevelopment/sustainable-development-goals/.

[130] See, for example, statements by the International Council of Chemical Associations (ICCA), which refer to its endorsement of Responsible Care® as evidence of its commitment to sustainable development. Information available at www.icca-chem.org/sustainable-development/.

[131] For example, Art. 4(3) of the Barcelona Convention (Convention for the Protection of the Marine Environment and the Coastal Region of the Mediterranean, Barcelona (Spain), 16 Feb. 1976, in force 12 Feb. 1978, at http://wedocs.unep.org/bitstream/handle/20.500.11822/7096/Consolidated_BC95_Eng.pdf?sequence=1&isAllowed=y).

[132] Heather C. Lovell, 'Governing the Carbon Offset Market' 2010(1) *WIRES Climate Change*, pp. 353–362, at 359.

managerial strategies, such as environmentally sound management (ESM). This operationalisation chiefly concerns sustainable development when applied as a second-order principle to govern the decision-making behaviour of TER addressees, including public and private entities. For instance, ESM is heavily emphasised in the Basel Convention on Hazardous Waste;[133] the Minamata Convention on Mercury and the OECD Guidelines for MNEs, which explicitly portray ESM as an implementation of sustainable development.[134] Most significantly, however, sustainable development has been linked to a nascent principle of progression in TER.

The past decade has witnessed the emergence of progression as an operationalisation of sustainable development within TER regimes. Requirements of progressive ambition are most prominent in climate change regulation. They are embedded within, for example, the Paris Agreement, which requires its member countries to submit progressively more ambitious NDCs for each global stocktake;[135] the EU ETS and the RGGI, which are organised around a gradual lowering of the overall emissions cap for regulated sectors; and in the CNP, which calls for the development of progressively more ambitious mitigation targets over time.[136] However, progression as a TER principle has also made inroads beyond the climate change context. For example, the OECD Guidelines for MNEs exhort its subscribers to 'continually seek to improve corporate environmental performance';[137] ISEAL requires standard scheme owners to adopt a 'continuous improvement approach' towards standardisation;[138] and the Responsible Care® Global Charter emphasises the regime's commitment to continuous improvement in chemicals product safety and stewardship.

The proliferation of 'progression' and 'continuous improvement' expectations in TER heralds a subtle but significant shift in the sustainability ethos of environmental regulation. On the one hand, their incrementalism could easily accommodate a weakening of the effective level of environmental protection delivered through

[133] By way of a cross reference to Cairo Guidelines and Principles for the Environmentally Sound Management of Hazardous Wastes.

[134] OECD Guidelines Commentary on Section VI (Env): 61. Sound environmental management is an important part of sustainable development, and is increasingly being seen as both a business responsibility and a business opportunity.

[135] See Chapter 5.1.2.

[136] Natural Capital Partners (NCP), *The Carbon Neutral Protocol. The Global Standard for Carbon Neutral Programmes*, Jan. 2017, available at https://assets.naturalcapitalpartners.com/downloads/The-CarbonNeutral-Protocol-Jan2017.pdf, p. 28: 'GHG reduction plans should be reviewed periodically to assess progress against planned actions and to assess the feasibility for further reductions, taking into account the availability of new technologies, enabling policies and incentives provided by government, and the overall business context'.

[137] 2011 version, section IV.6: 'also part of sustainable development is: b) establishment of measurable objectives and, where appropriate, targets for improved environmental performance and resource utilisation, including periodically reviewing the continuing relevance of these objectives; where appropriate'.

[138] ISEAL Code for standard setting.

sustainability, since environmentally harmful or insufficiently protective rules and regulations could yet be deemed 'sustainable' provided they are less damaging or permissive than their predecessors. On the other hand, a concept of continuous improvement grates against the Coasian assumptions embedded within weak sustainability as it eschews the possibility of a pareto-optimal point between development and environmental protection, beyond which more ambitious regulation is unwarranted.[139] Hence, the introduction of progression as a TER principle, and its connection to sustainability, have the potential to transform not only the operationalisation but also the rationalisation of sustainable development in a transnational context.

8.4 A MANAGERIAL TURN IN TER GOVERNANCE

The overview of TER principles in the preceding section is admittedly selective, both in terms of the source material reviewed and the principles identified for discussion. However, it is sufficiently rich to support a number of important new insights regarding the role of principles, and the role of law, in transnational environmental regulation.

A first key conclusion from the inductive analysis is that transnational environmental regimes are reasonably forthcoming in disclosing the principles which govern their own decision making and that of their regulatory addressees. Organisations such as the Global Tourism Council or RSPO are under no legal obligation to communicate and, consequently, expose to scrutiny their operating principles, yet many do as a minimum affirm a commitment to transparency, stakeholder participation and sustainable development in their standard-setting and decision-making practices. Moreover, among public, private as well as hybrid transnational regulators, communications about, particularly, first-order principles appear to become more explicit and extensive over time. Evidently, exceptions occur, most noticeably in scenarios where TER is effectuated through contractual means, as in the case of conservation contracting. To date, it remains highly difficult to obtain information about the content of transnational conservation contracts, let alone to draw lessons about the governance principles observed by the contracting parties in their negotiations.[140] In general, however, the analysis of TER regimes uncovered sufficient information to identify a core set of governance principles that transnational environmental regulators claim to espouse.

There is a strong overlap in content between the principles identified via a deductive approach, and those thrown up in an inductive analysis, with the highest

[139] Ronald H. Coase, 'The Problem of Social Cost' (1960) 3(1) *The Journal of Law & Economics*, pp. 1–44.

[140] Cf. Natasha Affolder, 'Looking for Law in Unusual Places: Cross-Border Diffusion of Environmental Norms' (2018) *Transnational Environmental Law*, 1–25. doi: 10.1017/S2047102518000080.

correlation occurring between inductive TER principles and the cohort of principles which form part of the constitutional, administrative and international public law disciplines mapped out in Section 8.2.3. This is not altogether surprising: in organising their exercise of authority, transnational regulators would be inclined to take inspiration from the rules and principles that govern state-based regulators, which are rooted in constitutional and administrative law. These are the very same sources that animate the development of global constitutionalism, global administrative law and, to a lesser degree, international institutional or public law. Yet while unsurprising, the overlap remains important to observe because the affinity between deduced and induced principles bolsters the relevance of legal experience and legal scholarship to support the further articulation of TER principles. Moreover, it strengthens the legitimacy of established legal principles as benchmarks against which to assess not just the governance quality but also the legality of TER decision making.

These are encouraging observations. Evidently, the TER sphere is not an unprincipled void, and no gaping discrepancy separates how the responsibilities of transnational regulators are gradually being defined within legal discourse on the one hand, and how they are emerging through TER self-definition and practice on the other. However, any conclusion that, consequently, it is possible to legalise the transnational environmental regulatory sphere swiftly and legitimately, would be overly hasty. First, the success of established legal principles, procedural and substantive, in disciplining the exercise of public authority in a manner commensurate to their aspirations and promises, is open to question. For example, decision making in compliance with sustainable development is a widely recognised legal requirement in many jurisdictions, yet even the most well-disposed commentator would hesitate to agree that society is making good on its commitment not to compromise future generations' ability to meet their needs. By the same token, the extent to which public participation provisions have contributed to a genuine enhanced democratisation of decision making, are regularly called into question.[141] Similar issues will undoubtedly plague the application of legal principles in the transnational sphere.

The inductive analysis of TER regimes already gives some indication of the particular weaknesses and biases that might influence and, potentially, scupper the effectiveness of TER principles in securing the legitimate exercise of

[141] E.g. Yvonne Rydin & Mark Pennington, 'Public Participation and Local Environmental Planning: The Collective Action Problem and the Potential of Social Capital' (2000) 5(2) *Local Environment: The International Journal of Justice and Sustainability*, pp. 153–169; Judith E. Innes & David E. Booher, 'Reframing Public Participation: Strategies for the 21st Century' (2004) 5(4) *Planning Theory & Practice*, pp. 419–436; Cary Coglianese, 'Citizen Participation in Rulemaking: Past, Present and Future' (2006) 55 *Duke Law Journal*, pp. 943–968; Roger Few, Katrina Brown & Emma L. Tomkins, 'Public Participation and Climate Change Adaptation: Avoiding the Illusion of Inclusion' (2007) 7(1) *Climate Policy*, pp. 46–59.

transnational regulatory authority. It was noted that general procedural principles predominate in the TER regulatory sphere, whereas substantive environmental principles are less firmly embedded. TER regimes could therefore be particularly vulnerable to underdelivering on environmental quality. This risk may be all the more pronounced where transnational regulators embrace a concept of sustainable development that decouples sustainability from the overall and external objective of ensuring adequate provision for future generations, and instead internalises the benchmark through its conversion into a managerial goal of incremental improvement from an arbitrary baseline.

Indeed, the tendency towards managerial interpretations of legal principles arguably spreads beyond the concept of sustainable development. The inductive analysis showed that TER regimes chiefly conceptualise transparency and participation as active responsibilities of public engagement; not as logical consequences of the exercise of third party rights.[142] Opacity and elitism must be managed because they constitute credibility risks to the TER enterprise, and this management is effectuated through concessions to openness and inclusivity. However, the extent and the terms of engagement remain firmly within the regulator's control. The same managerial inclination can be detected in the arrangements for contestation in TER regimes, which tend to favour conciliation over adjudication, and internal review over external dispute settlement.

The potential consequences of a managerial turn in the interpretation of TER principles are manifold and complex. In first instance, it could cause tensions between the fields of TER (and transnational governance generally) and human rights law, since managerialised forms of access and engagement are at odds with a rights-based approach to the disciplining of authority. The dearth of externality, or, the limited provision of external contestability in TER regimes, is particularly concerning in this context, since it restricts opportunities for this managerial turn to be effectively challenged and scrutinised. Moreover, it is important to recall the dialectic nature of exchanges between law and regulation: as transnational regulators draw on various legal disciplines to distil operating principles that may organise their work and enhance the legitimacy of their actions, so do legal disciplines draw on regulatory practice to infuse these principles with meaning. Hence, managerialised interpretations may over time leak into the legal discourse and shift the goalposts against which the legality and legitimacy of authority are measured, not only within the context of TER but far beyond.

[142] Cf. Auld and Gulbrandsen, whose analysis of MSC and FSC decision making leads them to conclude that the former uses transparency instrumentally, whereas the FSC sees it more 'as an end in itself': Graeme Auld & Lars H. Gulbrandsen, 'Transparency in Non-State Certification: Consequences for Accountability and Legitimacy' (2010) 10(3) *Global Environmental Politics*, pp. 97–119.

9

Environmental Regulation Transformed

Environmental regulation has transformed from a practice mostly associated with state authority, technical prescriptions and a dominant reliance on deterrence as a mode of enforcement into a much more diverse, more complex and more fascinating field. This book focused on a key factor of that transformation, the proliferation of environmental regulation 'beyond the state'. In these final pages, we revert to the original question driving the investigation into the purpose, the strategies and the principles of TER, and consider whether the variety of profiles uncovered have sufficient cohesion to constitute a distinctive model of regulation. Additionally, these closing paragraphs reflect briefly on the potential feedback loops between the study of TER and our equally evolving understanding of 'traditional' environmental regulation performed by state authorities, and explore its potential to further debates about the authority, legitimacy and effectiveness of regulation.

9.1 THE IDENTITY OF TRANSNATIONAL ENVIRONMENTAL REGULATION

The primary aim of this book was to conduct a quest for the identity of TER and to determine whether it constitutes a cohesive field with shared features, or one only connected by the sheer fact of being different from state-based regulation, but otherwise too disjointed to constitute a model of regulation. To answer this question, the field of TER was analysed through various lenses that focused on key aspects constitutive of regulatory identity: its actors, purpose, strategies and its normativity.

Inevitably, the investigations confirmed the profound wealth of diversity in TER: we identified five actor-based cohorts of TER; five different types of purpose pursued by transnational regulators; extensive variety in how TER initiatives are operationalised and effectuated at different stages of regulatory activity; a variety in intensity of legal challenges that TER represents; and differences in the depth of engagement with and in the content of governance principles espoused by different regulatory frameworks. However, the analyses also uncovered a significant number of shared themes and overlaps, some of which surprisingly intense, to the extent that it is possible to answer the question as to TER's distinctive identity with a confident affirmative. If the threshold for bestowing a positive identity is the existence of an identical set of features that is shared by each and every example of TER, then the investigation may fall short. However, if we treat TER characteristics as a 'bundle of sticks', with each frameworks having at least some branches in common with every other, then TER handsomely passes the test and constitutes a distinctive model of regulation.

Shared features arguably came to the fore most forcefully in Chapter 8 on TER principles, which confirmed the pivotal role of, particularly, transparency and inclusiveness requirements across TER of every colour and creed. However, shared characteristics go significantly beyond a commitment to general governance principles. Chapter 3 concluded that, although transnational regulators launch TER with a range of different intentions, the circumstances in which they operate rarely foster environmental ambition. With few exceptions, TER is therefore likely to display a bias towards conservative standard setting. The investigation into TER strategies revealed network dependency as an essential aspect of TER operationalisation. It also showed that, notwithstanding the great variety in normalisation, TER heavily uses standardisation by reference and methodological standardisation and that its engagement strategies, however diverse, are typically heavily invested in bonding and facilitation. Finally, regarding TER's relation to law, the analysis indicated that some variants of TER are much more problematic for mainstream conceptualisations of law than others, but the difference is one of degree rather than occurrence as no instance of TER was found to be entirely unproblematic. In sum, even in the absence of a fixed set of universally shared characteristics, TER regimes display key features that are sufficiently prevalent, and sufficiently distinctive, to justify the treatment of TER as a meaningful category of regulation.

The existence of a flexible but unmistakable positive identity of TER is a key result of the analyses conducted in the preceding chapters. Its realisation constitutes a vital foundation for further research and knowledge building in the field of environmental regulation generally. Yet the lesson does not end there. The repeated remapping of the field of TER from different perspectives – an actor-based organisation; an intentionality-based categorisation; an activity-based deconstruction and a normative perspective – also uncovered the beginnings of a potential range of significant pairings of characteristics across analytical divides. Most prominently, the study showed a high degree of overlap between actor-based and intentionality-based groupings: many of the examples of public/public TER were also cases of collective action TER; a considerable segment of public/private TER is trade facilitation TER; and substitute and risk management TER are most prominent in the cohorts of private TER. Additionally, there is a less pronounced but still noticeable correlation between hybrid TER and enhancement TER. Hence, information about the actors involved in transnational regulatory initiatives can serve as a useful first indicator of their intentions, and vice versa. There were other significant patterns too. The activity-based analysis revealed that the strategic operationalisation of private TER, when reviewed through the filters of goal setting, normalisation, engagement, learning and response, has greater affinity with the command-and-control model than either public or hybrid TER, and in terms of strategic choices arguably has more in common with 'traditional, state-based' environmental regulation than with so-called flexible governance initiatives. Thirdly, an inductive search for TER principles indicated a possible pairing between actor-based and normative organisation, since it showed that public TER is typically less effusive in its affirmation of governance principles than private TER, with the exception of public TER that is motivated by the objective of trade facilitation.

This is an admittedly incomplete picture for several reasons, many of which were flagged up at the start of the book. The study cast its net widely, but inevitably many examples of TER will have escaped attention, for reasons not least related to the limits of my knowledge and experience, and the UK-based, Euro-centric context in which the research in support of the investigation took place. Also, regulation can be defined by more than its actors, purpose, strategies, principles and relation to law. It is possible to think of other perspectives, or filters, to fine-tune the study (such as outcomes, interaction and survival). Nevertheless, the study significantly advances our knowledge about the distinctive nature of TER and opens up pathways for more detailed and advanced explorations. Further research could test the resilience of the preliminary connections which this work identified, such as those between actors and intentions in TER, or between intentions and governance principles. Alternatively, it could probe into the relation between compliance building and effectiveness in TER. This issue has raised significant interest in the past decade, but many questions remain to be answered. Also, there is scope for a more expansive and detailed analysis of transnational regulatory conceptualisations of governance principles, and of the complex interactions between TER and legal conceptualisations. Ultimately, the conclusions of this work and the fruits of further labour may help us to, if not find answers, then at least discover new ways to grapple with the overarching question of whether these new developments in regulation are capable of helping our global society in reorienting itself towards a more environmentally sustainable future and, if so, how best to harness this potential.

9.2 TER AND STATE REGULATION

The investigations in this book are in pursuit of a defined mission to identify and discuss the key features of TER. Faced with an already sprawling range of study subjects, they do not include a dedicated assessment of the impact of TER on the role and functions of state regulation, nor do they systematically review the relation between TER and state environmental regulation in terms of the latter's intentionality, strategies or normativity. However, the study does highlight a number of interesting aspects of the complex relationship between state and transnational environmental regulation and points the way towards areas ripe for further exploration. In general terms, the analyses in this book tend to corroborate co-extensive over rivalry-based accounts of the state/non-state regulatory dynamic. In fact, the study suggests that state/non-state interdependencies run deep and potentially explain more about the design, operationalisation and normalisation of transnational regulation than anticipated.

A first important observation flows from the study of TER strategies, which affirmed the inherently networked nature of environmental regulation beyond the state. Network features are commonly associated with regulatory measures that form part of a multi-level governance structure, but they also characterise regulatory initiatives that are typically treated as autonomous, such as private TER regimes. Moreover, the analysis illustrated that 'the state' plays a rich variety of roles throughout the recursive stages of TER activity. We encounter the state as a subject of normalisation to which many of TER's rich body of meta- and principle-based standards are addressed, yet it is also a source of normalisation in cases of standardisation by reference. States feature as regulatory addressees and, correspondingly, as the target of engagement strategies; as sources of feedback and as facilitators of and conduits for individualised responses. It is certainly not new to claim a role for the state in TER, but it is equally undeniable that our understanding of contemporary regulation could be significantly enhanced by further study of the complexity and multi-faceted character of the relationship between state and transnational regulatory authority. For example, the analysis drew our attention to the fact that, whereas market-based mechanisms are typically thought of as introduced to solicit endorsement and support from the private sector, the primary regulatory addressees of the overwhelming majority of TER initiatives in which such mechanisms are established or promoted are, in fact, state authorities. This raised the question whether, conceivably, a favouring of market-based strategies responds to public actor demands as much, if not more, than to private desiderata and is in the first place designed to bind national public authorities to the transnational regulatory scheme. In this context, the fact that the establishment of market-based strategies typically requires the kind of legal infrastructure that only the state can provide, assumed particular relevance. More generally, a fuller engagement with the notion of the state as an addressee of TER may help to foster a deeper understanding of transnational regulatory effectiveness. It is reasonable to assume that public actors respond to different stimuli from those motivating private actors, yet discussions of regulatory effectiveness rarely address or test this assumption.[1] Further research in this direction

[1] There is an interesting body of literature on the varying responsiveness of regulatory addressees to enforcement actions (see, for instance, Robert Baldwin & Julia Black, 'Really Responsive Regulation' (2008) 71(1) *The Modern Law Review*, pp. 59–94 and Gary Lynch-Wood & David

could forge new and productive interdisciplinary connections between scholarship on state compliance with international law on the one hand, and regulatory enforcement and effectiveness studies on the other.

A second intriguing lesson from the analysis is that some exemplars of private TER show a greater strategic affinity with command-and-control regulation, which is still chiefly associated with state authority, than with other variants of TER. Through the standardisation of industrial and commercial processes, in combination with third-party certification, private TER has developed a functional equivalent to the licensing and permitting regimes that constitute the bread and butter of state environmental regulators. Moreover, although the comparison is less evident at the stages of learning and, particularly, response, the contractual ties between private regulator and regulatee enable the agreement of a sanctions regime that serves a purpose very similar to administrative fines and that, like regulatory provisions, can be backed up through court action. Hence, experience with state environmental regulation may hold greater relevance and constitute a more pertinent source of learning for private TER than it does for public or hybrid TER.

Finally, the realisation of a more articulated identity of TER enables further inquiries into the extent to which TER is a transformative force upon state regulation. The suggestion has been mooted earlier in commentaries that the widespread reliance on'alternative' regulatory strategies at the transnational level validated and strengthened a corresponding interest in greater strategic experimentation at the national level.[2] The point has also been made that, in the case of market-based instruments, TER's engagement often takes the shape of an explicit encouragement of their introduction at the domestic level, which secures the engagement of state authorities.[3] Moreover, the scope for a transformative impact of TER on state regulation should equally be explored with reference to governance principles. Indeed, it is in this area more than any other that the transformative potential of TER comes to the fore. The inductive investigation in Chapter 8 revealed a thriving practice among transnational regulators of explicitly committing to governance principles, with endorsements of transparency, inclusiveness and sustainable development in particular reaching levels of near-ubiquity. This development can be witnessed across the board of TER activity; regardless of the regulator's public, private or hybrid composition, their intentionality or favoured strategies. It clearly – and consciously – underlines the proximity between TER and 'traditional' state environmental regulation, since a great many national environmental regulatory agencies, too, are bound to uphold these very same requirements of transparency,

Williamson, 'The Receptive Capacity of Firms – Why Differences Matter' (2011) 23(3) *Journal of Environmental Law*, pp. 383–413), but it is not focused on the distinction between public and private actors as regulatory addressees.

2 Stuart Bell, Donald McGillivray & Ole W. Pedersen, *Environmental Law*, 8th edn. (2013, Oxford University Press), p. 288.

3 See Chapter 6.3.

public participation in decision making and compatibility with sustainable development. However, it equally transpired that the meaning and implementation of governance principles in the TER context can differ significantly from that of state-based comparators. With regard to procedural guarantees, TER governance principles place a stronger emphasis on active information distribution and rarely include a commitment to granting access to environmental information in response to unsolicited third party requests. Transnational regulators increasingly consult stakeholders in decision making, but they tend to firmly control the stakeholder selection and participation process. As to contestability, those TER arrangements that offer an opportunity to regulatory addressees or third parties to challenge TER policies or decisions more frequently rely on internal review mechanisms that are primarily geared towards mediation and reconciliation of differences, and less towards securing accountability.

In Chapter 8, I suggested that this particular interpretation of procedural guarantees is indicative of a pivot to managerialism in the conceptualisation of regulatory governance, which also echoes in TER interpretations of sustainable development and in the growing emphasis on progression as a regulatory benchmark. From a managerial perspective, due process requirements such as access to information and participation are not only guarantees devised on behalf of the public, they also serve as legitimacy-building mechanisms through which regulators broadcast a carefully crafted image of themselves, engage with addressees and third parties, and persuade the public of the credibility and righteousness of the regulatory endeavour. In the same vein, well-publicised stakeholder events can harness the regulator's image as an open and inclusive decision maker, while the disruptive potential of public participation exercises is managed through strategic participant selection and choice of participation media. Contestation is handled internally and channelled through processes that are primarily geared towards mediation and inter-party conflict resolution; not towards a finding of (un)lawfulness of regulatory behaviour.

Not every instance of TER reflects this managerial approach to procedural guarantees, but the phenomenon is nonetheless prominent, particularly among private and hybrid regimes. Conversely, it is not as if state regulators have so far been blissfully unaware of the potential benefits that accompany shrewd information dissemination strategies, targeted consultation and discreet conflict resolution. However, it is essential to be alert to broader tonal shifts. As TER regimes proliferate and managerial approaches to due process expectations become more embedded in the regulatory landscape, the bonds between the governance principles of transparency, inclusiveness and contestability on the one hand, and individual fundamental rights to access to information, participation and access to justice on the other, may fray. Conceivably, this could not only alter the significance of governance principles at the transnational level itself, but could tilt the balance from passive to active, from reactive to proactive, from rights-based to managerial, across the scales of environmental regulation. There might be advantages to environmental regulators deftly using governance principles to manage their image and public relations, but questions need to be asked about the consequences of such development for the continued utility of these same principles as disciplining tools for the exercise of public authority. It therefore appears that the rapidly spreading incorporation of governance principles in TER does not so much solve transnational legitimacy deficits as reformulate them. Moreover, by opening the door towards subtle but significant shifts in the ethos of procedural guarantees, this development may create new and different legitimacy challenges for state regulation.

9.3 THE TRANSFORMATIVE IMPACT OF TER: REFLECTIONS ON AUTHORITY

The results of the investigation into the nature of TER offer new perspectives and raise new questions regarding major topics of debate in the study of regulation and governance. They span from inquiries into the nature of regulatory authority and how to secure the legitimacy of regulation to the ever-challenging question of what constitutes regulatory effectiveness, how to measure it and how to enhance it. The lessons flowing from the investigations in the preceding chapters are not of a nature to definitively settle any of these debates – as arguably no single set of lessons ever could or should – but they do lead to interesting fresh viewpoints and, in so doing, map out avenues for further exploration.

One of the most obvious ways in which the transformative impact of TER is felt, is in how it forces us to rethink authority; the relation between authority and regulation; and the relation between authority, regulation and law. As Chapter 2 discussed, the very notion of transnational regulation reflects a growing consensus that authority, or the power to command observance, is not solely vested in agents of the state. Moreover, and more contentiously, it was asserted that the presence of authority is not necessarily preconditioned on the existence of a legislative mandate that labels regulatory communications as officially binding and secures their enforceability with the threat of state-sanctioned violence. Instead of tethering the possibility of authority exclusively to state-based authorship and legal enforceability through the threat of violence, this study sought to identify authority, as a constitutive element of regulation, with reference to the consequences of cooperating or not cooperating with regime for the prospective regulatory addressees, and taking into account the impact of the regime, arrangement or initiative on third parties.

The shift in focus from formal status to real impact enables a more direct engagement with and problematisation of the organised exercise of power. After all, the main reason why we care about regulation and have concerns and expectations about its conduct, is because regulation is powerful. The fact that it is often performed by state bodies and enforced through the apparatus of the state is subsidiary to this essential concern. A decentred, impact-oriented approach to regulation thus keeps the focus on regulation's most problematic attribute. However, as acknowledged in Chapter 2,[4] it also unquestionably complicates the exercise of identifying and mapping regulation, since decision-shaping impact does not allow itself to be as straightforwardly ascertained as does authorship or formal status. In this book, I have taken a consciously inclusive approach towards the identification of regulatory authority and have explained this choice as both advisable in the light of the book's primary research mission, and as the reflection of a normative stance not to dismiss the possibility of authority lightly.

The activity-based model of regulation, as developed in Chapter 4, and the subsequent analyses and commentary in Chapters 5 and 6, can make a strong contribution to this evolving understanding of regulatory authority as a decentred phenomenon that is primarily identified by its impact. The identification of a set of processes and technologies which are geared towards *engaging* the regulatory addressee, and which in the transnational regulatory context typically transcend simple attempts at communication to include deliberate bonding and facilitation exercises, makes clear that tying regulatory addressees to a regulatory scheme is not just an ex-post assignment whereby enforcement and deterrence measures are slapped onto the regulatory framework. Instead, in TER regimes the connections between regulation and regulatory addressees tend to be carefully forged and layered, and constitute a dense web of steering, persuasive and cautionary messages. Together, they build an edifice that becomes difficult to escape, even if the gate is officially left unmanned. Application and further development of the activity-based model may help to pinpoint with greater clarity at which stages and through which mechanisms credibility is built and power is consolidated within the regulatory process. Application across a broader cohort of samples may help to achieve greater insights into the relative impact of different bonding, facilitation and response strategies, and to identify particularly successful or counterproductive combinations of strategies. Ultimately, such investigations could result in the development of new, alternative proxies to ascertain the presence of regulatory authority, which are less beholden to the official status of the regulator or the formal connection of the regime to the apparatus of the state, and more alive to the reality of the accumulation and exercise of force in a transnational context.

The study of TER also urges renewed reflection upon the relation between regulation, authority, and law. Chapter 7 discussed the phenomenon of transnationalisation of law by laying bare the battery of pressures that TER places upon key attributes of law, from its territoriality to its structural conceptualisation, and explored three different responses to transnationalisation. This discussion made two different types of claims about the pressures caused by transnational regulation; one less controversial, the other significantly more so. The first line of critique

[4] See Chapter 2.3.

engaged with TER as a subject of law and examined the various difficulties of locating the appropriate legal sources and disciplines to govern transnational regulatory behaviour. However, the discussion also raised the possibility that TER constitutes or at least includes acts of lawmaking, even if the regulating entity in question has not been officially bestowed with legislative authority. This is much more contentious, as it challenges the continued appropriateness of the stable conventions by means of which we distinguish law from alternative authoritative communications. The prospect of revisiting and destabilising these conventions is daunting, as it implacably confronts us with longstanding yet eternally unsettled essential questions about the nature and meaning of law. Yet not doing so, and stubbornly toeing the line that the conventions by which we currently distinguish lawmaking from non-lawmaking (or soft lawmaking) activity are sealed off to any form of re-examination, is deeply myopic. In the first place, the deployment of non-negotiable, binary categorisations may constrain our ability to fully engage with and to think critically about new generations of principles for global environmental governance, such as the Oslo Principles and other like-minded initiatives. As such initiatives are currently rapidly proliferating, that is a serious missed opportunity. Moreover, in a quickly changing geopolitical context, it is right that we remain open to question the rationality, the continued appropriateness and the consistency with which we draw boundaries between law and non-law, even if – or perhaps all the more so when – the outcome were to reaffirm the validity of prevailing conventions.

9.4 THE TRANSFORMATIVE IMPACT OF TER: REFLECTIONS ON LEGITIMACY

Reflections on the authority of regulation and law inevitably feed into legitimacy debates. The preceding chapters at some points refer to the connection between legitimacy and TER. Chapter 3 identifies particular legitimacy challenges in the wake of different types of intentionality, and Chapter 8 highlights the legitimacy-harnessing potential of TER governance principles. On the whole, however, this book has been rather restrained in its discussion of the legitimacy of TER. In examining regimes such as the CNP and the RGGI in Chapter 5, for example, the focus stays tightly on identifying the recursive activities of regulation, and does not move towards questioning the adequacy or acceptability non-state actors deploying particular regulatory strategies. Chapter 7 reviews different responses to the transnationalisation of law, but stops short of advocating one among them as the preferred approach. The reason for this restraint is not that the legitimacy of TER is considered irrelevant, or taken for granted. Rather, this work understands its key contribution to legitimacy debates as delivering an expanded, better articulated and more systematically organised knowledge base, which may serve as a platform for more productive explorations of the legitimacy challenges of transnational regulation.

As observed in Chapter 1, since normative expectations for 'good regulation' have predominantly matured in a state-centric context,[5] the benchmarks deployed to identify legitimate regulation and, conversely, alert us to problematic situations, incorporate assumptions about the role and nature of regulation that are broadly valid for state regulation, but may be less appropriate in a transnational context. If the underlying assumption is that non-compliance by regulatory addressees results in a range of deterrence interventions such as fines or revoked licenses, this may give rise to very different legitimacy concerns and, correspondingly, trigger calls for different types of countervailing guarantees than if the starting assumption is that non-compliance primarily leads to greater investment in facilitation, or in the removal of a logo. This may be so even if all responses are similarly successful in eliciting compliance. The variety in legitimacy concerns and reactions does not render all traditional legitimacy benchmarks for regulation automatically inappropriate as assessment tools for all manner of TER, but it does mean that their undifferentiated application easily leads to foregone conclusions.[6] Equipped with a better understanding of the purpose of TER, of how TER strategies unfold and how authority is built and consolidated in TER networks, we can now inject a greater level of nuance into legitimacy debates and make them more meaningful. The following paragraphs identify a set of potential contributions to legitimacy debates flowing from the discussions in this book, and indicate avenues for further exploration.

In first instance, lessons from Chapters 2 and 3 can enrich debates regarding the legitimacy of TER generally. A frequent point of departure in normative discussions of the goods and ills of regulation is that regulation limits the freedom of regulatory addressees, and therefore must be justified with reference to public imperatives of overriding importance. Hence, what is taken to be most concerning about regulation, and consequently serves as the key trigger for legitimation demands, is its coercive potential vis-à-vis a target audience which did not choose and cannot avoid to be thus constrained. From this vantage point, the question can be posed whether TER needs as much justification as state regulation. As illustrated in the actor-based overview in Chapter 2, transnational environmental regulators tend to communicate with similarly situated addressees; there are more instances of public/public and private/private TER, than public/private and private/public TER. Self-restraint may be less ethically problematic than external coercion. It is intriguing to consider, in

5 See, for example, the thorough review of regulatory legitimacy literature, including contributions from Robert Baldwin, Mariano-Florentino Cuéllar, Jerry Mashaw, Martin Shapiro and Cass Sunstein, in Bronwen Morgan & Karen Yeung, *An Introduction to Law and Regulation* (2007, Cambridge University Press), pp. 221–280.

6 Cf. Armin von Bogdandy, Matthias Goldmann & Ingo Venzke, 'From Public International to International Public Law: Translating World Public Opinion into International Public Authority' (2017) 28(1) *European Journal of International Law*, pp. 115–145, at 122, reflecting that the global governance perspective does not offer a way of distinguishing legitimate from illegitimate governance.

this context, the observed strong overlap between public/private TER and trade facilitation TER, coupled with the discovery in Chapter 8 that trade facilitation TER tends to be more effusive about its governance principles than collective action TER. Conceivably, the former's stronger externally coercive potential creates a stronger demand for legitimation, to which the adoption of governance principles constitutes a response. These considerations open up further lines of inquiry into the relation between the actor-based composition, intentionality and legitimation of TER and transnational regulation generally. For instance, it would be instructive to explore whether, as public/public and private/private regimes hybridise, legitimation pressures intensify, remain unaffected, or abate.

Regulation's coercive potential vis-à-vis regulatory addressees is a key impetus for legitimation demands, but it is not the only one. The legitimacy of regulation can also be assessed with reference to its external impacts; its effect on third parties who see their opportunities, choices and circumstances shaped by regulatory initiatives and their outcomes. From this angle, too, the analyses in the preceding chapters contribute a range of interesting perspectives. First, it is important to ask whether the consideration of legitimation needs vis-à-vis third parties is, and should be, informed by an expanded understanding of transnational regulatory intentionality. Should the legitimacy of, for example, substitute TER be measured by the same yardsticks as that of risk management TER, or should expectations of legitimation be stronger in one scenario than the other? In a similar vein, are public expectations regarding the probity of collective action TER identical to those for enhancement TER and, if not, should they be? Arguably, the legitimacy of a regulatory intervention could be affected not only by how this intervention is orchestrated, but also by the nature of the problem to which it is responding. Put more concretely, perhaps we are willing to put up with a few more legitimacy deficits in the context of substitute TER than in the case of risk management TER. Perhaps we can overlook legitimacy concerns more easily in the pursuit of collective action goals than for the sake of regulatory enhancement. These reflections are not without risk as they might open the door to blunt 'beggars can't be choosers' thinking which places certain categories of TER beyond the reach of scrutiny. However, such risk does not obviate the question whether, and how, intentionality and third-party legitimacy interact.

Finally, better insights into the nature of TER can helpfully inform case-by-case legitimacy assessments. There exists no single, universally agreed set of criteria against which to gauge the legitimacy of regulatory measures, but there is a strong consensus in regulatory practice and in the literature that meaningful benchmarks include: conformity of the regulation with a legislative mandate; accountability; respect for due process; expertise and efficiency. Additional frequently used criteria associate legitimacy with proportionality, congruence between regulatory objectives and outcomes, and consistency between regulatory provisions or frameworks. Whereas some of these benchmarks also work in a transnational context, others are less responsive, a challenge that has been duly discussed by authors such as Julia

Black and Anne-Marie Slaughter.[7] The aim of these concluding remarks is not to start a full-length investigation into the applicability of legitimacy benchmarks to TER, but here, too, the results of the analyses conducted in preceding chapters offer promising points of departure for future study. First, it is evident from the investigation of TER's relation to law that many transnational regulatory initiatives come into being in the absence of a legislative mandate. This is not a new point in the literature on transnational and decentred regulation, but the discussion in Chapter 7 does strengthen our awareness that, if the absence of a clear legislative mandate is a problem, it is one without a straightforward solution. Each of the three different responses to transnationalisation – reclaiming, reconstructing and reconceptualising – has serious political consequences and triggers a host of new challenges, all of which invite further exploration and debate.

A related point regards the accountability of transnational environmental regulators. TER institutions rarely have representative bodies to report to, either directly through parliamentary reporting duties or indirectly via the establishment of an ombudsman with a transnational 'jurisdiction'. Moreover, the pathways towards judicial review of TER decisions typically are few and inhospitable. These factors feed widespread concerns regarding the accountability and, consequently, the legitimacy of TER. On the other hand, it has been noted that accountability practices may blossom in exchanges other than those between the regulator and the legislature or the regulator and the judiciary. In this regard, the examination of TER strategies and governance principles highlights a range of institutional interfaces which could embed alternative accountability practices. For example, the frequently deployed practice of standardisation by reference forges linkages between different TER regimes. Widespread reliance on certification and independent accreditation of certifiers fosters interrelations between autonomous actors with different mandates and missions but a shared dependence on the credibility of the regulatory enterprise. The establishment of quasi-autonomous financial, technology and transparency 'mechanisms' under the auspices of MEAs, coupled with the proliferation of internal reporting duties, potentially multiplies instances when different branches of transnational regulation could give account to each other. The growing expectation of the contestability of TER decisions, and the corresponding establishment of, most frequently, internal review and mediation practices, further contribute to the emergence of alternative accountability opportunities. The point here is not to claim that these alternative accountability networks are functionally equivalent to state-based archetypes, but precisely to emphasise the

[7] Julia Black, 'Constructing and Contesting Legitimacy and Accountability in Polycentric Regulatory Regimes' (2008) 2(1) *Regulation and Governance*, pp. 1–28; Anne-Marie Slaughter, 'Disaggregated Sovereignty: Towards the Public Accountability of Global Government Networks' (2004) 39(2) *Government & Opposition*, pp. 159–190.

need for further study to understand better the potential for contribution and the vulnerabilities of alternative accountability arrangements in a transnational regulatory context.

Two final observations relate to due process and proportionality as legitimacy benchmarks. Chapter 8 indicated that TER investment in legitimacy building has strongly concentrated on procedural guarantees, with a clear emphasis on transparency and inclusiveness. However, it also transpired that commitments to due process can acquire different interpretations in a transnational context. This raises urgent questions whether more managerial approaches to due process leave untouched or instead erode the legitimacy-building force of procedural guarantees and, if so, to what extent. Finally, Chapter 8 documented a growing prominence of progression as a TER governance principle, and already flagged up its potential tensions with Coasian reasoning and proportionality. The tensions moreover invite us to consider the challenging role of proportionality benchmarks in the context of TER generally. Expectations that regulatory interventions will only happen if they can shown to be 'necessary' and if they represent the 'least restrictive option available'[8] are problematic in a range of different TER contexts. Claiming the necessity of substitute TER, for example, may set such regulatory initiatives on a collision course with local governments whose judgment is indirectly impugned by the alleged necessity of private regulatory interventions. By the same token, enhancement TER which embraces a target of outperforming binding regulatory standards is likely to struggle with the requirement that the regulatory interventions constitute the least restrictive option. Hence, in future debates of the legitimacy of TER, it will be essential to address the role and scope for proportionality as a legitimacy benchmark for transnational regulation, and investigate how its ethos of regulatory restraint can be reconciled with the multi-layered structure and increasingly progressivist ethos of TER.

9.5 THE TRANSFORMATIVE IMPACT OF TER: REFLECTIONS ON EFFECTIVENESS

A firmer grip on the nature and functions of TER can also enable a better understanding of requirements for and obstacles on the path towards regulatory effectiveness. The closing paragraphs of this book consider how the insights built up in the course of the preceding chapters might shed new light on regulatory effectiveness debates, and identify trajectories for further research and reflection.

First, since effectiveness relates to whether, and how well, decisions and practices achieve the goals for which they were undertaken, a better understanding of the intentionality of TER can vitally inform effectiveness assessments. The importance of understanding intentionality is illustrated most vividly in the case of risk management TER. Prominent examples of this variant of TER, such as Responsible Care®

[8] Cf. Gráinne de Búrca, 'The Principle of Proportionality and Its Application in EC Law' (1993) 13(1) *Yearbook of European Law*, pp. 105–150.

and the environmental chapters of CSR codes of conduct, are regularly critiqued for being ineffective and for, at the very least, under-delivering as environmental regulatory instruments. From an environmental protection perspective, such objections may be amply warranted, but it is key to realise that, from a risk management perspective, a satisficing instead of optimising strategy may be more effective. This does not imply that there is no validity to concerns about the environmental performance of risk management TER, but their failure to engage with and respond to the rationality that underlies risk management TER undeniably curtails their resonance. Understanding better what regulatory effectiveness means in different TER contexts can help in the formulation of more targeted critiques that are harder for transnational regulators to sideline.

A related point regards assumptions about the causes of transnational regulatory under-performance and regulatory failure. Because TER regimes are widely known to be light on deterrence measures, failures of TER regimes to make a discernible difference in terms of environmental outcomes are easily explained away as enforcement failures. However, a closer examination of the consequences of different types of regulatory intentionality for the organisation and evolution of TER decision making reminds us that TER regimes fall short in delivering environmental outcomes for a variety of reasons, many of which are unrelated to enforcement of deterrence. Collective action TER and trade facilitation TER, for example, face significant risks of stagnation that no amount of 'toughening up' on deterrence will remedy. A better understanding of TER can help to pinpoint the causes of regulatory failure with greater accuracy which, in turn, fosters more productive reflections on possible responses. In the same vein, supplementing conventional categorisations of TER strategies with a more granular, activity-based analysis of regulatory strategies, may considerably boost endeavours to enhance regulatory effectiveness. It lifts the lid on the expanse of distinctive decisions, actions and practices that together constitute the regulatory process and, correspondingly, uncovers a much wider range of potential intervention points for reform initiatives, rather than leaving reformers with a reductionist choice between 'command-and-control' or its handful of alternatives.

Advanced knowledge about TER will help the development of regulatory reform proposals that are more responsive to the transnational context. Like thoughts on regulatory legitimacy, ideas on how to enhance regulatory effectiveness are typically developed with reference to state regulation. Kenneth Abbott and Duncan Snidal have broken new ground in this debate and argued that responsive regulation, one of the most widely influential models for regulatory reform and optimisation, is rooted in a state-oriented conceptualisation of regulation. Its proposals cannot simply be transported into a transnational regulatory context without significant loss of utility.[9] Indeed, even some of the most recent, state-of-the-art contributions on regulatory

[9] Kenneth W. Abbott & Duncan Snidal, 'Taking Responsive Regulation Transnational: Strategies for International Organizations' (2013) 7(1) *Regulation & Governance*, pp. 95–113.

effectiveness, such as Cary Coglianese's work on Achieving Regulatory Excellence,[10] overwhelmingly take state regulation as a point of departure. Hence, there is a pressing need for the development of optimisation proposals that fully embrace the important role of TER in society.

Finally, in this context, there are great opportunities to be seized from studying the dynamics between TER principles and regulatory outcomes. As transnational regulatory regimes become powerful behaviour-shaping forces which, as explored in Chapter 7, defy easy categorisation and submission to the disciplining force of law, we increasingly place our faith in governance principles as alternative, transnational guarantors of good regulation. This development lends urgency to the question whether adherence to governance principles results in better transnational regulatory outcomes. Chapter 8 made a step towards understanding TER governance principles, not only as they are discussed in the legal literature but also as conceptualised and interpreted within TER regimes. One of the more encouraging lessons to take away from the investigation was that, even when they are under no formal obligation to do so, TER initiatives increasingly embrace and articulate governance principles. It moreover transpired that, in adopting governance principles, TER regimes draw inspiration from established bodies of international, human rights, constitutional and administrative law. Of course, this does not imply that all TER regimes develop the same practices to deliver, for instance, transparency, or that concepts of transparency within TER circles are identical to those in administrative law. Indeed, the more managerial take on transparency in TER has been noted and discussed. The point here, however, is that these conditions of similarity and differentiation unlock wonderful opportunities for innovative comparative work, which could vitally enhance our understanding of whether and the conditions under which governance principles are effective in enhancing regulatory performance, both as measured against the intentions of the regulator and against the externally professed goals of the regime.

9.6 CLOSING REMARKS

The model of TER developed in this book clarifies and organises thought about the scale and range of transnational regulation. It helps us understand the conditions under which TER initiatives will emerge, the mechanisms through which they are operationalised, and the normative challenges they provoke. Admittedly, the sheer act of understanding does not solve any of the critical environmental problems of the age. However, it is an indispensable ingredient in the quest towards a well-governed and sustainable world.

[10] Cary Coglianese (ed.), *Achieving Regulatory Excellence* (2017, Brookings Institution Press).

Bibliography

Abbott, Kenneth W., 'Strengthening the Transnational Regime Complex for Climate Change' (2014) 3(1) *Transnational Environmental Law*, pp. 57–88.

Abbott, Kenneth W. & Duncan Snidal, 'Hard and Soft Law in International Governance' (2000) 54(3) *International Organization*, pp. 421–456.

'Strengthening International Regulation through Transnational New Governance: Overcoming the Orchestration Deficit' (2009) 42 *Vanderbilt Journal of Transnational Law*, pp. 501–578.

'Taking Responsive Regulation Transnational: Strategies for International Organizations' (2013) 7(1) *Regulation & Governance*, pp. 95–113.

Abramowicz, Michael & Thomas B. Colby, 'Notice and Comment Judicial Decision Making' (2009) 76(3) *University of Chicago Law Review*, pp. 965–1036.

Ackerman, Bruce A. & Richard B. Stewart, 'Reforming Environmental Law' (1985) 37(5) *Stanford Law* Review, pp. 1333–1365.

Adelman, Sam, 'Human Rights in the Paris Agreement: Too Little, Too Late?' (2018) 7(1) *Transnational Environmental Law*, pp. 17–36.

Affolder, Natasha, 'Transnational Conservation Contracts' (2012) 25(2) *Leiden Journal of International Law*, pp. 443–460.

'Transnational Conservation Contracts: A Primer' (2012) 106 *Proceedings of the Annual Meeting (American Society of International Law)*, pp. 508–511.

'Looking for Law in Unusual Places: Cross-Border Diffusion of Environmental Norms' (2018) *Transnational Environmental Law*, 1–25.doi:10.1017/S2047102518000080.

Albareda, Laura, 'Corporate Responsibility, Governance and Accountability: From Self-Regulation to Co-Regulation' (2008) 8(4) *Corporate Governance: The International Journal of Business in Society*, pp. 430–439.

Alemanno, Alberto, "The Shaping of European Risk Regulation by Community Courts", Jean Monnet Working Paper No. 18 (2008), available at https://papers.ssrn.com/sol3/papers.cfm?abstract_id=1325770.

Alford, John, 'The Multiple Facets of Co-Production: Building on the Work of Elinor Ostrom' (2014) 16(3) *Public Management Review*, pp. 299–316.

Alm, Alvin L., 'A Need for New Approaches. Command-and-Control Is No Longer a Cure All' (1992) 18(2) *EPA Journal*, pp. 7–11.

Anderson, Christopher, 'Contrasting Models of EU Administration in Judicial Review of Risk Regulation' (2014) 51(2) *Common Market Law Review*, pp. 425–454.

Andonova, Liliana, Michele Betsill & Harriet Bulkeley, 'Transnational Climate Governance' (2009) 9(2) *Global Environmental Politics*, pp. 52–73.

Anton, Don & Dinah Shelton, *Environmental Protection and Human Rights* (2011, Cambridge University Press).

Armeni, Chiara, 'Global Experimentalist Governance, International Law and Climate Change Technologies' (2015) 64(4) *International & Comparative Law Quarterly*, pp. 875–904.

Arnold, Denis G., 'Corporations and Human Rights Obligations' (2016) 1(2) *Business and Human Rights Journal*, pp. 255–275.

Arup, Christopher & Hao Zhang, 'Lessons from Regulating Carbon Offset Markets' (2015) 4(1) *Transnational Environmental Law*, pp. 69–100.

Auld, Graeme & Lars H. Gulbrandsen, 'Certification Schemes and the Impacts on Forests and Forestry' (2008) 33 *Annual Review of Environment and Resources*, pp. 187–211.

'Transparency in Non-State Certification: Consequences for Accountability and Legitimacy' (2010) 10(3) *Global Environmental Politics*, pp. 97–119.

Ayres, Ian & John Braithwaite, *Responsive Regulation: Transcending the Deregulation Debate* (1992, Oxford University Press).

Bäckstrand, Karin, 'Accountability of Networked Climate Governance: The Rise of Transnational Climate Partnerships' (2008) 8(3) *Global Environmental Politics*, pp. 74–102.

Baker, Betsy & Brooks Yeager, 'Coordinated Ocean Stewardship in the Arctic: Needs, Challenges and Possible Models for an Arctic Ocean Coordinating Agreement' (2015) 4(2) *Transnational Environmental Law*, pp. 359–394.

Baldwin, Robert, 'Why Rules Don't Work' (1990) 53(3) *The Modern Law Review*, pp. 321–337.

'Regulation: After Command and Control' in Keith Hawkins (ed.), *The Human Face of Law* (1997, Oxford University Press).

'Regulation Lite: The Rise of Emissions Trading' (2008) 2(2) *Regulation & Governance*, pp. 193–215.

Baldwin, Robert & Julia Black, 'Really Responsive Regulation' (2008) 71(1) *The Modern Law Review*, pp. 59–94.

Baldwin, Robert, Julia Black & Gerard O'Leary, 'Risk Regulation and Transnationality: Institutional Accountability as a Driver of Innovation' (2014) 3(2) *Transnational Environmental Law*, pp. 373–390.

Baldwin, Robert, Martin Cave & Martin Lodge, *Understanding Regulation: Theory, Strategy, and Practice*, 2nd edn. (2012, Oxford University Press).

Bansard, Jennifer, Philipp Pattberg & Oscar Widerberg, 'Subnational Climate Networks, Who They Are and What They Do', paper presented at the 2014 Amsterdam Conference Beyond 2015: Exploring the Future of Global Climate Governance, available at www.indiaeu-climategovernance.org/Reports/Subnational-networks_Bansard.pdf.

Barral, Virginie, 'Sustainable Development in International Law: Nature and Operation of an Evolutive Legal Norm' (2012) 23(2) *European Journal of International Law*, pp. 377–400.

Barrett, Scott, 'The Political Economy of the Kyoto Protocol' (1998) 14(4) *Oxford Review of Economic Policy*, pp. 20–39.

Bartley, Tim, 'Certifying Forests and Factories: States, Social Movements, and the Rise of Private Regulation in the Apparel and Forest Products Fields' (2003) 31(3) *Politics and Society*, pp. 433–464.

Bell, Stuart, Donald McGillivray & Ole W. Pedersen, *Environmental Law*, 8th edn. (2013, Oxford University Press).

Benvenisti, Eyal, 'The Future of International Law Scholarship in Germany: The Tension between Interpretation and Change' (2007) 67 *ZaöRV*, pp. 585–598.

'The Conception of Law as a Legal System' (2008) Tel Aviv University Law School Faculty Papers 83.

The Law of Global Governance (2014, Hague Academy of International Law).

Berger, Klaus Peter, *The Creeping Codification of the New Lex Mercatoria*, 2nd edn. (2010, Center for Transnational Law).

Berman, Paul Schiff, *Global Legal Pluralism: A Jurisprudence of Law beyond Borders* (2014, Cambridge University Press).

Bethlehem, Daniel, 'The End of Geography: The Changing Nature of the International System and the Challenge to International Law' (2014) 25(1) *European Journal of International Law*, pp. 9–24.

Betsill, Michele & Harriet Bulkeley, 'Transnational Networks and Global Environmental Governance: The Cities for Climate Protection Program' (2004) 48(2) *International Studies Quarterly*, pp. 471–493.

'Cities and the Multilevel Governance of Global Climate Change' (2006) 12(2) *Global Governance*, pp. 141–159.

Beyerlin, Ulrich & Thilo Marauhn, *International Environmental Law* (2011, Hart Publishing).

Biermann, Frank & Philipp Pattberg, *Global Environmental Governance Reconsidered* (2012, MIT Press).

Black, Celeste M., 'Taxation of Cross-Border Transfers of Carbon Emission Allowances under Linked Emissions Trading Schemes' (2017) 6(2) *Transnational Environmental Law*, pp. 335–361.

Black, Julia, '"Which Arrow?": Rule Type and Regulatory Policy' (1995) *Public Law*, pp. 94–117.

'Constitutionalising Self-Regulation' (1996) 59(1) *The Modern Law Review*, pp. 24–55.

'Critical Reflections on Regulation' (2002) 27(1) *Australian Journal of Legal Philosophy*, pp. 1–35.

'Constructing and Contesting Legitimacy and Accountability in Polycentric Regulatory Regimes' (2008) 2(2) *Regulation & Governance*, pp. 137–164.

'Forms and Paradoxes of Principles-Based Regulation' (2008) 3(4) *Capital Markets Law Journal*, pp. 425–457.

'The Role of Risk in Regulatory Processes' in Robert Baldwin, Martin Cave & Martin Lodge (eds.), *The Oxford Handbook of Regulation* (2010, Oxford University Press).

Black, Julia, Martin Lodge & Mark Thatcher, *Regulatory Innovation: A Comparative Analysis* (2005, Edward Elgar).

Bleicher, Samuel, 'An Overview of International Environmental Regulation' (1972) 2(1) *Ecology Law Quarterly*, pp. 1–90.

Bodansky, Daniel, 'Is There an International Environmental Constitution?' (2009) 16(2) *Indiana Journal of Global Legal Studies*, pp. 565–584.

The Art and Craft of International Environmental Law (2010, Harvard University Press).

Bodansky, Daniel & Jessica C. Lawrence, 'Trade and Environment', in Daniel Bethlehem, Isabelle Van Damme, Donald McRae & Rodney Neufeld (eds.), *The Oxford Handbook of International Trade Law* (2009, Oxford Universiy Press).

Bogojević, Sanja, 'Ending the Honeymoon: Deconstructing Emissions Trading Discourses' (2009) 21(3) *Journal of Environmental Law*, pp. 443–468.

Bomhoff, Jacco & Anne Meuwese, 'The Meta-Regulation of Transnational Private Regulation' (2011) 38(1) *Journal of Law and Society*, pp. 138–162.

Börzel, Tanja A. & Thomas Risse, 'Governance without a State: Can It Work?' (2010) 4(1) *Regulation & Governance*, pp. 113–134.
Bosselmann, Klaus, *The Principle of Sustainability: Transforming Law and Governance*, 2nd edn. (2016, Routledge).
Braithwaite, John & Peter Drahos, *Global Business Regulation* (2000, Cambridge University Press).
Branger, Frédéric, Oskar Lecuyer & Philip Quirion, 'The European Union Emissions Trading Scheme: Should We Throw the Flagship out with the Bathwater?' (2015) 6(1) *WIREs Climate* Change, pp. 9–16.
Brütsch, Christian & Dirk Lehmkuhl (eds.), *Law and Legalization in Transnational Relations* (2007, Routledge).
Brütsch, Christian & Dirk Lehmkuhl, 'Complex Legalization and the Many Moves to Law', in Brütsch & Lehmkuhl (eds.), *Law and Legalization in Transnational Relations* (2007, Routledge).
Cadbury, Adrian, 'Corporate Social Responsibility' (2006) 1(1) *Twenty-First Century Society: Journal of the Academy of Social Sciences*, pp. 5–21.
Cadman, Timothy, Lauren Eastwood, Federico Lopez-Casero Michaelis, Tek Narayan Maraseni, Jamie Pittock & Tapan Sarker (eds.), *The Political Economy of Sustainable Development: Policy Instruments and Market Mechanisms* (2015, Edward Elgar).
Cafaggi, Fabrizio, 'New Foundations of Transnational Private Regulation' (2001) 38(1) *Journal of Law and Society*, pp. 20–49.
'Enforcing Transnational Private Regulation: Models and Patterns' in Fabrizio Cafaggi (ed.), *Enforcement of Transnational Regulation: Ensuring Compliance in a Global World* (2012, Edward Elgar), pp. 75–130.
'Transnational Private Regulation and the Production of Global Public Goods and Private "Bads"' (2012) 23(3) *European Journal of International Law*, pp. 695–717.
(ed.), *Enforcement of Transnational Regulation: Ensuring Compliance in a Global World* (2012, Edward Elgar).
Calliess, Gralf-Peter & Moritz Renner, 'Between Law and Social Norms: The Evolution of Global Governance' (2009) 22(2) *Ratio Juris*, pp. 260–280.
Calliess, Gralf-Peter & Peer Zumbansen, *Rough Consensus and Running Code: A Theory of Transnational Private Law* (2010, Bloomsbury Publishing).
Campbell, Denis & Rowena Mason, 'Jeremy Hunt Ditches Four-Hour Target as A&E Crisis Deepens' 9 Jan. 2017, *The Guardian*, available at www.theguardian.com/society/2017/jan/09/labour-party-jeremy-hunt-nhs-waiting-time.
Carlarne, Cinnamon, *Climate Change Law and Policy: EU and US Approaches* (2010, Oxford University Press).
Carothers, Claire, 'United We Stand: The Interstate Compact as a Tool for Effecting Climate Change' (2006) 41(1) *Georgia Law Review*, pp. 229–260.
Cashore, Benjamin, 'Legitimacy and the Privatization of Environmental Governance: How Non–State Market–Driven (NSMD) Governance Systems Gain Rule–Making Authority' (2002) 15(4) *Governance*, pp. 503–529.
Casini, Lorenzo, 'Down the Rabbit-Hole: The Projection of the Public/Private Distinction beyond the State' (2014) 12(2) *International Journal of Constitutional Law*, pp. 402–428.
'Beyond Drip-Painting? Ten Years of GAL and the Emergence of a Global Administration' (2015) 13(2) *International Journal of Constitutional Law*, pp. 473–477.
Cassese, Antonio, 'States: Rise and Decline of the Primary Subjects of the International Community' in Bardo Fassbender & Anne Peters, *The Oxford Handbook of the History of International Law* (2012, Oxford University Press), pp. 49–70.

Cassese, Sabino, 'Administrative Law without the State? The Challenge of Global Regulation' (2005) 37 *NYU Journal of International Law & Politics*, pp. 663–694.

Castells, Manuel, *The Rise of the Network Society: The Information Age*, 2nd edn. (2010, Wiley Blackwell).

Castro, Paula, 'Common but Differentiated Responsibilities beyond the Nation State: How Is Differential Treatment Addressed in Transnational Climate Governance Initiatives?' (2016) 5(2) *Transnational Environmental Law*, pp. 379–400.

Čavoški, Aleksandra, 'Assessment of Compliance Strategies' (2016) *European Law Review*, pp. 254–261.

Chalmers, Damian, Gareth Davies & Giorgio Monti, *European Union Law*, 3rd edn. (2014, Cambridge University Press).

Chayes, Abram & Antonia Handler Chayes, 'Compliance without Enforcement: State Behavior under Regulatory Treaties' (1991) 7(3) *Negotiation Journal*, pp. 311–330.

Cheit, Ross E., *Setting Safety Standards: Regulation in the Public and Private Sectors* (1990, University of California Press).

Cheremisinoff, Nicholas, Paul Rosenfield & Anton Davletshin, *Responsible Care: A New Strategy for Pollution Prevention and Waste Reduction Through Environment* (2008, Burlington: Elsevier Science).

Chircop, Aldo et al., 'Governance of Marine Protected Areas in East Africa: A Comparative Study of Mozambique, South Africa, and Tanzania' (2010) 41(1) *Ocean Development & International Law*, pp. 1–33.

Chiti, Eduardo, 'Where Does GAL Find Its Legal Grounding?' (2015) 13(2) *International Journal of Constitutional Law*, pp. 486–491.

Christoforou, Theofanis, 'The Precautionary Principle and Democratizing Expertise: A European Legal Perspective' (2003) 33(1) *Science and Public Policy*, pp. 205–211.

Churchill, Robin R. & Geir Ulfstein, 'Autonomous Institutional Arrangements in Multilateral Environmental Agreements: A Little-Noticed Phenomenon in International Law' (2000) 94(4) *American Journal of International Law*, pp. 623–659.

Coase, Ronald H., 'The Problem of Social Cost' (1960) 3(1) *The Journal of Law & Economics*, pp. 1–44.

Coglianese, Cary, 'Is Consensus an Appropriate Basis for Regulatory Policy?' in Eric W. Orts & Kurt Deketelaere (eds.), *Environmental Contracts: Comparative Approaches to Regulatory Innovation in the United States and Europe* (2001, Kluwer Law International).

'Citizen Participation in Rulemaking: Past, Present and Future' (2006) 55 *Duke Law Journal*, pp. 943–968.

(ed.), *Achieving Regulatory Excellence* (2017, Brookings Institution Press).

Coglianese, Cary & Evan Mendelson, 'Meta-Regulation and Self-Regulation' in Robert Baldwin, Martin Cave & Martin Lodge (eds.), *The Oxford Handbook of Regulation* (2010, Oxford University Press), pp. 146–168.

Cohen, Michael D., James G. March & Johan P. Olsen, 'A Garbage Can Model of Organizational Choice' (1972) 17(1) *Administrative Science Quarterly*, pp. 1–25.

Cole, Daniel H. & Peter Z. Grossman, 'When Is Command-and-Control Efficient? Institutions, Technology, and the Comparative Efficiency of Alternative Regulatory Regimes for Environmental Protection' (1999) *Wisconsin Law Review*, pp. 887–983.

Cotterrell, Roger, 'What Is Transnational Law' (2012) 37(2) *Law & Social Inquiry*, pp. 500–524.

Craig, Paul, *EU Administrative* Law, 2nd edn. (2013, Oxford University Press)

Croci, Eduardo (ed.), *The Handbook of Environmental Voluntary Agreements* (2005, Springer).

Cross, Frank B., 'Paradoxical Perils of the Precautionary Principle' (1995) 53(3) *Washington and Lee Law Review*, pp. 851–928.

CSBT Commission, Report of the Fifteenth Meeting of the Scientific Committee, 11 Sept. 2010 (Narita, Japan), available at www.ccsbt.org/userfiles/file/docs_english/meetings/meeting_reports/ccsbt_17/report_of_SC15.pdf.

Curtin, Deirdre, 'Holding (Quasi-)Autonomous EU Administrative Actors to Public Account' (2007) 13(4) *European Law Journal*, pp. 523–541.

Daily, Gretchen C., Stephen Polasky, Joshua Goldstein, Peter M. Kareiva, Harold A. Mooney, Liba Pejchar, Taylor H. Ricketts, James Salzman & Robert Shallenberger, 'Ecosystem Services in Decision Making: Time to Deliver' (2009) 7 *Frontiers in Ecology and the Environment*, pp. 21–28.

Dashwood, Hevina S., 'Canadian Mining Companies and Corporate Social Responsibility: Weighing the Impact of Global Norms' (2007) 40(1) *Canadian Journal of Political Science*, pp. 129–156.

d'Aspremont, Jean & Tanja Aalberts (eds.), 'Symposium on Soft Law' (2012) 25(2) *Leiden Journal of International Law*, pp. 309–378.

De Sadeleer, Nicolas, *EU Environmental Law and the Internal Market* (2014, Oxford University Press).

De Schutter, Olivier, 'Corporate Social Responsibility European Style' (2008) 14(2) *European Law Journal*, pp. 203–236.

Deakin, Simon & Richard Hobbs, 'False Dawn for CSR? Shifts in Regulatory Policy and the Response of the Corporate and Financial Sectors in Britain' (2007) 15(1) *Corporate Governance: An International Review*, pp. 68–76.

de Búrca, Gráinne, 'The Principle of Proportionality and Its Application in EC Law' (1993) 13(1) *Yearbook of European Law*, pp. 105–150.

deLeon, Peter, 'The Stages Approach to the Policy Process: What Has It Done? Where Is It Going?' in Paul A. Sabatier (ed.), *Theories of the Policy Process* (1999, Westview Press).

Delimatsis, Panagiotis, *The Law, Economics and Politics of International Standardisation* (2015, Cambridge University Press).

Delmas-Marty, Mireille, *Ordering Pluralism: A Conceptual Framework for Understanding the Transnational Legal World*, translated by Naomi Norberg (2009, Hart Publishing).

Dernbach, John & Federico Cheever, 'Sustainable Development and Its Discontents' (2015) 4(2) *Transnational Environmental Law*, pp. 247–287.

Desgagné, Richard, 'Integrating Environmental Values into the European Convention on Human Rights' (1995) 89(2) *American Journal of International Law*, pp. 263–294.

Dilling, Olaf, 'Legitimacy Collisions in 3D: Some Queries with the Third Dimension of Joerges' Conflicts Law' in Christian Joerges & Tommi Ralli (eds.), *After Globalisation: New Patterns of Conflict and Their Sociological and Legal Reconstructions* (2011, RECON Report Series).

Dimitrov, Radoslav S., 'International Coral Reef Initiative' in Thomas Hale & David Held (eds.), *Handbook of Transnational Governance: Institutions & Innovations* (2011, Polity Press), pp. 182–189.

Domingo, Rafael, *The New Global Law* (2010, Cambridge University Press).

Drew, Jacqueline M. & Michael E. Drew, 'Establishing Additionality: Fraud Vulnerabilities in the Clean Development Mechanism' (2010) 23(3) *Accounting Research Journal*, pp. 243–253.

Dupuy, Pierre-Marie, 'Formation of Customary International Law and General Principles' in Daniel Bodansky, Jutta Brunnée & Ellen Hey (eds.), *The Oxford Handbook of International Environmental Law* (2008, Oxford University Press), pp. 450–465.

Ebeling, Johannes, 'Risks and Criticisms of Forestry-Based Climate Change Mitigation and Carbon Trading' in Charlotte Streck et al. (eds.), *Climate Change and Forests: Emerging Policy and Market Opportunities* (2008, Chatham House).

Eberlein, Burkhard, Kenneth W. Abbott, Julia Black, Errol Meidinger & Stepan Wood, 'Transnational Business Governance Interactions: Conceptualization and Framework for Analysis' (2014) 8(1) *Regulation & Governance*, pp. 1–21.

Eberlein, Burkard & Edgar Grande, 'Beyond Delegation: Transnational Regulatory Regimes and the EU Regulatory State' (2005) 12(1) *Journal of European Public Policy*, pp. 89–112.

Egede, Edwin, 'Common Heritage of Mankind', *Oxford Index on International Law*, see http://oxfordindex.oup.com/view/10.1093/obo/9780199796953–0109.

Eisner, Marc Allen, 'Private Environmental Governance in Hard Times: Markets for Virtue and the Dynamics of Regulatory Change' (2011) 12(2) *Theoretical Inquiries in Law*, pp. 489–515.

Ekins, Paul & Terry Barker, 'Carbon Taxes and Carbon Emissions Trading' (2002) 15(3) *Journal of Economic Surveys*, pp. 326–376.

Ellinas, Antonis A. & Ezra N. Suleiman, 'Supranationalism in a Transnational Bureaucracy: The Case of the European Commission' (2011) 49(5) *Journal of Common Market Studies*, pp. 923–947.

Eriksen, Erik Oddvar & John Erik Fossum (eds.), *Democracy in the European Union. Integration through Deliberation* (Routledge, 2002).

Esty, Daniel C. & Damien Geradin, 'Market Access, Competitiveness, and Harmonization: Environmental Protection in Regional Trade Agreements' (1997) 21(2) *Harvard Environmental Law* Review, pp. 265–336.

Regulatory Competition and Economic Integration: Comparative Perspectives (2001, Oxford University Press).

Falkner, Robert, 'The Paris Agreement and the New Logic of International Climate Politics' (2016) 92(5) *International Affairs*, pp. 1107–1125.

Farag, Mohamed, 'Three Companies Win in First Phase of Solar Feed-In Tariff Project' 27 Feb. 2017, *Daily News Egypt*, available at https://dailynewsegypt.com/2017/02/27/three-companies-win-first-phase-solar-feed-tariff-project/.

Ferraro, Paul J., 'Global Habitat Protection: Limitations of Development Interventions and a Role for Conservation Performance Payments' (2001) 15(4) *Conservation Biology*, pp. 990–1000.

Few, Roger, Katrina Brown & Emma L. Tomkins, 'Public Participation and Climate Change Adaptation: Avoiding the Illusion of Inclusion' (2007) 7(1) *Climate Policy*, pp. 46–59.

Finnis, John, *Natural Law and Natural Rights*, 2nd edn. (2011, Oxford University Press).

Fiorino, Daniel J., 'Regulatory Negotiation as a Policy Process' (1988) 48(4) *Public Administration Review*, pp. 764–772.

Fisher, Elizabeth, Bettina Lange & Eloise Scotford, *Environmental Law: Text, Cases and Materials* (2013, Oxford University Press).

Fleurke, Floor, 'What Use for Article 95(5) EC? An Analysis of *Land Oberosterreich* and *Austria v Commission*' (2008) 20(2) *Journal of Environmental Law*, pp. 267–278.

Flinders, Matthew & Jim Buller, 'Depoliticization, Democracy and Arena Shifting' in Tom Christensen & Per Lægreid (eds.), *Autonomy and Regulation: Coping with Agencies in the Modern State* (2006, Edward Elgar).

Francioni, Francesco, 'International Human Rights in an Environmental Horizon' (2010) 21(1) *European Journal of International Law*, pp. 41–55.

Fredriksson, Per G. & Daniel L. Millimet, 'Is There a "California effect" in US Environmental Policymaking?' (2002) 32(6) *Regional Science and Urban Economics*, pp. 737–764.

Friedrich, Jürgen, *International Environmental 'Soft Law'* (2013, Springer Verlag).

Fuller, Lon L., 'Law and Human Interaction' (1977) 47(3/4) *Sociological Inquiry*, pp. 59–89.

Galle, Brian, 'Tax, Command ... or Nudge? Evaluating the New Regulation' (2014) 92(4) *Texas Law Review*, pp. 837–894.

Gereffi, Gary, Ronie Garcia-Johnson & Erika Sasser, 'The NGO-Industrial Complex' (2001) 125 *Foreign Policy*, pp. 56–65.

Gereffi, Gary & Frederick Mayer, 'Globalization and the Demand for Governance', in Gereffi, *The New Offshoring of Jobs and Global Development* (2006, IILS).

Giest, Sarah & Michael Howlett, 'Comparative Climate Change Governance: Lessons from European Transnational Municipal Network Management Efforts' (2013) 23 *Environmental Policy & Governance*, pp. 341–353.

Gilad, Sharon, 'It Runs in the Family: Meta-Regulation and Its Siblings' (2010) 4(4) *Regulation & Governance*, pp. 485–506.

Glicksman, Robert L. & Thoko Kaime, 'A Comparative Analysis of Accountability Mechanisms for Ecosystem Services Markets in the United States and the European Union' (2013) 2(2) *Transnational Environmental Law*, pp. 259–283.

Gollata, Judith A. M. & Jens Newig, 'Policy Implementation through Multi-Level Governance: Analysing Practical Implementation of EU Air Quality Directives in Germany' (2017) 24(9) *Journal of European Public Policy*, pp. 1308–1327.

Goulder, Lawrence H. & Andrew R. Schein, 'Carbon Taxes versus Cap and Trade: A Critical Review' (2013) 4(3) *Climate Change Economics*, pp. 1–28.

Gowdy, John M., 'Progress and Environmental Sustainability' (1994) 16(1) *Environmental Ethics*, pp. 41–55.

Gray, Wayne B. & Jay P. Shimshack, 'The Effectiveness of Environmental Monitoring and Enforcement: A Review of the Empirical Evidence' (2011) 5(1) *Review of Environmental Economics and Policy*, pp. 3–24.

Green, Jessica F., 'Order out of Chaos: Public and Private Rules for Managing Carbon' (2013) 13(2) *Global Environmental Politics*, pp. 1–25.

Rethinking Private Authority. Agents and Entrepreneurs in Global Environmental Governance (2014, Princeton University Press).

Grimm, Dieter, 'Proportionality in Canadian and German Constitutional Jurisprudence' (2007) 57(2) *University of Toronto Law Journal*, pp. 383–397.

Gulbrandsen, Lars H., 'The Emergence and Effectiveness of the Marine Stewardship Council' (2009) 33(4) *Marine Policy*, pp. 654–660.

Transnational Environmental Governance. The Emergence and Effects of the Certification of Forests and Fisheries (Edward Elgar, 2010).

Gunningham, Neil, 'Environmental Law, Regulation and Governance: Shifting Architectures' (2009) 21(2) *Journal of Environmental Law*, pp. 179–212.

Gunningham, Neil & Cameron Holley 'Next-generation Environment Regulation: Law, Regulation and Governance' (2016) 12 *Annual Review of Law and Social Science*, pp 273–293.

Gunningham, Neil & Joseph Rees, 'Industry Self-Regulation: An Institutional Perspective' (1997) 19(4) *Law & Policy*, pp. 363–414.

Gunningham, Neil, Peter Grabosky & Darren Sinclair, *Smart Regulation: Designing Environmental Policy* (1998, Oxford University Press).

Habermas, Jürgen, *Theorie des kommunikativen Handlens* (1981, Surhkamp).

Hahn, Robert W. & Kenneth R. Richards, 'The Internationalisation of Environmental Regulation' (1989) 30(2) *Harvard International Law Journal*, pp. 421–446.

Hahn, Robert W. & Robert N. Stavins, 'Incentive-Based Environmental Regulation: A New Era from an Old Idea?' (1991) 18(1) *Ecology Law Quarterly*, pp. 1–41.

Haites, Eric, 'Harmonisation between National and International Tradeable Permit Schemes', in OECD, *Greenhouse Gas Emissions Trading and Project-Based Mechanisms* (OECD, 2004), pp. 105–118.

Halpérin, Jean-Louis, 'L'Histoire de la Fabrication du Code le Code: Napoléon' (2003) 4(107) *Pouvoirs*, pp. 11–21.

Handl, Gunther, 'Compliance Control Mechanisms and International Environmental Obligations' (1997) 5 *Tulane Journal of International and Comparative Law*, pp. 29–50.

Harbo, Tor-Inge, 'The Function of Proportionality in EU Law' (2010) 16(2) *European Law Journal*, pp. 158–185.

Hardin, Garrett, 'The Tragedy of the Commons' (1968) 162(3859) *Science*, pp. 1243–1248.

Harrop, Stuart R., 'The International Regulation of Animal Welfare and Conservation Issues Through Standards Dealing with the Trapping of Wild Mammals' (2000) 21(3) *Journal of Environmental Law*, pp. 333–360.

Hart, H. L. A., *The Concept of Law*, 2nd edn. (1994, Oxford University Press).

Hawkins, Keith, *Environment and Enforcement* (1984, Oxford University Press).

Held, David & Anthony McGrew (eds.), *Governing Globalization: Power, Authority and Global Governance* (2002, Polity Press).

Herwig, Alexia, 'The Contribution of Global Administrative Law to Enhancing the Legitimacy of the Codex Alimentarius Commission' in Olaf Dilling, Martin Herberg & Gerd Winter (eds.), *Transnational Administrative Rule-Making. Performance, Legal Effects and Legitimacy* (2011, Hart).

Heyen, Dirk A., 'Influence of the EU Chemicals Regulation on the US Policy Reform Debate: Is a "California Effect" within REACH?' (2013) 2(1) *Transnational Environmental Law*, pp. 95–115.

Heyes, Anthony, 'Implementing Environmental Regulation: Enforcement and Compliance' (2000) 17(2) *Journal of Regulatory Economics*, pp. 107–129.

Heyvaert, Veerle, 'Codification and Centralisation of Environmental Law: A UK Perspective' (2005) 5 *Rivista Italiana di Diritto Pubblico Comunitario*, pp. 1329–1343.

'Facing the Consequences of the Precautionary Principle in European Community Law' (2006) 31(2) *European Law Review*, pp. 185–206.

'Globalizing Regulation: Reaching beyond the Borders of Chemical Safety' (2009) 36(1) *Journal of Law and Society*, pp. 110–128.

'Levelling Down, Levelling Up, and Governing Across: Three Responses to Hybridization in International Law' (2009) 20(3) *European Journal of International Law*, pp. 647–674.

'Governing Climate Change: Towards a New Paradigm for Risk Regulation' (2011) 74(6) *The Modern Law Review*, pp. 817–844.

'Regulatory Competition: Accounting for the Transnational Dimension of Environmental Regulation' (2012) 25(1) *Journal of Environmental Law*, pp. 1–31.

'What's in a Name? The Covenant of Mayors as Transnational Environmental Regulation' (2013) 22(1) *Review of European, Comparative & International Environmental Law*, pp. 78–90.

Heyvaert, Veerle & Thijs Etty, 'Introducing Transnational Environmental Law' (2012) 1(1) *Transnational Environmental Law*, pp. 1–11.

Hickman, Kristin E. & Mark Thomson, 'Open Minds and Harmless Errors: Judicial Review of Postpromulgation Notice and Comment' (2016) 101(2) *Cornell Law Review*, pp. 261–324.

Hillman, Kirsten, 'International Control of Persistent Organic Pollutants: The UN Economic Commission for Europe Convention on Long-Range Transboundary Air Pollution, and Beyond' (1999) 8(22) *Review of European Community and International Environmental Law*, pp. 105–112.

Hobolth, Mogens & Dorte Sindbjerg Martinsen, 'Transgovernmental Networks in the European Union: Improving Compliance Effectively?' (2013) 20(10) *Journal of European Public Policy*, pp. 1406–1424.

Holzinger, Katharina, Christoph Knill & Thomas Sommerer, 'Environmental Policy Convergence: The Impact of International Harmonization, Transnational Communication, and Regulatory Competition' (2008) 62(4) *International Organization*, pp. 553–587.

Honkasalo, Antero, 'The EMAS Scheme: A Management Tool and Instrument of Environmental Policy' (1998) 6(2) *Journal of Cleaner Production*, pp. 119–182.

Hood, Christopher, *Explaining Economic Policy Reversals* (1984, Open University Press).

Hood, Christopher, Henry Rothstein & Robert Baldwin, *The Government of Risk: Understanding Risk Regulation Regimes* (2001, Oxford University Press).

Huber, Bruce R., 'How Did RGGI Do It? Political Economy and Emissions Auctions' (2013) 40(1) *Ecology Law Quarterly*, pp. 59–106.

Huggins, Anna, 'The Desirability of Depoliticization: Compliance in the International Climate Regime' (2015) 4(1) *Transnational Environmental Law*, pp. 101–124.

Hutter, Bridget M., *Compliance: Regulation and Environment* (1997, Oxford University Press).

Innes, Judith E. & David E. Booher, 'Reframing Public Participation: Strategies for the 21st Century' (2004) 5(4) *Planning Theory & Practice*, pp. 419–436.

Ivanova, Antonina & Manuel Angeles, 'Trade and Environment Issues in APEC' (2006) 43(4) *The Social Science Journal*, pp. 629–642.

Jack, Brian, 'Article 260(2) TFEU: An Effective Judicial Procedure for the Enforcement of Judgements?' (2013) 19(3) *European Law Journal*, pp. 404–421.

Jacoby, Wade & Sophie Meunier, 'Europe and the Management of Globalization' (2010) 17(3) *Journal of European Public Policy*, pp. 299–317.

Jasanoff, Sheila, 'The Idiom of Co-Production' in Sheila Jasanoff (ed.), *States of Knowledge. The Co-Production of Science and Social Order* (2004, Routledge).

Jessup, Philip, *Transnational Law* (1956, Yale University Press).

Job, Jenny, Andrew Stout & Rachael Smith, 'Culture Change in Three Taxation Administrations: From Command-and-Control to Responsive Regulation' (2007) 29(1) *Law & Policy*, pp. 84–101.

Jordan, Andrew, 'The Implementation of EU Environmental Policy: A Policy Problem without a Political Solution?' (1999) 17 *Environment and Planning C: Government and Policy*, pp. 69–90.

Jordan, Andrew, Rüdiger K.W. Wurzel & Anthony R. Zito, *New Instruments of Environmental Governance?: National Experiences and Prospects* (2003, Frank Cass).

'Still the Century of "New" Environmental Policy Instruments? Exploring Patterns of Innovation and Continuity' (2013) 22(1) *Environmental Politics*, pp. 155–173.

Kaeding, Michael & Alan Hardacre, 'The European Parliament and the Future of Comitology after Lisbon' (2013) 19(3) *European Law Journal*, pp. 382–403.

Kähler, Lorenz, 'Contract-Management Duties as a New Regulatory Device' (2013) 76(2) *Law & Contemporary Problems*, pp. 89–103.

Kaime, Thoko, 'Symposium Foreword: Framing the Law and Policy for Ecosystem Services' (2013) 2(2) *Transnational Environmental Law*, pp. 211–216.

Kambhu, John, 'Regulatory Standards, Noncompliance and Enforcement' (1989) 6(1) *Journal of Regulatory Economics*, pp. 103–114.

Kang, Moon Jung & Jihyoun Park, 'Analysis of the Partnership Network in the Clean Development Mechanism' (2013) 52 *Energy Policy*, pp. 543–553.

Kanie, Norichika & Frank Biermann (eds.), *Governing through Goals: Sustainable Development Goals as Governance Innovation* (2017, The MIT Press).

Karavias, Markos, 'Interactions between International Law and Private Fisheries Certification', (2018) 7(1) *Transnational Environmental Law*, pp. 165–184.

Kardasheva, Raya, 'Package Deals in EU Legislative Politics' (2013) 54(4) *American Journal of Political Science*, pp. 858–874.

Karkkainen, Bradley C., 'Information as Environmental Regulation: TRI and Performance Benchmarking, Precursor to a New Paradigm' (2001) 89(2) *Georgetown Law Journal*, pp. 257–370.

Kaul, Inge, Isabelle Grunberg & Marc A. Stern (eds.), *Global Public Goods: International Cooperation in the 21st Century* (1999, published for the United Nations Development Programme by Oxford University Press).

Kellow, Aynsley & Anthony R. Zito, 'Steering through Complexity: EU Environmental Regulation in the International Context' (2002) 50(1) *Political Studies*, pp. 43–60.

Keohane, Nathaniel O., Richard L. Revesz & Robert O. Stavins, 'The Choice of Regulatory Instruments in Environmental Policy' (1998) 22(2) *Harvard Environmental Law Review*, pp. 313–367.

Keohane, Robert O. & David G. Victor, 'The Regime Complex for Climate Change' (2011) 9(1) *Perspectives on Politics*, pp. 7–23.

Ketchen, James C., 'Revisiting Fuller's Critique of Hart: Managerial Control and the Pathology of Legal Systems: The Hart-Weber Nexus' (2003) 53 *University of Toronto Law Journal*, pp. 1–35.

Kica, Evisa, 'The Drive towards Nanotechnology Standardization: Shifting Roles in Governance and Key Challenges', (2012) 3(2) *European Journal of Risk Regulation*, pp. 227–234.

Kingsbury, Benedict, 'The Concept of "Law" in Global Administrative Law' (2009) 20(1) *European Journal of International Law*, pp. 23–57.

Kingsbury, Benedict, Nico Krisch & Richard B. Stewart, 'The Emergence of Global Administrative Law' (2005) 68(3/4) *Law and Contemporary Problems*, pp. 15–61.

Kingston, Suzanne, Veerle Heyvaert & Aleksandra Čavoški, *European Environmental Law* (2017, Cambridge University Press).

Klabbers, Jan, *An Introduction to International Institutional Law*, 2nd edn. (2009, Cambridge University Press).

Kleinheisterkamp, Jan, 'Financial Responsibility in European International Investment Policy' (2014) 63(2) *International & Comparative Law Quarterly*, pp. 449–476.

Knappa, Kenneth J., R. Franklin Morris, Jr., Thomas E. Marshall & Terry Anthony Byrd, 'Information Security Policy: An Organizational-Level Process Model' (2009) 28 *Computers & Security*, pp. 493–508.

Knill, Christoph & Dirk Lehmkuhl, 'Private Actors and the State: Internationalization and Changing Patterns of Governance' (2002) 15(1) *Governance*, pp. 41–63.

Knopf, Brigitte et al., 'The European Emissions Trading System (EU ETS): Ex-Post Analysis, the Market Stability Reserve and Options for a Comprehensive Reform', 19 Sept. 2014, *FEEM Working Paper* No. 79.2014. Available at SSRN: https://ssrn.com/abstract=2499457 or http://dx.doi.org/10.2139/ssrn.

Koenig-Archibugi, Matthias, 'Transnational Corporations and Global Accountability' (2004) 39(2) *Government and Opposition*, pp. 234–259.

Koop, Christel & Martin Lodge, 'What Is Regulation? An Interdisciplinary Concept Analysis' (2017) 11(1) *Regulation & Governance*, pp. 85–101.

Koremenos, Barbara & Timm Betz, 'The Design of Dispute Settlement Procedures in International Agreements' in Jeffrey L. Dunoff & Mark A. Pollack (eds.), *Interdisciplinary Perspectives on International Law and International Relations: The State of the Art* (2012, Cambridge University Press), pp. 371–393.

Korkea-Aho, Emilia, 'Laws in Progress? Reconceptualizing Accountability Strategies in the Era of Framework Norms' (2013) 2(2) *Transnational Environmental Law*, pp. 363–385.

Kosoy, Nicolás & Esteve Corbera, 'Payments for Ecosystem Services as Commodity Fetishism' (2010) 69 *Ecological Economics*, pp. 1228–1236.

Kotsakis, Andreas, 'Change and Subjectivity in International Environmental Law: The Micro-Politics of the Transformation of Biodiversity into Genetic Gold' (2014) 3(1) *Transnational Environmental Law*, pp. 127–147.

Kotzé, Louis, 'Arguing Global Environmental Constitutionalism' (2012) 1(1) *Transnational Environmental Law*, pp. 199–233.

Global Environmental Governance: Law and Regulation for the 21st Century (2012, Edward Elgar).

Krisch, Nico, *Beyond Constitutionalism: The Pluralist Structure of Postnational Law* (2010, Oxford University Press).

'Who Is Afraid of Radical Pluralism? Legal Order and Political Stability in the Postnational Space' (2011) 24(4) *Ratio Juris*, pp. 386–412.

'The Decay of Consent: International Law in an Age of Global Public Goods' (2014) 108(1) *American Journal of International Law*, pp. 1–40.

Kulovesi, Kati, *The WTO Dispute Settlement System: Challenges of the Environment, Legitimacy and Fragmentation* (2011, Kluwer Law International).

Kulovesi, Kati, Elisa Morgera & Miquel Muñoz, 'Environmental Integration and Multi-Faceted International Dimensions of EU Law: Unpacking the EU's 2009 Climate and Energy Package' (2011) 48(3) *Common Market Law Review*, pp. 829–891.

Kuo, Ming-Sung, 'From Administrative Law to Administrative Legitimation? Transnational Administrative Law and the Process of European Integration' (2012) 61(4) *International & Comparative Law Quarterly*, pp. 855–879.

Kurtzer, Paulette & Alice Cooper, 'Consumer Activism, EU Institutions and Global Markets: The Struggle over Biotech Foods' (2007) 27(2) *Journal of Public Policy*, pp.103–128.

Kysar, Douglas, 'Sustainable Development and Private Global Governance' (2005) 83(7) *Texas Law Review*, pp. 2109–2166.

Ladeur, Karl-Heinz, 'The Evolution of General Administrative Law and the Emergence of Postmodern Administrative Law' (March 21, 2011). Osgoode CLPE Research Paper No. 16/2011. Available at SSRN http://ssrn.com/abstract=1792062 or http://dx.doi.org/10.2139/ssrn.1792062.

Laing, Timothy, Misato Sato, Michael Grubb & Claudia Comberti, 'The Effects and Side-Effects of the EU Emissions Trading Scheme' 2014 5(4) *Wiley Interdisciplinary Reviews: Climate Change*, pp. 509–519.

Lanctot, Catherine J., 'The Good Cause Exceptions: Danger to Notice and Comment Requirements under the Administrative Procedure Act' (1980) 68(3) *Georgetown Law Journal*, pp. 765–782.

Lasswell, Harold, *The Decision Process: Seven Categories of Functional Analysis* (1956, University of Maryland Press).

Latin, Howard, 'Ideal versus Real Regulatory Efficiency: Implementation of Uniform Standards and "Fine-Tuning" Regulatory Reforms' (1985) 37(5) *Stanford Law* Review, pp. 1267–1332.

Latour, Bruno, *Science in Action: How to Follow Scientists and Engineers through Society* (1987, Harvard University Press).

Legg, Andrew, *The Margin of Appreciation in International Human Rights Law. Deference and Proportionality* (2012, Oxford University Press).

Leino, Päivi, 'Efficiency, Citizens and Administrative Culture: The Politics of Good Administration in the EU' (2014) 20(4) *European Public Law*, pp. 681–710.

Lemos, Maria Carmen & Arun Agrawal, 'Environmental Governance' (2006) 31 *Annual Review of Environment and Resources*, pp. 297–325.

Levi-Faur, David & Jacint Jordana, 'The Rise of Regulatory Capitalism: The Global Diffusion of a New Order' (2005) 598(1) *The ANNALS of the American Academy of Political and Social Science*, pp. 200–217.

Levy, David L., 'Business and International Environmental Treaties: Ozone Depletion and Climate Change' (1997) 39(3) *California Management Review*, pp. 53–71.

Lewis, Tammy L., 'Transnational Conservation Movement Organizations: Shaping the Protected Area Systems of Less Developed Countries' (2000) 5(1) *Mobilization: An International Journal*, pp. 103–121.

Lian, Koh Kheng, 'Transboundary and Global Environmental Issues: The Role of ASEAN' (2012) 1(1) *Transnational Environmental Law*, pp. 67–82.

Light, Sarah E. & Eric Orts, 'Parallels in Public and Private Environmental Governance' (2015) 5(1) *Michigan Journal of Environmental & Administrative Law*, pp. 1–72.

Lodge, Michael, David Johnson, Gwenaëlle Le Gurun, Markus Wengler, Phil Weaver & Vikki Gunn, 'Seabed Mining: International Seabed Authority Environmental Management Plan for the Clarion–Clipperton Zone. A Partnership Approach' (2014) 49 *Marine Policy*, pp. 66–72.

Lovell, Heather C., 'Governing the Carbon Offset Market' 2010(1) *WIRES Climate Change*, pp. 353–362.

Lowe, Mary Frances, 'Toward a Globally Harmonized System: Negotiating to Promote Public Health, Environmental Protection, and International Trade', (2003) 27 *Fletcher Forum of World Affairs*, pp. 195–208.

Lurie, Jonathan, *The Chicago Board of Trade 1895–1905: The Dynamics of Self-Regulation* (1979, University of Illinois Press).

Lynch-Wood, Gary & David Williamson, 'The Receptive Capacity of Firms – Why Differences Matter' (2011) 23(3) *Journal of Environmental Law*, pp. 383–413.

Maduro, Miguel Poiares, 'The Importance of Being Called a Constitution: Constitutional Authority and the Authority of Constitutionalism' (2005) 3(2/3) *International Journal of Constitutional Law*, pp. 332–356.

Maignan, Isabelle & David A. Ralston, 'Corporate Social Responsibility in Europe and the U.S.: Insights from Businesses' Self-Presentations' (2002) 33(3) *Journal of International Business Studies*, pp. 497–514.

Maimaris, Joanne, 'ISEAL Membership Linked to Improved Transparency, Accessibility and Rigour of a Standards Systems' (14 July 2017), available at www.isealalliance.org/sustainability-news/iseal-membership-linked-improved-transparency-accessibility-and-rigour.

Majone, Giandomenico, 'The Rise of the Regulatory State in Europe' (1994) 17(3) *West European Politics*, pp. 77–101.

Marcussen, Martin, 'OECD Governance through Soft Law' in Ulrika Mörth (ed.), *Soft Law in Governance and Regulation: An Interdisciplinary Analysis* (2004, Edward Elgar), pp. 103–128.

Marmor, Andrei, 'Legal Conventionalism' (1998) 4(4) *Legal Theory*, pp. 509–531.

Marx, Axel & Dieter Cuypers, 'Forest Certification as a Global Environmental Governance Tool: What Is the Macro-effectiveness of the Forest Stewardship Council?' (2010) 4(4) *Regulation & Governance*, pp. 408–434.

May, James R. & Erin Daly, *Global Environmental Constitutionalism* (2014, Cambridge University Press).

McBarnet, Doreen & Christopher Whelan, 'The Elusive Spirit of the Law: Formalism and the Struggle for Legal Control' (1991) 54(6) *The Modern Law Review*, pp. 848–873.

Mehling, Michael & Erik Haites, 'Mechanisms for Linking Emissions Trading Schemes' (2009) 9(2) *Climate Policy*, pp. 169–184.

Meidinger, Errol E., 'Forest Certification as a Global Civil Society Regulatory Institution' in Errol Meidinger, Chris Elliot & Gerhard Oesten (eds.), *The Social and Political Dimensions of Forest Certification* (2003, Remagen-Oberwinter).

'The New Environmental Law: Forest Certification' (2003) 10 *Buffalo Environmental Law Journal*, pp. 211–300.

'Beyond Westphalia: Competitive Legalization in Emerging Transnational Regulatory Systems', in Christian Brütsch & Dirk Lehmkuhl (eds.), *Law and Legalization in Transnational Relations* (2007, Routledge), pp. 121–143.

Menon, Anand & Stephen Weatherill, 'Transnational Legitimacy in a Globalising World: How the European Union Rescues Its States' (2008) 31(3) *West European Politics*, pp. 397–416.

Michaels, Ralf, 'The Re-Statement of Non-State Law: The State, Choice of Law, and the Challenge from Global Legal Pluralism' (2005) 51(3) *The Wayne Law Review*, pp. 1209–1258.

Michalopoulos, Sarantis, 'EU member states still divided over endocrine disruptor regulation' 22 Dec. 2016, *EURACTIV*, available at www.euractiv.com/section/health-consumers/news/eu-member-states-still-divided-over-endocrine-disruptor-regulation/.

Miliband, David, 'The New Politics of Economics', in Colin Crouch & David Marquand, *Ethics and Markets: Co-operation and Competition within Capitalist Economies* (1993, Oxford Blackwell).

Millennium Ecosystem Assessment, *Ecosystems and Human Well-Being: The Assessment Series* (2005, Washington, DC, Island Press).

Misonne, Delphine, 'The Importance of Setting a Target: The EU Ambition of a High Level of Protection' (2015) 4(1) *Transnational Environmental Law*, pp. 11–36.

Mol, Arthur P.J., 'Environmental Deinstitutionalization in Russia' (2009) 11(3) *Journal of Environmental Policy and Planning*, pp. 223–241.

Möllers, Christoph, 'European Governance: Meaning and Value of a Concept' (2006) 43(2) *Common Market Law Review*, pp. 313–336

'Ten Years of Global Administrative Law' (2015) 13(2) *International Journal of Constitutional Law*, pp. 469–472.

Morgan, Bronwen & Karen Yeung, *An Introduction to Law and Regulation* (2007, Cambridge University Press).

Morgera, Elisa, 'Bilateralism at the Service of Community Interests? Non-Judicial Enforcement of Global Public Goods in the Context of Global Environmental Law' (2012) 23(3) *European Journal of International Law*, pp. 743–767.

Murphy, David F. & Jem Bendell, *In the Company of Partners: Environmental Groups and Sustainable Development Post-Rio* (1997, Polity Press).

Natural Capital Partners (NCP), *The Carbon Neutral Protocol: The Global Standard for Carbon Neutral Programmes*, Jan. 2017, available at https://assets.naturalcapitalpartners.com/downloads/The-CarbonNeutral-Protocol-Jan2017.pdf.

Nehl, Hanns Peter, *Principles of Administrative Procedure in EC Law* (1999, Hart Publishing).

Nicolaidis, Kalypso & Gregory Shaffer, 'Transnational Mutual Recognition Regimes: Governance without Global Government' (2005) 68(3/4) *Law & Contemporary Problems*, pp. 263–317.

Noortmann, Math, August Reinisch & Cedric Ryngaert (eds.), *Non-State Actors in International Law* (2015, Hart Publishing).

Nwapi, Chilenye, 'Jurisdiction by Necessity and the Regulation of the Transnational Corporate Actor' (2013) 30(78) *Utrecht Journal of International and European Law*, pp. 24–43.

O'Gorman, Roderic, 'Environmental Constitutionalism: A Comparative Study' (2017) 6(3) *Transnational Environmental Law*, pp. 435–463.

Ong, David M., 'From "International" to "Transnational" Environmental Law? A Legal Assessment of the Contribution of the "Equator Principles" to International Environmental Law' (2010) 79 *Nordic Journal of International Law*, pp. 35–74.

Organisation for Economic Cooperation and Development, *The Governance of Regulators, OECD Best Practice Principles for Regulatory Policy* (2014, OECD Publishing).

Orlitzky, Marc, Frank L. Schmidt & Sara L. Rynes, 'Corporate Social and Financial Performance: A Meta-analysis' (2003) 24(3) *Organization Studies*, pp. 403–441.

Ostrom, Elinor, 'Polycentric Systems for Coping with Collective Action and Global Environmental Change' (2010) 20(4) *Global Environmental Change*, pp. 550–557.

Ostrom, Elinor, Marco A. Janssen & John M. Anderies, 'Going beyond Panaceas' (2007) 104(39) *Proceedings of the National Academy of Sciences of the United States of America*, pp. 15176–15178.

Osuji, Onyeka K., 'Corporate Social Responsibility, Juridification and Globalisation: "Inventive Interventionism" for a "Paradox"' (2015) 11(3) *International Journal of Law in Context*, pp. 265–298.

Overdevest, Christine & Jonathan Zeitlin, 'Assembling an Experimentalist Regime: Transnational Governance Interactions in the Forest Sector' (2014) 4(1) *Regulation & Governance*, pp. 22–48.

Parker, Christine, *The Open Corporation: Effective Self-regulation and Democracy* (2002, Cambridge University Press).

Parker, Christine & Vibeke Lehmann Nielsen, 'Compliance: 14 Questions' in Peter Drahos (ed.), *Regulatory Theory: Foundations and Applications* (2017, The Australian National University Press), pp. 217–232.

Partnership for Market Readiness & International Carbon Action Partnership, *Emissions Trading in Practice: A Handbook on Design and Implementation* (2006, World Bank).

Patterson, Dennis & Ari Afilalo, *The New Global Trading Order: The Evolving State and the Future of Trade* (2008, Cambridge University Press).

Pauwelyn, Joost, Ramses A. Wessel & Jan Wouters, *Informal International Lawmaking* (2012, Oxford University Press).

'When Structures Become Shackles: Stagnation and Dynamics in International Lawmaking' (2014) 25(3) *European Journal of International Law*, pp. 733–763.

Peel, Jacqueline, Lee Godden & Rodney J. Keenan, 'Climate Law in an Era of Multi-Level Governance' (2012) 1(2) *Transnational Environmental Law*, pp. 245–280.

Pelkmans, Jacques, 'The New Approach to Technical Harmonization and Standardization' (1987) 25(3) *Journal of Common Market Studies*, pp. 249–269.

Penca, Jerneja, 'Marketing the Market: The Ideology of Market Mechanisms for Biodiversity Conservation' (2013) 2(2) *Transnational Environmental Law*, pp. 235–257.

Peters, Anne, The Constitutionalist Reconstruction of International Law: Pros and Cons (NCCR International Trade Working Paper No. 11(July 2006).

Pirker, Benedikt, 'Access to Justice in Environmental Matters and the Aarhus Convention's Effects in the EU Legal Order: No Room for Nuanced Self-Executing Effect?' (2016) 25(1) *RECIEL*, pp. 81–91.

Porter, Tony & Karsten Ronit, 'Self-Regulation as Policy Process: The Multiple and Criss-Crossing Stages of Private Rule-Making' (2006) 39(41) *Policy Sciences*, pp. 41–72.

Power, Michael, 'The Risk Management of Everything' (2004) 5(3) *The Journal of Risk Finance*, pp. 58–65.
Prosser, Tony, 'Regulation and Social Solidarity' (2006) 33(3) *Journal of Law and Society*, pp. 364–387.
The Regulatory Enterprise: Government Regulation and Legitimacy (2010, Oxford University Press).
Purnhagen, Kai, 'Mapping Private Regulation – Classification, Market Access and Market Closure Policy and Law's Response', (2015) 49(2) *Journal of World Trade*, pp. 309–324.
Rabson, Mia, 'Federal Carbon Tax Plan to follow Alberta Program, Include Individual Rebates', 9 May 2017, *The Globe and Mail*, available at www.theglobeandmail.com/news/politics/federal-carbon-tax-plan-to-follow-alberta-program-include-individual-rebates/article34939245/.
Rahim, Mia Mahmudur, 'Meta-Regulation Approach of Law: A Potential Legal Strategy to Develop Socially Responsible Business Self-Regulation in Least Developed Common Law Countries' (2011) 40(2) *Common Law World Review*, pp. 174–206.
Ranson, Matthew & Robert N. Stavins, 'Linkage of Greenhouse Gas Emissions Trading Systems: Learning from Experience' (2016) 16(3) *Climate Policy*, pp. 284–300.
Ratner, Stephen R., 'Corporations and Human Rights: A Theory of Legal Responsibility' (2001) 111(3) *Yale Law Journal*, pp. 443–545.
Raustiala, Kal, 'The Architecture of International Cooperation: Transgovernmental Networks and the Future of International Law' (2002) 43(1) *Virginia Journal of International Law*, pp. 1–92.
Ray, Christopher, 'Transnational Co-operation between Rural Areas: Elements of a Political Economy of EU Rural Development' (2001) 43(3) *Sociologia Ruralis*, pp. 279–295.
Rayfuse, Rosemary, 'Precaution and the Protection of Marine Biodiversity in Areas beyond National Jurisdiction' (2012) 27(4) *The International Journal of Marine and Coastal Law*, pp. 773–781.
Raz, Joseph, *The Morality of Freedom* (1986, Clarendon Press).
Razzaque, Jona, 'Payments for Ecosystem Services in Sustainable Mangrove Forest Management in Bangladesh' (2017) 6(2) *Transnational Environmental Law*, pp. 309–333.
Reid, Colin T., 'Between Priceless and Worthless: Challenges in Using Market Mechanisms for Conserving Biodiversity' (2013) 2(2) *Transnational Environmental Law*, pp. 217–233.
Reynard, Pierre Claude, 'Public Order and Privilege: Eighteenth-Century French Roots of Environmental Regulation' (2002) 43(1) *Technology and Culture*, pp. 1–28.
Richardson, Benjamin J., 'Socially Responsible Investing for Sustainability: Overcoming Its Incomplete and Conflicting Rationales' (2013) 2(2) *Transnational Environmental Law*, pp. 311–338.
Roessing Neto, Ernesto, 'Linking Subnational Climate Change Policies: A Commentary on the California-Acre Process' (2015) 4(2) *Transnational Environmental Law*, pp. 425–437.
Rosen, Amanda M., 'The Wrong Solution at the Right Time: The Failure of the Kyoto Protocol on Climate Change' (2015) 43(1) *Politics & Policy*, pp. 30–58.
Rudder, Catherine E., 'Private Governance as Public Policy: A Paradigmatic Shift' (2008) 70(4) *The Journal of Politics*, pp. 899–913.
Ruggie, John Gerard, *Just Business: Multinational Corporations and Human Rights* (2013, W.W. Norton & Company).
Runge, C. Ford, 'Trade Protectionism and Environmental Regulations: The New Nontariff Barriers' (1990) 11 *Northwestern Journal of International Law and Business*, pp. 47–61.
Rydin, Yvonne & Mark Pennington, 'Public Participation and Local Environmental Planning: The Collective Action Problem and the Potential of Social Capital' (2000) 5(2) *Local Environment: The International Journal of Justice and Sustainability*, pp. 153–169.

Sabel, Charles F. & David G. Victor, 'Governing Global Problems under Uncertainty: Making Bottom-up Climate Policy Work' (2017) 144(1) *Climatic Change*, pp. 15–27.
Sachs, Noah M., 'Jumping the Pond: Transnational Law and the Future of Chemical Regulation', (2009) 62 *Vanderbilt Law Review*, pp. 1815–1869.
Salzman, James & Buzz Thomson, 'Teaching Policy Instrument Choice in Environmental Law: The Five P's' (2013) 23(3) *Duke Environmental Law & Policy Forum*, pp. 363–376.
Samaan, Andrew Watson, 'Enforcement of International Environmental Treaties: An Analysis' (1993) 5 *Fordham Environmental Law Journal*, pp. 261–283.
Sands, Philippe & Jacqueline Peel, *Principles of International Environmental Law* (2012, Cambridge University Press).
Sato, Hajime, 'The Advocacy Coalition Framework and the Policy Process Analysis: The Case of Smoking Control in Japan' (1999) 27(1) *Policy Studies Journal*, pp. 28–44.
Sauder, Michael & Wendy Nelson Espeland, 'The Discipline of Rankings: Tight Coupling and Organizational Change' (2009) 74(1) *American Sociological Review*, pp. 62–82.
Savaresi, Annalisa, 'The Paris Agreement: A New Beginning' (2016) 34(1) *Journal of Energy & Natural Resources Law*, pp. 16–26.
Scharpf, Fritz, 'Negative and Positive Integration in the Political Economy of European Welfare States' in Martin Rhodes & Yves Mény (eds.), *The Future of European Welfare* (1996, Springer).
Schepel, Harm, *The Constitution of Private Governance: Product Standards in the Regulation of Integrating Markets* (2005, Hart Publishing).
Schiffman, Howard S. & Briony Patricia MacPhee, 'The Southern Bluefin Tuna Dispute Revisited: How Far Have We Come?' (2014) 3(2) *Transnational Environmental Law*, pp. 395–396.
Schlag, Pierre, 'Rules and Standards' (1985) 33(2) *UCLA Law Review*, pp. 379–430.
Schreuer, Christoph, 'The Waning of the Sovereign State: Towards a New Paradigm for International Law?' (1993) 6(4) *European Journal of International Law*, pp. 447–471.
Schultz, Thomas, *Transnational Legality: Stateless Law and International Arbitration* (2014, Oxford University Press).
Scott, Colin, 'Analysing Regulatory Space: Fragmented Resources and Institutional Design' (2001) *Public Law*, pp. 329–353.
Scott, Craig, '"Transnational Law" as Proto-Concept: Three Conceptions' (2009) 19(7) *German Law Journal*, pp. 859–876.
Scott, Joanne, 'From Brussels with Love: The Transatlantic Travels of European Law and the Chemistry of Regulatory Attraction' (2009) 57(4) *American Journal of Comparative Law*, pp. 897–942.
Seidenfeld, Mark, 'Demystifying Deossification: Rethinking Recent Proposals to Modify Judicial Review of Notice and Comment Rulemaking' (1997) 75(3) *Texas Law Review*, pp. 483–524.
Shäfer, Armin, 'Resolving Deadlock: Why International Organisations Introduce Soft Law' (2006) 12(2) *European Journal of International Law*, pp. 194–208.
Shaffer, Gregory (ed.), *Transnational Legal Ordering and State Change* (2012, Cambridge University Press).
'How the WTO Shapes Regulatory Governance' (2015) 9(1) *Regulation & Governance*, pp. 1–15.
'Theorizing Transnational Legal Ordering' (2016) 12 *Annual Review of Law and Social Science*, pp. 231–253.
Shaffer, Gregory & Mark A. Pollack, 'Hard vs. Soft Law: Alternatives, Complements, and Antagonists in International Governance' (2010) 94 *Minnesota Law Review*, pp. 706–799.

Sieberson, Stephen C., 'Inching towards EU Supranationalism? Qualified Majority Voting and Unanimity under the Treaty of Lisbon' (2010) 50(4) *Virginia Journal of International Law*, pp. 919–996.

Sinclair, Darren, 'Self-Regulation versus Command and Control? Beyond False Dichotomies', (1997) 19(4) *Law & Policy*, pp. 529–559.

Slager, Rieneke, Jean-Pascal Gond & Jeremy Moon, 'Standardization as Institutional Work: The Regulatory Power of a Responsible Investment Standard' (2012) 33 (5–6) *Organization Studies*, pp. 763–790.

Slaughter, Anne-Marie, 'International Law in a World of Liberal States' (1995) 6(3) *European Journal of International Law*, pp. 503–538.

'Disaggregated Sovereignty: Towards the Public Accountability of Global Government Networks' (2004) 39(2) *Government & Opposition*, pp. 159–190.

Sofronova, Ekaterina, Cameron Holley & Vijaya Nagaran, 'Environmental Non-governmental Organizations and Russian Environmental Governance: Accountability, Participation and Collaboration' (2014) 3(2) *Transnational Environmental Law*, pp. 341–371.

Soltau, Friedrich, 'Common Concern of Humankind' in Cinnamon P. Carlarne, Kevin R. Gray & Richard Tarasofsky (eds.), *The Oxford Handbook of International Climate Change Law* (2016, Oxford University Press), pp. 203–211.

Somek, Alexander, 'Constituent Power in National and Transnational Contexts' (2012) 3(1) *Transnational Legal Theory*, pp. 31–60.

Starr, Randy, Jim Newfrock & Michael Delurey, 'Enterprise Resilience: Managing Risk in the Networked Economy' (2005) *Strategy and Business*, pp. 1–11, available at http://theicor.org/art/present/art/ARORRM00030.pdf.

Steiner, Henry J. & Detlev F. Vagts, *Transnational Legal Problems*, 2nd edn. (1976, Foundation Press).

Steinzor, Rena I., 'Reinventing Environmental Regulation: The Dangerous Journey from Command to Self-Control' (1998) 22(1) *Harvard Environmental Law Review*, pp. 103–202.

Sternberg, Claudia Schrag, *The Struggle for EU Legitimacy* (2013, Palgrave Macmillan).

Stewart, Richard B., 'Controlling Environmental Risks through Economic Incentives' (1988) 13(2) *Columbia Journal of Environmental Law*, pp. 153–170.

'Models for Environmental Regulation: Central Planning Versus Market-Based Approaches' (1992) 19(3) *Boston College Environmental Affairs Law Review*, pp. 547–562.

'Remedying Disregard in Global Regulatory Governance: Accountability, Participation, and Responsiveness' (2014) 108(2) *American Journal of International Law*, pp. 211–270.

'The Normative Dimensions and Performance of Global Administrative Law' (2015) 13(2) *International Journal of Constitutional Law*, pp. 499–506.

Stokes, Elen, 'The EC Courts' Contribution to Refining the Parameters of Precaution' (2008) 11(4) *Journal of Risk* Research, pp. 491–507.

Streck, Charlotte & Jolene Lin, 'Making Markets Work: A Review of CDM Performance and the Need for Reform' (2008) 19(2) *European Journal of International Law*, pp. 409–442.

Suder, Gabriele, 'Regional Trade Agreements and Regionalisation: Motivations and Limits of a Global Phenomenon' (2013) 4 (1) *ANU Centre for European Studies Briefing Paper Series*, available at http://ces.anu.edu.au/research/publications/regional-trade-agreements-and-regionalisation-motivations-and-limits-global-ph.

Sunstein, Cass R., *Laws of Fear: Beyond the Precautionary Principle* (2005, Cambridge University Press).

Sweet, Alec Stone, 'The New *Lex Mercatoria* and Transnational Governance' (2006) 13(5) *Journal of European Public Policy*, pp. 627–646.

Tallberg, Jonas, 'Paths to Compliance: Enforcement, Management, and the European Union' (2002) 56(3) *International Organization*, pp. 609–643.

Tamm Hallström, Kristina & Magnus Boström, *Transnational Multi-Stakeholder Standardization: Organizing Fragile Non-State Authority* (2010, Edward Elgar).

Taylor, Christopher, Simon Pollard, Sophie Rocks & Andy Angus, 'Selecting Policy Instruments for Better Environmental Regulation: A Critique and Future Research Agenda' (2012) 22(4) *Environmental Policy and Governance*, pp. 268–292.

Terpan, Fabien, 'Soft Law in the European Union – The Changing Nature of EU Law' (2015) 21(1) *European Law Journal*, pp. 68–96.

Teubner, Gunther (ed.), *Global Law without a State* (Ashgate, 1997).

'The Project of Constitutional Sociology: Irritating Nation State Constitutionalism' (2013) 4(1) *Transnational Legal Theory*, pp. 44–58.

Thornhill, Chris, 'National Sovereignty and the Constitution of Transnational Law: A Sociological Approach to a Classical Antinomy' (2013) 3(4) *Transnational Legal Theory*, pp. 394–460.

Tietenberg, T. H., 'Economic Instruments for Environmental Regulation' (1990) 6(1) *Oxford Review of Economic Policy*, pp. 17–33.

Torres, Pedro Ballesteros & Roman Doubrava, 'The Covenant of Mayors: Cities Leading the Fight against the Climate Change' in Maryke Van Staden & Francesco Musco (eds.), *Local Governments and Climate Change* (2010, Springer), pp. 91–98.

Trubek, David M. & Louise G. Trubek, 'New Governance & Legal Regulation: Complementarity, Rivalry, and Transformation' (2007) 13(3) *Columbia Journal of European Law*, pp. 539–564.

van Asselt, Harro, 'Pluralism, Informality and Transnational Environmental Law' (2014) 3(1) *Transnational Environmental Law*, pp. 173–189.

The Fragmentation of Global Climate Governance: Consequences and Management of Regime Interactions (2014, Edward Elgar).

Van Erp, Judith, Toine Spapens & Karin van Wingerde, 'Legal and Extralegal Enforcement of Pollution by Seagoing Vessels' in Tanya Wyatt (ed.), *Hazardous Waste and Pollution. Preventing Green Crimes* (2016, Springer International).

Vankrunkelsven, P., K. Merckx, M. De Meyere & J. J. Amy, 'De Orde van geneesheren op een keerpunt: hervormen of verdwijnen' (2012) 68(2) *Tijdschrift voor Geneeskunde*, pp. 57–65.

Verbruggen, Paul, 'Gorillas in the Closet? Public and Private Actors in the Enforcement of Transnational Private Regulation' (2013) 7(4) *Regulation & Governance*, pp. 512–532.

Verschuuren, Jonathan, 'Contribution of the Case Law of the European Court of Human Rights to Sustainable Development in Europe' in Werner Scholtz & Jonathan Verschuuren (eds.), *Regional Integration and Sustainable Development in a Globalised World* (2015, Edward Elgar), pp, 363–385.

Vogel, David, 'The Private Regulation of Global Corporate Conduct' (2010) 49(1) *Business & Society*, pp. 68–87.

Trading Up: Consumer and Environmental Regulation in a Global Economy (1997, Harvard University Press).

von Benda-Beckmann, Franz & Keebet von Benda-Beckmann, 'The Dynamics of Change and Continuity in Plural Legal Orders' (2006) 53(4) *Journal of Legal Pluralism & Unofficial Law*, pp. 1–44.

von Bogdandy, Armin, Matthias Goldmann & Ingo Venzke, 'From Public International to International Public Law: Translating World Public Opinion into International Public Authority' (2017) 28(1) *European Journal of International Law*, pp. 115–145.

von Bogdandy, Armin & Stephan Schill, 'Overcoming Absolute Primacy: Respect for National Identity under the Lisbon Treaty' (2011) 48(1) *Common Market Law Review*, pp. 1–38.

von Homeyer, Ingmar, 'Emerging Experimentalism in EU Environmental Governance' in Charles F. Sabel & Jonathan Zeitlin (eds.), *Experimentalist Governance in the European Union* (2010, Oxford University Press), pp. 121–150.

Vos, Ellen (ed.), *European Risk Governance: Its Science, Its Inclusiveness and Its Effectiveness*, Connex Report Series No. 6 (2008).

'Making Informal International Law Accountable: Lessons from the EU' in Joost Pauwelyn, Ramses A. Wessel & Jan Wouters (eds.), *Informal International Lawmaking* (2012, Oxford University Press), pp. 369–381.

Weber, Franziska, 'European Integration Assessed in the Light of the "Rules vs Standards Debate"' (2013) 35(2) *European Journal of Law & Economics*, pp. 187–210.

Weiler, Joseph H. H., 'The Geology of International Law – Governance, Democracy and Legitimacy,' (2003) 63 *Zeitschrift für ausländisches öffentliches Recht und Völkerrecht*, pp. 547–562.

Wennerås, Pål, *The Enforcement of EC Environmental Law* (2007, Oxford University Press).

Wiener, Jonathan Baert, 'Global Environmental Regulation: Instrument Choice in Legal Context' (1999) 108(4) *The Yale Law Journal*, pp. 677–800.

Windholz, Eric & Graeme A. Hodge, 'Conceptualising Social and Economic Regulation: Implications for Modern Regulators and Regulatory Activity' (2012) 38(2) *Monash University Law Review*, pp. 212–237.

Winter, Gerd, 'Transnational Administrative Comitology: The Global Harmonisation of Chemicals Classification and Labelling' in Olaf Dilling, Martin Herberg & Gerd Winter (eds.), *Transnational Administrative Rule-Making* (2011, Hart Publishing).

World Commission on Environment and Development, *Our Common Future* (1987, Oxford University Press).

Wurzel, Rüdiger K. W., Anthony R. Zito & Andrew J. Jordan, *Environmental Governance in Europe* (2013, Edward Elgar).

Yoshida, Osamu, 'Soft Enforcement of Treaties: The Montreal Protocol's Noncompliance Procedure and the Functions of Internal International Institutions' (1999) 1 *Colorado Journal of International Environmental Law and Policy*, pp. 95–142.

Zumbansen, Peer, 'Transnational Legal Pluralism' (2010) 1(2) *Transnational Legal Theory*, pp. 141–189.

'Neither "Public" Nor "Private", "National" Nor "International": Transnational Corporate Governance from a Legalist Pluralist Perspective' (2011) 38(1) *Journal of Law and Society*, pp. 50–75.

'Transnational Private Regulatory Governance: Ambiguities of Public Authority and Private Power' (2013) 76(2) *Law & Contemporary Problems*, pp. 117–138.

Zúñiga Schroder, Humberto, *Harmonization, Equivalence and Mutual Recognition of Standards in WTO Law* (2011, Kluwer Law International).

Index

For EU product safety concerns, contact us at Calle de José Abascal, 56–1°, 28003 Madrid, Spain or eugpsr@cambridge.org.

www.ingramcontent.com/pod-product-compliance
Lightning Source LLC
LaVergne TN
LVHW011526200926
848484LV00001B/163